INFORMATION SYSTEMS MANAGEMENT
Handbook

JAE SHIM • JOEL SIEGEL

ANIQUE QURESHI • ROBERT CHI

PRENTICE HALL

Library of Congress Cataloging-in-Publication Data

Information systems management handbook / Jae K. Shim . . . [et al.].
        p. cm.
    Includes index.
    ISBN 0-13-913989-3
    1. Information resources management—Handbooks, manuals, etc.   I. Shim, Jae K.
T58.64.I5338   1999
658.4'038—dc21   98-40741
                                                                                     CIP

Acquisitions Editor: *Susan McDermott*
Production Editor: *Jacqueline Roulette*
Formatting/Interior Design: *Robyn Beckerman*

© 1999 by Prentice Hall

This publication is designed to provide accurate and authoritative information in regard to
the subject matter covered. It is sold with the understanding that the publisher is not engaged
in rendering legal, accounting, or other professional service. If legal advice or other expert
assistance is required, the services of a competent professional person should be sought.

*. . . From the Declaration of Principles jointly adopted by a Committee of the American Bar Association
and a Committee of Publishers and Associations.*

Printed in the United States of America

10 9 8 7 6 5 4 3

ISBN 0-13-913989-3

90000

9 780139 139895

ATTENTION: CORPORATIONS AND SCHOOLS

Prentice Hall books are available at quantity discounts with bulk purchase for educational, business, or sales promotional use. For information, please write to:
Prentice Hall Special Sales, 240 Frisch Court, Paramus, New Jersey 07652. Please
supply: title of book, ISBN, quantity, how the book will be used, date needed.

PRENTICE HALL
Paramus, NJ 07652

On the World Wide Web at http://www.phdirect.com

DEDICATED TO:

SUSAN M. McDERMOTT
Excellent Editor

DAVID GORIN, PARTNER, ARTHUR ANDERSEN, LLP
An Extremely Helpful and Caring Alumnus

ROBERTA M. SIEGEL
Loving Wife, Colleague, and Computer Genius

SHAHEEN QURESHI
Loving and Supportive Wife

USMAN, SAQIB, NAEMA, SAIMA, and HANA
Wonderful Nephews and Nieces

ACKNOWLEDGMENTS

We express our appreciation to our editor, Susan M. McDermott, for her excellent editorial work and input on this book. We appreciate her efforts. Donna Park assisted with Chapter 10. Saori Hamilton contributed an example of a neural network application.

Thanks also go to Roberta M. Siegel for her expertise in computer technology and applications. She provided very helpful comments. We are grateful to Allison Shim for her word processing and spreadsheet assistance.

Special thanks is due to Gus Garcia at the AICPA Library.

CONTENTS

Chapter 4 Hiring and Outsourcing   95

Chapter 5 Project Management   125

Chapter 11 Artificial Intelligence and Expert Systems 319

Chapter 12 Auditing Information Technology 353

Chapter 13 Electronic Commerce   367

Chapter 14 Special Issues in Doing Business on the Web 389

Chapter 15 Legal and Ethical Considerations   401

ABOUT THE AUTHORS

Jae K. Shim, Ph.D., is a Professor of Business Administration and Computer Science at California State University, Long Beach. Dr. Shim received his Ph.D. degree from the University of California at Berkeley. He is the President of the National Business Review Foundation, a management and computer consulting firm. Dr. Shim has published about 50 articles in professional journals, including *Journal of Systems Management, Financial Management, Journal of Operational Research, Omega, Data Management, Management Accounting, Simulation and Games, Long Range Planning, Journal of Business Forecasting, Decision Sciences, Management Science,* and *Econometrica.* Dr. shim has over 45 books to his credit and is a recipient of the Credit Research Foundation Outstanding Paper Award for his article on financial modeling. He is also a recipient of a Ford Foundation Award, Mellon Research Fellowship, and Arthur Andersen Research Grant. For over twenty years Dr. Shim has been an industrial consultant in the areas of information systems development and applications, corporate planning, modeling, business forecasting, and financial modeling.

Joel G. Siegel, Ph.D., CPA, is a computer consultant to businesses and Professor of Accounting and Information Systems at Queens College of the City University of New York. He was previously associated with Coopers and Lybrand, LLP, and Arthur Andersen, LLP. He served as a consultant to numerous organizations including Citicorp, International Telephone and Telegraph, Person-Wolinsky Associates, and the American Institute of CPAs. Dr. Siegel is the author of about 55 books. His books have been published by Prentice-Hall, Richard Irwin, McGraw-Hill, HarperCollins, John Wiley, Macmillan, Probus, International Publishing, Barron's, Glenlake, and the American Institute of CPAs. He has authored approximately 200 articles on business and computer topics. His articles have appeared in various journals including *Computers in Accounting, Decision Sciences, Financial Executive,*

Financial Analysts Journal, The CPA Journal, National Public Accountant, and *Practical Accountant.* In 1972, he received the Outstanding Educator of America Award. Dr. Siegel is listed in *Who's Who Among Writers* and *Who's Who in the World.* Dr. Siegel is the former chairperson of the National Oversight Board.

Anique Qureshi, Ph.D., CPA, CIA, is a computer consultant to companies and Associate Professor of Accounting and Information Systems at Queens College of the City University of New York. Dr. Qureshi has contributed chapters to books published by Prentice-Hall and McGraw-Hill. His articles have appeared in *Accounting Technology, The CPA Journal, National Public Accountant, Management Accountant,* and *Internal Auditing.* Dr. Qureshi is proficient in programming languages such as C/C++, Java, and Visual Basic. Besides having expertise with many software packages, he maintains the Web page for the Department of Accounting and Information Systems at Queens College.

Robert T. Chi, Ph.D., is Associate Professor of Information Systems at California State University at Long Beach. He received his Ph.D. in Management Science and Information Systems from the University of Texas at Austin. His experience includes artificial intelligence applications, data communications, decision support systems, and executive information systems. Dr. Chi has coauthored a computer book for Prentice-Hall. He has published in the *Journal of Management Information Systems, Journal of Expert Systems with Applications, Journal of Operational Research, International Journal of Intelligent Systems, Journal of Knowledge Based Systems,* and *Journal of Decision Support Systems.*

WHAT THIS BOOK WILL DO FOR YOU

The *Information Systems Management Handbook* is a valuable reference for information systems professionals. Information systems professionals include anyone whose job responsibilities require applying computing and communications technologies to manage information.

Information is data that has been processed and is useful to an organization. Processing of data means that it has been collected, processed, transmitted, and stored. It must also be retrieved and distributed among users of the organization. Information is a resource, like energy, capital, personnel, raw materials, etc. Its management is vital to the operation and management of organizations.

This book covers information systems in all phases of business and in all functional areas to analyze and solve business problems in the "real world." The objective of this handbook is to provide information systems professionals with an up-to-date compendium of current technologies and applications. New and emerging trends are also considered. This book is designed as a practical "how-to" guide. We provide extensive examples to illustrate practical applications. The tools and techniques in this handbook can either be adopted outright or modified to suit your needs. Checklists, charts, graphs, diagrams, report forms, schedules, tables, exhibits, sample documents and computer printouts, illustrations, and step-by-step instructions enhance the handbook's practical use. Answers to commonly raised questions are also given.

The combination of growth in systems, the rapid changes in technology, and the complexity of organizations has expanded the scope of the duties of information systems professionals. The role of information systems is no longer limited to supporting the organization. Information systems are expected to transform the organization. The investment of information technology should not only increase efficiency and reduce costs, but should also lead to new markets, new products, and new ways of doing business.

Information systems professionals must prepare themselves for these new challenges. The increased knowledge requirements place a heavy workload of readings on the information systems professional. This handbook serves to reduce that workload by providing information systems professionals with a compact yet comprehensive resource.

Information systems management requires the executive to be knowledgeable about both the technology and its management. Special consideration has been given to balancing these two needs. We cover both traditional and emerging issues in technology and management of that technology. Traditional technology topics, such as data communications, information systems security, network capacity planning, and data management in a distributed environment are presented. Emerging management issues, such as business reengineering, outsourcing, electronic commerce, data warehousing, voice communications, total quality management, and the legal environment of information systems are also included.

Planning is critical in effective information systems management. Information systems are not simply a collection of software, hardware, and personnel. Information systems should fit an organization's strategy and structure. The systems development life cycle has to be considered. Therefore, this handbook gives special emphasis to strategic and operational planning information systems, including guidance for estimating current requirements and forecasting future demands. Help desks, as well as planning process and plan contents, are discussed. The various methods for pricing information services are also presented.

Factors that contribute to an "optimal" structure and the extent of centralization/decentralization are included. This is especially important in the contemporary telecommunications environment. In the past, this technology was primarily based on central mainframes and underdeveloped communications equipment. The technological constraints severely restricted management's ability to dictate the distribution of information systems. A decentralized organization, for example, had to accept a centralized information system. Recent advances in microcomputers and network computers have made it easy for management to select the degree of such distribution. Management philosophy, rather than technology, is now the primary factor that influences the distribution of information systems.

This handbook offers guidance on improving information systems productivity. Improving productivity means increasing or improving output for a given level of input. Potential benefits of improving productivity are significant. Also covered are causes of low productivity, along with potential means of improving the level and quality of output, such as quality circles, suggestion systems, rewards, recognition, etc., are discussed.

Quality control, including total quality management, is an important part of information systems management. Anyone who manufactures a product or offers a service must have a quality control function to ensure that the product or service conforms to standards. Quality control considerations are explicitly considered in this handbook.

The book applies to all sizes of organizations, whether they are large, medium-sized, or small. It is a working guide as to what to look for, what to do, and how to apply what you know.

In conclusion, the *Information Systems Management Handbook* will serve as a valuable reference and a handy guide for daily use. It is comprehensive, informative, authoritative, and practical. The material in this handbook is clear, concise, and useful. The uses of this book are as varied as the topic areas presented.

1
INFORMATION RESOURCE MANAGEMENT

WHAT ARE INFORMATION RESOURCES?

In the past decade firms have realized that information goes far beyond the information itself. The topics covered in this chapter form the basis of managing information resources. *Information resources management* (*IRM*) is an activity that is pursued by managers on all levels of the firm for the purpose of identifying, acquiring, and managing the information resources needed to satisfy information needs. Traditionally, information management emphasized data management because database management was widespread in the IS field. Most people believed that, if they managed their data by implementing computer-based DBMS, they would, in effect, manage their information.

Then another view of information resources emerged: that is, IS professionals should manage information by managing the resources that produce the information. In other words, rather than concentrating on input and output, professionals should pay attention to the processing element in information systems. The processing element includes hardware, software, people who develop and operate the system, and the facility that houses the resources.

In general, information resources consist of the following elements: computer hardware, computer software, IS professionals, end users, data or database, information, and facilities.

To become a good information resources manager, a person must be able to identify the elements in a computerized information system, the resources available to achieve a certain goal, the trade-off if limited resources are available, and how to achieve the desired goal with current resources.

MANAGEMENT OF INFORMATION RESOURCES

In general, the *CIO* (*chief information officer*) is the manager of information services who contributes managerial skills to solving problems relating not only to the information resources but also to other areas of the firm's operations. Major duties of the CIO are to:

1. deliver reliable information services,

2. integrate business operations with information technologies,

3. build business partnerships with business units and line management, and

4. improve business operation by reengineering.

STRATEGIC PLANNING FOR INFORMATION RESOURCES MANAGEMENT

Strategic planning is generally long-term planning. The objective of strategic planning is to give the business a beneficial future direction so that the business becomes competitive.

Integrating Strategic Plans from Different Functional Areas

It is easy to develop a strategic plan for each business function and then integrate all strategic plans into one whole. The drawback of this approach is that it does not guarantee that all substrategic plans will work together as synchronized subsystems. Figure 1-1 shows how different strategic plans from different business functional areas affect each other.

Information Systems (IS) Strategic Plans Form a Company's Master Strategic Plan

This approach treats the IS strategic plan as part of the company's strategic plan. In general, the company develops a strategic plan and sets up goals to be achieved. The CIO then develops plans to provide enough information services to achieve the goals of the company's strategic plan. The disadvantage of this approach is that the functional areas do not always have the resources to ensure the accomplishment of the company's strategic goals. (See Figure 1-2.)

Figure 1-1.
INTEGRATION OF STRATEGIC PLANS

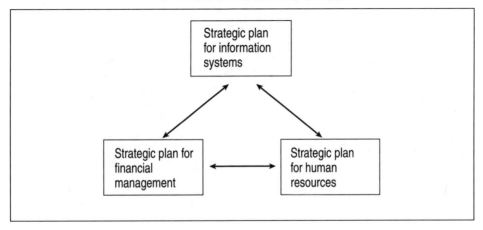

Figure 1-2.
STRATEGIC PLAN

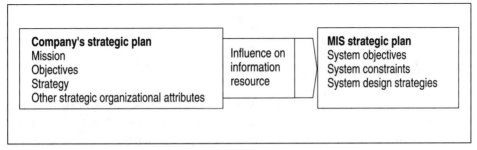

Source: William King, "Strategic planning for management information systems," *MIS Quarterly* 2 (March 1978), p. 28.

Strategic Planning for Information Resources

To avoid the disadvantages of these two approaches, William King of the University of Pittsburgh developed strategic planning for information resources (SPIR). The company's plan is developed concurrently with the IS strategic plan. As a result, the company's plan reflects the support that can be provided by the information division. The information strategic plan reflects the future demands for systems support. (See Figure 1-3.)

Figure 1-3.
STRATEGIC PLANS AND STRATEGY

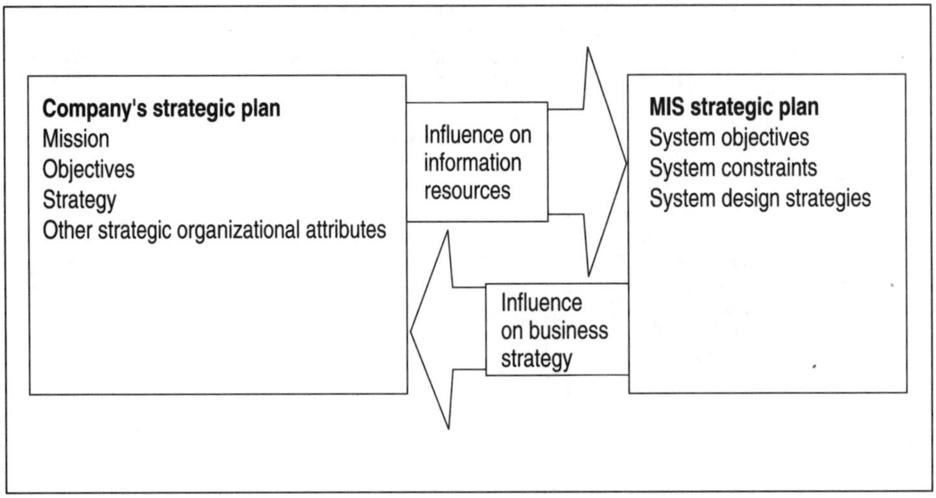

Source: William King, "Strategic planning for management information systems," *MIS Quarterly* 2 (March 1978), p. 28.

IS FUNCTIONS IN THE ORGANIZATION

The corporate IS team is responsible for providing business solutions using computer technologies. These services include designing, developing, operating, and maintaining information requirements for the organization. In addition, the acquisition and adaptation of software is part of the job descriptions of the IS department.

What Do Information Systems Do for Organizations?

Information systems in organizations are designed to support business operations in managing general knowledge workers. These workers use data provided by information systems to make decisions daily, weekly, monthly, and annually. The quality of information provided by the information system can change the quality of decisions that further affect the organization's effectiveness and efficiency. For example, in many retail stores, the point-of-sales system supports the operations conducted at sales registers. An information system automatically triggers electronic orders for store merchandise to be replenished, transmitting information from the store's computer directly to the computer of the firm's suppliers.

Capabilities of Information Systems

Fast and Accurate Information Processing with Mass Information Storage and Communications Computer information systems can process massive volumes of business transactions and generate management reports for decision making. Data processing by computer information systems is much faster than with manual processing. For example, AT&T takes less than 1/10 of a second to allocate a customer's record among millions of customers by using telephone numbers. An employee could need more than a day to allocate the same record manually. The storage capacity is beyond a human being's imagination. A typical hard drive of 5 gigabytes of information can store 5 billion English characters or 25 million copies of résumés. In addition, this stored information can be retrieved very quickly. Internet technology makes most computers connected through networks. This makes communication easier. Today, e-mail has become one of the most popular means to communicate, and it includes image, voice, and video transmission over the network.

Instantaneous Access to Information Computer information systems allow users to access information on a timely basis—and not just for local storage devices, such as the hard drive in the user's computer. Through the telecommunication capacity, a query may be directed to a remote site where the data are actually stored without the user's awareness. Moreover, the presentation of data may be individualized for a particular user with various forms of graphics, text, voice, or even videos. In addition, many organizations are accumulating their business data into so-called data warehouses to make the data accessible to managers and other users.

Decision-Making Support The manager performs decision-making and coordination functions, which require timely and accurate information. Computers process data and generate information for managers so that better decisions can be made. There are decision support systems developed in various problem domains. For example, marketing decision support systems help sales representatives collect detailed sales data for better stocking of inventory mix so that more sales can be generated.

Support Organizational Memory and Learning *Organizational memory* is the means by which knowledge from the past exerts influence on present organizational activities. This memory preserves the experience the company has cumulated in delivering its product and services to the marketplace. Because of this memory, the company can continue its operations in spite of employee turnover. This is because the company's memory is not only in the mind of employees but also in the firm's structure that casts these employees into appropriate roles. As an organization acquires knowledge and modifies its behavior during the learning process, information systems play an important role in providing information for this process.

Improve Organizational Practice Information systems allow business operations to be handled in a specific way. E-mail systems and computer conferencing provide a protocol for the interaction of people within an organization. Information systems not only "computerize" business operations, but also routinize business operations. However, "routinizing" does not mean casting in concrete: Properly designed systems should enable an organization to evolve its practice as the environment changes.

UNDERSTANDING THE IS ARCHITECTURE

Centralized IS management

A *centralized IS department* performs IS functions mainly by the IS professionals in the department. Software packages such as database systems, accounting information systems, inventory management systems, and marketing information systems are developed and operated in the IS department. End-users are not required or trained to understand or modify any software in the system. All information requirements are sent to the IS department for processing. As a result, IS staff design and operate the system, which may not be suitable for other departments. The workers in other departments, due to their lack of IS knowledge, do not know what can be done by the IS department. The gap between the IS department and other departments can drastically reduce the potential benefits that IS can bring to the company.

Distributed IS Function

Distributed IS department controls are important to IS functionality. Minor or nonessential IS functions are performed by end-users throughout the whole organization. Thanks to drastically improved software technology, the development and implementation of software packages can be achieved by non-IS professionals. For example, the graphical user interface (GUI) is extremely well designed. Most end-users can learn how to install or use a software package on their own. Thus, IS functions can be distributed into other functional departments. For example, the financial department can have its own operators for the financial information systems, and the operators can perform easier computer-related tasks, such as individual software installation and modification. However, network operations and major IS functions that involve the whole company should still be under the control of the IS department. The benefits of this approach include lessening the workload of the IS department, reducing the gap between other departments and the IS department, and improving the efficiency of IS operations. More and more corporations adopt this approach to balance the IS operations with other functional areas and to improve the effectiveness and efficiency of IS operation. As a result, client/server systems, not traditional mainframe or midrange systems, become the major computing architecture in corporations.

IS PROFESSIONAL AND JOB DESCRIPTIONS

There are many career choices in the area of information systems. The demand for IS professionals will continue to grow due to fast developments in this field and the increasing demand for information functions in business and organizations. New graduates from information systems usually start their careers as programming analysts who participate in the programming process for information projects and then help design and construct information systems. After several years of experience in programming and system analysis, they can select from various career paths:

1. Systems development positions, such as programmers and system (programming) analysts.
2. Advanced positions, such as project leaders, IS directors, chief information officers, database administrators, webmasters, and network managers.

Some graduates spend several years in commercial companies or government agencies, and then leave and start their own consulting businesses. A career in information systems is rewarding in two ways. One is the challenge of creating new systems that can improve business operations and help people do their jobs more efficiently. Second, the financial rewards are well above those for other professionals.

An IS career is no longer limited to the IS field. Often, IS managers advance to high positions in other fields. Some have become the presidents of their organizations. The U.S. Department of Labor predicts that, by the year 2000, there will be demand for 700,000 computer analysts.

Systems Development Positions

Programmer A programmer is an IS professional who is trained to write programming codes for different tasks. A good programmer can write the most efficient code to achieve a certain task without errors. However, in reality, error-free code may be very difficult to achieve. The revolution in programming language has brought programming languages from first-generation language (machine code) to fourth-generation language (natural language). However, most programmers use third-generation languages with object-oriented features such as Visual Basic or Visual C++. To eliminate possible programming errors and reduce programming efforts, codes are modulated into different segments. Individual segments can then be tested and debugged without interfering with other segments. As the result, many programmers can share in generating a large piece of code.

System (Programming) Analyst   This type of IS professional has a very strong background in system development. Given an information requirement, he or she has the ability to analyze and design an IS so that information can be processed efficiently. A good programming background is necessary to estimate and manage the system. (Programmers do most programming tasks.) In addition, a knowledge of hardware is very helpful since new hardware may be purchased to achieve the goals of the software.

Advanced Positions

Project Leader   A project leader is an IS professional who manages and controls the IS project to ensure that the project is on schedule and quality is controlled. A project leader should have knowledge in computer hardware and software, programming languages, system integration, and data communication. In addition, good oral communication skills and pleasant personality are important.

Chief Information Officer (CIO)   The CIO, the most powerful person in the corporation in terms of the management of information systems, is responsible for long-term or strategic IS planning. He or she has to have a good vision of the future of IS service and the impact on other departments. In addition, new technology may cause opportunities for the company or present it with new risks. The CIO should be able to pursue opportunities strategically.

IS Director   The IS director is the manager of the IS department. This person makes sure that the following IS functions are performed well: IS development, IS operation, and customer service.

- *IS development* includes new system design and implementation of customized software packages and off-the-shelf packages. Sometimes, existing systems need to be modified based on the current environment.

- *IS operation* involves the daily IS information requirements and operation. Redundant systems should be used for backup if unpredictable system failures occur.

- *Customer service* involves customer problem solving, consultation, and customer training. End-user computing can sometimes reduce the workload of customer problem solving but may increase the customer training being requested by end-users.

Database Administrator   The database administrator is responsible for the management and operation of database systems to ensure that the data is available when needed. Different DBMS require different skills and knowledge to operate, and acquiring those skills may require many years of experience.

Network Manager   The network manager is in charge of the computer network. A computer network consists of computers and telecommunication equipment. The connectivity and compatibility of the equipment is the major challenge for a network manager. Since many users on the network share resources with other users, security is essential to the network. To prevent network errors or virus infection through the network, software (such as *firewalls*) and hardware (such as *routers*) are installed for better security. A network manager should have a broad knowledge in terms of different operating systems and platforms so that incompatibility can be avoided.

Webmaster   The webmaster is in charge of webpage design, web maintenance, e-mail facility, on-line transactions with database connection, and eventually electronic commerce capability. Webmasters should have knowledge of HTML, JAVA, Internet browsers, domain name service, and other web editing tools. In addition, data communication equipment such as routers, switches, media, modem, leased line, and ISDN services should be included in their background knowledge.

ESTABLISHING AN IS REQUIREMENT

Cost-Benefit Analysis

Since IS is an investment that should be justifiable economically, cost-benefit analysis is used to estimate the payoff from an information system. This technique, widely used because of its simplicity, evaluates whether the benefit will outweigh the cost. However, due to the nature of IS projects and the intangible benefit from the IS project, the attempt to quantify financial outcomes with any precision is almost doomed to fail. The basic stages of cost-benefit analysis of IS projects are discussed in the following sections.

Identification of the Costs of Acquisition and Operation of the Proposed System

Fixed costs include one-time costs of acquiring system resources (software and hardware), systems development, systems implementation, and training. These expenditures need to be made before the system becomes operational.

Operating costs are incurred on an ongoing basis after the system is fully implemented. Costs such as operation and maintenance labor, facility usage, and supplies are classified as operating costs.

Identification of Benefits that Will Be Derived from the Use of the System

Benefits from IS can be classified as tangible and intangible. *Tangible benefits* are easy to express in dollars, and *intangible benefits* are difficult to quantify. Tangible benefits are reduced labor costs, reduced hardware costs, inventory reduction, increased sales, market expansion, and increased revenue. Intangible benefits are strategic advantage in the marketplace, improved work coordination, improved resource control, improved customer service, higher-quality decision making, and improved strategic planning.

Comparison of Costs with Benefits

After the costs and benefits are quantified, a cost-benefit evaluation technique is applied. To fairly compare costs and benefits, all dollar amounts must be converted into present value. For example, $100 worth of benefit a year from now is worth only, say, $91 today. By subtracting the present value of the costs from the present value of the benefits, the real cost-benefit analysis can be generated. If a positive value is obtained, the project has merit.

METHODS OF ACQUIRING IS

Traditionally, information systems are developed by in-house IS professionals using a lifecycle organization of the development process. This step-by-step process ultimately generates an IS. However, the drawback of the life-cycle approach is the time consumed and the costs of development.

To overcome these disadvantages, other information development strategies have emerged. Some of them use a quick development strategy and others subcontract development to other vendors. The most popular strategies are internal development by IS professionals using a life-cycle methodology, internal development by IS professionals using a prototyping approach, internal development by end-user computing, outsourcing, and purchase of a package.

Internal Development by IS Professionals Using a Life-cycle Methodology

The typical or formal means of system development is the life-cycle methodology. Despite the drawbacks of the life-cycle approach, some large-scale IS projects still use this methodology for system development. The life-cycle consists of four stages:

1. *System analysis:* Before an IS project can be designed, a survey must be made to understand what needs to be done. What opportunities and problems are involved in this project? What type of information is required? This stage can be very time consuming and expensive. However, if system analysis is not well done, the rest of the stages may encounter more difficulties, or the project may even become infeasible.

2. *System design:* After the information requirement is fully understood, the design of the system begins. This stage provides a blueprint of what the system should be. The economics of the system should also be considered. To satisfy the information requirement, there may be different approaches to designing the system. The trade-off between a less expensive system and a more sophisticated one with a longer life span could be the issue.

3. *Coding and testing:* The individual software modules of the system are coded, tested, and then integrated into an operational system as further levels of testing proceed to ensure continuing quality control. System documentation is produced as the project progresses.

4. *Installation, training, and maintenance:* After the programming stage, the integration of different pieces of program should be put together. The integration and testing should be conducted in the actual environment where it will be developed and conversion of operations done to fit the new system.

Internal Development by IS Professionals Using a Prototyping Approach

A *prototype* is a preliminary working system that is built quickly and inexpensively, with the intention of modifying it. The initial prototype is particularly helpful in the development of the user interface. The prototype is turned over to users, who work with it and make suggestions for modifications. During this learning process, both users and developers discover the actual user requirements.

Internal Development by End-User Computing

End-users may be classified in terms of how the software is used:

1. *Sophisticated use of information technology by end-users:* This is the lowest level of end-user computing since end-users use existing software as it has been installed.

2. *End-user control of systems:* This, the second level of end-user computing, allows end-users to take control of their system that they are using. The advantage of such systems is that end-users can install or modify the systems as they want them to be. This dramatically improves the effectiveness of IS usage if end-user control is properly implemented. However, the disadvantage for some end-users is a lack of IS knowledge, which results in a poorly functioning IS with no professional maintenance.

3. *End-user development of certain applications:* This is often a highly productive approach, and it can place IS into end-users' hands more quickly than an IS professional can. By developing their own systems, end-users avoid the multiyear backlogs of systems development projects awaiting the attention of IS units in many firms. If the end-user coexists with the IS professional properly, the communication gap between end-users and the IS professional shrinks or even disappears. In addition, development and training costs can be reduced. Certain applications are suitable for end-user development. The characteristics of applications software that are suitable for end-user development are as follows:

   a. The complexity and the size of the IS project should be fully evaluated and calculated. A very complicated IS may fail without professional IS people involved.

   b. The application software should be for limited use, such as personal use or within a specific organization.

   c. There are no high security, privacy, or data integrity demands.

   d. The application software does not involve a large number of transactions. It should be for management support, such as in decision support systems or executive information systems.

Because more and more information systems are developed by end-users, there has been some concern about the risk involved in end-user development. The risk, however, can be reduced if certain management controls are implemented. Possible risks are:

1. *Poor system analysis process:* Without proper training and real-life experience in system development, end-users can make mistakes such as:

     Identifying the right problem

     Applying the wrong analytical method to the problem

     Overlooking or underlooking a potential problem

     Using the wrong software tool

   However, more training and experience can reduce the risk of these risks.

2. *Poor system design process:* The benefit of information systems comes from the right combination of computer hardware, software, and infrastructure of the company. How to create an environment that provides a compatible system is one of the most immportant and difficult tasks. For example, different database management systems may not be able to share information with each other, or they may downgrade the performance of the whole system. Therefore, enterprise standards should be established for hardware, software, and network acquisition. Departure from such standards can be made only for valid reasons.

3. *Inefficient use of financial resources.*

Outsourcing

The use of contract programmers or IS companies to develop application systems, rather than a firm's employees, is a long-established practice.

Known as *outsourcing,* this is the practice of contracting out the operation of a firm's IS center, communication networks, and application software development to external vendors, which can be individual programmers, system analysts, or IS service companies. Outsourcing arrangements may give the firm access to experienced IS specialists working for the vendor due to specialization and economies of scale. For example, an IS company with experts in a specific database management system may provide services to many companies with similar application software, thereby distributing the costs of hiring the experts. Therefore, by buying services from an outsourcing vendor, a firm may invest its resources more productively elsewhere and the client may pay for only the IS services it actually uses, resulting in further economies and flexibility, as compared with running an underutilized IS center.

The drawbacks are the lack of control when a company's IS center is outsourced due to a dependency on the outsourcing vendor, the lack of expected access to the technological talents, and unrealized savings.

The key successful factors are:

- *The selection of IS components to be outsourced:* The critical components with competitive strength for the firm should not be outsourced. For example, strategic IS components should not be outsourced since they have been consistently modified to challenge competitors in the marketplace. If the company loses control of strategic IS functions, the competitive advantages are no longer available and this greatly affects the future of the company.

- *How the outsourcing decision can be reversed if, in the future, the arrangement does not work out:* Appropriate contractual provisions are necessary, but not sufficient, for this contingency. Indeed, termination services to be delivered at the conclusion of the contract should be considered a part of an outsourcing contract.

- *Negotiation of the outsourcing contract with utmost care since it will affect a company's critical operation:* A typical outsourcing contract consists of:

    Baseline services, including routing IS services and basic IS functions.

    Extra services, including special ad hoc requirements and advanced IS services. Extra services usually require payment of extra fees. It is crucial to carefully examine the nature, volume, and quality of the baseline services to avoid excess charges in the future.

The trend for outsourcing has been promoted by the idea of "To specialize around your own core business and let experts in other fields handle what you do not specialize in." Long-term corporate partnerships may generate trust and satisfaction. Major companies that provide outsourcing services are Experian, Anderson Consulting, Computer Associates, Electronic Data Systems, and IBM.

Purchase and Customization of a Software Package

A company can choose to purchase a software package that satisfies most of its IS requirements instead of spending money and risking all its efforts in developing its own application software. However, packages are designed to fit most potential customers' needs; some features may not be good for this company and some may be too much for current IS requirements. In general, two types of software packages are based on customer segmentation:

- *Horizontal market:* This market focuses on general customers regardless of the industry they are in. For example, word processing packages and spreadsheet software are in this category.

- *Vertical market:* This type of software concentrates on a specific business or industry. An example is a package designed for retail management systems or gas station operations.

How software is sold can be different:

- *Site license:* Site license allows users to use a package in a certain area without the limitation of the number of licenses. Users usually purchase an agreement to use this software as long as it is used within a particular area.

- *Individual license:* One license allows one installation of the software with one concurrent user.

There are two ways of purchasing software:

- *One-time purchase:* This purchase allows users to purchase the software without future upgrades.

- *Upgradable purchase:* With a premium paid, the user can purchase a license with an upgradable agreement for a number of years. In other words, the user can get free upgraded software when it is available within the contractual time period.

There are two ways of purchasing in terms of how software is installed:

- *Individual installation:* A copy of the software is installed in each computer.
- *Network installation:* A copy of the software is installed in the network server. Many client computers can then access the server computer for the usage of the software.

The principal advantages of a package purchase over internal development are that the purchase is generally less expensive and it takes much less time for implementation. Once properly installed, a purchased software package is almost ready to use. The disadvantages are that it is not flexible in adapting the software to the evolving needs of the enterprise and it does not support special functions required by the company.

CONCLUSION

Information resources management is very important. The success of information systems depends not just on the resources itself but mainly on how the resources are properly managed. It is a difficult task because of the complexity of information resources. A good way to improve the management of information resources is to understand the full capability of information technology and the interactivity between end-users and computer systems. The ultimate goal is to integrate users' expectations and information technology in every functional area in the company so that the IS strategic plan can fully embrace the strategic plan of the company.

2 RISK MANAGEMENT

Risk management helps an organization avoid accepting risk simply out of ignorance. It helps in making informed risk-management decisions. Risk-analysis techniques may be quantitative or qualitative. The common objectives of risk management include:

- Avoiding, reducing, or transferring risk.
- Reducing the cost of managing risk.
- Actively managing risk in a consistent manner throughout the organization.
- Providing senior management with reports on risk-management activities within the organization.

While it is virtually impossible to foresee or predict all risk events, care should be taken to ensure a minimum acceptable level of risk analysis. This can often be achieved by classifying the risk into various categories and subcategories. For example, risk may be categorized into (a) internal threats, (b) external threats, and (c) environmental threats. Internal threats may then be further classified as (a) intentional or (b) unintentional, and so on. The process of categorizing risk events helps ensure the completeness of risk analysis.

Risk may also be analyzed and categorized in terms of assets. For example, a list can be prepared of an entity's assets and the types of risks to which they may be vulnerable. Yet another way to categorize risk is by the outcome of each threat. Possible outcomes, for example, are (a) damage or contamination to data files, (b) disclosure of sensitive or private information, and (c) theft of computer hardware, etc.

Risk management is used to balance the information security and information access needs of the organization. The resources expended on security should be cost effective. While this appears to be obvious, many organizations do not perform a cost-benefit analysis. For example, many organizations devote considerable resources to protect their computer system from "outsiders," whereas an organization is typically much more susceptible to threats from "insiders."

THE RISK-ANALYSIS PROCESS

The risk-analysis process consists of four steps. The risk analyst needs to determine:

- The scope of analysis.
- The assets to be protected.
- The risks and vulnerabilities.
- The safeguards to be implemented.

Scope

The risk analyst determines the scope of the analysis through discussions with top management. At this stage, a decision should be made about the parts of a company that are to be evaluated. Information should be collected about equipment and facilities, policies and procedures, and the security practices of the company. It is also appropriate to discuss security policies with top management, including determining the acceptable level of risk. Some questions to ask are:

- How are risk-management activities organized?
- Are risk-management activities being coordinated?
- Which individuals are responsible for managing risk?
- What's the level of senior management's involvement in risk management?

Assets

The assets that need to be protected are determined next. This is typically done by interviewing company personnel. The accounting department should also be able to provide a list of assets and their historical cost.

Assets provide probable future economic benefits, and they may be tangible or intangible. *Tangible assets* include hardware, software, documentation, property, plant, and equipment. *Intangible assets* include goodwill, patents, and trademarks. Tangible assets have physical substance while intangible assets lack physical substance. Such distinction, however, is not always clear. For example, the data or information owned by a company is extremely important and would probably best be classified as intangible.

The risk analyst should determine the value and importance of each asset. A determination should be made of the consequences if the integrity of assets is compromised. Customers might be lost. There may be a threat of lawsuit for violation of privacy laws. Fines might be imposed by government and regulatory agencies. Even human lives might be lost. Most organizations face the following threats with respect to assets, which may be accidentally or intentionally:

- Destroyed
- Unavailable
- Modified
- Misused
- Disclosed

Risks and Vulnerabilities

Assets are vulnerable to loss. Potential risks need to be identified. Threats usually come from three sources: (a) internal threats, (b) external threats, and (c) environmental threats. Internal and external threats may be intentional or accidental. Such threats include human error, equipment malfunction, theft, vandalism, fraud, viruses, and other malicious acts. Environmental threats include loss due to flood, fire, earthquake, etc. The job of identifying potential risks can be facilitated by categorizing risk events. It is essential that the risk analyst check for completeness in analysis. The probability and the magnitude of potential loss should be assessed. This typically involves the following assessments:

- *Exposure factor (EF):* This represents the degree of loss in the value of an asset resulting from occurrence of a risk event. Its value ranges from 0% to 100%.

- *Annual expected frequency (AEF):* This represents the number of times a risk event is expected to occur per year. For example, if a risk event is expected to occur 10 times per year, *AEF = 10.* If a risk event is expected to occur once every five years, *AEF = 1/5 = .20.* If *AEF = 0,* then the risk event is not expected to occur. It is a measure of certainty that a risk event will occur. AEF, however, is not the same as probability; probabilities are, by definition, limited to 100%. AEF, on the other hand, has no ceiling and can increase very rapidly. For example, consider a small company with 10 employees, where each employee makes unintentional errors that violate the integrity of assets about twice a month. The AEF, in this instance, is equal to 240 ($10 \times 2 \times 12$). This value is determined using statistical data on the occurrence of past events and the analyst's judgment.

- *Single loss exposure (SLE):* SLE represents the monetary loss exposure from a single risk event. It is calculated as follows:

    SLE = Monetary value of asset × Exposure factor

- *Annual loss expectancy (ALE):* ALE represents the total annual expected monetary loss from all risk events. The annualized loss number can be used to plan budgets for risk management/reduction activities. The ALE is calculated as follows:

    ALE = SLE × AEF

Safeguard Selection and Implementation

The final step involves identifying, evaluating, and implementing safeguards to minimize the effect of risk events. A vulnerability, such as unauthorized access to data or unprotected hardware, exists in a system generally because one or more safeguards are missing.

There are various general types of safeguards. *Preventive safeguards* aim to eliminate the risk event. After the occurrence of a risk event, safeguards may be used to *mitigate* the effect of the risk event. *Detective safeguards* are used to become aware of the occurrence of a risk event. Finally, *recovery safeguards* are used to bring things back to normal after the occurrence of a risk event.

There is no standard method for determining optimal safeguards. Expert judgment is needed to determine the appropriate set of safeguards. Many risk-analysis software packages provide such recommendations.

The total cost of a safeguard must be identified to determine if a safeguard is cost effective. It is very difficult to determine the amount that should be spent on safeguards. When determining the cost of a safeguard, it is important to consider that many safeguards actually reduce costs by enhancing productivity, improving performance, and reducing errors and irregularities; the cost of a safeguard should therefore be computed net of such savings. In fact, it is even possible that implementing a safeguard may result in net savings rather than costs.

Safeguards should be designed such that little or no human involvement is needed for their effective operation. A safeguard that does not involve human intervention is generally stronger than one that relies on human involvement. The human involvement should be considered not only during the operation of the safeguard but also during its servicing.

The safeguards should contain some sort of automatic or manual override capabilities in the event that safeguards are violated. It should be possible to shut down every type of safeguard. No safeguard should be so completely protected that it is impossible for humans to shut it down completely in a cost-effective and safe manner. It should also be possible to disable a safeguard for servicing and maintenance. Of course, care should be taken to ensure that servicing and maintenance are performed by authorized individuals, and the actions of these individuals should be audited. Fail-safe safeguards that automatically reverse in the event of a failure should also be used. No safeguard should harm humans unless an even greater harm is posed by the violation of the safeguard. In an emergency or natural disaster, the failure of a safeguard should never result in loss of life.

It should be possible to monitor safeguards to ensure that they are operating properly and to identify any failures or violations. Any failure or violation should be immediately reported to information systems management. A record should be kept of past violations or attempted violations.

Even well-designed safeguards can fail due to unforeseeable events. It is therefore imperative that the safeguard contain instrumentation, such as a periodic report, to monitor its functioning. The lack of proper instrumentation may lead to a great danger of a negative safeguard; that is, the computer system may be assumed to be functioning effectively when, in fact, it is not. An added benefit of instrumentation is that the individuals responsible for monitoring the safeguard are constantly updated about its correct functioning and are immediately made aware when something goes wrong, such as if a violation is attempted or the safeguard fails. The instrumentation should not be voluminous; otherwise, it will tire and distract the user. It should be as concise and usable as possible.

Complete specifications and instructions should be available for each safeguard. The specifications should describe the purpose of the safeguard and what it is capable of doing. The specifications should also state what the safeguard is not supposed to do. The relationship between safeguards should also be documented. It is better for the safeguards to be independent of each other. A failure in one safeguard should not necessarily result in the failure of other safeguards. Some safeguards depend on each other, and the serial nature of the safeguards should be considered. As the value of an asset increases, so should the number of safeguards that would need to be violated to access the asset. Moreover, violation of a safeguard in a series of safeguards should generate an alert as well as strengthen other related safeguards. Violators may attempt to attack several safeguards at once. Serial safeguards are generally simpler to design and may be used to replace more complex design structures. Of course, by keeping the design of safeguards simple, you increase reliability, reduce costs, and reduce implementation errors.

Safeguards should be applied uniformly and have a minimum of exceptions. As exceptions are created for safeguards, one decreases the effectiveness of the safeguards and increases the possibility of failures. While exceptions are sometimes necessary, they should be kept to a minimum and be well documented.

For safeguards to be effective, there should be segregation between those who control the safeguards and those who are controlled by it. In smaller organizations it can be especially difficult to achieve such segregation. Under such circumstances, two or more individuals can be involved in each safeguard. Multiple control sometimes offers advantages over complete segregation. For example, two individuals must sign a check over a certain limit, such as $10,000.

It is important to ensure that safeguards do not excessively interfere with normal job performance. Otherwise, workers naturally tend to bypass, override, or avoid the safeguard. A safeguard that is part of the worker's normal routine is more likely to be followed than a safeguard that requires a special effort on the worker's part.

The effectiveness of a safeguard should not depend on the secrecy of its mechanism. An effective safeguard protects the system even when violators know of its existence and its design mechanism. For example, cryptographers assume that the code breakers are just as knowledgeable as the designers. Therefore, they do not rely on the secrecy of the encoding method, but rather on the complexity of each key used. If a safeguard must rely on design secrecy, then certain key variables should be changed on a periodic basis to deter violators.

Some organizations find entrapment a useful technique. However, on balance, it is probably best to avoid such a strategy. Under this strategy, one or more of a system's vulnerabilities are made especially attractive to potential intruders. The intruder is expected to choose to exploit one of these vulnerabilities. These vulnerabilities are therefore heavily monitored, and it is generally possible to detect and stop the intrusion. This strategy can fail simply because the intruder may decide to attack a safeguard that is not heavily monitored. The intruder and the organization may not necessarily agree on what is really a weakness or vulnerability in the system. This strategy also may be at least partially unethical. Making a vulnerability attractive may in fact entice an otherwise innocent individual to attack the system. In general, it is best to avoid any strategy that encourages individuals to attack the system.

A safeguard's effectiveness should have longevity. It should be as effective after several years of use as it is on its first day. Automated safeguards tend to possess this characteristic. In safeguards involving humans, boredom or fatigue may set in and reduce the effectiveness of the safeguard. One must constantly keep humans motivated to keep the safeguard effective.

Accountability for each safeguard should be assigned to at least one person. No individual should be assigned responsibility for too many safeguards or the likelihood of violations increases. In addition, responsibility for the safeguard should be directly integrated, whenever possible, with the worker's normal routine.

Since workers can often override safeguards, the personnel must accept the safeguards. The workers must feel that the safeguards are important, and it is the management's job to convince the workers. Management should follow the same safeguards that they expect from their workers. Automatic safeguards that require minimal human intervention should be used whenever possible. It is dangerous to have a safeguard that appears attractive to violate; you don't want the workers to see the safeguard as a challenge and have the workers try to violate it.

Safeguards should also be periodically audited to ensure compliance with specifications. Each safeguard should be auditable, and criteria should be established to test them. Auditors should play a significant role in evaluating the auditability of safeguards. A conflict of interest results when the auditors involved in designing the safeguards also test the safeguards; it is essential that different auditors be used in each of the design and testing phases. The total cost of testing a safeguard should be explicitly considered. Such testing also helps to determine whether the safeguards are functioning as expected. Some safeguards may behave unexpectedly. For example, safeguards may reveal sensitive information to attackers that would help the attackers in future attacks on the computer system.

Some safeguards expend themselves in the process of protecting assets. For example, halon gas may be released automatically in a minor fire. After the fire, there is still a need to protect the assets and the halon gas may need to be recharged. Consideration must be explicitly given to protecting the assets in the interim period.

Safeguards should be selected based on their primary risk-reduction function. Frequently, however, two or more safeguards appear to be equally effective. Under such circumstances, their secondary functions should be considered.

COST-BENEFIT ANALYSIS

From a conceptual perspective, cost-benefit analysis is very simple. For an analyst to undertake a task, such as implementing a safeguard or undertaking a project, the benefits from implementation should exceed the costs. However, from a practical perspective, cost-benefit analysis can be very difficult to perform. The measurement of costs and benefits is generally quite complex. Sometimes the costs and benefits are difficult to quantify. Furthermore, there may be timing differences and the time value of money needs to be considered. For example, an immediate expenditure may benefit the organization over several years. One needs to consider both the initial and ongoing cost of implementing safeguards. While the measurement of costs and benefits can be complicated, the risk analyst needs this information to conduct a formal quantitative analysis.

Consider the two examples in Figure 2-1. The risk analyst has made estimates of the costs and benefits of undertaking the project. The same costs and benefit figures are used in both examples. Without considering the time value of money, the net benefit in both examples is $6,500 over a five-year period. However, when the time value of money is considered, Example A shows net benefits of $2,667 and Example B shows a net loss of

Figure 2-1.
DISCOUNTED COST-BENEFIT ANALYSIS

Example A: Discount Rate: 10%

Year*	Benefit	Cost	Net Benefit	PV Discount Factor**	Discounted Net Benefit
0	$ —	$ 5,000	$ (5,000)	1.0000	$ (5,000)
1	$ 3,000	$ 2,000	$ 1,000	0.9091	$ 909
2	$ 4,000	$ 6,000	$ (2,000)	0.8264	$ (1,653)
3	$ 8,000	$ 3,500	$ 4,500	0.7513	$ 3,381
4	$ 3,500	$ 2,500	$ 1,000	0.6830	$ 683
5	$ 9,000	$ 2,000	$ 7,000	0.6209	$ 4,346
Total	$27,500	$21,000	$ 6,500		$ 2,667

Example B: Discount Rate: 25%

Year*	Benefit	Cost	Net Benefit	PV Discount Factor**	Discounted Net Benefit
0	$ —	$ 5,000	$ (5,000)	1.0000	$ (5,000)
1	$ 3,000	$ 2,000	$ 1,000	0.8000	$ 800
2	$ 4,000	$ 6,000	$ (2,000)	0.6400	$ (1,280)
3	$ 8,000	$ 3,500	$ 4,500	0.5120	$ 2,304
4	$ 3,500	$ 2,500	$ 1,000	0.4096	$ 410
5	$ 9,000	$ 2,000	$ 7,000	0.32777	$ 2,294
Total	$27,500	$21,000	$ 6,500		$ (473)

*Cash flows are assumed to occur at the end of each year. Year 0 represents cash flows at the beginning of year 1.

**The discount factor is the present value of a single sum. It is calculated as follows:

$$PV = \frac{1}{(1 + i)^n}$$

where,

i = discount rate

n = number of periods (years)

$473. The difference is due to the discount rate. The discount rate reflects the time value of money. The discounted rate should be based on factors such as the inflation rate and the opportunity cost of alternatives.

Sensitivity analysis may be performed to investigate the effects of variability in making cost-benefit decisions. A small change in the discount rate may have a significant effect on the overall net present value, as shown in Figure 2-2. As the discount rate increases, the net present value (NPV) decreases.

Figure 2-2. SENSITIVITY ANALYSIS:
THE EFFECT OF INTEREST DISCOUNT RATE ON NET PRESENT VALUE

Year*	Net Benefit	Discounted Net Benefit**						
		7%	8%	9%	10%	11%	12%	13%
0	$(10,000)	(10,000)	(10,000)	(10,000)	(10,000)	(10,000)	(10,000)	(10,000)
1	$ 7,000	6,542	6,481	6,422	6,364	6,306	6,250	6,195
2	$ (3,000)	(2,620)	(2,572)	(2,525)	(2,479)	(2,435)	(2,392)	(2,349)
3	$ 4,000	3,265	3,175	3,089	3,005	2,925	2,847	2,772
4	$ 9,000	6,866	6,615	6,376	6,147	5,929	5,720	5,520
5	$ (4,890)	(3,487)	(3,328)	(3,178)	(3,036)	(2,902)	(2,775)	(2,654)
Net present value	$ 2,110	$ 566	$ 372	$ 183	$ 0	$ (177)	$ (350)	$ (517)

*Cash flows are assumed to occur at the end of each year. Year 0 represents cash flows at the beginning of year 1.

**The discounted net benefit is the present value factor of a single sum multiplied by the undiscounted net benefit. It is calculated as follows:

$$Discounted\ net\ benefit\ =\ \frac{1}{(1+i)^n}\ \times\ Net\ benefit$$

where,

i = discount rate

n = number of periods (years)

A small change in or deviations from estimated costs and benefits may have a significant effect on net benefits. Figure 2-3 shows the net benefits for a three-year period while the estimates for the costs and benefits vary considerably. This analysis assumes that each outcome is equally likely. It is easy to incorporate probabilities into one's analysis when the outcomes are not equally likely. Monte Carlo simulation may be used for more extensive analysis.

Figure 2-3. SENSITIVITY ANALYSIS:
THE EFFECT OF CHANGES IN COSTS AND BENEFITS ON NET BENEFITS

Cost/Benefit Matrix of Net Benefits for Year 1

		Benefit						
		$ 5,000	$ 7,000	$ 8,000	$ 8,500	$ 9,000	$10,000	$11,200
	$ 2,500	2,500	4,500	5,500	6,000	6,500	7,500	8,700
	$ 3,000	2,000	4,000	5,000	5,500	6,000	7,000	8,200
	$ 3,320	1,680	3,680	4,680	5,180	5,680	6,680	7,880
Cost	$ 5,000	—	2,000	3,000	3,500	4,000	5,000	6,200
	$ 8,000	(3,000)	(1,000)	—	500	1,000	2,000	3,200
	$ 9,000	(4,000)	(2,000)	(1,000)	(500)	—	1,000	2,200
	$15,000	(10,000)	(8,000)	(7,000)	(6,500)	(6,000)	(5,000)	(3,800)

Cost/Benefit Matrix of Net Benefits for Year 2

		Benefit						
		$ 6,520	$ 7,100	$ 7,800	$ 8,450	$ 8,750	$ 9,000	$ 9,500
	$ 3,500	3,020	3,600	4,300	4,950	5,250	5,500	6,000
	$ 4,000	2,520	3,100	3,800	4,450	4,750	5,000	5,500
	$ 4,250	2,270	2,850	3,550	4,200	4,500	4,750	5,250
Cost	$ 4,600	1,920	2,500	3,200	3,850	4,150	4,400	4,900
	$ 5,100	1,420	2,000	2,700	3,350	3,650	3,900	4,400
	$ 5,300	1,220	1,800	2,500	3,150	3,450	3,700	4,200
	$ 5,500	1,020	1,600	2,300	2,950	3,250	3,500	4,000

Cost/Benefit Matrix of Net Benefits for Year 3

		Benefit						
		$ 2,550	$ 2,800	$ 3,300	$ 3,650	$ 4,000	$ 4,225	$ 4,500
	$ 1,250	1,300	1,550	2,050	2,400	2,750	2,975	3,250
	$ 1,600	950	1,200	1,700	2,050	2,400	2,625	2,900
	$ 2,250	300	550	1,050	1,400	1,750	1,975	2,250
Cost	$ 3,000	(450)	(200)	300	650	1,000	1,225	1,500
	$ 3,350	(800)	(550)	(50)	300	650	875	1,150
	$ 3,755	(1,250)	(955)	(455)	(105)	245	470	745
	$ 4,800	(2,250)	(2,000)	(1,500)	(1,150)	(800)	(575)	(300)

Determining the benefits of safeguards is generally more difficult than determining their cost. The benefits are basically loss reductions in the effect of risk events. Sometimes it is possible to measure the benefit in monetary terms. Other times, such as when goodwill or other intangible assets are lost, the benefits derived from safeguards may not be determinable in monetary terms.

INSURANCE AND RISK ACCEPTANCE

Generally, the risk of loss can never be totally eliminated or avoided. Any formal analysis should explicitly consider the types and levels of risks that a company is willing to accept. Insurance may be purchased to transfer or assign the risk to another entity. Risk may also be transferred to another party more adequately prepared to assume such risks. For example, document storage may be transferred to another entity that is better prepared to store or archive records.

Criteria should be established for risk acceptance. A threshold limit should be set and no risk beyond that threshold should be accepted in the absence of a specific exception. For example, it may be decided that the threshold is a 3% chance of losing $500,000. A specific informed decision should then be made if a risk entails, for example, a 5% chance of losing $500,000. The acceptance of risk should be well documented. While rarely done in practice, senior management should be asked to sign the document stating that they are willing to accept responsibility for the risk. Periodically, the original decision should be reassessed to determine whether accepting the risk is still warranted.

Most organizations purchase some type of insurance for their computer systems. Frequently, however, small but significant gaps exist in coverage. Typically, you rely on an insurance professional's advice concerning the type and amount of coverage. Many companies do not realize how much coverage they need till they suffer a loss and have to file a claim. The rapid changes in technology further complicate an accurate assessment of coverage needs.

In comparing possible insurance policies, ask the following questions:

- How long does it take to collect on the policy?
- What records must be maintained?

- Is there reimbursement for using substitute equipment and software after the original system was damaged or destroyed and the new system is installed?

- How many losses on the policy will it take for the insurer to cancel the policy or decline to renew coverage?

- What exactly does the policy include or exclude? For example, what happens if someone improperly accesses the online database for purposes of obtaining information or changing it?

- What exclusions exist in the policy? For example, does the company's own negligence prevent recovery?

- What is the usual percentage increase in premiums per year?

- Do premiums decrease if there are no losses over the years?

- Who are the insurance carrier's existing clients?

- Does this insurance carrier specialize in your industry?

- Is the insurance carrier financially strong? How is it rated?

Conventional business insurance policies do not address the real cost of computer systems and the business risks associated with them. For example, a conventional insurance policy may not include threats caused by viruses, electrical surges, flooding, lightning, etc. A standard policy also may not cover possible business interruptions. However, it is generally possible to extend coverage to cover such risks. Cost-benefit analysis should always be performed to determine whether it is prudent to pay a third party to cover such risks. The higher the deductible of a policy, the lower is the insurance premium. The decision to accept a risk should always result from an informed decision rather than simple ignorance.

The amount of insurance coverage should be based on the cost to replace the computer system, both temporarily and permanently. The rapid changes in technology mean that hardware and software are frequently upgraded. The replacement value of computer systems also changes rapidly. The insurance policy should cover all the new systems. Moreover, make sure that you are not paying for coverage on systems that have been moved to another location/division, replaced, or retired. Insurance records should be reviewed periodically and updated accordingly. Insurance records include information about payments, refunds, write-offs, premiums paid, losses, settlements, values of insured items, claim status, policy dates, and inspections.

The following types of coverages may be needed by your organization and should be discussed with your insurance professional.

- *Loss of income,* or business interruption insurance covers losses due to computer failure, including lost profits during shutdown, continuing fixed costs, incremental cost to replace computer equipment, and overtime. Policies typically restrict the length of time this type of coverage will apply as a result of physical loss or damage to electronic records. What is the limit on losses covered?

- *Extra expense* coverage pays for expenses incurred in excess of ordinary business expenses. These expenses are typically incurred to continue business operations after suffering a loss. Such expenses include the cost of obtaining temporary space and computer equipment while the covered equipment is being replaced or repaired.

- *Valuable papers and records* insurance covers the cost of researching and replacing lost data when a backup does not exist. A conventional insurance policy generally limits coverage for damage to electronic media, such as magnetic tapes/disks and CD-ROMS, to the value of the physical media. In other words, the insurance will not pay for the *value of data* stored on the media unless that coverage is specifically included.

- *Theft/disappearance* insurance covers not only theft but also accidental loss. While all computer equipment should be insured for theft, it is especially important for portable computer equipment.

- *Utility interruption* insurance coverage is necessary for damages caused by electrical surges and lightning that enters through electrical lines.

- *Computer programming errors* are typically excluded from coverage. Software vendors should be asked to provide a certificate of insurance to confirm that they have an error-and-omissions policy.

- *Temporary locations* should be covered by extending insurance coverage. Many policies do not cover computer equipment that is in transit or off premises at a temporary location. Company-owned equipment is sometimes permanently located at an employee's home and it, too, may not be covered. Coverage should be included for computers at client offices. A *floater coverage* may be purchased for such items. A *mobile equipment* coverage should be purchased for computer equipment that is permanently installed in trucks and motor vehicles.

- *Fidelity bonds* covering employees insure against the theft of equipment by staff.

The amount of insurance coverage depends on many factors, including the frequency of brownouts in the area, the likelihood of unauthorized use, the honesty and competence of staff, the incidence of crime in the locality, and the need for a continuous working environment. In conclusion, getting the right insurance is as important in obtaining the best computer system with the best service contract.

A plan should be established to assess risk on a regular and periodic basis. In a dynamic environment, risk should be assessed at least annually. In a less dynamic environment, risk should still be assessed every two or three years.

TOOLS FOR RISK ANALYSIS

Risk-analysis techniques are used to evaluate loss exposure to an enterprise's assets. Risk analysis and management involve determining the following:

- What assets must be protected?

- From whom should the assets be protected?

- How are the assets to be protected?

- Are the benefits derived from protecting the assets greater than the costs of protecting the assets?

Various automated tools are available for managing the risk exposure of computer systems. These tools help risk analysts measure and evaluate risk in computer environments using qualitative, quantitative, or both approaches. *Quantitative tools* typically express the results in monetary terms, while *qualitative tools* express the results in linguistic terms. Quantitative techniques typically require an assessment of the probability and the loss magnitude for each risk event to determine annual loss expectancy. The loss exposure is then ranked by the level of severity. Qualitative techniques may be used to rank the relative importance of an organization's various assets. They are typically used when it would be inappropriate or impossible to quantify the data. There is no consensus among risk analysts as to which approach is better.

Given the many choices, it is often difficult to compare the various tools. A system with shortcomings in one area may have significant features in another area. The following guidelines should help in selecting appropriate risk-analysis tools.

Usability and User-Friendliness   This is perhaps the most important criterion. The tools must be usable and provide an intuitive interface. Risk-management tools are unlikely to be used so frequently as a word processor or spreadsheet. Since risk-management tools are not used so frequently, the user will experience a learning curve each time he or she uses the package if the software lacks user-friendliness. For example, the user's manual should not be needed after the initial training. The system should allow the user to concentrate on the task and not be burdened with learning the intricacies of the system.

- The software should not rely on technical jargon and terminology; it should use clear and familiar terminology for input and output. Risk-analysis tools tend to use their own terminology. Look for software that defines the terms carefully. Also make sure that the questionnaires are well written.

- The system should be able to anticipate mistakes users are likely to make and allow them to correct errors easily.

- At any given point, users should know exactly where they are and what options are available next.

- The system should never "lock" users into an option. It should always enable them to "escape" or back out of an option. It should always be possible to undo an action; preferably, the system should allow users to "undo" several last actions.

- The system should be effective in handling errors. Error messages should be clear and easy to understand. The system should provide suggestions and context-sensitive help, as appropriate.

- There should be flexibility in data entry formats, including providing default values for data input.

- The system should prevent the user from accidentally damaging, deleting, or modifying data.

- The system should support various types of access features, such as read-only, read and write, etc.

Vendor   When conducting a thorough review in selecting a risk-analysis system, it is essential to consider not only the system, but also the supplier (see sidebar on the following pages for list of vendors).

- Look for a company with a history of performance. However, with the rapid changes in technology, it may be better to go with a newcomer to the industry if their product is superior.

- Consider the market size of the company, such as the number of clients they have or their revenues, and the company's experience with your industry. It is also a good practice to ask for and check references.

Support   Users often overlook technical customer support. Consider the type of support provided by the vendor. Here are some questions to ask when checking references:

- Does the vendor provide any type of initial training to users, including live instruction, video tapes, and online tutorials?

- How large is the support staff and what is the quality of response?

- What are the hours of operations?

- How easy is it to get through to the vendor?

- Is it possible to reach the vendor through different means, including telephone, fax, e-mail, and interactive online?

- What is the quality of written documentation?

- Is online help available and what is its quality?

- Is source code available for custom modifications?

- How frequently is the software typically updated?

- When was the last version released?

- How long is technical support free? What are the charges after the free period?

Risk Analysis Vendors

ANALYSIS 2000
Business Resumption Planners
San Carlos, CA

**Automated Risk Evaluation System
(ARES)**
Air Force Communications and
    Computer Security Management
    Office
Kelly AFB, TX

**Bayesian Decision Support System
(BDSS)**
Ozier, Peterse & Associates
Petaluma, CA

The BUDDY Risk Analysis System
Countermeasures, Inc.
Hollywood, MD

Control Matrix
Jerry Fitzgerald & Associates
Redwood City, CA

Control-It
Jerry Fitzgerald & Associates
Redwood City, CA

**CCTA Risk Analysis and Management
    Methodology (CRAMM)**
Executive Resources Association
Arlington, VA

COSSAC
Computer Protection Systems, Inc.
Plymouth, MI

CRITI-CALC
International Security Technology
Reston, VA

GRA/SYS
Nander Brown & Co.
Reston, VA

IST/RAMP
International Security Technology
Reston, VA

JANBER
Eagon, McAllister Associates, Inc.
Lexington Park, MD

**Los Alamos Vulnerability and Risk
    Assessment (LAVA)**
Los Alamos National Laboratory
Los Alamos, NM

LRAM
Livermore National Laboratory
Livermore, CA

MARION
Coopers & Lybrand
London, England

Micro Secure Self Assessment
Boden Associates
East Williston, NY

MINIRISK
Nander Brown & Co.
Reston, VA

continued

Predictor Concorde Group International Westport, CT	**@RISK** Palisade Corp. Newfield, NY
PRISM Palisade Corp. Newfield, NY	**RISKCALC** Hoffman Business Associates, Inc. Chevy Chase, MD
QuickRisk Basic Data Systems Rockville, MD	**RISKPAC** Computer Security Consultants, Inc. Ridgefield, CT
RANK-IT Jerry Fitzgerald & Associates Redwood City, CA	**RISKWATCH** Expert Systems Software, Inc. Long Beach, CA
RA/SYS Nander Brown & Co. Reston, VA	**SOS** Entellus Technology Group, Inc. Longwood, FL

Education and Training   Most risk-analysis packages offer some type of instruction on computer security. The users might become more aware of security issues by completing the input requirements of the package. Some developers require security questionnaires to be distributed to team members with diverse backgrounds and responsibilities, and this approach has proven to be effective. Training should be an important consideration in selecting the risk-analysis tool. The effective use of any tool is limited if the risk analyst lacks appropriate training. A comprehensive online tutorial helps considerably in training risk analysts in the proper use of the software.

Technical Expertise   The technical expertise needed to use risk-analysis tools varies. It is your responsibility to ensure that your organization either has or can bring in the needed technical expertise. Inaccurate results may be derived if the tools are used by individuals lacking technical experience in security problems.

Analysis Techniques   Risk-analysis tools typically use techniques such as probabilistic analysis, fault trees, event trees, matrix representation, and fuzzy set theory. Many tools approach these techniques in different ways. Fuzzy sets are typically used in tools that accept qualitative verbal inputs. The analysis methodology should be technically proven, reliable, and mathematically sound. The risk-analysis system should not rely on an experimental methodology; the methodology should have been successfully used and have a proven track record. A reliable system yields consistent results even if another methodology is used. A package that uses both qualitative and quantitative methods is preferable to one that uses only one approach. The package should also provide assistance with many aspects of computer security risk management, including cost-benefit analysis and safeguard selection.

Likelihood Assessment   Assessing the likelihood or frequency that a risk event will incur is an important part of risk analysis. Likelihood assessments represent one's confidence in the probability that a threatening event will occur. Many risk-analysis packages ignore likelihood assessment considerations. While such assessments are difficult to make, some estimate is nonetheless needed for risk analysis. It is desirable for the risk-analysis software to address the issue of likelihood assessments.

Flexibility   Useful features in risk-analysis software include the ability to write ad hoc reports, import and export data in a wide variety of formats, modify the questionnaire, redefine specific vulnerabilities or safeguards, add new fields to data, perform user-defined database query, etc. The software's utility is greatly enhanced if it allows changes to certain parts of the methodology without modifying its algorithms or mathematics. This is essential because there is no single universal criterion for selecting the combination of safeguards necessary to result in acceptable reductions in vulnerability. The software package should be adaptable to the needs of the user without direct intervention from the vendor.

Expansibility   The vendor should be able to offer a wide variety of tools that can be integrated with the risk-analysis software. Some tools may be needed immediately; others, later.

Customizability   The availability of source code is desirable. Vendors may also be willing to customize software.

Environments   The risk-analysis system should be capable of handling a variety of environments, such as distributed systems, applications, small system environments, and mainframe systems.

What-If Analysis   The what-if capability of the risk-analysis software allows the analyst to estimate the effect of certain proposed safeguards on risk.

Comprehensiveness   The system should be complete and provide comprehensive and reliable coverage of risk analysis. Most tools recommend how to decrease risk. The better risk-analysis tools also measure risk. The software should help the analyst in selecting appropriate safeguards. Its reports should list risks or vulnerabilities, as well as recommend safeguards. It should help the analyst determine what each proposed action will cost and the extent to which it will reduce risk and loss exposure.

Security   The software should provide means to limit access, such as thorough passwords. Multilevel passwords that restrict user's access by functions are desirable. Audit trail capabilities are a must.

Cost   The cost of risk-management software varies from a few hundred to several hundred thousand dollars. These packages vary in the complexity and the volume of data they are capable of processing. Many software packages offer modules for specialized functions at an additional cost. In addition to the basic cost of the software license, additional costs are typically incurred for the hardware, installation, training, or supplies.

Timing of Charges   The timing of charges may also vary considerably. It is possible to purchase the software system outright or to timeshare. One-time charges are often incurred for the software license, installation, and training. Additional ongoing charges are incurred for ongoing support and telecommunications. Variable charges may be incurred for timesharing usage or per claim.

3 SECURITY MANAGEMENT

INCREASING CONCERN FOR SECURITY THREATS

Security concerns have heightened in recent years. News events about computer-related data errors, thefts, burglaries, fires, and sabotage pervade the news. The nature of the computing environment has changed significantly. The increased use of networked computers—including the Internet, Intranet, and the Extranet—has had a profound effect on computer security. The greatest advantage of remote access via networks is convenience. This convenience makes the system more vulnerable to loss. As the number of points from which the computer can be accessed increases, so does the threat of attack. More caution is clearly needed to counter such threats. Weak computer security and lack of internal controls increase an organization's vulnerability to:

- Commission of fraud

- Theft of electronic information

- Theft of physical information, such as printed outputs or computer disks/tapes

- Invasion of privacy

- Damage to computers and peripherals

- Interception of communications

41

- Illegal recording of electromagnetic emanations from computers and peripherals
- Unintentional data errors due to carelessness or negligence
- Loss of information integrity through unauthorized alterations and modifications to data
- Sabotage by disgruntled employees or competitors
- Power failure

THE STEPS IN MANAGING COMPUTER SECURITY

The first step in managing computer security is to *identify the resources that need to be protected.* For example, the resource to be protected might be CPU cycles or computer time. This is unlikely to be the objective of most attackers or hackers. Frequently, hackers are interested in obtaining access to private or confidential information. Sometimes the organization may not even consider the information to be "valuable" to anyone else and may not be willing to take security precautions. This is a serious mistake. Hackers often steal or destroy data or information simply because it is there! Other hackers delete or destroy files in an attempt to cover their illegal activity. This leads to just one conclusion: A casual attitude towards computer security is never justified.

The second step in managing computer security is to *determine against whom you want to protect the system.* The security needs of a military computer system are likely to be significantly different from the security needs of a corporation. Are you trying to protect your computer system against teenagers "playing around" or corporate spies and industrial espionage?

The third step in managing computer security is *balancing the costs and benefits* of various security safeguards. In other words, how much are you willing to spend on security? Clearly, it is prudent to spend more on protecting the resources that are of greater value to the organization. The cost of security safeguards include not only the direct cost of the safeguards, such as equipment and installation costs, but also indirect costs such as employee morale and productivity. It is important to recognize that increasing security typically results in reduced convenience. For example, employees may resent the inconvenience that results from implementing security safeguards. Too much security can be just as detrimental as too little security; a balance must be maintained.

The last step in managing computer security is *contingency planning*. Assuming that security is violated, how do you recover? What are the data backup policies? What are the legal consequences? What will be the financial impact?

A risk analysis should be performed in planning computer security policies and financial support. Computer security risks fall into one of three major categories: destruction, modification, and disclosure. Each of these may be further classified into intentional, unintentional, and environmental attacks. The threat comes from computer criminals and disgruntled employees who intend to defraud, sabotage, and "hack." It also comes from computer users who are careless or negligent. Lastly, the threat comes from the environment; an organization must protect itself from disasters such as fire, flood, and earthquakes.

An effective security plan must consider all three types of threats: intentional attacks, unintentional attacks, and environmental attacks. What is the company's degree of risk exposure? Insurance policies should be taken out to cover such risks as theft, fraud, intentional destruction, and forgery.

Business interruption insurance covers lost profits during downtime. A computer system can fail for several reasons, including:

- Operator mistakes

- User mistakes

- Malicious acts

- Hardware malfunction

- Software bugs

- Environmental factors such as lightning, fire, earthquake, or power outage

When discussing computer reliability, distinguish among errors, failures, and faults in a computer system. An *error* occurs when there is a deviation from expectations. Some errors are acceptable because they can be overcome; others are not. An unacceptable error is a *failure*. If the failure can have serious consequences, it is considered a *critical failure*. A *fault* is a condition that results in a failure.

System reliability is distinct from system security. Security is designed to protect against intentional misuse and does not consider malfunction.

Improving one factor often enhances the other factor. Both factors need to be considered in managing risk.

ESTABLISHING A SECURITY POLICY

Every organization should have a security policy that defines the limits of acceptable behavior and the organization's response to violations of such behavior. Its purpose is to assign accountability and delegate authority across the organization. Security policy naturally differs from organization to organization, based on unique needs. For example:

- There may be an edict barring the playing of computer games on corporate computers.
- There may be a policy against visiting adult websites on the Internet using corporate Internet accounts or computers.
- Some organizations may wish to restrict the use of a specific protocol because it cannot be administered securely.
- Employees may be prohibited from taking copies of certain corporate data off office premises.
- There may be a policy prohibiting the use of pirated software.

The security policy should not only define acceptable behavior, but also contain the organization's response to violations. How will the violators be reprimanded? Will the organization reprimand violators inside the organization differently from violators outside the organization? What type of civil or criminal actions might be taken against violators?

The security policy should be a broad statement that guides individuals and departments in achieving certain goals. The specific actions needed to realize the goals are contained in supporting standards rather than in the policy document. The security policy should be concise and to the point, generally not exceeding ten pages. It should be easy to understand. Its focus should be on emphasizing the role of individuals and departments in achieving the objectives. The purpose of the security policy is not to educate or train individuals. Such an objective is better served through training seminars.

The background for developing a security policy should be discussed, including the purpose of security and why data integrity must be maintained. The importance of maintaining the confidentiality and privacy of information resources should be emphasized. The continuous availability of information is important for the organization, and any interruption can have serious financial consequences.

Employees should understand that computer security is everyone's responsibility. The scope of the computer security policy should encompass all locations of the company and all its subsidiaries. Security is only as strong as its weakest link and therefore the same set of standards should be used throughout the organization. This means that the standards should be flexible enough so that they can be used in a wide variety of circumstances and conditions, yet they should provide consistency and quality across the organization.

The security policies apply to all computer facilities and the data they contain, including standalone computers, Internet and Intranet sites, local area networks (LANs), and wide area networks (WANs). All forms of electronic communication, including e-mail, fax, and data transmissions, are covered by the security policy. Other printed material, such as documentation and technical specifications, should be included in the security policy.

Computer security should be viewed as a means to an end and not an end itself. Computer security is an integral component of an organization's overall risk-management strategy. The responsibilities of various departments and individuals should be identified in the security policy. The policy established should be evaluated on a periodic basis to incorporate changes in technology or circumstances. The authority for issuing and amending the security policy should rest with a committee such as the Information Technology Management Committee. This committee should be responsible for determining when circumstances justify departure from the policy; all exemptions and exceptions should be approved by the committee.

Active participation by individuals and departments is needed for a security policy to succeed. It is well established that individuals are more likely to accept the security policy if they have had input during its creation. The real benefit of participation is that employees or departments will make a positive contribution to the policy by imparting their knowledge. Senior management's support and cooperation are critical in implementing the policy.

The relationship between the computer security policy and other corporate policies should be described. For example, the computer security policy should be used in conjunction with the firm's policies for:

- The internal control structure

- Contingency plans, including business resumption planning

- Privacy and confidentiality

- Compliance with local and federal laws and regulations

A process should be in place to ensure compliance with laws and regulations. Privacy and confidentiality issues have a serious effect on computer security. Increased governmental regulation should be expected in the future. The legal department should assist department heads in complying with laws and regulations.

The responsibilities of the information systems department and its security personnel should be defined in the security policy document. These responsibilities include:

- Ensuring that security personnel have the training and skill needed to perform duties required by the security policy

- Providing computer security assistance to other departments

- Being responsible for all computer networks and communications

- Providing systems development methodology for security needs

- Being responsible for all cryptographic methods and keys

- Providing and managing virus detection software for networked and standalone computers

- Being responsible for acquiring hardware or operating systems that are not currently part of the organization's architecture

- Authorizing the use of the network, including the Internet and Intranet

- Reviewing, evaluating, and approving all contracts with third parties concerning information systems

For personal computer systems, additional precautions are needed and should be addressed in the security policy. Some points to consider include:

- All original data should be backed up on a periodic basis.
- Personal computers connected to a network may be a source of viruses; virus detection software should always be used, especially before copying data or programs onto the network.
- Confidentiality and privacy of data must never be compromised.
- Certain types of confidential or important data should never be stored on a local hard drive. Such data should be stored on the network, on floppy or compact disks, or on removable hard drives so that it may be removed and stored in a secure place.
- Standards should be established for remote access.
- Personal computers should not be directly connected to the Internet since the Internet is a source of virus infections and hackers may be able to gain access through it. Internet access should be only through the company's Internet server, which is capable of protecting itself.

FINANCIAL LOSS AND THE COST-BENEFIT CRITERION

The danger of financial loss to a company can be greatly reduced by increasing computer security. In all likelihood, not investing in appropriate security measures will prove to be far more expensive for a company than investing in the appropriate security measures. It would even be appropriate for a company to consider the cost of investing in computer security as a form of insurance.

The cost of security measures must always be compared with the benefits received. As Figure 3-1 illustrates, the optimal level of security expenditure is when the combined cost of security measures and financial loss is minimized. The law of diminishing returns clearly applies. Expenditures on security measures beyond a certain point are not likely to be cost effective. While appropriate security measures can greatly reduce the likelihood of a financial loss, security measures by themselves cannot guarantee against every type of damage and accident; a certain degree of risk will always have to be accepted.

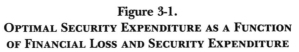

Figure 3-1.
OPTIMAL SECURITY EXPENDITURE AS A FUNCTION
OF FINANCIAL LOSS AND SECURITY EXPENDITURE

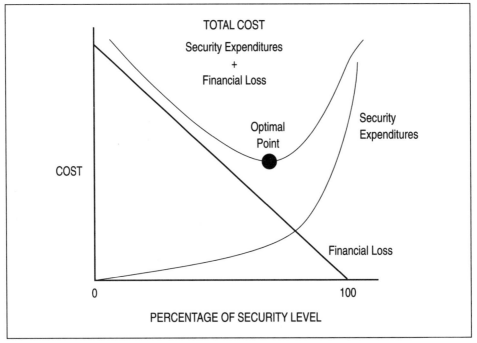

The cost-benefit criterion dictates that a company formally assess the risks it faces. The following three questions must be answered by the organization:

- What types of threats may affect our organization?
- What is the probability that a threat will occur?
- What is the potential liability for each threat?

For each type of threat, the expected loss may be calculated as follows:

Loss expectancy = Probability of loss × Amount of loss

Using this formula, expected losses may be placed into three categories. As shown in Figure 3-2, loss expectancy is highest for category A and lowest for category C. Clearly, considerable attention must be directed toward category A since both the amount of loss and its probability are high.

In contrast, little attention needs to be given to category C items, which seldom occur and whose associated loss is small. Professional judgment is required to determine which items in category B require attention.

Figure 3-2.
LOSS EXPECTANCY

		High	Low
	High	A	B
	Low	B	C

(Amount of Loss on vertical axis)

While this model is theoretically appealing, it has serious practical limitations. The model relies heavily on estimating future probabilities and costs; it is extremely difficult to make such estimates with reasonable accuracy. When implementing the model, it is also possible for the user to overlook many serious indirect consequences of the threat.

IDENTIFYING PHYSICAL SECURITY AND DATA SECURITY

Physical security is the first line of defense in protecting a computer system; it encompasses the plant, equipment, and personnel. Data security is also of vital concern to an organization; data integrity, data accuracy, and data privacy are of paramount importance. Both physical and data security considerations are equally important. An effective security system will prevent a security breach. However, if in spite of proper protection, a system is successfully attacked, the system should create an audit trail to allow prompt investigation.

Computer Room

The *computer room* is the structure that houses the computer facilities. Unauthorized access to the computer room should be restricted. Sensing and surveillance devices may be installed. The plant should be designed to protect the computer environment, including heating, cooling, dehumidifying, ventilating, lighting, and power. Air ducts of air conditioning units should be secured against access with heavy-gauge screens.

Appropriate care must be taken to protect the plant from harm from accidents and disasters such as fires and floods. Adequate emergency lighting should be available for safe evacuation in case of fire or other disaster. Consideration must be given to the loss or damage to computer equipment and peripherals. Media, such as disks, tapes, and output, should be protected. User manuals for equipment and software must be protected to maintain the continuity of proper operations. Surge protectors should be used to protect the computer system against power line disturbances. Finally, the organization must consider the loss of or injury to its personnel.

Not only must the organization be concerned about the physical safety of its employees, it must also consider the threat of psychological dissatisfaction. Disgruntled employees may do intentional damage. Moreover, job turnover associated with dissatisfied employees disrupts the routine operation and maintenance of computer systems.

The layout of computer facilities is important in planning for computer security as well as for achieving cost savings. As computers become smaller, they can be housed in smaller areas and this changes how facilities are designed and planned. For example, it is no longer necessary to have raised floors in the computer room. If wiring is a concern, cables can generally be installed along the walls. If flooding is a concern, aluminum channels or I-beams can be used to raise components and cabinets. Cabling costs can be saved by placing the network equipment next to the processing equipment. Smaller components may be stacked vertically to conserve floor space and reduce cable costs.

The computer room should be housed in a building's core area near wire distribution centers. Care should be taken to avoid locations where water or steam pipes cross either vertically or horizontally. The room should be sealed to keep out smoke and dust.

Only one door should be used for access into a secured area. The door should be self-closing and it should not have a hold-open feature. A combination or programmable lock may be sufficient. An alarm system should be installed. There should not be any direct access from public places.

Protecting Information

The integrity, accuracy, and privacy of data must be protected. Data integrity is essential to computer security. Data lacks *integrity* if it is missing, incomplete, inconsistent, or if it is poorly designed in a database environment. The concept of accuracy is distinct from that of integrity. Data is *accurate* if it is reliable and the data is what it purports to be. *Privacy* means that only authorized individuals have access to data. Programmers should not have free access to the computer area or library due to possible data manipulation. Important diskettes should be locked up.

Wires and Cables

With the increase in distributed computing, it is even more essential to protect the wiring system. Wires and cables are generally made of either copper or optical fiber. Fiber optics offer significant performance and security advantages. However, they cost more to install. Still, if considerable data needs to be transferred, the cost disadvantage of fiber optics rapidly diminishes.

Cables and wires are fragile. They can be easily damaged. It is not possible to repair damaged wires; they must be replaced. The electrical properties of cables may also be affected and the data may become unreliable. Alternate paths should always be provided for cables linking important or critical paths.

Fiber optics offer better security protection. Someone who can obtain access anywhere along the length of copper lines can wiretap them relatively easily. Such wiretaps are very difficult to detect. In contrast, it is difficult and expensive to wiretap fiber optics. Moreover, normal operations are disturbed in a fiber optics tap and can therefore be detected more easily. Even with fiber optics, a skilled individual with proper equipment can tap the system undetected. Fiber optics provide a deterrent, but should not be viewed as perfectly secure. Of course, the best way to protect sensitive data is to use some type of encryption.

Fiber optics are not affected by electrical or magnetic interference. Copper wires have to be shielded with cabling and grounded metal conduits have to be provided.

The ends of all fiber optic cables must be microscopically smooth. They have to be exactly aligned and positioned. This requires the use of expensive special equipment and highly trained personnel.

Data wiring should be certified by a knowledgeable and experienced individual. Such an individual should:

- Perform a visual inspection.
- Check that each cable is connected correctly.

- Check that there are no crossed pairs.
- Use a reflectometer to detect if there are any constrictions, bad terminations, or external interference.

Purchase orders for any wiring should specify:

- Who will certify the wiring.
- What equipment will be used to test the wiring.
- What standards will be followed.

Destroying Data

Once data is no longer needed, it must be properly destroyed. Information on magnetic media is typically "destroyed" by overwriting. While the information appears to have been destroyed, there are many subtleties to consider. For example, if the new file is shorter than the old file, information may remain on the magnetic media beyond the new file's end-of-file marker. Any information beyond the end-of-file can be easily retrieved. A safe method is to overwrite the entire media. However, overwriting the entire media is time-consuming and other methods, such as degaussing, should be used. *Degaussers* are essentially bulk erasure devices and, when used within their specification, provide adequate protection.

Formatting a disk does not safely destroy all information. It is important to note that magnetic media may retain a latent image of the preceding bit value after the write insertion of a new bit value. This occurs due to the inability to completely saturate the magnetization. While normal read/write operations are not affected by this limitation, it does pose a security threat and anyone with sophisticated equipment could exploit it.

Papers and other soft materials, such as microfiche and floppy disks, can be shredded. Some shredders cut in straight lines or strips. Others offer cross-cutting and particle-producing. Some shredders disintegrate the material by repeatedly cutting and passing it through a fine screen. Shredders may also grind the material and make pulp out of it.

Burning is still another way to destroy sensitive data that is no longer needed. As with shredding, burning means that the storage media can no longer be reused. Even burning requires caution. It is possible, for example, to retrieve printed information using special techniques from intact paper ashes, even though the information may no longer be visible to the human eye.

ENVIRONMENTAL CONSIDERATIONS

Computer facilities are susceptible to damage from environmental factors. Fire security is especially important and is discussed in detail in a separate section. Other important factors include heat, water, humidity, dust, and power failure.

- *Heat* can cause electronic components to fail. Air conditioning is generally essential for reliable operation. Simple precautions should be taken to ensure that air vents are not blocked and that the air is allowed to circulate freely. Backup power should be available for air conditioning if the computer system will be used even if the primary power fails.

- *Water* is an obvious enemy of computer hardware. Floods, rain, sprinkler system, burst pipes, etc., could do significant damage. Attention should be given to the routing of water pipes and the location of the computer facilities. Instead of a traditional sprinkler system, consider using an alternate fire-extinguishing agent that will not damage the hardware.

- *Humidity* at either extreme is harmful to the hardware. High humidity is likely to lead to condensation, which can corrode metal contacts or cause electrical shorts. Low humidity is likely to permit the buildup of static electricity. Computer facilities should either be housed on bare floors or floors covered with antistatic carpeting. Humidity should be continuously monitored and kept at acceptable levels.

- *Dust, dirt, and other foreign particles* can ruin computer hardware. For example, dust can interfere with proper reading and writing on magnetic media. Personnel should not be permitted to eat or drink near the computer facilities. Air should be filtered and filters replaced at appropriate intervals.

- *Power failure* can render all equipment useless. Brownouts and blackouts are the most visible sign of power failure. However, voltage spikes are much more common and can cause serious damage. Spikes may be produced by lightning, and they may either damage equipment or randomly alter or destroy the data. A drop in line voltage can also lead to malfunction of computer equipment and peripherals. Voltage regulators and line conditioners should be used if electrical fluctuations occur. Use of uninterruptible power supplies should be considered.

Maintenance and Preventive Care

Facilities should be protected against adverse effects of the weather and other environmental factors. Regular maintenance can help prevent unexpected downtime. Diagnostic programs should be run as part of regular maintenance. Maintenance logs should be kept. Recurring problems can be quickly identified by scanning the logs. The maintenance log should include at least the following information:

- Description of equipment serviced
- Company identification number of equipment serviced
- Date of service
- Services performed, including the results of diagnostic tests
- A note indicating whether the service was scheduled or unexpected

Computer areas should be properly cleaned and dusted. Eating, drinking, and smoking should be prohibited in computer areas. Personnel should be trained in proper handling of computer equipment and peripherals. They should also be trained in the proper handling of magnetic media and CD-ROMs. For example, magnetic media should not be placed on top of or near telephones, radios, and other electric equipment. Labels should be prepared prior to placing them on a disk; many untrained personnel will affix the label to the disk and then write on the label using a ballpoint pen.

Computers and peripheral equipment should be cleaned on a regular basis using cleaning products recommended by the manufacturer. Electrical equipment should never be sprayed directly with cleaning liquids. Keyboard surfaces should be cleaned with a damp cloth and vacuumed using special computer vacuums.

Magnetic media devices, especially the read/write heads and transport rollers, should be cleaned using commercially available cleaning products for such purpose. Dust, smoke, fingerprints, and grease can build up on recording surfaces and lead to crashes or permanent damage to the equipment and magnetic media. Printers may need to be cleaned to remove fibers, dust particles, and lint.

Simple precautions, such as using static-resistant dust covers, protect the computer equipment and peripherals. Such covers should be used only when the equipment is not in use. Otherwise, the equipment may overheat and be damaged.

Water Alert Systems

Water alert systems should be installed where water might damage computer equipment. Generally, water alert systems should be installed in the basement or in floors above the computer systems. Water-sensing systems are especially useful in protecting electrical cables under the floor. Water sensors should be installed within suspended ceilings and inside water-cooled computer cabinets and process cooling equipment. The water sensors should activate an alarm as well as some type of drainage pump.

Static Electricity

Static electricity results from an excess or deficiency of electrons. An individual could easily become charged to several thousands of volts. While the current from electrostatic discharges is too low to harm humans, electronic equipment could easily be damaged.

Protective measures against electrostatic discharges include grounding, shielding, filtering, and limiting voltage. Vinyl flooring is generally better than carpeting to avoid the buildup of static electricity. Simple precautions can minimize the dangers from static electricity; these include:

- Using antistatic spray
- Grounding computer equipment
- Using antistatic floor and table mats
- Maintaining the proper level of humidity

Humidity Control

Humidity should be tightly controlled and maintained at an optimal level. When the air is too dry, static electricity is generated. When humidity is too high, generally at levels above 80% relative humidity, there may be problems with electric connections, as a process similar to electroplating starts to occur. Silver particles start to migrate from connectors onto copper circuits, thus destroying electrical efficiency. A similar process affects the gold particles used to bond chips to circuit boards. Generally, an optimal relative humidity level is about 40–60%.

IMPLEMENTING EFFECTIVE FIRE PROTECTION

According to insurance companies, fire is the most frequent cause of damage to computer centers. No combustible material should be allowed in the computer room. This means special care should be taken in selecting office furniture. Waste receptacles of any kind should not be in the computer room. Instead, waste receptacles should be located nearby, just outside the computer room.

Fire and Smoke Detection Devices

Fire detectors should be installed in appropriate locations and connected to an automatic fire alarm system. Fire detectors sense either changes in temperature or thermal combustion and its byproducts. Fire detectors may be actuated by smoke, heat, or flame.

Smoke-actuated devices provide early warning for slowly developing fires. Smoke detectors should be installed in air conditioning and ventilating systems. Smoke detectors typically rely on either photoelectric devices or radioactive devices.

- *Photoelectric smoke detectors:* Variations in the intensity of light cause changes in electric current in the photoelectric cell. Photoelectric smoke detectors are generally of three types:
  - *Area-sampling* photoelectric devices draw in air from the area to be protected. If smoke is present in the sampled air, the light reflections on the photoelectric cell trigger the alarm.
  - *Beam* photoelectric devices focus a beam of light onto a photoelectric cell across the protected area. The smoke causes an obstruction in the light, which activates the alarm.
  - *Spot* photoelectric devices, unlike beam photoelectric devices, contain the light source and the receiver in one unit. Light is not projected across the protected area. Instead, smoke entering the detector causes the light to reflect onto the photoelectric cell, activating the alarm.

- *Radioactive smoke detectors:* These smoke detectors contain a minute amount of radioactive material in a special housing. Smoke interacts with the radioactive material and changes its ionization, thus activating the alarm. Radioactive detectors are most commonly the spot type.

The response time for radioactive smoke detectors is affected by several variables, including the stratification of air currents and the nature of products of combustion. Generally, the heavier the particles resulting from combustion, the longer it takes them to reach the ceiling where the smoke detectors are usually attached and the longer the response time of the unit. *Note:* The danger from radiation from such detectors is minimal and all detectors must meet or exceed government standards.

Heat-actuated detectors can be of two types. The first type activates the alarm when the temperature reaches a fixed predetermined value. The second type of detector senses the rate of change in temperature. Typically when the rate of rise in temperature exceeds 15–20° F, the alarm is activated.

For highly combustible areas, the rate-of-rise temperature detectors are recommended due to their faster response time. However, fixed temperature detectors tend to be more reliable and are not so prone to false alarms. Some heat-actuated detectors contain both types of sensors.

Heat-actuated detectors are available in line or spot coverage styles. *Line* detectors usually rely on heat-sensitive cables or a pneumatic tube. *Spot* detectors are placed at fixed intervals in each zone.

Flame-actuated detectors are of two types: flame-radiation-frequency and flame-energy. *Radiation-frequency* detectors sense the flame-related flicker caused by combustion. These sensors tend to be expensive and are therefore suitable under limited circumstances. *Flame-energy* detectors sense the infrared energy of the flame. These are also expensive and tend to be suitable for protecting expensive equipment. The principal advantage of flame-energy detectors is their superfast detection of infrared energy of flame. These detectors are also capable of producing enough voltage to trigger the release of an extinguishing agent.

Types of Extinguishing Agents

Different types of fires require different types of extinguishing agents. Using the wrong extinguishing agent can do more harm than good.

- Fires involving ordinary *combustible materials,* such as wood, paper, plastics, and fabric, can be safely extinguished using water or triclass (ABC) dry chemical.

- Fires involving *flammable liquids and gases,* such as oil, grease, gasoline, or paint, can generally be safely extinguished using triclass (ABC) and dry chemical, Halon, FM-200, and carbon dioxide.

- Fires involving *live electrical equipment* should be extinguished using a nonconducting extinguishing agent, such as triclass (ABC), regular dry chemical, Halon, or carbon dioxide.

Electrical Fires

Most computer room fires are electrical, caused by overheating of wire insulation or other components. Smoke from an electrical fire may be toxic and it should be avoided in even small quantities. Generally electrical fires cannot be extinguished until the heat source is eliminated.

A power panel with circuit breakers for the major pieces of equipment should be placed at an easily accessible location, preferably inside the computer room. The circuits should be clearly labeled so that equipment can be shut down quickly in an emergency. Redundant devices should be on separate circuits. There should be one emergency switch to shut down everything in the event of a fire.

In the event of a major fire or explosion, the only concern should be the safety of human life. Computer equipment and wiring are likely to be destroyed by the intense heat. Backup copies of disks and data should always be kept at off-site locations. Off-site backup not only helps when attempting to recover from a fire, but it can also prevent personnel from attempting to save backup data by risking their lives.

Halon has the potential of depleting the ozone layer. While Halon is still in use, an international agreement was reached to stop its manufacture as of January 1, 1994. FM-200 is now available as a Halon substitute. Both Halon and FM-200 systems tend to be expensive, and governmental approval is often required. These systems are also not very effective against electrical fires. In an electrical fire, it is essential that the power be shut off because a fire extinguishing system will only suppress the fire until power is stopped.

Water Sprinklers

Water sprinkler systems are simple and a relatively inexpensive protection against fire. Most new buildings are required by code to have a sprinkler system. Accidental activation of the sprinkler system can cause substantial damage and it may take a long time before normal operations are resumed. In an electrical fire, water may even intensify the fire and cause greater damage. Sensors should be installed to cut off electrical power before sprinklers are turned on. It should be possible to activate sprinkler heads individually to prevent damage to a wide area. There should be a shut-off valve inside the computer room so that water can be turned off when it is no longer needed. This will minimize damage in the event of accidental activation.

Cleanup after a Fire

Carbon dioxide, Halon, and FM-200 extinguishers do not require any clean-up after discharge. However, carbon dioxide discharge can suffocate humans. Foam or dry chemicals can be hard to remove. Hand-held fire extinguishers should be mounted on walls. Self-contained breathing apparatus should also be mounted on the wall.

Smoke Removal

Quick removal of smoke should be a priority. Special fans and blowers should automatically be activated by the smoke or fire alarm.

Extinguishing Microcomputer Fires

If computer equipment starts smoking, the first step should be to cut off the equipment's electrical power. This is frequently sufficient and the fire will probably extinguish by itself. If there are visible signs of fire, or if you can feel the heat, an appropriate fire extinguisher should be used. Carbon dioxide extinguishers are often recommended for microcomputer-related fires. When using a carbon dioxide extinguisher, do not spray the extinguishing agent directly onto the glass surface of the CRT, because it will lead to a sudden drop in temperature and shatter the glass.

Training Personnel

Personnel should be trained for fire emergency. Company policy should state exactly what action should be taken in the event of a fire or smoke alarm. Personnel should be strictly forbidden from risking injury or loss of life to protect data or equipment.

Reducing Insurance Premiums

The following steps can reduce the damage caused by fire and, in the process, reduce insurance premiums:

- Safes for the storage of documents should have a minimum four-hour fire rating.

- The walls, floors, and ceilings of computer facilities should have a minimum two-hour fire rating.

- The fire alarm should ring simultaneously at the computer facility and the nearest fire department. In addition, fire alarm signals should be located where prompt response is assured.

- Vaults used for storing backup tapes and records should be located in a separate building at a sufficient distance.

- Smoke and ionization detection systems should be installed throughout the ceiling of the computer facilities. Water detection systems should be installed under the floor of computer facilities.

- Halon, FM-200, or a similar fire extinguishing system should be installed throughout the computer facilities. Automatic sprinkler systems can be used in the supply and support areas. In case of destruction, there should be a disaster recovery plan.

- Building code and fire marshal regulations must be adhered to strictly.

CONTROLLING ACCESS AGAINST TAMPERING AND IMPROPER USE

Access controls guard against the improper use of equipment, data files, and software. The oldest method of restricting physical access is by using a lock. Locks may be classified into two types: preset and programmable.

With *preset locks,* the access requirements cannot be changed without physically modifying the locking mechanism. *Programmable locks* may be either mechanical or electronic. The combination on the programmable locks can be more easily changed as security needs change. A basic problem with such locks is that the entry codes are frequently easy to obtain by an observer. Some types of electronic locks overcome this problem by using a touch screen that randomly varies the digit locations for each user and by restricting directional visibility to basically a perpendicular angle.

Security guards and security dogs are another way to restrict access in a wide variety of situations. The physical presence of guards and dogs serve as a deterrent. In the event of a problem, the guard is able to respond appropriately. Preemployment screening and bonding are essential when hiring security guards. Certain states, such as New York, have mandatory training requirements for guards.

Limitations with such methods are well known. Guards can become easily bored with the routine work and may not fulfill their duties as expected. It is easy for someone to forge identification and be let in by a guard. Another limitation of guards is that they may not be informed and through procedural error allow unauthorized individuals access to restricted areas.

Guard dogs are also very useful and act as deterrents. Dogs have excellent hearing and a keen sense of smell. Guard dogs can be trained to "hold" intruders until security personnel arrive. One disadvantage of security dogs is that additional liability insurance must be purchased. Training and maintaining dogs is expensive. Finally, guard dogs generally cannot differentiate between authorized and unauthorized visitors.

Still, security is enhanced if guards and/or dogs patrol the facilities frequently and at random intervals. The use of guards and dogs contribute to psychological deterrence. It lets potential attackers or intruders know that they might be caught. Determined attackers, of course, are unlikely to be deterred by psychological deterrents and security should always be supplemented through other means.

Something as simple as lighting greatly enhances security. Lights improve the ability of security personnel to carry out surveillance and deter intruders from entering the facilities. Either lights may be left on all the time, on timer control, on ambient control, or they may be activated by motion detectors or manually operated.

To limit access, a security system must be able to discriminate between authorized and unauthorized individuals. Access can be limited using three general methods:

- *Identification:* Identification is based on comparing the physical characteristics of the individual with previously stored information. For example, an individual's signature, code, voice print, palm print, fingerprint, teeth print, or other personal trait could be verified before allowing access. Secondary authentication, such as the user's place of birth, may be required for highly sensitive information.

- *User's name and password:* Passwords are based on some memorized combination of letters or numbers. There should be no logic to the password, so that it cannot be easily guessed. Individuals are authorized based on what they know. Passwords should be changed regularly. Inactive passwords (e.g., more than four months old) should be deleted. Passwords should be changed and confidential data withdrawn from terminated employees. If a user changes a password, controls must exist to assure that the user does not use an old password. Passwords should not be shared. Access control software may be used to have a minimum password time period in which either a new password cannot be changed or a new password that matches an old one will be rejected.

- *Cards/keys:* Access can also be limited through the use of cards, keys, badges, etc.; individuals are authorized based on what they possess. Improper access may be signaled by an alarm. An unauthorized access pattern should be evaluated. *Smart cards* may be used; users enter both their identification number and a randomly generated code that changes each time the card is used or over a stated time period.

Computer and terminal access controls include:

- *Automatic shut-off:* The system signs itself off if the user fails to sign off after the transmission is completed.

- *Call-back:* A phone call is made to the terminal site to verify the user's identity before access is granted to the system.

- *Time lock:* Access is denied to the system during specified hours, such as after normal business hours.

Within the plant, areas containing sensitive data should be accessible only to authorized personnel. These areas, including the computer room, should have a single entry door, which can be operated only by an appropriate encoded magnetic-strip ID card. Physical controls include having a librarian keeping a log. A lockout should occur with repeated errors. Logs should automatically be kept of the ID number, time of access, and function performed. Further, data dictionary software provides an automated log of access to software and file information. Intrusion detection devices, such as cameras and motion detectors, should be used to monitor sensitive and high-risk areas against unauthorized individuals.

Are controls over processing, records maintenance, and file or software modification being diligently followed? Each function (such as accounts receivable or payroll) may have its own password so that users have access to limited areas of their authorization. The computer can keep an internal record of the date and time each file was last updated. This internal record should be compared against the log. The hours to access "key" microcomputer files should be limited. This prevents unauthorized access after normal working hours. Files should be categorized in terms of different levels of confidentiality and security such as top secret, confidential, internal use only, and unrestricted. Confidential information should not be displayed on the screen. To control access to sensitive data, access requirements to the system components should be mapped. Access rights should be based on job function, and there should exist an appropriate segregation of duties. Temporary employees should be restricted to a specific project, activity, system, and time period.

INSTITUTING A HARDWARE SECURITY PROGRAM

Computer hardware has improved in reliability and speed tremendously. These technological advances, however, have not always had a beneficial impact on computer security and data integrity.

Parity checks and data redundancy are critical for error-free data processing. Extra bits are included at predetermined locations to help catch certain types of errors when data is moved back and forth between different devices or from storage to registers.

- *Vertical redundancy checks* (*VRCs*) are used frequently despite problems. VRCs are simple and inexpensive to implement. A determination is initially made as to whether there should be an odd or an even number of 1 bits in each character's binary code. An error is detected if the correct number (either odd or even) of bits is not transmitted. A basic flaw with such an approach is that two offsetting errors may cause the error to go unnoticed. Furthermore, there is no standardization of the use of odd or even parity among manufacturers or suppliers.

- *Longitudinal redundancy checks* (*LRCs*) provide an additional safeguard since VRCs may not detect all the errors. This technique involves the use of an extra character that is generated after a predetermined number of data characters. The bits in the extra character provide parity for its corresponding row. An LRC approach has its limitations. It cannot correct multiple errors or errors in ambiguous positions (ambiguous bit is correct for VRC but incorrect for LRC), or errors that do not result in both a VRC or LRC indication.

- *Cyclical redundancy checks* (*CRCs*) are typically used when extra assurance of data accuracy is needed. A large number of redundant data bits are used. This requires longer transmission times and extra space in memory. The primary advantage of this technique is that any single error, whether in data bit or parity bit, is detected.

Hardware typically also has several features to protect the data during input, output, and processing:

- *Dual-read* involves reading the same data twice and comparing the two results. Any discrepancy indicates an error.

- *Read-after-write* requires reading the data immediately after it is recorded to verify the accuracy of the write function.

- *Echo check* is used to verify the reception of a signal when data is transmitted to another computer or peripheral devices such as printers.

- *Replication* is an important feature for critical applications. A backup computer or site is used in the event of failure of the primary computer. Fault-tolerant or fail-safe computers contain at least two processors that operate simultaneously; if one processor fails, the other processors pick up the load. When a critical application requires extensive communication facilities, the backup equipment should contain both communication equipment and a processor. Repairs or replacement of the malfunctioning equipment should be undertaken immediately.

- *Overflow* may result when an arithmetic operation, such as dividing by zero, results in values beyond a computer's allowable range. This function is typically built into the computer hardware.

- *Interrupts* are generated when the hardware detects deviations. Interrupts are used to maintain the integrity of the data processing system. For example, input/output (I/O) interrupts result when a previously busy device becomes available. A check is made after each I/O interrupt to determine if the data has been written or read without error. I/O interrupts are also generated when the Escape or Enter key is pressed. From a security perspective, such intervention can affect logs or result in the execution of unauthorized programs.

Other types of interrupts include program check interrupts, machine check interrupts, and external interrupts. *Program check interrupts* terminate the program and occur as a result of improper instructions or data. *Machine check interrupts* are generated as a result of defective circuit modules, open drive doors, and parity errors. *External interrupts* result from pressing an Interrupt key, from a signal from another computer, or by timer action. From a security perspective, for example, the built-in electronic clock in the processor can be used to generate an interrupt at a specified interval to ensure that sensitive jobs do not remain on the computer long enough to be manipulated or modified. Appropriate action should be taken to ensure that loss of data does not result because of interrupts.

Security Record Keeping

Most integrated circuit chips on hardware equipment appear to be inscrutable to a layperson. There are hundreds of thousands of transistors on a small semiconductor. Still, a bug can be planted into electronic equipment, and it may be very difficult to detect. Several techniques may be used to seal the hardware against tampering.

Records should always be kept of hardware failure and computer downtimes. Regular maintenance should be performed periodically and records should be maintained. If computer equipment frequently requires servicing, personnel might be tempted to bypass controls and take shortcuts. The possibility of human errors therefore increases considerably. Records should be analyzed to determine if an unfavorable trend is observed in downtime or if the equipment frequently requires unscheduled service.

Records should be kept for all computer equipment and peripherals. The hardware inventory logs should contain at least the following information:

- A description of the hardware
- Manufacturer's name
- Model number
- Serial number
- Company identification number
- Date of purchase
- Name, address, and phone number of stores where the item was purchased
- Date warranty expires
- The department or location where the hardware equipment will be used
- The name and title of responsible individual
- The department name
- The signature of the responsible individual or department head
- If the equipment is taken off premises, the date and time the equipment is checked out, and the date and time the equipment is returned, along with the signature of the authorized individual

The hardware inventory logs should be stored in a secure location. A copy of the logs should also be stored in an off-site location. All hardware should be etched or engraved with the company name, address, telephone number, manufacturer's serial number, and company's identification number. To prevent theft, locking devices should be used to secure computer equipment and peripherals.

INSTITUTING A SOFTWARE SECURITY PROGRAM

Program Development and Maintenance

Segregation of duties is essential in protecting computer programs during the development and modification stages. When software is developed and maintained internally, changes are frequently made to meet evolving requirements. The source code is generally stored in the source library, while the compiled and executable version of the program is stored in the production library. The source library is under the control of the programmer, whereas the production library should be under the control of computer operations or a similar entity that does not have programming responsibilities.

All programs and data files should have date and time stamps, including both production and test versions. Date and time stamps make it possible to determine the current version of the program in the event of an error or malfunction.

The transfer of programs from test to production status should be accompanied by management authorization. The quality assurance department should do a formal review before releasing the final production version.

Whenever modifications to a program are required, the reasons and requirement must be documented to prevent fraudulent modification. Requests for modification should include at least the following information:

- Description of the change

- Why the change is needed

- How the change will benefit the department or organization

- Name, title, and department of individual requesting the change

- Approval of department head or another authorized individual

- Date of request

- Date of desired completion (the time by which modifications should be made)

Once the information systems department receives the request to modify a program, it should determine:

- The priority of modification and the estimated date of completion

- The cost to make the modifications and the charge to the user department

The user department should be notified of the budgeted cost and the estimated completion time. The user department should approve the estimated completion time and budgeted cost.

A control sequence number should be assigned to the modification. Change requests should be tracked from the time they are initially submitted to the time the changes are completed. A programmer or analyst should be assigned the primary responsibility for making the changes. A determination should be made as to how the modified program will be tested. This generally requires the cooperation of the user department.

Small changes or emergency modifications should be possible without going through the full formal control procedure. Such changes should be carefully monitored. At a minimum, the following information about the modification should be documented:

- Description of modification
- Approval of the user department
- Review of source code changes by a supervisor

Password Security

Passwords are subject to attack using several techniques. One technique, which relies on brute force, was frequently used in the past. All possible combinations were tried until the attacker was successful. To prevent such unauthorized access, the number of unsuccessful tries should be limited. Moreover, unsuccessful log-in attempts should be audited.

A hacker is often able to guess the correct password because many individuals select words or strings of characters that have a logical association with the individual under attack. For example, individuals often select the following easily guessable words:

- Spouse's, girlfriend's, or boyfriend's name
- A child's name
- Pet's name
- Social security number
- Phone number
- Own birthday, or a loved one's birthday
- Words like "password" or "code"

It is best to select a password that does not appear in a dictionary. It is also a good idea to include numbers or characters, such as a question mark or a percentage or a dollar sign in the password.

It is sometimes possible for a hacker to edit the password file and insert bogus user names and passwords. To protect against such an attack, the password file should be properly protected against unauthorized writing.

The passwords should always be kept in an encrypted format. Otherwise, it is easy for someone to scan for commands that are followed by passwords, such as log-ins, to capture passwords either from storage or as they are typed or routed.

A serious design flaw can sometimes result in the creation of a "universal password." Such a password satisfies the requirements of the log-in program without the hacker actually knowing the true and correct password. In one case, for example, a hacker could enter an overly long password. The overly long password would end up overwriting the actual password, thus allowing the hacker unauthorized access.

Saboteur's Tools

While in recent years ingenious procedures have been developed to preserve computer security, many computer systems are still astonishingly insecure. Saboteurs may use a wide variety of tools and techniques to overcome security. Some of the methods are as follows:

- *Trojan horse:* The saboteur places a hidden program within the normal programs of the business. The computer continues to function normally, while the hidden program is free to collect data, make secret modifications to programs and files, erase or destroy data, and even cause a complete shutdown of operations. Trojan horses can be programmed to destroy all traces of their existence after execution.

- *Salami techniques:* The perpetrator can make secret changes to the computer program that cause very small changes that are unlikely to be discovered but whose cumulative effect can be substantial. For example, the perpetrator may steal ten cents from the paycheck of each individual and transfer it to his own account.

- *Back door or trap door:* During the development of a computer program, programmers sometimes insert a code to allow them to bypass the standard security procedures. Once the programming is complete, the code may remain in the program either accidentally or intentionally. Attackers rely on their knowledge of this extra code to bypass security.

- *Time bomb/logic bomb:* A code, inserted into a computer program, may cause damage when a predefined condition occurs.

- *Masquerade:* A computer program is written that masquerades or simulates the real program. For example, a program may be written to simulate the log-in screen and related dialogue. When a user attempts to log in, the program captures the user's ID and password and displays an error message prompting the user to log in again. The second time, the program allows the user to log in, and the user may never know that the first log in was fake.

- *Scavenging:* A computer normally does not erase data that is no longer needed. When the user "deletes" data, that information is not actually destroyed; instead, the space is made available for the computer to write on later. A scavenger may thus be able to steal sensitive data, which the user thought had been deleted, but was actually still available on the computer.

- *Viruses:* Viruses are similar to Trojan horses, except the illegal code is capable of replicating itself. A virus can rapidly spread throughout the system, and eradicating it can be expensive and cumbersome. To guard against viruses, care must be taken using programs on diskettes or in copying software from bulletin boards or outside the company. Only disks from verified sources should be used. The best precaution is to use a commercial virus scanner on all downloaded files before using them. An example is McAfee's virus scan. Virus protection and detection are crucial.

- *Data manipulation:* The most common and easiest way of committing fraud is to add or alter the data before or during input. The best means of detecting this type of computer crime is to use audit software to scrutinize transactions and to review audit trails indicating that additions, changes, and deletions were made to data files.

  Batch totals, hash totals, and check digits can also help prevent this type of crime. A *batch total* is a reconciliation between the total of daily transactions processed by the microcomputer and a manually determined total by an individual other than the computer operator. Material deviations must be investigated. A *hash total* is a total of values that would not typically be added so that the total has no meaning other than for control purposes. Examples are employee and product numbers. A check digit is used to ascertain whether an identification number (such as an account number or employee number) has been correctly entered by adding a calculation to the identification number and comparing the outcome to the check digit.

- *Piggybacking:* Piggybacking is frequently used to gain access to controlled areas. Physical piggybacking occurs when an authorized employee goes through a door using his magnetic-strip ID card, and an unauthorized employee enters the premises behind him. The unauthorized employee is then in a position to commit a crime. Electronic piggybacking may also occur. For example, an authorized employee leaves her terminal or desktop, and an unauthorized individual uses it to gain access.

INSTITUTING A COMMUNICATIONS SECURITY PROGRAM

Communication systems are used to link data between two or more sites. The communication system should be reliable, private, and secure. Communication systems are frequently affected by environmental factors, hardware malfunction, and software problems.

Attacks on computers that do not require physical access fall under the domain of communications security. The increased use of computer technology has also increased dependence on telecommunications. All types of data, including sound, video, and traditional data, are transferred between computers over networks. Communications security means ensuring that the physical links between the computer networks function at all times. This also means preventing breakdowns, delays, and disturbances during data transmission. Care must be taken to prevent unauthorized individuals from tapping, modifying, or otherwise intercepting data transmission. Six considerations in communications security are:

1. *Line security:* Line security is concerned with restricting unauthorized access to the communication lines connecting the various parts of the computer systems.

2. *Transmission security:* Transmission security is concerned with preventing the unauthorized interception of communication.

3. *Digital signature:* This is used to authenticate the sender or message integrity to the receiver. A secure digital signature process is comprised of (a) a method of signing a document that makes forgery infeasible and (b) validating that the signature is the one it is supposed to be.

4. *Cryptographic security:* Cryptography is the science of secret writing. The purpose of cryptographic security is to render the information unintelligible if unauthorized individuals intercept the transmission. When the information is to be used, it can be decoded. Security coding (*encryption*) of sensitive data is necessary. A common method is the *Data Encryption Standard* (*DES*). For even greater security, *double encryption* may be used, in which encryption is processed twice using two different keys. (One may also encrypt files on a hard disk to prevent an intruder from reading the data.)

5. *Emission security:* Electronic devices emit electromagnetic radiation, which can be intercepted, without wires, by unauthorized individuals. Emission security is concerned with preventing the emission of such radiation.

6. *Technical security:* Technical security is concerned with preventing the use of devices such as microphones, transmitters, or wiretaps to intercept data transmission. Security modems allow only authorized users to access confidential data. A modem may have graduated levels of security, with users assigned different security codes. There can be password and call-back features, as well as built-in audit trail capabilities allowing users to monitor who is accessing private files.

Many companies are now using *value-added networks* (*VANs*), which offer both communication services and specialized data processing. It is important to consider the security provided by VANs. Generally, a company has no direct control over a VAN's security, but its security has a direct effect on the client organization's overall security.

DEVELOPING EFFECTIVE CONTROLS

Controls are used to reduce the probability of attack on computer security. As additional controls are placed, the overall operating costs are likely to increase. As discussed earlier, cost-benefit considerations require a careful balance of controls:

1. *Deterrent controls:* The aim of deterrent controls is to create an atmosphere conducive to control compliance. For example, the organization could impose penalties whenever a control is disregarded, regardless of the actual damage. Deterrent controls are inexpensive to implement, but their effectiveness is difficult to measure. These controls complement other controls and are not sufficient by themselves.

2. *Preventive controls:* Preventive controls are designed to reduce the probability of an attack. They serve as the first line of defense. Effective preventive controls will thwart a perpetrator from getting access to the computer system.

3. *Detective controls:* Once a system has been violated, detective controls help identify the occurrence of harm. These controls do nothing to insulate the system from harm; they serve only to focus attention on the problem. For example, a bait file will identify unauthorized use. Here, a "dummy" nonexistent record is put into processing. The standard run time and actual run time for an application are compared to spot possible misuse.

4. *Corrective controls:* After a loss has occurred, corrective controls serve to reduce the impact of the threat. Their purpose is to aid in recovering from damage or in reducing the effect of damage. For instance, lost information on floppies may be restored with utility programs.

Application Controls

Application controls are built into software to deter crime and minimize errors. Application controls typically include input controls, processing controls, change controls, testing controls, output controls, and procedural controls.

- *Input controls:* The purpose of input controls is to ensure that each transaction is authorized, processed correctly, and processed only once. An edit program substantiates input by comparing fields to expected values and by testing logical relationships. A missing data check assures that all data fields have been used. A valid character check verifies that only alphabetical, numeric, or other special characters are present in data fields. In dual-read, duplicate entry or key verification verifies the accuracy of some critical field in a record by requiring that a data item is entered twice. A valid code check compares a classification (e.g., asset account number) or transaction code (e.g., credit sale entry) to a master list of accounts (master file reference) or transaction codes.

Input controls include rejecting, correcting, and resubmitting data that were initially wrong. Is input information properly authorized? Character validation tests may be programmed to check input data fields to see if they contain alphanumerics when they are supposed to have numerics. A preprocessing edit check verifies a key entry by a second one or a visual examination. There may be a limit test check of input data fields to make sure that some predetermined limit has not been exceeded (e.g., employee weekly hours should not be automatically processed if the sum of regular and overtime hours per individual exceeds 60).

- *Processing controls:* Processing controls are used to ensure that transactions entered into the system are valid and accurate, that external data is not lost or altered, and that invalid transactions are reprocessed correctly. Sequence tests may be performed to note missing items. Batch totals are used to ensure that the counted and totaled number and value of similar data items are the same before and after processing in batch or sequential processing. In a parity check, because data is processed in arrays of bits (binary digits of 1 or 0), we add a parity bit, if needed, to make the total of all the 1 bits even or odd. The parity bit assures that bits are not lost during computer processing. Parity checks prevent data corruption. External and internal file identification labels may be used. The program may check to see if an item in a record is within the correct range. Crossfooting tests apply to logical tests for information consistency (e.g., sum totals to column totals). Application reruns assure that the initial run was correct.

- *Change controls:* Change controls safeguard the integrity of the system by establishing standard procedures for making modifications. For example, a log file can be maintained to document all changes. A report may be prepared showing the master file before and subsequent to each update.

- *Testing controls:* Testing controls ensure that reliance can be placed on a system before the system becomes operational. For example, limited test data could be processed and tested using the new system. Utility programs should be used to diagnose problems in application software.

- *Output controls:* The purpose of output controls is to authenticate the previous controls; this is to ensure that only authorized transactions are processed correctly. Random comparisons can be made of output to input to verify correct processing. For example, an echo check involves transmitting data received by an output device back to its source. Output controls presume information is not lost or improperly distributed. Errors by receivers of output, such as customers, should be investigated.

- *Procedural controls:* Procedural controls safeguard computer operations, reduce the chance of processing mistakes, and assure continued functioning if a computer failure occurs. Processing errors must be thoroughly evaluated. Output should be distributed to authorized users of such information. A record retention and recovery plan must also exist.

UNDERSTANDING ELECTRONIC DATA INTERCHANGE

Electronic data interchange (*EDI*) is the electronic transfer of business information among trading partners. Thousands of businesses use EDI to exchange information with suppliers and customers. The benefits of EDI are clear. The paperwork is greatly reduced, and the efficiency in accounting and processing functions is greatly enhanced.

The risk inherent in EDI is much greater than in standard computer processing systems. An EDI security system is only as strong as the weakest link among the trading partners. Some risks of EDI are as follows:

- Data could be lost in the interchange.

- Unauthorized changes may be made to the data.

- The lack of paperwork means a greater likelihood that the audit trail may not be maintained.

- Authorized individuals can initiate unauthorized transactions.

- Unauthorized individuals can gain access to the system through the weakest link among the trading partners.

MAINTAINING PERSONNEL SECURITY

Each employee should sign a nondisclosure agreement that obliges them not to reveal computer security information to those outside the business or to unauthorized staff within the firm. If staff leave the company, certain control procedures are required, including returning badges, keys, and company materials. Access codes, passwords, and locks may have to be changed.

Specific procedures should be established for recruiting and hiring computer data processing professionals. A security investigation should include contacting the applicant's work references, checking the applicant's background with appropriate authorities, and verifying the applicant's school references. New employees should be impressed with the importance of computer security with respect to every phase of computer data processing. For example, to indoctrinate new employees, security professionals can communicate the company's rules and procedures to new employees in educational seminars.

In addition, formal performance evaluation systems should be in place to ensure that employees' performances and skills are routinely reviewed. An effective review procedure can help prevent job frustration and stress. It can also help maintain employee morale. Discontentment often acts as a catalyst for computer crime. Possible indicators of discontentment include excessive absenteeism, late arrival, low-quality or low-production output, complaints, putting off vacations, and excessive unwarranted overtime. Quick action, such as communicating with the employee on a one-to-one basis, can minimize, if not eliminate, job discontentment.

Duties among staff should be segregated. For example, a programmer should not also serve as an operator. Rotate assignments with, for example, programmers doing different assignments and operators working different shifts. A function may require more than one operator to make it more difficult for an individual to perpetrate an improper act since others are involved. The development and testing of software should be done by separate employees.

ESTABLISHING AN AUDIT TRAIL

Audit trails contain adequate information regarding any additions, deletions, or modifications to the system. They provide evidence concerning transactions. An effective audit trail allows the data to be retrieved and certified. Audit trails give information regarding the date and time of the transaction, who processed it, and at which terminal.

Analyze transactions related to the physical custody of assets. Evaluate unusual transactions. Keep track of the sequential numbering of negotiable computer forms. Periodically test controls. For example, the audit trail requires the tracing of transactions to control totals and from the control total to supporting transactions. Computer-related risks affect the company's internal control structure and thereby affect the company's audibility.

In online electronic data interchange (EDI) systems, computers automatically perform transactions such as order processing and generating invoices. Although this can reduce costs, it can adversely affect a company's audibility because of the lessened audit trail.

The American Institute of Certified Public Accounts (AICPA) has issued control techniques to ensure the integrity of an EDI system. At the *application level* of an EDI system, the AICPA recommends controls over accuracy and completeness, including checks on performance to determine compliance with industry standards, checks on sequence numbering for transactions, reporting irregularities on a timely basis, verifying the adequacy of audit trails, and checking embedded headers and trailers at the interchange, functional group, and transaction set levels. At the *environment level,* control techniques include reviewing the quality assurance of vendor software, the segregation of duties, ensuring that software is virus-free, procuring an audit report from the vendor's auditors, and evidence of testing. To ensure that all the EDI transactions are authorized, the AICPA provides these *authorization* controls: operator identification code, operator profile, trading partner identifier, maintenance of user access variables, and the regular changing of passwords.

PLANNING NETWORK SECURITY

Computer networks play a dominant role in transmitting information within and between firms. A *network* is simply a set of computers (or terminals) interconnected by transmission paths. These paths usually take the form of telephone lines; however, other media, such as wireless and infrared transmission, radio waves, and satellite, are possible. The network serves one purpose: the exchange of data between the computers and/or terminals. The considerations in selecting a network medium are:

- Technical reliability
- The type of business involved
- The number of individuals who need to access or update accounting data simultaneously
- The physical layout of existing equipment
- The frequency of updating
- The number of micros involved
- Compatibility
- Cost
- Geographic dispersion
- The type of network operating software available and support
- Availability of application software
- Expandability in adding workstations
- Restriction to PCs (or can cheaper terminals be used?)
- Ease of access in sharing equipment and data
- The need to access disparate equipment like other networks and mainframes
- Processing needs
- Speed
- Data storage ability
- Maintenance
- Noise
- Connectivity mechanism
- The capability of the network to conduct tasks without corrupting data moving through it

Classifications of Networks

Networks may be broadly classified as either wide area networks (WANs) or local area networks (LANs). Network security is needed for both LANs and WANs. The computers in a WAN may be anywhere from several miles to thousands of miles apart. In contrast, the computers in a LAN are usually closer together, such as in a building or a plant. Data switching equipment might be used in LANs, but not so frequently as it is in WANs.

There must be positive authentication before a user can have access to the online application, network environment, nature of applications, terminal identification, and so on. Information should be provided on a "need to know" basis only.

Access controls should exist to use a specific terminal or application. Date and time constraints, along with file usage, may be enumerated. Unauthorized use may deactivate or lock a terminal. Diskless workstations may result in a safer network environment.

There must be a secure communication link of data transmission between interconnected host computer systems of the network. A major form of communication security on the network is cryptography to safeguard transmitted data confidentiality. Cryptographic algorithms may be either *symmetric* (private key) or *asymmetric* (public key). The two popular encryption methods are link-level security and end-to-end security. The former safeguards traffic independently on every communication link, while the latter safeguards messages from the source to the ultimate destination. Link-level enciphers the communications line at the bit level; data is deciphered upon entering the nodes. End-to-end enciphers information at the entry point to the network and deciphers it at the exit point. Unlike link-level, end-to-end security exists over information inside the nodes.

Security should be provided in different layers and must exist over networking facilities and telecommunication elements. Controls must be placed over both host computers and subnetworks.

Network traffic may be over many subnetworks, each having its own security level depending on confidentiality and importance. Therefore, different security services and controls may be required. The security aspect of each subnetwork has to be distributed to the gateways to incorporate security and controls in routing decisions.

The architecture of a network includes hardware, software, information link controls, standards, topologies, and protocols. A *protocol* relates to how computers communicate and transfer information. Security controls must exist over each component within the architecture to assure reliable and correct data exchanges. Otherwise, the integrity of the system may be compromised.

Backup capability is an especially important feature of networks. For instance, if one computer fails, another computer in the network can take over the load. This might be critical in certain industries such as the financial industry.

Data flow between networked computers in one of three ways:

- *Simplex* transmission is in one direction only. An example of simplex transmission is radio or television transmission. Simplex transmission is rare in computer networks due to its one-way nature.

- *Half-duplex* transmission is found in many systems. In a half-duplex system, information can flow in both directions. However, it is not possible for the information to flow in both directions simultaneously. In other words, once a query is transmitted from one device, it must wait for a response to come back.

- A *full-duplex* system can transmit information in both directions simultaneously; it does not have the intervening stop-and-wait aspect of half-duplex systems. For high throughput and fast response time, full-duplex transmission is frequently used in computer applications.

Data switching equipment is used to route data through the network to its final destinations. For instance, data switching equipment is used to route data around failed or busy devices or channels.

In designing the network, one must consider three factors. First, the user should get the *best response time and throughput.* Minimizing response time entails shortening delays between transmission and receipt of data; this is especially important for interactive sessions between user applications. Throughput involves transmitting the maximum amount of data per unit of time.

Second, the data should be transmitted along the *lowest-cost path* within the network, as long as other factors, such as reliability, are not compromised. The lowest-cost path is generally the shortest channel between devices and involves the use of the fewest number of intermediate components. Furthermore, low-priority data can be transmitted over relatively inexpensive telephone lines, while high-priority data can be transmitted over expensive high-speed satellite channels.

Third, *maximum reliability* should be provided to assure proper receipt of all data traffic. Network reliability includes not only the ability to deliver error-free data, but also the ability to recover from errors or lost data in the network. The network's diagnostic system should be capable of locating problems with components and perhaps even isolating the component from the network.

A good telecommunications program will have numerous protocol options, enabling communications with different types of equipment. Some communications programs do error checking on the information or software programs received. Desirable features in telecommunications programs include menus providing help, telephone directory storage, and automatic log-on and redial.

Network Topologies

The *network configuration,* or *topology,* is the physical shape of the network in terms of the layout of linking stations. A *node* refers to a workstation. A *bridge* is a connection between two similar networks. Network *protocols* are software implementations providing support for network data transmission. A *server* is a microcomputer or a peripheral performing tasks such as data storage functions within a local area network (LAN).

Network servers are of several types. A *dedicated* server is a central computer used only to manage network traffic. A computer that is used simultaneously as a local workstation is called a *nondedicated* server. In general, dedicated servers provide faster network performance since they do not take requests from both local users and network stations. In addition, these machines are not susceptible to crashes caused by local users' errors. Dedicated servers are expensive, and they cannot be disconnected from the network and used as standalone computers. Nondedicated servers have a higher price/performance ratio for companies that need occasional use of the server as a local workstation.

The most common types of network topologies are as follows:

- The *hierarchical* topology (also called vertical or tree structure) is one of the most common networks. The hierarchical topology is attractive for several reasons. The software to control the network is simple and the topology provides a concentration point for control and error resolution. However, it also presents potential bottleneck and reliability problems. Network capabilities may be completely lost in the event of a failure at higher level.

- The *horizontal* topology (or bus topology) is popular in local area networks. Its advantages include simple traffic flow between devices. This topology permits all devices to receive every transmission; in other words, a single station broadcasts to multiple stations. The biggest disadvantage is that, since all computers share a single channel, a failure in the communication channel results in the loss of the network. One way to get around this problem is through the use of redundant channels. Another disadvantage with this topology is that the absence of concentration points makes problem resolution difficult. Therefore, it is more difficult to isolate faults to a particular component. A bus network usually needs a minimum distance between taps to reduce noise. Identifying a problem requires the checking of each system element. A bus topology is suggested for shared databases but is not good for single-message switching. It employs minimum topology to fill a geographic area, while at the same time having complete connectivity.

- The *star* topology is a very popular configuration and it is widely used for data communication systems. The software is not complex and controlling traffic is simple. All traffic emanates from the hub or the center of the star. In a way, the star configuration is similar to the hierarchical network; however, the star topology has more limited distributed processing capabilities. The hub is responsible for routing data traffic to other components. It is also responsible for isolating faults, which is a relatively simple matter in the star configuration.

  The star network, like the hierarchical network, is subject to bottlenecking at the hub and may cause serious reliability problems. One way to minimize this problem and enhance reliability is to establish a redundant backup of the hub node. A star network is best when data has to be entered and processed at many locations, with day-end distribution to different remote users. Information for general use is sent to the host computer for subsequent processing. It is easy to identify errors in the system, since each communication must go through the central controller. While maintenance is easy, if the central computer fails, the network stops. There is a high initial cost in setting up the system because each node requires hookup to the host computer in addition to the mainframe's cost. Expansion is easy, since all that is needed is to run a wire from the terminal to the host computer.

- The *ring* topology is another popular approach to structuring a network. The data in a ring network flows in a circular direction, usually in one direction only. The data flows from one station to the next; each station receives the data and then transmits it to the next station. The main advantage of the ring network is that bottlenecks, such as those found in the hierarchical or star networks, are relatively uncommon. There is an organized structure. The primary disadvantage of the ring network is that a single channel ties all of the components in a network. The entire network can be lost if the channel between two nodes fails. This problem can usually be alleviated by establishing a backup channel. Or switches or redundant cables can be used to automatically route the traffic around the failed node.

A ring network is reliable and relatively inexpensive when there is a minimum level of communication between micros. This type of network is best when several users at different locations have to continually access updated data.

Since more than one data transmission can occur simultaneously, the system is kept current on an ongoing basis. For example, the ring network permits the firm's accountants to create and update shared databases. With a ring, there is a higher incidence of error compared with a star because data is handled by numerous intervening parties. In light of this, the accountant should recommend that data in a ring system make an entire circle before being removed from the network.

- The *mesh* topology provides a very reliable, though complex, network. Its structure makes it relatively immune to bottlenecks and other failures. The multiplicity of paths makes it relatively easy to route traffic around failed components or busy nodes.

The major differences between WANs and LANs result in their taking on different topologies. A WAN structure tends to be more irregular. Since an organization generally leases the lines at a considerable cost, an attempt is usually made to keep the lines fully utilized. To accomplish this, data is often routed for a geographical area through one channel; hence, the irregular shape of the WAN.

The LAN topology tends to be more structured. Because the channels in a LAN are relatively inexpensive, the owners of a LAN are generally not concerned with the maximum utilization of channels. In addition, because LANs usually reside within a building or a plant, such networks tend to be inherently more structured and ordered. LANs are flexible, fast, and compatible. They maximize equipment utilization, reduce processing cost, decrease errors, and provide ease of information flow. LANs use ordinary telephone lines, coaxial cables, fiber optics, and other devices like interfaces. Fiber optics result in good performance and reliability but are high in cost. LAN performance depends on physical design, protocols supported, and transmission bandwidth. *Bandwidth* is the frequency range of a channel and reflects transmission speed along the network. Transmission speed is slowed down as more devices become part of the LAN.

Two or more LANs may be interconnected and communicate with each other. Each node becomes a cluster of stations (subnetworks).

Advantages of interfacing networks include the following:

- Total network costs are lower.
- There is flexibility in having individual subnetworks meet particular needs.
- More reliable and higher-cost subnetworks can be used for critical activities and vice versa.
- If one LAN fails, the other LANs still function.

The disadvantages of interfacing networks include the following:

- Complexity is greater.
- Some network functions may not be able to go across network boundaries.

Network Security

Communication security may be in the form of:

- *Access control* guards against the improper use of the network. For example, KERBEROS is a commercial authentication software that is added to an existing security system to verify that a user is not an impostor. KERBEROS does this by encrypting passwords transmitted around networks. Password control and user authentication devices may be used, such as Security Dynamics' SecurID (800-SECURID) and Vasco Data Security's Access Key II (800-238-2726). Do not accept a prepaid call if it is not from a network user. Hackers do not typically spend their own funds. Review data communications billings and verify each host-to-host connection. Review all dial-up terminal users. Are the telephone numbers unlisted and changed periodically? Control specialists should try to make unauthorized access to the network to test whether the security is properly working.

- *Identification* identifies the origin of a communication within the network, such as identifying the entity involved through digital signals or notarization.

- *Data confidentiality* maintains confidentiality over unauthorized disclosure of information within the communication process.

- *Data integrity* guards against unauthorized changes (such as adding or deleting) of data at both the receiving and sending points, such as through cryptographic methods. Antivirus software should be installed at both the network server and workstations. Detection programs are available to alert users when viruses enter the system.

- *Authentication* substantiates the identity of an originating or user entity within the network. There is verification that the entity is actually the one being claimed and that the information being transmitted is appropriate. Examples of security controls are passwords, time stamping, synchronized checks, nonrepudiation, and multiple-way handshakes. Biometric authentication methods measure body characteristics with the use of equipment attached to the workstation. Retinal laser beams may also be used. Keystroke dynamics offer another possible means of identification.

- *Digital signature* messages are signed with a private key.

- *Routing control* inhibits data flow to unsecure network elements such as identified unsecure relays, links, or subnetworks.

- *Traffic padding* analyzes data traffic for reasonableness.

- *Interference minimization* involves the elimination or curtailment of radar/radio transmission interference. There are various ways to back up data in networks. For a small network, one workstation may be used as the backup and restore for other nodes. In a large network, backup may be done by several servers since the failure of one could have disastrous effects on the entire system. Access to backup files must be strictly controlled.

THE SECURITY ADMINISTRATOR'S RESPONSIBILITIES

The size and needs of the company dictate the size of the security administration department. Personnel in this department are responsible for the planning and execution of a computer security system. They ensure that the information system's data is reliable and accurate. The security administrator should possess a high level of computer technical knowledge as well as management skills and a general understanding of the organization's internal control structure.

A security administrator:

- Should interact with other departments to learn of the organization's changing needs and be able to maintain and update the security system efficiently.

- Is responsible for enacting and customizing policies and standards for the organization based on specific needs.

- Checks on performance and monitors staff to ensure that the policies and standards are being complied with.

In developing these policies and procedures, as well as the overall information computer security system, the security administrator must perform a risk assessment.

CONTINGENCY PLANNING

Many man-made and natural disasters can strike a company. A *disaster* is defined as anything that will create a significant disruption in an organization's ongoing activities for a considerable period of time. Proper contingency planning can help minimize the loss of human life, data, and capital. Preparedness is the key to recovering from disaster.

The primary focus of computer security should always be to take preventive, not corrective, action. Nonetheless, preventing every security breach is impossible. It is virtually impossible to anticipate every problem, and even if a problem can be anticipated, the cost-benefit criterion may not justify taking preventive action. Sometimes the precautionary measures may prove to be ineffective because of human or other error. Productivity and efficiency may also be sacrificed if precautionary measures are taken too far.

For each possible type of disaster, emergency procedures should be established, and a determination should be made about the effect of the disaster on data processing and business operations. In other words, how long will the service be interrupted? At what level would the company be able to operate?

LEGAL ISSUES TO CONSIDER

Legal issues are important in considering computer security. Substantial liability may be incurred by a company for violating legal requirements. Sometimes management may even be held personally liable.

Privacy and other personal rights may be violated due to a lack of computer security. The public is very concerned about privacy, and this concern is reflected in the ever increasing legal requirements and regulations.

The general rule at the federal level is that all government files are open to the public unless there is a specific reason, enacted by the legislature, to keep the information secret. The Freedom of Information Act makes it possible for citizens and organizations to obtain access to most government records.

The federal government has passed legislation to protect private information. The Financial Privacy Act of 1978 was one step in this direction. The 1987 Computer Security Act showed further commitment to computer security. This act states that, "improving the security and privacy of sensitive information in the federal computer systems is in the public interest." This objective by no means should be limited to the federal government. Those in the private sector have to play their part in ensuring that private information is kept private. The public is very concerned about information getting into the wrong hands, and is concerned when asked to provide sensitive information.

With the 1987 Computer Security Act, the *National Institute of Standards and Technology (NIST)* was assigned the responsibility to develop cost-effective standards and guidelines to protect sensitive information in the federal databases. The Act also created a twelve-member panel to help the NIST perform its role. The private sector and the corporate world as a whole should not rely entirely on the government to take the steps toward improving security. To ensure that individual privacy is protected, the following needs to be considered:

- Classification of information
- Accuracy
- Protection of sensitive information

Once information is determined to be sensitive, it should be verified for accuracy before being put into a database. Such information should be afforded the necessary protection to keep it confidential and adequately protected.

The Federal Privacy Act applies to records maintained by certain branches of the federal government. When contracting with agencies subject to the Federal Privacy Act, the Act applies to the contract. The contractor and its employees are subject to the same requirements. Agency and criminal penalties may result from failure to comply.

Most states have public records acts similar to the federal Freedom of Information Act. Several states have also enacted Fair Information Practices Acts regulating the information that state agencies, and those contracting with the state agencies, may maintain about individuals.

At the international level, especially in Europe, there are laws covering both governmental and private records. Computerized data banks must be licensed and certain laws apply only to them. Rules concerning disclosure are generally strict. There are frequently prohibitions against transferring information across national boundaries.

E-mail communications may be a source of claims of privacy violations. The organization should have a clearly stated policy about using computer systems for personal communications. For example, the organization may want to clearly state that the organization has the right to read all e-mail communications. Courts have generally held that the employer has the right to view employee e-mail; still it is prudent to have a written policy on this issue.

The *Computer Fraud and Abuse Act* is a federal law making it a crime for any unauthorized use (copying, damaging, obtaining database information, etc.) of computer hardware or software across state lines. Offenders can be sentenced to up to 20 years in prison and fined up to $100,000.

The *Foreign Corrupt Practices Act* (*FCPA*) of 1977 applies to all companies whose securities are registered or filed under the Securities Exchange Act of 1934. This Act requires companies to keep accurate accounting records and to maintain a system of internal control. In other words, this Act mandates that these companies maintain appropriate computer security of its accounting records. Criminal prosecution can result from willful violations.

Computer security-related legal liability may be incurred in a variety of situations, ranging from programming errors to civil or criminal violations. A company is expected to exercise due care, and violation of the due care standard could result in liability. Consider a computer program that was originally designed properly—bug-free and operating effectively. However, due to lack of appropriate security, an attacker is able to place a logic bomb that causes the system to crash at a specified time in the future. The organization and its senior management may be held personally liable for any damages arising from the crash of the program. Such damages may include, for example, loss in the market price of stock shares. Human life might also be affected if the program that crashed performed critical functions, such as a medical diagnosis system.

Consider another scenario in which the attacker is able to modify the database of a construction company. Assume the database contains information about the strength of various types of steel that will be used to construct an office building. Engineers may rely on the modified database and use steel that is not strong enough. The building eventually collapses and human life is lost. The liability that may result in such circumstances is likely to be astronomical, especially if it is proven that appropriate security could have prevented modification of the database.

The National Institute of Standards and Technology has published several national standards in the area of computer security. Some of the standards include:

- Password usage
- Physical security and risk management
- Data encryption standards
- User authentication techniques
- Contingency planning
- Electrical power for computer facilities
- Key management
- Automated password generators
- Digital signature standard

The Department of Defense (DOD) also publishes booklets, known as the *Rainbow Series,* to help developers, evaluators, and users of trusted systems. It includes information on networks, databases, and other problems with distributed computer systems. Similar guidelines are issued by other countries. The governments of Britain, Netherlands, France, and Germany have jointly issued detailed Information Technology Security Evaluation Criteria (ITSEC).

It is prudent to consider using these standards in managing computer security. In a lawsuit alleging breach of security, failure to follow these standards may be used by plaintiffs to prove negligence, even if your organization was not required to follow these standards.

CONCLUSION

Computer security is intended to safeguard software, data, hardware, and personnel. Monitoring and control measures and devices are needed. Duties should be segregated and proper training should exist. Computer equipment, including peripherals, should be properly maintained. Someone should be in charge of monitoring computer security for the entire company. Periodic and surprise computer security audits should be undertaken. Employees not following computer security guidelines should be identified and disciplined.

Insurance coverage should not be inadequate or excessive. If inadequate, there is a great risk of loss. If excessive, insurance costs are exorbitant. Insurance coverage depends on numerous factors including risk level, loss exposure, cost, time period, and policy provisions. Is there insurance coverage for errors and omissions? An example is a loss arising from mistakes and omissions of personnel. Table 3-1 provides a checklist for microcomputer security.

Table 3-1.
MICROCOMPUTER SECURITY CHECKLIST

(A *no* response indicates a potential vulnerability.)

	Yes	*No*
Organizational		
1. Is management's attitude toward microcomputer security, as reflected by its actions, appropriate?	☐	☐
2. Has the organization prepared a coordinated plan of implementation for microcomputers addressing such factors as:		
• Hardware compatibility within and between departments?	☐	☐
• Software compatibility within and between departments?	☐	☐
• Future expansion?	☐	☐
• A manual of standard practices?	☐	☐
3. Are duties rotated to increase the chance of exposure of errors and irregularities and to give depth to microcomputer operations?	☐	☐
4. Are vacations mandatory to reduce the likelihood of fraud or embezzlement resulting from increased chance of exposure?	☐	☐

	Yes	No

5. Do personnel policies include background checks to reduce the likelihood of hiring dishonest employees? ☐ ☐

6. Have employees who have access to sensitive data been bonded? ☐ ☐

7. Is there a quality control program? ☐ ☐

8. Are exception reports to procedures and policies prepared? ☐ ☐

Hardware

1. Is theft and hazard insurance covering microcomputers adequate? ☐ ☐

2. Which of the following theft deterrence techniques are in operation:

   • Limiting computer access to employees with a defined need? ☐ ☐

   • Installing computers only in areas that are locked and kept under surveillance when not in use? ☐ ☐

   • Bolting computers to desks or tables? ☐ ☐

   • Placing lockable covers on computers? ☐ ☐

   • Installing alarms and motion detectors in areas with a high concentration of computer equipment? ☐ ☐

   • Placing internal trip alarms inside computers? ☐ ☐

3. Which of the following factors for the physical protection of hardware are present:

   • Elementary surge suppressors or noise filtering devices to protect against surges and spikes? ☐ ☐

   • Line conditioners to smooth out power? ☐ ☐

   • Uninterruptible power supply units to supply power during power outages? ☐ ☐

   • Antistatic mats and pads to neutralize static electricity? ☐ ☐

   • Halon fire extinguishers to reduce losses from fire? ☐ ☐

   • Placement of equipment away from the sprinkler system to avoid water damage? ☐ ☐

   • Waterproof covers to avoid water damage? ☐ ☐

   • Implementation of a smoking ban, or the use of a small fan around the computer to blow any smoke away from the system? ☐ ☐

   • Avoidance of other potential pollutants (e.g., dust, food, and coffee) around the computer? ☐ ☐

4. In the event of equipment breakdown, is substitute equipment available? ☐ ☐

	Yes	No

Software

1. Does present insurance cover software? ☐ ☐

2. Is insurance carried to cover the cost of a business interruption resulting from a computer mishap? ☐ ☐

3. Are backups and working copies maintained on site? ☐ ☐

4. Do software backups, like originals, have write-protect tabs in place? ☐ ☐

5. Are originals placed in off-site storage (e.g., a safe deposit box or the home of the owner or chief executive officer)? ☐ ☐

6. Are steps taken to avoid unauthorized copying of licensed software? ☐ ☐

7. Are steps taken to avoid the use of bootleg software? ☐ ☐

8. Is software tested before use? ☐ ☐

Data and Data Integrity

1. Are backups in data files routinely prepared? ☐ ☐

2. Is documentation duplicated? ☐ ☐

3. Are backups placed in off-site storage (e.g., a safe deposit box or the home of the owner or chief executive officer)? For particularly important files, a third copy may be kept. ☐ ☐

4. Are backups of sensitive data that are stored off-site encrypted to reduce the chance of unauthorized exposure? ☐ ☐

5. Do hard disks include an external hard disk or a cassette tape as a backup? ☐ ☐

6. Is a program such as Ship or Park used when removing the read-write head from the hard disk and software to reduce the likelihood of a crash? ☐ ☐

7. Has the Format command been left off the hard disk? ☐ ☐

8. Have Debug and other utilities that provide a means of accessing restricted software or data been left off the disk? ☐ ☐

9. Has data encryption been considered for sensitive data (e.g., payroll)? ☐ ☐

10. Is work on sensitive data limited to private offices to reduce the likelihood of exposure? ☐ ☐

		Yes	*No*
11.	Are sensitive data placed only on distinctly marked diskettes or removable hard disks?	☐	☐
12.	Are diskettes or cartridges removed from unattended computers?	☐	☐
13.	Does the organization have a designated custodian for sensitive data disks?	☐	☐
14.	Are unattended microcomputers turned off when data is removed from the system?	☐	☐
15.	Is reformatting of the disk or overwriting of the file required for destruction of sensitive data?	☐	☐
16.	Have legally binding confidentiality agreements been drafted by the employer and signed by microcomputer users with access to sensitive data (e.g., customer lists)?	☐	☐
17.	Are diskettes or cartridges stored in a secure cabinet or fire-rated safe?	☐	☐
18.	Which of the following are required before decisions are made based on microcomputer-generated reports:		
	• Validating the accuracy of customized microcomputer programs and imbedded formulas?	☐	☐
	• Dating changes to databases?	☐	☐
	• Dating reports with the date of production and the date of the database?	☐	☐
	• Independent validation of the data input?	☐	☐
19.	In the event of downtime, are there alternative processing arrangements with service bureaus?	☐	☐
20.	Does a preventive maintenance program exist?	☐	☐
21.	Have data been processed out of sequence or priority?	☐	☐
22.	Do transactions not fit a trend (e.g., too little, too much, too often, too late, illogical)?	☐	☐
23.	Are compiled data in conformity with legal and regulatory dictates?	☐	☐
24.	Did anyone attempt access above their authorization level?	☐	☐

Source: T. E. Buttress and M. D. Ackers, "Microcomputer security," *Journal of Accounting and EDP,* Spring 1990.

4

HIRING AND OUTSOURCING

Companies have always competed for skilled workers. The process of locating, selecting, and hiring employees is complex. Strategic planning is required to perform this function in a timely and efficient manner. It is imprudent to wait until a vacancy occurs before planning how to fill it. Effective human resource planning mandates that data be collected and analyzed to determine the number of people and their skill levels that will be needed by the organization. Projected need can then be filled either internally or externally.

The human resource function plays an important role in setting an organization's goals and standards. This function is responsible for assisting the departments in setting consistent, objective, and uniform standards. It provides the central control for employee evaluations. Human resource function is responsible for controlling costs and should actively participate in the budget planning process. It should also control budget allocations for hiring, training, transfers, and so forth for all departments, including the information systems department. Human resource personnel should act as consultants in the hiring of employees, in determining their positions, and in determining their salaries.

SEARCHING FOR QUALIFIED CANDIDATES

The process of attracting and hiring candidates can be streamlined by establishing sound procedures that are consistently followed and preferably automated. An employment manual that explains in detail the procedures and standards to be followed should be developed. The manual should contain copies of all forms and letters to be used. After doing a systematic job analysis, the duties and responsibilities for each job position should be clearly specified.

The organization itself is often an excellent place to start when beginning the search process. In addition to promoting candidates within the organization, other individuals may be interested in lateral moves.

If it is necessary to go outside the organization, several approaches may be utilized. Advertising is effective in attracting qualified candidates. Of course, care must be exercised in selecting the right media: daily newspapers, trade journals, professional magazines, and so forth. Advertising on the Internet is highly effective and should not be overlooked by the information systems department.

Private employment agencies and executive search firms may also be contacted. Many employment agencies specialize in specific professions, including computers and information systems. Executive search firms generally tend to focus on recruiting for high-level positions requiring specialized experience. It is critical to use the right employment agency or executive search firm. Such a decision should be undertaken after extensive research. Of course, the firm's fee and related expenses should be agreed upon in writing before the search is begun.

It is advisable to develop a special recruiting plan for minorities and women. For example, some advertisements should be placed in media aimed at minorities and women. Attempts should also be made to actively recruit from colleges and universities with a large concentration of minorities.

The following is a list of websites of firms that specialize in jobs for information technology professionals. While most of these firms operate at the national level, some are very localized and serve only a specific metropolitan region (such as New York, Atlanta, San Francisco, Boston, etc.), or specialize in attracting international candidates:

- www.computerjobs.com
- www.computerdirections.com
- www.dynamichost.com/jobs
- www.hcsjobs.com
- www.hotjobs.com
- www.icpa.com

- www.rhic.com/jobsRHIC/index.html
- www.jobs-online.net/
- www.cplusplusjobs.com/
- www.coboljobs.com/
- www.contract-jobs.com/
- javajobs.com/
- www.charm.net/~web/Jobs.html
- www.visualbasicjobs.com/
- www.softwarejobs.com/
- www.mas-jobs.com/
- www.internet-solutions.com/itjobs.htm
- www.wco.com/~cri/
- www.computerstaff.com/
- www.schulenburg-assoc.com/
- www.astin.nl/
- www.softskills.ie/
- www.beardsleygroup.com/
- www.dice.dlinc.com/bedford/
- www.tech-lease.com/
- www.techsearch.com/
- www.andex.com/
- www.ilsglobe.com/
- www.masterteam.com/jobs
- www.matrixres.com/
- jobs-usa.com/
- www.webcom.com/mco/
- www.testart.com/

TEMPORARY AND PART-TIME EMPLOYEES

Temporary and part-time employees are often necessary to meet variations in work demand. The organization does not have to make the same level of commitment to temporary or part-time employees. These employees benefit from the flexibility of such an arrangement. *Temporary* employees normally work full-time but for a short duration. The time period may be agreed upon in advance or based on work demand. *Part-time* employees generally do not work a full 40-hour week. Their work assignment is more permanent in nature than temporary employees. Many individuals prefer part-time work because they may have other commitments, such as a family, another job, or college. Temporary and part-time employees may be given the opportunity to become regular full-time employees when positions become available. This gives the company the opportunity to evaluate a prospective employee's work before making a more permanent commitment.

Many companies routinely engage part-time or freelance programmers. Such programmers are typically paid an hourly or daily rate. It should be clear that the work product, such as software and documentation, belongs to the company, not to the programmer. The company should require programmers to assign their work product exclusively and irrevocably to the company.

OBTAINING COMPLIANCE WITH GOVERNMENT REGULATION

The selection of the right candidate means making an informed decision about hiring the individual with the greatest possibility of success. Background information such as experience, education, abilities, and personal characteristics must be collected. Such information is typically collected using application forms, interviews, and formal tests. Congress, the courts, and many state and local legislative bodies have placed limits on what employers may do in hiring employees. The basic aim of this legislation is to prohibit (1) the hiring or firing of employees because of "status" factors such as age, race, sex, national origin; (2) discrimination against employees who are exercising their legal rights; or (3) the discrimination against individuals who have filed a grievance with a federal agency. Your organization must make sure it does not violate any federal, state, or local laws.

Civil Rights Act of 1964

The Civil Rights Act of 1964 is the most important means of fighting discrimination. Title VII of the Act prohibits discrimination based on race, religion, or national origin. Exceptions to Title VII coverage include drug or alcohol abusers and foreign nationals. While the act does not say much about sexual discrimination, Equal Employment Opportunity Commission (EEOC) guidelines state that it is a violation of Title VII to discriminate because of sexual stereotyping. For example, employers cannot mention in help-wanted ads an employee's sex unless sex is a bona fide qualification for the job. A 1978 amendment to the Act prohibits discriminating against employees on the basis of medical condition, especially pregnancy and childbirth. The Civil Rights Act of 1964 applies to all entities, whether foreign or domestic, doing business in the United States.

The Federal Rehabilitation Act of 1973

This Act prohibits discrimination against individuals with disabilities if they work for the federal government, for organizations that hold federal contracts, or for programs that receive federal funds. Employers may not discriminate against individuals with a physical or mental disability if they are otherwise qualified to perform job responsibilities.

Age Discrimination in Employment Act of 1967

Age discrimination in the Employment Act of 1967 prohibits discrimination against employees between the ages of 40 and 70. Public and private companies with 20 or more employees and labor unions with 25 or more members must conform to this law. This Act does not apply to jobs for which age is a genuine occupational qualification. It is also reasonable for the employer to ask employees to undergo a physical exam if the job requires physically demanding work. The Act prohibits employers from discriminating against employees because of a benefit plan. Many states have enacted laws that further enhance the federal act and protect against age discrimination.

PREEMPLOYMENT HIRING GUIDELINES

It is important to be candid with prospective employees. Let them know what is and is not acceptable behavior. If any type of testing is to be done, let them know about it immediately. Of course, never make any promises, written or verbal, that you have no means or intention of keeping. While it is perfectly acceptable to emphasize the strong points of the job, be clear and honest about the bad points. Tell the candidate about his or her chances of advancement or success in the organization. Inform the candidate before he joins the organization if there is a probationary period or if the job is otherwise of a temporary nature. Also, let the prospective employee know if the company may be planning reductions in the work force, such as closing a branch or a department.

It is illegal to refuse to hire candidates because they have been involved in a lawsuit, other administrative action, or complaint against a previous employer. Similarly, it is illegal to refuse to hire an individual who has testified on behalf of a coworker, is active in a union, or is serving on jury duty.

All applicants should be asked to fill out the company's job application. The application form should be designed for your company's and department's specific needs. You will generally want to request at least the following information:

- What's the full name and address of the applicant? How long has he/she lived there? What were the applicant's previous addresses and how long did the applicant live there?

- Has the applicant used different names or aliases? What is the applicant's maiden name?

- What are the names of the applicant's spouse and children? What are the names of the applicant's parents?

- Who should be notified in the event of an emergency?

- Has the applicant served in the military? Did the applicant receive an honorable discharge?

- Is the applicant a U.S. citizen or does he/she have authorization to work in the United States?

- What is the education level of the applicant? Where did the applicant get his/her education?

- What is the applicant's work experience?
- Does the applicant speak any foreign languages?
- How familiar is the applicant with the Internet and World Wide Web?
- Does the applicant know any programming languages?
- What is the applicant's familiarity with software and hardware?
- Who are the applicant's character references?

To discourage applicants from later stating that they did not fill out the application, candidates should be required to sign the application in the presence of a responsible company official or notary. The applicant should also be asked to provide additional information such as transcripts and personnel records. Inform the candidate that any misstatement or omission will be sufficient reason for not hiring the applicant or, if he/she is hired, for dismissal. Written consent should be obtained from the applicant to check his/her background. Applicants should be informed that the company may legally, with some exceptions, monitor employees' telephone calls and electronic mail and that their acceptance of this is a specific condition for their employment.

The law allows employers to place certain restrictions on their employees. For example, the law allows you to refuse to hire any candidate not willing to work on Saturdays or Sundays, as long as the employer is not singling out members of a specific religious community. You may also refuse to hire any candidate who is unwilling to work the hours required of other employees. You may require prospective employees to be bondable, if the job requires fidelity bonding. Candidates with poor credit histories may be denied the job if the job requires handling money or other valuables. Any candidate who is unwilling to allow you to conduct a job-related preemployment investigation does not have to be hired. An individual who does not accept reasonable efforts by the employer to accommodate the individual's religious practices may be denied the job. You may ask candidates about their salary history. You may also inquire about performance reports of previous employers.

All candidates whom you intend to hire should be given a copy of the corporate guidelines, personnel manuals, company handbook, and any other relevant material that explains the condition of the employment and holds the employee to them. Even if the employee does not actually read all the material, he or she acknowledges acceptance of the terms and conditions by receiving it.

The employment material should not contain any references to "permanent" employees; instead use terms such as "full-time" or "regular" employees. This gives you the option of dismissing employees with substandard work performance. Disclaimers should also be added; while they are not guaranteed to help during litigation, they cannot hurt. The employment agreement should stipulate reasons for dismissal as well as procedures for resolving disputes, such as the use of arbitration. The hiring practices should be uniform and applied consistently and equitably. They should not appear to favor one set of workers over another. An organization is responsible for the actions of its managers and staff. Ensure that company personnel understand the basic guidelines in hiring and recruiting candidates.

UNDERSTANDING PRIVACY ISSUES

As an information systems manager involved with hiring and managing employees, you must understand the privacy rights of prospective applicants. A balance must be struck between your organization's right to know and the candidate's privacy. Prospective employees have rights through both common law and legislation. This includes the right not to be portrayed in a false or misleading way, the right to prevent public disclosure of private information, and the right to be free from unnecessary intrusion.

Personnel Records

Employees have a right to sue their employer and perhaps even get punitive damages if they can show that the employer gave out false or misleading information about them or if the employer holds a grudge against the employee and acted maliciously. Privacy laws protect almost all types of personal information, including personnel files, college transcripts, and other private, sensitive, or personal information. It is unwise to release any such information to a prospective employer about a former employee without that employee's written permission. In fact, an employee needs only to show that the information released was unauthorized and that it caused some type of damage to win a suit. An employee does not need to show that the information was false, just unauthorized. It is prudent to review an employee's record for incorrect or misleading statements before releasing it to avoid defamation of character suits.

Federal Records

Federal agencies collect a vast amount of data on individuals. Under the Freedom of Information Act (FIA), it is possible to access many government files, including criminal conviction records. Some types of information, such as an individual's personnel or medical records, cannot be accessed under the FIA. The FBI's Identification Division contains the largest repository of criminal records in United States. Employers can request a criminal check for prospective employees. Most states prohibit employers from inquiring about an applicant's juvenile crime records, arrests that did not result in a conviction, or misdemeanor convictions older than five years as long as the individual did not have any convictions in the meantime.

Financial Records

Financial and credit records of prospective applicants can be accessed through credit bureaus and private investigative agencies. The Fair Credit Reporting Act governs investigative consumer reports that are frequently used by prospective employers to screen candidates. In compiling these reports, the agency may communicate with neighbors, employers, and others to collect personal information about individuals and their habits. The agency that compiles this information must inform applicants of the employer's request to access this information. Written consent should be obtained from applicants.

Educational Records

School records, including college transcripts, are protected by privacy laws. The Federal Family Educational and Privacy Act of 1974 states that only the candidate (or the parents of the candidate if the candidate is under 18 years old) may obtain records from any educational institution receiving money from the federal government. A school may legally release some types of information about a candidate. For example, an educational institution may tell if and when an individual graduated, how long the individual attended that institution, what type of degree the individual received, and the major or minor of the individual. An educational institution may not release any information about the candidate's rank or grade point average. Of course, it is a crime to obtain educational records under false pretenses. It is also a crime, generally a misdemeanor, for prospective employees to lie about their educational background. After hiring someone, you may dismiss the employee if you learn that the applicant lied about his or her educational background.

Medical Records

All medical information about your employees is protected by federal and state laws. The basic exception to this is when the medical information has a genuine bearing on applicants' ability to perform their duties. For example, you may not ask a female employee if she is, or intends to become, pregnant. Questions about AIDS are typically forbidden in many states. However, you may ask the employee medical questions if the job requires great physical ability, quick reflexes, or above-average hearing or vision. In certain industries, such as aviation, individuals may be asked about their drinking or drug habits. The need to examine medical information may be justified for jobs that are physically or psychologically demanding. Permission should always be obtained from the candidate, and the medical information should be relevant to the job qualifications.

Protecting Your Organization

Corporate policy on privacy in hiring should be formulated and the managers and staff should be educated. Prospective applicants should be informed of the company's privacy policy and how it would be used to screen the candidates. All information collected should be directly relevant to the job. Sensitive personal information should be kept confidential and secure. Access to an applicant's records should be limited only to authorized individuals, and no information should be released without the employee's written permission.

CHECKING A PROSPECTIVE EMPLOYEE'S BACKGROUND

A significant percentage of applicants lie on their résumés or during interviews. Many individuals with criminal pasts will not divulge that information to prospective employers. If an employee commits a criminal act while employed, the employer may be held liable. It is therefore imperative that an applicant's background be thoroughly checked. In fact, employers have a legal obligation to thoroughly investigate their employees' backgrounds without, of course, violating their privacy.

Work History

Many applicants lie about their work history. They may increase the amount of time they have spent at a job, create fictitious employers, and boost their salary levels. They may tell you that their employer has gone out of business. Check to see how long the company was actually in business. Also check to see whether the applicant's experience matches the time the company was actually in business. Exaggerating one's job duties and inflating job titles is also common. Many individuals falsely claim to be self-employed or independent consultants. These individuals may have been unemployed for a long time, or worse, in prison. In the information systems and computer industry, self-employment is very common. Employers therefore need to put in extra effort to check these claims. You should check the applicant's previous address, professional associates, bank references, credit history, and corporate records.

Education and Professional Experience

Candidates sometimes fabricate educational credentials and professional experience. Individuals who have attended only a year or two of college might claim that they have a bachelor's degree. Some individuals may even assume the identity of a real graduate or an established professional. Candidates may have bought their degrees from unaccredited mail-order universities. Some applicants may have degrees from mail-order colleges and universities with names similar to prestigious universities. Foreign credentials may also require extra scrutiny. Individuals may fabricate honors and awards. Some may list fake publications on their résumé. You should ask applicants to provide copies of their publications and proof of their honors or awards. The advances in desktop publishing make it especially easy for individuals to create false records. College transcripts, for example, should always come directly from the college.

Recommendations from Former Employers

Letters of recommendation from previous employers should be viewed with skepticism. Former employers may be hesitant about telling the truth about an employee in writing. They may also want to simply pass a problem worker on to you. A broad general letter recommending a candidate may signal a problem. Such an employer might be afraid to put any specifics in writing. Candidates may give the names of friends and relatives as previous supervisors. This is especially difficult to check if these friends work for the same company as the applicant.

Reference Checks

Checking references is an important step in investigating an individual's background. Many employers do a poor job of checking references. They either don't bother checking the references or just barely check them. To avoid legal hassles, all applicants should be required to sign a release form. The applicants should permit you to check their references and promise to hold their references harmless for what they say. Of course, all references should be thoroughly checked before any formal offer is made. If the reference check is not acceptable, you do not have to give candidates a reason why they were not selected. Records should be kept of reference checks to refute allegations of discriminatory or illegal actions. A conscientious reference check may also be used to defend your company if at a later stage your company is involved in litigation due to that employee's actions. Even if the references lie outright, you may be able to read between the lines and ascertain from your communication that the references are not being truthful.

Applicants should be told clearly that you will be checking their references. Inform applicants about whom you intend to contact, what you will ask them, and why you need that information. Applicants should be aware that information of a sensitive and personal nature may be collected. When contacting the references, emphasize why you need that information and how that information will be used to evaluate the candidate. Always communicate in a professional manner, and avoid using any language that might be construed as discriminatory.

Public Records

Employers can check a prospective employee's background from hundreds of public sources, which does not require the applicant's permission. To save time and effort, a corporation's in-house security department may be used or an external private investigative agency may be hired. The public records will show whether the employee has a conviction record and, in some jurisdictions, even an arrest record. A conviction record is generally not a sufficient reason to deny the applicant the job. The applicant's conviction should have something to do with the job the applicant is seeking. Denying individuals a job just because they have been arrested but not convicted is even more dangerous.

Corporate records and limited partnership records are also available publicly. One can ascertain from these records whether the applicant actually owned his own business and for how long. You can also ascertain if the applicant really worked for an out-of-business corporation by comparing the time the applicant said she worked for the business and the time the business was active.

Court records are another useful source. They contain both civil and criminal litigation records. From the litigation records you can learn whether the applicant was a participant in any litigation. To learn about a candidate's financial situation, you can look through city and county filings for liens against the applicant. Additional sources of a candidate's financial situation are real property records and tax rolls.

Work Authorization Requirements

All employees must have authorization to work in the United States. This generally means that the applicant must be a U.S. citizen, hold a "green card," or have specific work authorization. Employers may incur serious civil and criminal penalties for violating the immigration and work authorization laws if they hire illegal aliens. Employers are required to verify that the applicant is authorized to work in the U.S. by filling out Form I-9 of the Immigration and Naturalization Service.

Using Private Investigators

If your firm utilizes private investigators to check on an individual's background, make sure that the investigators comply with the privacy laws. Your organization may be liable if the investigators act negligently and commit illegal acts. A written contract that outlines the investigative firm's responsibilities should be used. Nonetheless, your firm might still be held liable since the investigators are acting as your agents. Appendix A provides a list of selected companies that perform background verification for pre-employment screening.

CONDUCTING INTERVIEWS

Interviewing is a skill that requires talent. To be an effective interviewer, you should take charge of the interview and control the line of questioning. Your questions should be direct and to the point. Speak slowly and clearly. Maintain a friendly tone and don't talk down to the interviewee. You should talk about only one topic at a time and ask only one question at a time. Questions should be unambiguous and easy to understand. Give the candidate an opportunity to ask questions and answer them honestly.

Because interviewees may not be completely honest in their answers, look out for vague and evasive answers. Candidates may also contradict themselves by giving inconsistent answers to similar questions. Note candidates' emotional reactions to questions. Watch out for individuals who switch jobs frequently. Assess whether they are reluctant to talk about their education or work experience. Observe the candidate's body language.

Keep interviewees relaxed and give them plenty of time to answer your questions. Do not rush them. By putting candidates at ease, you can elicit much more information. It is important to take good notes during the interview. Write down anything pertinent to the job. You may also want to consider videotaping the interview.

During the interview you may ask candidates to comment on their work experience. You may ask about their future plans. Candidates should be informed about the company's code of ethics and other rules. Candidates may be asked if they are willing to accept those rules. For example, if your company does not allow smoking, candidates may be asked if they would be willing to refrain from smoking while on the job.

Many topics should be avoided during an interview. Do not say or joke about anything that may be construed as discriminatory. Questions about one's religion and political affiliation should be avoided. Sometimes candidates bring up the question of religion, such as requesting something to accommodate their religious needs. Let them know whether your company will be able to accommodate them. You may also want to let candidates know that your company is under no legal obligation to accommodate those needs.

Questions about sex, including an individual's sexual preference, should also be avoided. Such questions might be construed by some individuals as sexual harassment. Questions about an individual's marital status, including cohabitation, are generally not relevant and should not be asked. You should generally avoid questions about health, unless health is an issue in job performance. You should also not ask female candidates whether they are pregnant or plan to become pregnant.

In short, your questions should be directly relevant to the job. Further, you should ask the same questions and apply the same standard to everyone you interview regardless of race, sex, religion, or ethnic background.

Some general interview questions include:

- "Tell me about yourself."
- "Why should I hire you?"
- "Why did you choose information systems as your career?"
- "What do you consider to be your greatest strengths and weaknesses?"
- "Where do you see yourself two, five, or ten years from now?"
- "Describe a challenging project you have worked on."
- "Describe your most rewarding accomplishment."
- "What qualifications or skills do you have that will help you make a positive contribution to this company?"
- "Why are you interested in working for our company?"
- "What do you know about our company?"
- "What factors are most important to you in a job?"

It is also acceptable to ask technical questions. You can ask candidates how they would solve a hypothetical problem. The primary purpose of the interview, however, should be to assess the personality and problem-solving ability of the candidate. Candidates' technical competence should be assessed primarily through other means such as the candidate's education, work experience, and certification.

SKILLS-ASSESSMENT EXAMS AND CERTIFICATION

Many employers require candidates to take a skills-assessment examination. Such testing can be developed in-house or purchased from specialty companies. Many software vendors also offer proficiency or certification exams for their products.

Microsoft (www.microsoft.com/mcp/) offers several different types of certifications. Its *Microsoft Office User Specialist Program* certifies candidates' skills in using Microsoft Office products at both Proficient and Expert user levels. For computer professionals, Microsoft offers the *Microsoft Certified Professional Programs;* certification is currently offered in:

- Microsoft Certified Professional
- Microsoft Certified Systems Engineer
- Microsoft Certified Solution Developer
- Microsoft Certified Professional + Internet
- Microsoft Certified Systems Engineer + Internet
- Microsoft Certified Trainer

Sun Microsystems offers certification for Solaris system administrators and Java programmers. The Sun Java Certification Program is based on Java Development Kits and is available at two levels: the *Sun Certified Java Programmer* and the *Sun Certified Java Developer.* The *Sun Certified Java Programmer* tests for overall Java knowledge and is a prerequisite for the *Sun Certified Java Developer* certification. The *Sun Certified Java Developer* tests one's ability to perform complex programming tasks.

Appendix B lists the names of some companies involved in testing information systems professionals. Most companies generally tend to concentrate on testing only computer programmers.

JOB OFFER AND EMPLOYMENT CONTRACT

Acceptance of a written or verbal job offer creates an employment contract. The terms of the contract define the relationship between the employer and the employee. Care must be taken in drafting this agreement to avoid potential problems. You must clearly communicate to the prospective employees what would be expected from them. Prospective employees should be given a complete job description and the scope of the duties should be explained. The employee should understand that the employee:

- Is expected to devote all energies, skills, and efforts only to the performance of duties assigned by the employer.
- Is expected to work exclusively for the employer.

- May not work for any competitive organization, including after hours, on weekends, or during vacations without prior written permission.

- May not render services or engage in any type of business transaction for anyone else's or personal benefit, regardless of the scope of services, whether or not compensation is received.

- Will not be interfering with the rights of third parties by accepting employment with you, including the misuse of proprietary information or trade secrets belonging to third parties.

In addition:

- The employment is terminable at will by either the employer or the employee.

- The employer may make changes in personnel, benefits, and assignments at any time.

If a written contract is being signed, the contract should contain all terms and conditions. The contract should also make reference to the company's policies and procedures manual and to the personnel handbook. If no written agreement exists, the terms of employment should be communicated during the interview and in any written communication.

Employees should be told the physical location where they are expected to work. Compensation and fringe benefits should also be included in the contract. It is important to stress to employees that pay is determined by experience and qualification and that race, sex, ethnic origin, and religion have no influence on pay scales. The contract should also include whether you will require the employee to work on a weekend.

All paid holidays should be specified in advance. If the employee requests time off for religious observances, you have two options. If you allow members of one faith to take paid time off, you must allow members of all faiths paid time off. Alternatively, you may allow the employee to take unpaid time or use a personal day. The law only requires employers to make a reasonable effort to accommodate the religious observances of its employees. In fact, your company is under no compulsion to hire anyone who refuses to or is unable to perform the job for whatever reason, including religious observances.

The organization must ensure that any software or other work product developed by the employees or contractors is the property of the company. Software development is unique. It requires creativity and support of the personnel who create it. It is very easy for employees to copy the employer's software for their own benefit or for the benefit of competitors. A written agreement can help reduce the likelihood of misconduct by employees, and provide added protection when trying to recover damages. It is sometimes difficult to obtain protection through trade secret laws with such an agreement. You may ask employees to sign agreements turning over any software, inventions, or patents to the employer. Any work performed by the employee while being paid by your company belongs to your company, including the following:

- All existing proprietary rights in trademarks, trade secrets, patents, copyrights, and other intangible assets belonging to the employee at the inception of employment should be specified in the agreement.

- All other work product, including software, documentation, technology, and other intellectual property, belongs to the employer.

- The employee agrees to transfer, perfect, and defend the employer's ownership of work product, during or after employment, as necessary.

- The employee must return all materials including software, documentation, disks, tapes, CDs, and other media, notes, records, letters, and memoranda to the employer.

- If the employee ever wants to develop a product with his/her own resources and time, the employee must obtain written clearance from the employer.

You may also ask employees to sign noncompete agreements. *Noncompete agreements* prevent your employees from setting up a directly competitive business or working for your rivals for a certain time period or within a certain geographic region. The law tends to favor an individual's freedom in selecting employment and will not for public policy reasons allow overreaching "noncompete" covenants.

- After the employment terminates, the employee should be required to notify the employer if the employee wishes to accept an engagement that violates the noncompete covenants.

- The employer may, at its discretion, allow the employee to accept such an engagement.

Employees and contractors are often entrusted with confidential information, and precautions should be taken to prevent abuse of such information. If the employee will have access to confidential information or trade secrets, you may want to have the individual sign a confidentiality agreement. The confidentiality agreement, at a minimum, should include:

- An understanding that the employee is to be entrusted with secret, confidential, and proprietary information involving trade secrets.

- The trade secrets include all types of technical and nontechnical data, programs, source code, and compilations, techniques and methods, financial or technical plans, and lists of actual or potential customers and suppliers.

- The employee agrees not to use or disclose the trade secrets of the employer for personal benefit or for the benefit of competitors.

- The employee agrees to use the information only for authorized purposes.

The basis for termination should be specified in the contract to avoid a wrongful discharge suit. Before hiring prospective employees, let them know what types of behavior would be grounds for termination. Explain severance policies to them. Finally, include in the contract the means of resolving disputes, such as arbitration.

As part of normal exit procedures, departing employees should be asked to acknowledge their obligations to the organization. They should acknowledge that any proprietary information of the company will remain so and will not be used or disclosed. For example, the copyright to any software developed during the employees' tenure at the company belongs to the company and may not be used by employees for any purpose once their relationship with the company is terminated. This procedure reminds departing employees of their responsibilities to the company.

Departing employees should sign an agreement acknowledging that:

- They have received or been exposed to confidential and proprietary information of considerable value.

- Such information includes, but is not limited to, data, source code, algorithms, manuals and documentation, data structures, training materials, formulas, techniques, and methods.

- Any proprietary information developed during the course of employment is the property of the company, and any interest the employee has in such property is conveyed to the company.

- The employee will refrain from using or disclosing the proprietary information in the future, either for personal benefit or for the benefit of third parties.

- The employee will not reverse-engineer binary or object versions of software programs.

- The employee has returned all proprietary information and other property of the company.

THE PROS AND CONS OF EMPLOYING AN INDEPENDENT CONTRACTOR

Many computer consultants prefer to work as independent contractors rather than as employees. This allows the consultant to retain control over the manner and method of performing the work.

There are also significant tax advantages to being an independent contractor. While an employee can take only a few deductions, an independent contractor is treated as a business owner and can deduct all expenses involved in earning income. These deductions can greatly reduce taxable income and taxes. The main tax disadvantage to being an independent contractor is having to pay both the "employer's" and "employee's" share of social security and medicare taxes. Still, the tax advantages typically far outweigh any disadvantages.

Many companies prefer to use independent contractors. Independent contractors allow the company to obtain specialized expertise for a short period, thus enabling the company to complete one-time tasks and projects. By using independent contractors, the company does not have to:

- Withhold taxes

- Pay the "employer's" share of social security and medicare taxes

- Pay for worker's compensation or unemployment or disability insurance

- Pay fringe benefits, including pension benefits and health insurance

- Worry about antidiscrimination laws, labor laws, or other governmental regulations concerning employer–employee relations

- Deal with unions and their demands

- Commit to long-term employment

The Internal Revenue Service (IRS) is very concerned about employers and employees abusing the independent contractor status. If the IRS finds that independent consultants should have been classified as employees, the company will be assessed penalties and interest on payroll taxes that the company should have withheld. In fact, it does not matter that the consultant has already paid the required taxes on those same earnings.

The IRS has developed a set of guidelines that companies and workers can use to determine whether workers should be considered employees or independent contractors. These guidelines consist of twenty questions that determine whether workers' relationships with the company are more like an employee's or an independent business owner's. These questions essentially determine how much risk workers assume and how much control they have on their work. An independent contractor is typically hired on a project or job basis, offers services to the general public, derives its revenues typically from several clients, operates as a separate business, and does not have a long-term obligation to a specific client.

The IRS uses the following twenty factors to determine if an employer–employee relationship exists. Note that no single factor is conclusive evidence. Each factor may not be relevant for some occupations. The weight given to each factor varies depending on the occupation and other circumstances:

1. Does the hiring firm provide detailed instructions about when, how, and where the worker is supposed to work? Employees may be given detailed instructions. Contractors may be provided with specifications but not given detailed instructions.

2. Does the hiring firm train the worker? Employees may be trained, but independent contractors must not be trained.

3. Does the service have to be rendered personally? Contractors may hire others to provide the desired results.

4. The hiring, supervising, and payment of assistants is done by contractors.

5. Contractors should not have a continuous relationship with the hiring firm. A permanent employee relationship may exist even if the work is part-time or seasonal or of short duration. Contractors provide services at irregular intervals or whenever work is available. Such engagements can be frequent but should not be continuous.

6. The hiring firm's core operations must not depend on the use of contractors.

7. Contractors establish their own hours whereas employees work a fixed number of hours.

8. Contractors do not have to devote themselves full-time to the hiring firm. Contractors have enough time to pursue work with other firms.

9. Contractors control where they work. Working on the hiring firm's premises does not necessarily imply that the work is being controlled by the hiring firm. However, work done off the hiring firm's premises indicates some freedom of control.

10. The order and sequence of work to be performed are determined by the contractor. An employer controls, or has the right to control, the routines and schedules of its employees.

11. Contractors are paid per project or by the job. Payment based on fixed time typically indicates an employer–employee relationship.

12. Contractors are hired for results. Contractors are not required to turn in interim or progress reports. Having to provide oral or written reports suggests that the person is subject to controls and supervision.

13. The contractor is responsible for incidental business and travel expenses. An employee receives reimbursement for such expenses.

14. Contractors work for more than one firm at a time.

15. Contractors furnish their own tools and materials.

16. The services of contractors are available to the general public. Contractors may have their own offices, use assistants, possess business licenses, advertise, and have their own telephone numbers.

17. Contractors should not have to rely on the hiring firm's facilities to provide services. Contractors typically have a substantial investment in facilities, including equipment, furniture, machinery, etc.

18. Contractors may make or lose money. Their profit or "salary" is not guaranteed.

19. Employees may be discharged. However, contractors cannot be fired unless they fail to meet the results specified in the contract.

20. Employees can quit at any time. Contractors cannot terminate their relationship without satisfactorily completing the job. Contractors are not compensated if they do not complete the assignment.

OUTSOURCING BENEFITS AND CONSIDERATIONS

The processes that underlie traditional ways of doing business have changed. The advances in technology, the effect of changes in business practices, and the greater demands and expectations of customers are forcing organizations to explore new ways of doing business. To succeed, organizations must modify their structures.

In the past, most businesses utilized strategies proposed and enacted by their own organization's dedicated staff. However, to enhance their competitiveness and improve performance, many organizations are looking outside their own companies for talent. Internal staff are assuming different responsibilities and their accountability is being handled differently. The staff is expected to be more knowledgeable and willing to change. Flexibility is critical and the old hierarchies must be modified.

Mergers and acquisitions, as well as strategic alliances, are often used to obtain the skill, knowledge, and experience needed to enhance an organization's *core* business. If the desired talent and expertise do not exist within the company, it looks to outsiders to help the company produce and deliver its core products and services. To enhance effectiveness in an organization's *noncore* functions, outsourcing is frequently utilized. Outsourcing is contracting to others work that was formerly done within the information systems department. Outsourcing helps an organization obtain access to world-class services. The best business practices may be effectively implemented. Continuous improvements will help a company gain a competitive advantage in necessary yet noncore functions.

Before outsourcing information systems services, consideration should be given to sensibility, time concerns, sources of revenue, needs and expectations, the nature of item (e.g., critical importance), company objectives, compatibility, corporate culture, the degree of control sought, continuity of functions, innovation and creativity, employee morale, logistics, the desire to simplify operations, legal liability, legal aspects, and cost of redeployment and relocation.

Outsourcing information systems services allows a business to be more efficient and effective, reduce costs (e.g., staff), lower risk, streamline and simplify operations, improve quality, focus on core activities and competencies, free up capital and human resources, improve existing processes, enhance flexibility, obtain a competitive advantage, redeploy staff and assets, achieve economies, convert fixed costs to variable costs, and obtain improved up-to-date technology. Companies more suitable for outsourcing are those that are decentralized, engaged in restructuring, and out-of-date.

The outsourcing of information systems and its subfunctions was first popularized by Eastman Kodak when it outsourced its information systems operations to IBM, Businessland, and Digital Equipment Corp. Selective outsourcing has always been a part of information systems. Certain information system functions, such as programming, training, documentation, and disaster recovery, have been outsourced since the origin of electronic data processing. However, Kodak legitimized and popularized the total dismantling of internal information system departments.

Kodak's success started a bandwagon rolling. Senior executives everywhere wanted to emulate the strategic benefits enjoyed by Kodak and sought alliances with information systems outsourcing vendors. It seemed clear to everyone that information systems was a commodity service best provided by external suppliers. As a result, many companies signed long-term contracts and outsourced their entire information systems departments, frequently by transferring their employees, facilities, and hardware and software to external vendors. Many companies publicly announced as anticipated benefits drastic cost reductions of 10–50%, higher service levels, and access to emerging technologies and greater technical expertise.

However, outsourcing must be approached with caution. The outsourcing of information systems over the last decade has taught us many lessons. In the coming years outsourcing—in particular selective outsourcing—will continue to increase. In this chapter, we discuss the strategies for successful outsourcing, including its effect on cost reductions, service levels, and the utilization of new technologies. We separate the rhetoric from reality and examine the assumptions underlying outsourcing.

Cost Reductions

Senior management outsources information systems primarily to achieve significant cost reductions. It is argued that economies of scale will reduce costs. Mass production efficiencies and labor specialization are expected to reduce vendors' costs. Moreover, many vendors submit lower bids than existing information systems costs. However, the fact that external vendors need to produce a profit is often ignored. External contracting also generates additional transaction and sales costs. Frequently, companies are surprised by hidden costs in their contracts. Are there any conversion costs?

Major savings from outsourcing are generally the result of data center consolidation. An organization can realize similar savings by consolidating data centers on its own. Nowadays, economies of scale are no longer realized through hardware, and software licenses are usually corporation-specific.

Loose contracts are often disappointing in terms of cost savings. For example, hidden costs may be associated with a vendor's standard change-of-character clauses. If your organization changes from one word processor to another, your organization may be charged an extra fee to support the new word processing package. From the company's perspective, a word processor is a word processor and extra fees should not be charged. However, from the external vendor's perspective, a new software package means additional costs. The vendor may have to retrain its staff. More queries will also be generated as more users try to adapt to the new package. Such problems can be avoided by fully documenting in the contract the services and the service level expected from the vendor. It is also prudent to ask the vendor to demonstrate exactly how they plan to reduce costs. For example, ask them to show why they enjoy economies of scale.

Outsourcing may help control costs by reducing usage. Information systems costs are directly correlated with usage. Most organizations arbitrarily allocate information systems costs to user departments. Such allocation schemes are generally not tied to usage and result in the users' demanding and consuming excessive resources. External vendors' charges vary more directly with usage. Users are discouraged from requesting frivolous changes. User departments are forced to submit and justify their requests through a formal cost-control process.

Of course, this is likely to generate complaints from users that they now have to waste their time justifying something essential to performing their jobs. To alleviate such problems, senior management should work with the external vendors in prioritizing user requests. Such cost-control mechanisms can easily be implemented without outsourcing. However, outsourcing creates a formal relationship that is less prone to internal politics.

Outsourcing information systems is viewed by some senior executives as a way to restructure the information systems budget from a capital budget to an operating budget. Outsourcing provides the firm with greater financial flexibility by converting fixed costs into variable costs. As an added advantage, cash may be generated in the short term. An organization can sell its assets to the external vendor, which increases near-term cash flow. In return the organization signs a long-term contract, which, of course, reduces financial flexibility. External vendors generally require long-term contracts because they know that information systems costs will drop significantly over time. While the organization pays less in the first year than its existing costs, the organization pays more than it should in the latter years of the contract. Over time, the organization does not share in the benefits of performance/price increases because the organization pays the same fees over the life of the contract. It is therefore advisable to sign shorter-duration contracts, such as two to five years, rather than longer-term contracts of ten years or more. If a longer-term contract is signed, insist on the ability to reassess performance/price at reasonable intervals and renegotiate the contract accordingly.

Outsourcing also results in downsizing the information technology department, resulting in lower labor costs because of fewer employees.

Core Competencies

Many large organizations have abandoned their diversification strategies, once pursued to reduce risk, and have started to concentrate their energies on their core businesses. Most senior executives now believe in focusing on doing what their organizations do best and subcontracting all other functions. The most important sustainable advantage an organization has is its strategic focus.

Most senior executives see information systems as a noncore activity and want to outsource the entire department. However, certain information system functions, such as strategic planning and support of critical systems, should not be outsourced since they require detailed business knowledge. External vendors, while possessing the technology and expertise, do not generally possess detailed business knowledge.

Successful outsourcing is selective. Certain routine information system functions such as computer maintenance and data center processing may be outsourced, whereas nonroutine functions requiring business-specific knowledge should be kept in-house. Activities providing the information technology department with an existing or potential competitive advantage may be best kept within the company. Competitive differentiation is important to take into account. Innovation to develop internally is another key factor.

Improving Technical Services

Senior executives may outsource to improve the type or level of service, to gain access to new technology, or to utilize talent and expertise not available internally. In-house information system departments may create dissatisfaction by not responding to user requests promptly or within budget. To avoid disappointments, contracts should clearly state the type and level of service expected. External vendors may overwork their staff to contain costs, and overworked staff is more prone to making errors. It may not be unreasonable to specify in the contract the minimum number of individuals that the vendor will assign to the organization. Some companies go so far as to name the key individuals within the vendor's organization who will be responsible for and work with the company. Economies of scale are obtained using standardized software packages, and your organization may not be completely satisfied with such packages. Significant cash penalties may be used to ensure that the vendor conforms to the agreed-upon level of service. Penalties could be stipulated for delays or downtimes.

Access to technical expertise is an important factor in outsourcing. Many organizations find it difficult to find or retain highly qualified and talented individuals. Unfortunately, access to technical talent does not necessarily improve with outsourcing. Frequently, the technical expertise remains about the same because the internal staff has simply been transferred to the external vendor. The only way to ensure that extra technical expertise will be available is to specify it in the contract.

Many senior managers believe they will get access to new technologies by outsourcing but are frequently disappointed in this respect. In fact, a long-term outsourcing contract may motivate the vendor to use older technology as long as feasible. For example, a change from mainframe to client/server technology may be subject to the standard change-in-character clause and would result in additional fees for the organization. Access to new technology may then become prohibitively expensive. The best way to access new technology through outsourcing is to create technology-specific contracts. An external vendor may be hired specifically to assist in migrating to new technology. The organization keeps control over the entire process, but uses the vendor for technical expertise. This also enables the organizational staff to learn from the external vendor.

Another option to enhance access to new technology is to include incentives in the contract to share the benefits of new technology. For example, the firm and its external vendor could collaborate in developing new business applications involving state-of-the-art technologies whereby both the firm and vendor can share in the profits.

Political Consequences

Outsourcing may be undertaken for political reasons. Information system departments may undertake outsourcing evaluation to prove that they are operating efficiently, to justify acquisition of new resources, or to expose exaggerated claims. Senior management's reasons for outsourcing include eliminating a troublesome function or duplicating the success of other organizations.

Top management might view information systems as an overhead function and evaluate it strictly based on its cost-efficiency. The information systems department may desire a bid from external vendors to demonstrate to senior management that the department is cost-efficient. Top management is likely to view the results of such comparisons with skepticism. Senior management may feel that the information systems manager has selectively picked its best managed and most cost-efficient function for outsource comparison.

External vendors may also view outsourcing requests by the information systems department with suspicion. External vendors are concerned that the information systems department is inquiring about outsourcing just to obtain a free assessment. Therefore, vendors charge a significant amount to submit bids.

Information systems managers may use outsourcing to justify requests for additional resources. Senior management may be unwilling to provide new resources or information systems without extensive justification. IS managers might therefore attempt to show that demand cannot be satisfied efficiently through outsourcing and that the only choice is investment in new technology.

When the IS department initiates any outsourcing bids, senior management must actively participate in the process. Senior management's participation will add credibility to the external outsourcing evaluation request. The scope of the evaluation, as well as the bid criteria, should be verified by senior management. Senior management should also review and analyze the bid. Senior management should work with the IS department, but the information systems department must be involved. The IS department should specify the technical and financial details for the bid request, and it should help interpret the technical aspects of the external bids. The primary purpose of senior management's involvement is simply to minimize the politics.

Selecting an Outsourcing Vendor

In selecting an outsourcing vendor, consider reputation, stability, specialty and focus, contacts, references, reliability, experience, availability, time constraints, fees, flexibility, expertise (specialized skills), communications, cost, commitment, quality of service, capacity limitations, efficiency and effectiveness, contract provisions and restrictions (e.g., time period and cancellation penalty clauses), productivity, and "fit." Is the outsource vendor committed, creative, and innovative?

Ask the vendor for a "trial period" to see how things are going before entering into a regular contract. Even then, avoid long-term contracts, especially those whose terms are rigid. You want flexibility and do not want to be locked in for the long term. We recommend renewable short-term contracts. The contract should be updated as the environment and circumstances change.

Insist that outsourcing contracts contain provisions for performance expectations (e.g., scope of work, service level goals) and measurement guidelines. Undertake periodic performance appraisals.

Appendix C provides a listing of the names, addresses, and telephone numbers of selected outsourcing services in information technology.

5
PROJECT MANAGEMENT

Information systems managers must have the organizational skills needed to manage projects. Projects are exceptions to the routine work. In a project, you usually deal with unique problems, have a set of constraints, and often work with deadlines. Projects may involve extensive interaction with various departments within your organization.

In all projects, you are likely to encounter the following three elements:

- *Time schedule:* A project has a specific life span. It has a starting point and a stopping point. Controls must be used to ensure that all phases of a project are completed in a timely manner.

- *Budgetary constraints:* A project's budget is often separate from a departmental budget and gives the project team some independence. Capital budgets may be required in addition to expense budgets. The project manager assumes responsibility for the budget and any variance.

- *Results-oriented activities:* Projects are results-oriented. They are undertaken to achieve a specific objective. The project manager should identify and define the specific tasks that would lead to the desired results.

PLANNING AND CONTROLLING A PROJECT

The purpose of the project should be clearly defined. The management of a project requires proper planning and control of a project's completion

125

time, budgetary resources, and desired results. Without proper planning and control, it is highly unlikely that the project will be completed within the deadline or within resources, or that the desired results will be achieved.

In planning and controlling a project, ask the following questions:

Project Objective

- What are the desired results?
- What do we expect to achieve by undertaking this project?
- What problems are likely to be encountered?
- How will those problems be solved?

Time Considerations

- What is the magnitude of the project?
- Is it a large project or a small project?
- If it is a large project, how can it be divided into a series of shorter tasks?
- How long will it take to complete the project?
- What is the project's deadline?
- What are the consequences of a delay in deadline?
- For longer projects, when should each phase of the project be completed?

Financial Considerations

- What is the project's budget?
- What are the major categories of expenses?
- Will capital expenditures be undertaken?
- How much of the budget should be allocated to planned expenses?
- How much of the budget should be allocated to unexpected expenses and contingency planning?

- What are the consequences of going over or under budget?
- What resources, including human resources, are needed to complete the project?
- What tools and methods will be used to ensure that the project is within budget?

Management

- What is my responsibility?
- Who will be on my project team?
- What is the responsibility of each team member?
- Who will manage and coordinate the various activities in a project and ensure that they are proceeding as planned and will be completed before their deadline?
- Who will monitor that the project is proceeding as planned and within budget?
- How will variances be identified and corrected for?

Interim Analysis

- Are the intermediate results consistent with the final desired results?
- Is the project achieving the desired results at each major step along its completion path?
- How will you accelerate the pace of the work if your team falls behind schedule?
- How will you reduce expenses if actual costs exceed the budget?
- If problems are developing, what actions will be taken to correct them?

Final Report

- How will the results of the project be documented?
- What type of final report will be prepared and for whom?

To successfully complete the project, the project manager must have a clear understanding of the desired results and how these results will satisfy the needs of the end-user.

Project managers should assume a leadership position. Their aim should be not only to supervise but more importantly to coordinate the efforts of the team members. This often requires direct involvement in the major phases of the task so that the team works together, budgets do not show significant variances, schedules are kept, and deadlines are met.

A schedule of work should be prepared outlining responsibilities. Everything should be written down. Checklists should be used to ensure that all team members know their responsibilities and when the job must be completed.

Team members sometimes work on several projects simultaneously. Under these conditions, there may be conflicts among priorities, especially if they are working under different project managers. To minimize such conflicts, team members should be asked to let project managers know in advance about scheduling conflicts. Team members may then be reassigned to different tasks.

Team members should be given detailed instructions, and participation should be encouraged from the beginning. Their input should be solicited. Let the members propose solutions and assist in implementation. Active participation will motivate the project team, and when the ideas are good, the entire project benefits.

CONDUCTING THE INITIAL MEETING

Before starting the project, the project manager should meet with the team to set a positive tone and define the project's purpose. The meeting can help avoid misunderstandings and save time and effort later. It also clarifies the nature of the assignment, as well as the authority and responsibility of each individual.

Meetings should then be scheduled at regular intervals, but limited in time and frequency. If the project team spends all its time in meetings, not much else will be accomplished. At the same time, it is important to get together to review progress, resolve problems, and ensure adherence to budgets and schedules.

At the initial meeting, each team member should identify the problems he or she anticipates in working on the project. A list should be prepared of anticipated problems and team members should generate solutions. If additional data is needed, discuss who will research the data and from what sources. How will this information be verified? Possibly some of the data may be inaccurate, obsolete, or someone may have misinterpreted the data. Be sure to consider how much time it will take to gather additional data or to conduct research.

A list of initial tasks should be prepared and assigned to appropriate individuals. Whenever possible, let the team members volunteer; they are likely to be more motivated if they define their own roles. The entire team should gain an understanding of the scope of the entire project at the initial meeting.

For all major phases of the project, prepare an initial schedule. For each phase, as well as for the overall project, establish the anticipated start and completion dates. Some phases, of course, may overlap. Subgroups of the team may be working independently and the work of one subgroup may not depend on the work of another subgroup. Nonlinearity in a project and its overlapping phases offer tremendous flexibility in scheduling activities.

While deadlines should be established in the initial schedule, maintaining flexibility is also important. It is highly unlikely that everything will happen according to schedule. Furthermore, as the team starts its work, the members will gain a better understanding of the problems, and the schedule and budget may have to be modified.

An initial financial budget should be prepared for each phase of the project. The initial budget should be prepared after considering human, financial, and information resources. For capital expenditures, consider both purchasing and leasing, as appropriate. Variance analysis should be conducted at the end of each phase by comparing the actual to budget figures for costs, time, and productivity. This allows you to monitor actual expenditures and time, and to take corrective action, if necessary, to keep the project within budget.

ASSEMBLING THE PROJECT TEAM

The project team is a major determinant of the success or failure of a project. As the team increases in size, its diversity increases, the managing tasks become more difficult and complex, and the potential for conflict increases. There might be misunderstandings in communication. Different individuals have different motives and goals.

Team Assignment

As a project manager, you may or may not have control over the staff members assigned to the project team. If a team is being imposed, you should communicate with senior management and request that they allow you involvement in the selection process. For example, you could give them a list of individuals with whom you have worked successfully in the past. Emphasize the importance of having a cohesive project team and that such a team is critical to a project's success.

Of course, sometimes it just is not possible to put together a team of your choice and you have to do the best with those you are given. These individuals may be perfectly capable of doing the job. They may have been assigned to this project only because they were available. It is also possible that these individuals were assigned because of their interest or talent. In any event, you should give each individual a chance to do the best possible work, and you may be pleasantly surprised.

It is important to inspire and motivate team members. Your aim should be to help team members understand how the success of the project will affect their success. Primarily interested in themselves, team members will not commit themselves to the project if they do not anticipate personal gain. You need to specifically identify the benefits to the team members to motivate them and to focus their energies on the project. An ideal team member understands the desired results and is committed to making it happen.

Job Assignment

It is generally best to break a large project into several phases and each phase into distinct tasks. Each team member should then be assigned the responsibility of executing one or more of those tasks, which should not be highly structured. To motivate team members, assign them the responsibility for a given job and let them approach it the way they believe is best. This, of course, does not mean that you should not supervise them or give them guidance. Coordinate the activities and make sure the team members understand the goals and aims of the task. However, by providing team members with responsibility for certain tasks, you give them an incentive to put in their best efforts. This also lets them know that you trust them and that you have confidence in their abilities.

Delegating Duties

If you are too assertive and too controlling, you may stifle the freedom of your project team and impede its creativity. An effective project manager knows how to delegate the work. You should not insist that the project be done your way. Your role should be to monitor the team's work and coordinate its efforts, while watching the budget and the time schedule of each phase of the project. Of course, you should be available to help your team members, especially if they come to you with a problem.

Conflict Resolution

Conflicts sometimes develop among team members or groups of team members. For example, individuals may differ as to how to approach the project or to solve a problem, or groups may compete for credit for some work. As the project manager, your aim is to resolve conflicts and to make sure they do not destroy the project. Emphasize to your team that the success of the project is more important than the success of any individual. Stress that everyone benefits from the project's success and everyone loses from its failure.

Self-Directed Work Teams

The self-directed team structure is an alternate to the traditional team structure and has become popular. A *self-directed team* is a group of well-trained workers with full responsibility for completing a well-defined segment of work. This segment of work may be the entire finished product or an intermediate part of the whole. Every member of the team shares equal responsibility for the entire segment of work. Conceptually, self-directed teams are the opposite of traditional teams that work in an assembly-line manner. In an assembly line, each worker assumes responsibility for only a narrow technical function. In self-directed teams, each worker is equally responsible for the entire segment. This, of course, requires that the team members receive extensive training in administrative, technical, and interpersonal skills to maintain a self-managing group. Self-directed teams have many more resources available to them compared with traditional teams.

Traditional teams assign a narrow function to each member. Since a large number of people contribute to the finished product, individual workers see little relationship between their efforts and the finished product. This leads to apathy and alienation. All members in self-directed teams receive extensive cross-training, and they share in the challenging as well as routine activities for their segment of work.

OBTAINING SENIOR MANAGEMENT BUY-IN

Obtaining the cooperation of senior management is essential. Senior management's involvement and attitude toward projects differ from company to company and from person to person. Senior management might be very supportive of the project or couldn't care less about it. Senior management's attitudes may be classified as follows:

- "It is your project. You have to solve your own problems. I don't want to be bothered until it is completed."

- "I would be happy to work with you and resolve any problem you encounter."

- "Although I would like to help, there is nothing I can do. You will have to resolve this problem on your own."

- "Keep me apprised of the situation and any problems you encounter."

Regardless of senior management's attitude, you should be prepared to complete the project without any help. Frequently, you will have no choice but to do the best you can with available resources.

DEVELOPING A FEASIBLE BUDGET

The budgeting process may be a source of confusion and frustration for many project managers. There may be a great deal of pressure to remain within the budget. A *budget* is simply an estimate of the sources and uses of cash and other resources. Since the budget is an estimate, it is unlikely that the final expenditures will be exactly equal to the budget.

Preparing the budget at a realistic level is important. Agreeing to an inadequate budget is unwise. While it may be convenient at the formation stage to reduce or minimize conflict, you and your project will eventually suffer. You will be expected to explain unfavorable variances to senior management. Moreover, you will be perceived negatively when your project goes over budget.

The budget should always be developed by the project manager. It is unrealistic to work with an imposed budget. The project manager is generally in the best position to know what the project should cost and is responsible for explaining any resulting variances. Accordingly, you should always insist on developing your own budget and should not settle for an inadequate budget simply to minimize conflict at the outset. Otherwise, both you and your project will suffer in the long run.

Project budgets are typically more difficult to prepare and adjust than departmental budgets. Projects typically consist of nonroutine activities. Departmental budgets are generally prepared annually and are often revised quarterly or semiannually. In contrast, project budgets are generally for the life of the project and are not related to a fiscal year. Revisions to project budgets are uncommon in the absence of a mistake in the original budget or a major change in the scope of the project. Unfavorable variances in a project usually are noticed more than unfavorable variances in a departmental budget. At the departmental level, variances are often accepted as being inevitable, but similar variances in a project are often frowned upon. In general, a project manager is typically held to a higher level of accountability than a department manager.

The major expense in most projects is likely to be for human resources. When estimating labor expense, consider both the labor hours and the skill levels needed to complete each phase of the project. Multiplying the hours by the labor rate at each level will give the total labor cost.

Also for each phase of the project, prepare a detailed budget listing the materials, supplies, and equipment requirements, which vary widely. Some projects consist essentially of administrative tasks and do not require any special materials or supplies. Other projects may require considerable expenditures on property, plant, or equipment.

Fixed and variable overhead is another major category of expenses for most projects. Companies differ in how they allocate fixed overhead, but it is usually by formula. Overhead may be allocated based on labor hours, labor cost, machine hours, square feet, etc. Variable overhead is allocated to the project like other project-specific expenses. In general, overhead is more likely to be allocated for longer-term projects. For shorter-term projects, senior management may decide not to allocate overhead expenses. It is essential to identify significant variances from budgeted amounts. Most companies require formal variance analysis at the end of the project. You should do variance analysis at each phase of the project and take corrective action. If a phase is long, consider doing monthly variance analyses. All significant variances, whether favorable or unfavorable, should be investigated.

If actual expenses exceed budgeted expenses, investigate the cause. Budgets are closely tied to work schedules. Certain phases might be taking longer than estimated. You may have no choice but to demand more work from your team members. Also, your original assumptions and estimates might be wrong or a significant change might have occurred in the scope of the project. You could request senior management to revise the project budget. It is sometimes possible to absorb unfavorable variances from one phase into the next phase. Your personal involvement in future phases of the project might also enhance productivity. You may also need to initiate budgetary controls to curb spending.

It is important to investigate *all* significant variances, not just the unfavorable ones. Sometimes expenses turn out to be less than budgeted. Examine why you are under budget. Is your team more productive than anticipated? Was there a significant decline in the price of materials, supplies, or equipment? Were your original estimates accurate? Is quality being sacrificed in any way to obtain cost savings? Do you expect to incur expenses in later phases that might wipe out any savings from the earlier stages?

DETAILED TIME-SCHEDULE PREPARATION

Prepare a schedule for each phase of the project. You will be unable to complete your project on time without planning and controlling the time budget. Even a small delay in one phase of a project can have a significant effect on the overall completion time. Many tasks in a project are interdependent. A small isolated delay might perhaps not be a problem. However, when activities are interdependent, a small delay might throw off the entire schedule.

The schedule should be reasonable and realistic. Some projects are plagued by delays. If you have been unable to complete the initial phases on time, it is unlikely that you will complete the project on time. An effective project manager knows how to set up a realistic time budget and how to follow through on the budget. Time-management skills are essential characteristics of a good project manager.

When planning the initial schedule, budget a little slack. However, project deadlines are often imposed and you may have no choice but to work within the imposed guidelines. Sometimes a delay in one phase of the project simply has to be overcome in a later phase.

As the project manager, you are responsible for staying on schedule and meeting the deadline. It does not matter what caused the delay. You are personally responsible for controlling the activities, monitoring progress, anticipating problems, and taking corrective actions before delays cause you to miss the final project deadline.

Although your goal should be to meet the project deadline, it is unwise to let the quality of the project suffer. Your final results should be accurate and of high quality, even if it means that you need to request an extension. You should try, of course, to work faster, put in overtime, or modify your original plan to meet the deadline. However, if the trade-off is between meeting the deadline or doing quality work, the project's quality must not be sacrificed.

SCHEDULING TOOLS AND TECHNIQUES

Presenting the schedule information in a visual form helps you and your team understand the project workflow and time requirements.

Gantt Charts

A *Gantt chart* is a tool to monitor progress. Showing both planned and actual outcomes for each phase, a Gantt chart allows you to isolate and solve scheduling problems in a methodical manner. While the project as a whole might be overwhelming, a Gantt chart helps in managing a large project by breaking the project into a series of smaller phases. As each phase is completed, you can see if the final deadline is likely to be met. If you are behind schedule, you can attempt to get back on track by absorbing the delay in one phase by making it up in another phase. This tool should be used not only by the project manager, but by the entire team. Its use is most effective when everyone on the team uses it.

A Gantt chart may be constructed using several techniques involving different combinations of lines and symbols. The actual and planned beginning and ending points for each phase are plotted along a time line. The first phase is plotted at the top and the last phase is plotted at the bottom. Gantt charts may be constructed by hand or through computer software packages.

Networks

Most large projects can be represented by a network of activities. *PERT* (*Program Evaluation and Review Technique*) and *CPM* (*Critical Path Method*) *network techniques* are used extensively to aid in the planning and scheduling of large projects. PERT/CPM are probably the most commonly used of all quantitative techniques in management. Many extensions and modifications have been made to these tools to increase their usefulness and application.

PERT is a useful tool for planning and scheduling large projects involving:

- a large number of activities,
- with uncertainty about completion time,
- where the activities are independent of each other,
- and the activities must be completed in a certain order.

The CPM is closely related to PERT. Its focus is on the trade-off between cost and completion time for large projects. CPM considers:

- the relationship between the cost of using additional resources, and
- their effect on reducing the completion time of jobs within a project.

Unlike PERT, CPM assumes that the time to complete a job is known with certainty. It also assumes that the relationship between the amount of resources utilized and the amount of time needed to complete the project is known. CPM is concerned simply with the time–cost trade-offs.

The differences in the two techniques make them suitable for different applications. PERT is used more extensively in research and development projects, where completion times are uncertain. CPM is used more extensively in projects where the organization has experience in similar projects. Both techniques, however, require the project to consist of a set of independent activities that must be performed in a specific order.

PERT

Gathering and analyzing data are familiar tasks for the IS professional. Assume you are gathering and analyzing data and your project consists of five independent activities, or jobs. The project starts with determining the aim and scope of the project. Next, you prepare a mailing list of people to be surveyed. Note that you can start preparing the survey instrument alongside obtaining the mailing list. Neither activity is dependent on the other. After preparing the survey, you pilot-test the survey and correct the flaws. Finally, surveys are mailed and data is collected and analyzed.

Table 5-1 shows the activities and describes their flow. The immediate predecessor activity or group of activities is also shown for each activity. Note that each activity is represented by a letter. The table shows the amount of time needed to complete each activity.

Table 5-1.
PERT ACTIVITIES AND FLOW

Activity Name	Description	Immediate Predecessors	Time (Weeks)
a	Define the aim and scope of project.	—	2
b	Identify participants and prepare a mailing list.	a	4
c	Prepare a survey questionnaire.	a	5
d	Do pilot-testing and fix flaws in questionnaire.	c	7
e	Mail survey; collect and analyze data.	b, d	10

A PERT network may be generated from this information, as shown in Figure 5-1.

Figure 5-1.
SAMPLE PERT NETWORK

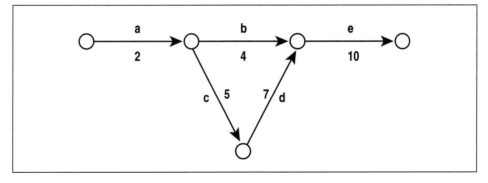

The minimum time required for completion of the whole project is given by the longest path in the network and is known as the *critical path*. As Figure 5-1 shows, there are two paths in this project: a-b-e and a-c-d-e. The completion time for a-b-e is 16 weeks and the completion time for a-c-d-e is 24 weeks. The path a-c-d-e is the critical path because it is the longer path in the network. *Slack* is determined by subtracting the completion time for the noncritical paths from the completion time for the critical path. Therefore, the slack for path a-b-e is 8 weeks. Slack information is extremely useful to project managers. It tells you how much flexibility you have in scheduling various activities.

More complex projects can have multiple critical paths. If there are two critical paths with no common activities, then at least two activities, one on each path, must be shortened to reduce the project's completion time. If the critical paths share one or more of the activities, shortening that activity reduces the entire project's completion time.

PERT specifically takes into account uncertainties inherent in completing activities. An estimate is made of the *Most Probable, Pessimistic,* and *Optimistic* completion times by a knowledgeable individual. The pessimistic estimate is based on a familiar assumption: Everything that can go wrong will go wrong. However, this estimate does not include the effect of catastrophic or highly unusual events, such as earthquakes or fires. The optimistic estimate is based on the assumption that everything goes right, and it represents the shortest possible time for the completion of the activity.

The three estimates, while not always easy to prepare, give important information about the expected uncertainties. For some activities, the three estimates will be close together and cover a narrow range; for other activities the estimates may be over a wide range. These estimates may or may not be symmetrical around the mean.

The expected completion time for each activity is calculated using the *beta* distribution, which is not based on empirical data. Since many projects occur only once, it is not possible to use historical data to empirically determine probabilities. Under these conditions, using the beta distribution is generally the best possible option.

The beta distribution assumes that the pessimistic and optimistic activity times occur with equal frequency. The most probable estimate occurs with a probability four times more likely than either the pessimistic or the optimistic. Applying these weights,

$$t_e = \frac{t_o + 4t_m + t_p}{6}$$

The *expected completion time* t_e is equal to the sum of the optimistic time estimate t_o, the pessimistic time estimate t_p, and four times the most probable time estimate t_m, divided by 6.

Continuing with our earlier example, assume the estimates shown in Table 5-2 were obtained for the optimistic t_o, most probable t_m, and pessimistic t_p times. The expected completion time t_e, based on the beta distribution, has been calculated. The *standard deviation S_t* and *variance V_t* are also shown. The network based on these new time estimates is shown in Figure 5-2.

Table 5-2.
NEW DISTRIBUTION ESTIMATES

Activity	t_o	t_m	t_p	t_e	S_t	V_t
a	2	4	10	4.7	1.3	1.8
b	2	8	11	7.5	1.5	2.3
c	4	5	7	5.2	0.5	0.3
d	6	6	12	7.0	1.0	1.0
e	4	10	16	10.0	2.0	4.0

Figure 5-2.
NETWORK BASED ON NEW TIME ESTIMATES

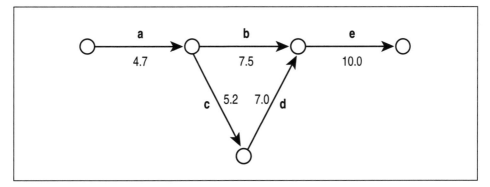

Standard deviation and variance are commonly used as measures of variability. The *variance* is the average squared difference of all the numbers from their mean, and *standard deviation* is simply the square root of variance.

The calculation of standard deviation and variance in PERT are even simpler because the beta distribution is represented by only three values. Standard deviation S_t can be estimated as follows:

$$S_t = \frac{t_p - t_o}{6}$$

In other words, S_t is one-sixth of the difference between the pessimistic and optimistic time estimates. The greater the uncertainty, the greater the range and the higher the S_t. A high standard deviation means that there is a great likelihood that the time to complete the activity will differ significantly from the expected completion time t_e. Variance V_t is the square of standard deviation.

The expected completion time and variance for a sequence of independent activities is the sum of their separate times and the sum of individual variances. The critical path and the expected completion time and variance for the project may be calculated by adding the time and variance for each activity along the path. If a project has more than one critical path, select the one with the largest variance.

CPM

CPM was developed to solve scheduling problems, and it is less concerned with the uncertainty problems of PERT. CPM is concerned with minimizing the costs of project scheduling. It is a deterministic model, unlike PERT, which is a probabilistic model.

CPM recognizes that most activities can be completed in a shorter time by utilizing additional resources, thus increasing the cost of the project. If the advantages outweigh the incremental costs, a job should be expedited, or *crashed*. In contrast, if a job has significant slack and there is no reason to shorten it, the job should proceed at its normal or most efficient pace and with fewer resources. Thus, only critical jobs should be expedited or crashed, and CPM is used to determine which jobs to crash and by how much.

Project costs may be classified into two categories. *Direct costs* are associated with individual activities in a project. *Indirect costs* are overhead items and fixed expenses. If a project's duration is shortened, *direct costs increase* and *indirect costs decrease*. This relationship is illustrated in Figure 5-3.

Figure 5-3.
DIRECT AND INDIRECT COSTS VERSUS DURATION

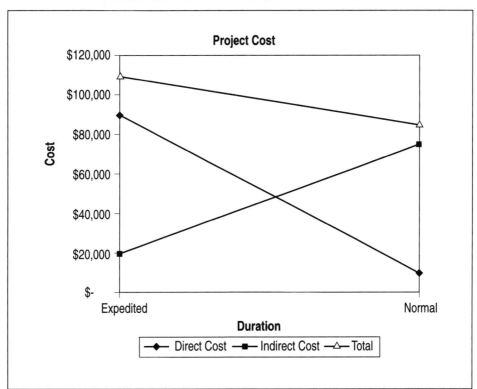

To illustrate the concept, assume that the time–cost trade-off is linear and that the relationship can be represented by a straight line. Figure 5-4 shows the time–cost trade-off for a typical job. The slope of the line gives us the cost of expediting an activity: the steeper the slope, the higher the cost. A vertical line represents an activity that cannot be shortened regardless of the extra resources. The vertical line in Figure 5-4 suggests that it is not possible to shorten the activity, no matter what additional resources are expended. A horizontal line indicates that shortening or expediting a job would require no extra resources. The horizontal line in Figure 5-4 indicates that slowing down the activity would decrease the direct costs only up to a certain extent, beyond which no additional savings are obtained. Costs may even start to increase if the activity is slowed excessively. Typically, we expect a line to slope downward to the right. The negative slope of the line indicates that there is a negative association between cost and time; costs go up as duration is shortened.

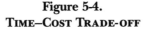

Figure 5-4.
TIME–COST TRADE-OFF

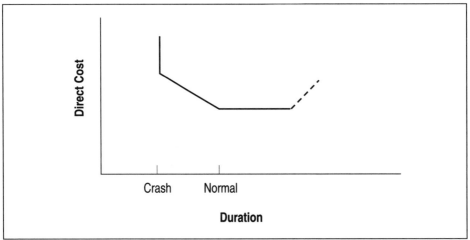

Using CPM we can determine the optimum project length, striking a balance between shortening jobs or not to minimize the direct and indirect costs. A preliminary schedule with maximum time length and normal resources is generated. This schedule is reduced by expediting one or more activities at an additional cost. If these additional costs are less than the savings in indirect costs from expediting the project, then the activities should be expedited. A new schedule is then generated and additional activities are expedited. This continues while net savings are realized in total cost. Improvements continue to be made using a stepwise method.

Only activities along the critical path affect a project's length, and thus only these activities are considered for crashing. The cost–time slope for each activity along the critical path is examined, and the one with the smallest slope is selected because it can be shortened with the least expenditure. Cost-benefit analysis is conducted to determine if net savings exist. This process is repeated until either no activity on the critical path can be shortened or the cost of shortening would exceed the resultant savings from shortening the project duration.

Consider a basic project with four activities, as shown in Figure 5-5. The normal and crash duration times, as well as the cost to crash, is given in Table 5-3 for each activity. The activity's normal time represents the number of weeks needed to complete the activity at an efficient pace. The crash time represents the minimum time that results from the use of additional resources. It is possible to have other times between the normal and crash durations. However, reducing the project time beyond the crash duration is not possible. The cost of crashing is the cost of the additional resources needed to shorten the activity completion time by *one week*. Figure 5-6 shows the cost–time trade-off for each activity. Recall that it is more expensive to crash activities with steeper slopes. As Figure 5-6 shows, activity a has the steepest slope, followed by activity c, activity d, and activity b.

Figure 5-5.
BASIC PROJECT DIAGRAM

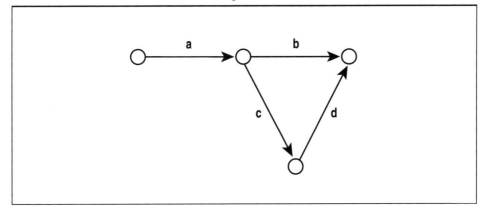

Table 5-3.
CRASH AND DURATION TIMES

Activity	Normal	Crash	Cost of Crashing
a	4	2	$6,000
b	9	4	$2,000
c	5	2	$5,000
d	6	3	$3,000

Figure 5-6.
COST–TIME TRADE-OFF FOR EACH ACTIVITY

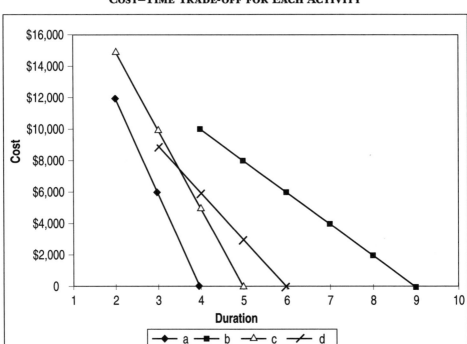

The critical path is represented by a-c-d. It takes 15 weeks to complete this project. Assume that the time-related indirect expenses for this project are $6,500 per week. If we don't expedite the project, total relevant cost is:

Total relevant cost = Cost of crashing + Cost of overhead
                          = $0   + $6,500 × 15 weeks
                          = $97,500

The total relevant cost is not necessarily the same as total cost. When considering the relevant cost for decision-making purposes, we can ignore the base cost of the project. The base cost has to be paid regardless of whether the project is expedited and is thus irrelevant.

The critical path is a-c-d and, since activity d has the smallest slope on the critical path, it is the least expensive to shorten. Activity b has two weeks of slack; therefore d can be shortened by two weeks before activity b becomes critical. By shortening d by two weeks, the project can now be completed in 13 weeks and its cost is as follows:

$$
\begin{aligned}
\text{Total relevant cost} &= \text{Cost of crashing} + \text{Cost of overhead} \\
&= \$3{,}000 \times 2 \text{ weeks} + \$6{,}500 \times 13 \text{ weeks} \\
&= \$90{,}500
\end{aligned}
$$

Although we incurred $6,000 for crashing activity d, we saved $13,000 by reducing overhead costs and realized a net savings of $7,000 ($90,500 versus $97,500).

Now we have two critical paths, a-b and a-c-d. Both paths must be reduced if we want to shorten our schedule. We have several choices, as shown in Table 5-4. Activity a is common to both paths and reducing it will shorten the overall project. Alternatively, we can reduce activities b and c or activities b and d. Clearly, the best alternative is to crash activities b and d; they have the lowest combined cost of crashing. Keep in mind that d can be crashed only one additional week since d cannot be less than three weeks and we have previously reduced it by two weeks. The total relevant cost for crashing b and d by one week is:

$$
\begin{aligned}
\text{Total relevant cost} &= \text{Cost of crashing b and d} + \text{Cost of overhead} \\
&= \text{b} \rightarrow \$2{,}000 \times 1 \text{ week} + \$6{,}500 \times 12 \text{ weeks} \\
&\quad\ \text{d} \rightarrow \$3{,}000 \times 3 \text{ weeks} \\
&= \$2{,}000 + \$9{,}000 \quad\ + \$78{,}000 \\
&= \$89{,}000
\end{aligned}
$$

Table 5-4.
ACTIVITY VERSUS COST

Crash Activity	Cost of Crashing (Per Week)
a	$6,000
b and c	$2,000 + $5,000 = $7,000
b and d	$2,000 + $3,000 = $5,000

As shown in Table 5-5, we now have two choices. Activity a can be shortened from four to two weeks:

Total relevant cost = Cost of crashing a, b and d   + Cost of overhead
         = b → $2,000 × 1 week   + $6,500 × 10 weeks
            d → $3,000 × 3 weeks
            a → $6,000 × 2 weeks
         = $2,000 + $9,000 + $12,000 + $65,000
         = $88,000

Table 5-5.
RELEVANT ACTIVITY VERSUS COST

Crash Activity	Cost of Crashing (Per Week)
a	$6,000
b and c	$2,000 + $5,000 = $7,000

The only alternative left is to shorten b and c. Recall b has already been shortened by one week, but it can be shortened by another four weeks. Activity c, however, can be shortened by only three weeks. If we reduce b and c by three weeks, then:

Total relevant cost = Cost of crashing a, b, c and d + Cost of overhead
         = b → $2,000 × 4 weeks   + $6,500 × 7 weeks
            d → $3,000 × 3 weeks
            a → $6,000 × 2 weeks
            c → $5,000 × 3 weeks
         = $8,000 + $9,000 + $12,000 + $15,000 + $45,000
         = $89,500

It does not make sense to crash b and c since the cost exceeds the benefit. Hence, our final schedule consists of ten weeks and requires crashing activities a, b, and d. The total relevant cost for the project is $88,000.

6

QUALITY AND PRODUCTION MANAGEMENT

Manufacturing is a broad and complicated subject. If a firm manufactures different products, its processes and operations may be extremely varied. The mission of a manufacturing information system is to apply computer technology to improve the process and the efficiency of a manufacturing system to increase the quality of products and to lower the costs to manufacture them. In other words, a manufacturing system takes material, equipment, data, management, and information systems technology as the input and uses manufacturing and information processes to generate better final products as output (see Figure 6-1).

Figure 6-1.
THE MODEL OF A MANUFACTURING INFORMATION SYSTEMS

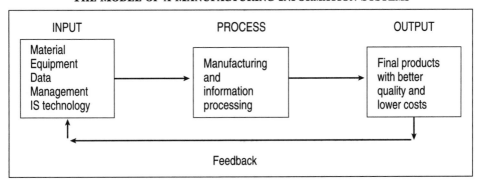

Manufacturing consists of many different disciplinary areas, including product engineering, facility design and scheduling, fabrication, and quality control management. Each area can be dramatically improved by using information systems.

UNDERSTANDING PRODUCT DESIGN AND ENGINEERING

Product engineering is the starting point of the manufacturing process, by which the design and technical specifications for the product are finalized. Recently, product design and engineering are becoming more computerized through computer software packages such as computer-aided design (CAD) and computer-aided manufacturing (CAM). With CAD, product designers use technologies to design a prototype of the product, test the product, and modify the design on the computer before it goes into production. The initial design can be input to the CAD system in various ways, including drawing sketches on a digital tablet, using a digital camera, or even scanning digitized photographs or pictures into the system. After the product is digitized, the design can then be simulated and tested under real-world conditions, which have been predefined by the designer. As changes are suggested, the original design can be modified—similar to editing a letter in a word processing program. Artificial intelligence (AI) has also been used in CAD systems AI agents can help human designers make changes, implement suggestions, or do tests based on different circumstances.

After the product has been designed, another important issue is how to produce the product efficiently and effectively. Designing products for easy and cheap assembly is critical since assembly often accounts for over half the total manufacturing costs. For example, by reducing the number of components by 30%, a manufacturer can drastically cut manual assembly times and manufacturing costs. Large corporations such as IBM, GM, Ford, HP, and GE have sophisticated product designs, which reflect how this product should be functioning as well as how it should be manufactured efficiently and economically.

FACILITY DESIGN AND SCHEDULING

After the product is designed, the facility or equipment used to produce the designed product should be arranged. This decision may be as simple as changing several tools or as complex as redesigning the entire plant. Some computer software packages can also arrange the plant layout based on the production information of the designed product. Many of the layout algorithms proposed use an improvement approach, a construction approach, or a simulation approach.

Improvement Approach

This approach requires users to specify initial conditions and parameters. A combinatory-based approach is then applied to improve the initial layout. This process is usually done by intelligent search techniques to try numerous alternatives to find the best possible solution. For example, machine A can be switched with machine B to see the effects on the manufacturing process.

Construction Approach

This approach builds one or more layout solutions from scratch with or without the user's initial suggestions. The best one is then selected.

Simulation

Monte Carlo simulation has also been used to solve facility layout problems. This approach simulates the real production environment based on the assumptions provided by the designer. This process requires lots of computer resources and the time to generate good results.

METHODS OF FABRICATION

Fabrication, or manufacturing, is the process of making new products from raw materials. There are two types of production methods: job shop production and process production.

Job Shop Production

Each work order is considered a job. Raw materials required to process these materials are routed to work centers depending on the production step required. The job shop is more flexible in terms of the products that can be produced. Therefore, a variety of products can be produced at the same time. Today, many computer software packages are able to generate a job shop schedule using mathematical programming or artificial intelligence technologies.

Flow Shop Production

One or a few products travel through a set of fabrication activities specially arranged for the products. This approach is suitable for repetitive manufacturing (e.g., an automobile assembly line) and process industries such as an oil refinery in which no significant stoppage in the flow of materials is evidenced, and the flow rate becomes the critical decision. The layout of the assembly line and the flow rate can be determined by expert systems with the rule base retrieved from many manufacturing experts.

COMPUTER-AIDED DESIGN AND COMPUTER-AIDED MANUFACTURING FUNCTIONS

CAD programs are software programs for the design of products. CAD programs can be found in all types of computers from mainframe systems to microcomputers. They are developed to help engineers design all kinds of products from airplanes to pens. The advantages of CAD software are that the design can be drawn in three dimensions, the design can be simulated in the computer, and design changes can be made very efficiently. Good CAD packages are AutoCAD, TurboCAD, and EasyCAD2.

Some CAD programs are developed for nonprogrammers. For example, a relatively unskilled person can use this type of software to design an office or even a home. These programs include libraries of options such as cabinetry, furniture, trees, and even shadows. Once the design is completed, users can "walk into the design" and view the structure from different points of view. This is similar to a virtual reality system.

"CAM" is an umbrella term that includes almost any use of computers in manufacturing operations. It consists of the following functions:

- *Monitoring:* Computers can be used to control and monitor manufacturing operations in a dangerous environment. For example, an oil refinery facility uses CAM to open and shut valves when a certain temperature is reached in a tank.

- *Numeric control:* Computer technology is used to control the manufacturing operations. For example, CAM can help manufacturing workers produce parts that require a high degree of precision because computers are used to improve the accuracy of manufacturing.

- *Optimization:* Many manufacturing operations involve finding the best solution among others. For example, oil refinery is looking for the cheapest way to mix crude oils to achieve a finished gasoline that meets certain restrictions. Auto assembly plants try to arrange the best schedule so that the operating costs can be minimized. With CAM techniques, optimization can be improved and the operation can be more economical and efficient.
- *Robotics:* Robotics is the use of computer-controlled machines to perform motor activities previously done by humans: welding a joint, painting, and fitting parts together. The automobile industry uses robotics to improve productivity and quality.

OVERVIEW OF FLEXIBLE MANUFACTURING SYSTEMS

Flexible manufacturing systems (FMS) was introduced to provide a shorter life-cycle manufacturing process and responsive manufacturing facilities to improve competition. For example, a VCR factory can use FMS to produce different models using similar facilities, which can be rescheduled and rearranged to fit into different manufacturing patterns. For some firms, FMS is an extension of Computer Integrated Manufacturing (CIM). With older systems, an assembly line was set up to make one type of product, and it could take days or months to change the equipment to manufacture another model or other products. The changeover process is also costly. Today, facilities are designed to be flexible and adaptive. One major advantage of an FMS is the ability to react to market needs or competition. FMS is implemented using computer systems, robotics, and other manufacturing techniques. The trend is to let the computer make the necessary changes to the equipment, assembly lines, and other processes.

PRODUCTION PLANNING AND CONTROL

Production Planning

Planning encompasses defining the organization's objectives or goals and establishing an overall strategy for achieving the goals. Planning can be classified into several categories:

- *Strategic versus operational:* Plans that apply to the entire organization to establish the organizational overall objectives are called strategic plans. Plans that specify the detailed process of how the strategic plan can be achieved are called operational plans.

- *Short-term versus long-term:* Plans that cover a longer time period are called long term and vice versa. Long-term plans tend to be strategic and short-term plans tend to be operational.

- *Specific versus directional:* Specific plans have clearly defined objectives while directional plans identify general guidelines. They provide focus but do not lock management into following specific objectives or specific courses of action.

Production planning consists of four key decisions—capacity, location, process, and layout.

Capacity Planning

Capacity planning deals with determining the proper size of your plant to satisfy the demand of the market. Capacity planning begins with making a forecast of sale demand and converting the projection into capacity requirements. (See Figure 6-2.) This model can be easily entered into a spreadsheet and results generated.

Figure 6-2.
CAPACITY PLANNING

Product	Units/Demand	Machine-Hours/Unit	Total Machine-Hours
A	200	3	600
B	400	2	800
C	100	7	700
		Total machine-hours =	2,100

Each machine is on for 24 hours a day with a breakdown rate of 5%
hours × Number of machines needed × 95% >= 2,100 machine hours
Number of machines needed = 93

Master Production Scheduling

Master production scheduling involves planning the production of individual products or services to fill orders and meet forecasts of other demand. A master schedule, often called a *master production schedule (MPS)*, is a schedule of planned completion of end-items. That means that it is concerned only with the final product (planning the production of parts and components will be left for detailed plans to follow). In services, the appointment book serves as the master schedule.

Computerized Scheduling Systems

In many cases, computer software packages for master production scheduling are an integral part of a large manufacturing information system—cost analysis, inventory information, and scheduling. IBM's *Communications Oriented Production and Control System (COPICS)* is an example. The system integrates forecasting, scheduling, inventory, and purchasing decisions into one large information system or planning and controlling all facets of the production system. Many computer programs also perform "what-if" (or sensitivity) analysis, which allows a production planner to determine how the production schedule would change with different assumptions concerning demand forecasts or cost figures.

Some recent computerized scheduling systems are gaining in popularity. Noteworthy among those are *Optimized Production Technology (OPT)* and *Disaster,* developed by Dr. Eli Goldratt in Israel, and *Q-Control,* developed by William E. Sandman. All of them concentrate their scheduling efforts on bottleneck operations.

Location Planning

When you determine the need for a new facility, you must determine where this facility should be installed. The location of the facility depends on which factors have the greatest impact on total production and distribution costs. These include availability of labor skills, labor costs, energy costs, proximity to suppliers or customers, and the like.

Process Planning

In process planning, management determines how a product or service will be produced. Process planning encompasses evaluating the available production methods and selecting the set that will best achieve the operating objectives.

Layout Planning

Layout planning deals with the access and selection among alternative layout options for equipment and work stations. The objective of layout planning is to find the best physical arrangement that will best facilitate production efficiency. There are three types of work-flow layouts:

- *Process layout:* Arrange manufacturing components according to similarity of function.
- *Product layout:* Arrange manufacturing components according to the progressive steps by which a product is made.
- *Fixed-position layout:* The product stays in place while tools, equipment, and human skills are brought to it.

Computerized Plant Layouts

The number of possible layout designs, even with a small number of departments, is so large that evaluating a considerable number of possibilities requires the aid of a computer. Several computer programs are available for developing and analyzing process layouts, including the ALDEP (Automated Layout Design Program), CORELAP (computerized relationship layout planning), and CRAFT (computerized relative allocation of facilities technique) programs. The first two programs employ the ranking of the desirability of closeness of departments to each other, while the CRAFT program uses the quantitative measure of minimizing the total transportation costs between them and material-handling costs.

The Line Balance Problem

Line balancing is the process of distributing the workloads evenly, that is, to group and/or subdivide activities or tasks in such a way that all job stations have an equal amount of work to do in terms of the time required to perform the tasks. The idea is to obtain the desired level of output with the minimum input of labor and other resources.

Much work has been done to develop models that produce optimally balanced lines. There have been a large number of proposals for theoretical and practical methods for solving the line balance problem. Some of the proposals have been attempts to deal with large-scale balance problems, particularly those involving 75–100 tasks or more and line lengths involving 10–15 or more stations. There is a model for handling very large problems, known as the *COMSOAL technique,* which is a computer-based sampling methodology.

COMSOAL uses a computer routine that generates a fairly large number of feasible solutions through a biased sampling method. The best solutions in the set become alternative solutions to the line balance problem. The universe from which we are sampling is, of course, all the possible feasible solutions to the particular line balance problem, and there is a finite probability that we can turn up optimal solutions in this fashion, a slightly large probability that we can turn up the next best solutions, and so on. The probability of developing excellent solutions is related to the size of the sample generated. Obviously, the trick is to generate feasible solutions rapidly and to bias the generation of these solutions toward the better ones rather than to simply generate feasible solutions at random. The COMSOAL technique has been implemented by Chrysler Corporation and other companies. It has been applied to a hypothetical line with 1,000 tasks and a known optimum of 200 stations with zero idle time, and a sequence requiring 203 stations resulting in 1.48 percent idle time.

PRODUCTION CONTROL STEPS

Control can be defined as the process of monitoring activities to ensure that they are being accomplished as planned and of correcting any significant deviations. The control process consists of three steps: (1) measuring actual performance, (2) comparing actual performance against a standard, and (3) taking managerial action to correct deviations or inadequate standards. There are three types of controls:

- *Feedforward* control prevents anticipated problems.
- *Concurrent control* occurs when an activity is in progress.
- *Feedback control* exists after an action has occurred.

All three types of control can be implemented by information systems.

MANAGING INVENTORY PLANNING AND CONTROL

A manufacturing company has three types of inventory: (1) raw material, (2) work-in-process, and (3) final products. One of the most common problems facing operations managers is that of inventory planning. This is understandable since inventory usually represents a sizable portion of a firm's total assets and, more specifically, on the average, more than 30% of total current assets in U.S. industry. Excessive money tied up in inventory is a drag on profitability.

Inventories may contain materials that have either dependent demand or independent demand. *Dependent demand* inventories consist of items whose demand depends on the demands for other items also held in inventory. Demand (or usage) of subassemblies and component parts is derived from the number of finished units that will be assembled. A classic example is demand for wheels for new automobiles. *Independent demand* items are the finished goods or other end-items. Demand is independent of the demand for any other item carried in inventory.

Economic Order Quantity and Reorder Point

The purpose of inventory planning is to develop policies that will achieve an optimal investment in inventory. This objective is achieved by determining the optimal level of inventory necessary to minimize inventory-related costs.

Inventory-related costs fall into three categories:

1. *Ordering costs* include all costs associated with preparing a purchase order.

2. *Carrying (holding) costs* include storage costs for inventory items plus the cost of money tied up in inventory.

3. *Shortage (stockout) costs* include costs incurred when an item is out of stock. These include the lost contribution margin on sales plus lost customer goodwill.

Many of the inventory planning models available try to answer basically the following two questions:

1. How much to order?

2. When to order?

They include the economic order quantity (EOQ) model, the reorder point, and the determination of safety stock.

Computers and Inventory Planning

Inventory planning, control, and management are done routinely by computers. IBM's Inventory Management Program and Control Techniques (IMPACT) and Communications Oriented Production and Control System (COPICS) are two prime examples of management information systems with embedded inventory packages. IMPACT is based on independent demand and therefore uses traditional or classical inventory analysis. The goal of IMPACT is to provide operating rules to minimize cost. To do this, the following functions are performed:

1. Forecast demand using various forecasting models such as exponential smoothing, trend, and seasonal (or cyclical) models. Forecasts are monitored based on the *mean absolute deviation (MAD)* and the tracking signal.

2. Determine the safety stock required for a specified level of service.

3. Determine the order quantity and time for reorder, using the EOQ and quantity discounts models.

4. Consider the effects of freight rates and quantity discounts.

5. Estimate the expected results of the inventory plan.

EFFECTIVE MATERIAL REQUIREMENTS PLANNING AND MANUFACTURING RESOURCES PLANNING

Material requirements planning (MRP) deals with inventory systems for dependent demand. It is a system that works backwards from the scheduled quantities. MRP needs dates for end-items specified in a *master production schedule (MPS)* to determine the requirements for components needed to meet the MPS. It is usually computerized because of the complex interrelationship among many products and their parts. Many MRP packages are available commercially. An expanded version of MRP is *manufacturing resources planning (MRP II)*. MRPII is an *integrated* computer system that links the regular MRP to other functional areas. In addition to the regular output of MRP, MRP II determines the costs of components and the cash needed to pay for those components; figures out cost of labor, equipment repair, energy, and tools; and generates a detailed, computerized budget.

JUST-IN-TIME GOALS

Just-in-time (JIT) is fast becoming as familiar and identifiable in the lexicon of manufacturing terminology as "mass production." Although the term is familiar to many people, the true meaning and definition remain clouded and unclear. The most common misunderstanding of just-in-time is to deliver inventory when it is needed. That means to reduce inventory while the operation is maintained. However, this is not the true meaning of just-in-time. The true definition of "just-in-time" is an awareness that true optimum manufacturing performance revolves around the dictate to eliminate waste in all of its many manifestations. The goals of JIT are to eliminate all manufacturing waste, which are to:

- Produce the product the customer wants.
- Produce the product when the customer wants it.
- Produce a good-quality product.
- Produce instantly—with no lead time.
- Produce with no waste of labor, material, or equipment.

The implementation of JIT can be enhanced using *electronic data exchange (EDI),* especially when internal business partners are involved. Some notable computer software for JIT include:

- *HP Manufacturing Management II* supports multilocation tracking and JIT component ordering, extensive MRP and inventory control, and interactions with budgeting, costing, and CAD/CAM applications.
- *Control manufacturing,* by Cincom Systems, supports multiple location JIT inventory control, MRP, financial management, and production scheduling.

PROJECT MANAGEMENT TOOLS AND TECHNIQUES

Project management involves planning and scheduling. *Project planning* includes all activities that result in a course of action for a project. Goals for the project must be set and their priorities established. Goals include resources to be committed, competition times, and activities. Areas of responsibility must be identified and assigned. Time and resource requirements to perform the work activities must be projected and budgeted. *Project scheduling*, compared with project planning, is more specific. Scheduling establishes the times and sequences of the various phases of the project.

Computer Software for Project Management

The management of projects is enhanced by tools such as Gantt charting, the Program Evaluation and Review Technique (PERT), and Critical Path Method (CPM). These tools are easily computerized and indeed dozens of commercial packages are on the market. The user inputs activity time estimates and procedure information, and the program outputs slack for each activity, duration, and variance for critical paths, and other useful project management information. Popular packages are:

1. *Harvard Project Manager,* Harvard Software Inc.
2. *Pertmaster,* Westminster Software Inc.
3. *PMSII/RMSII,* North America Mica Inc.
4. *Primavera,* Primavera Systems Inc.
5. *Project Scheduler 5000,* Scitor Corp.
6. *Pro-Jet 6,* Soft-Corp, Inc.
7. *Project Manager Workbench,* Applied Business Tech Corp.
8. *Project,* Microsoft Corp.
9. *MacProject & LisaProject,* Apple Computer Corp.
10. *VisiSchedule,* Paladin Software Corp.

INITIATING STATISTICAL QUALITY CONTROL

Quality control relates to activities that ensure that the final product is of satisfactory quality. The quality control function is concerned with detecting existing quality deficiencies and preventing future product quality problems. If the quantity produced is small and the final product is expensive, all products are inspected for quality control. However, if the units produced are in a large quantity and inexpensive (e.g., pencils and diskettes), a statistical sample is used to determine if the quality of this lot of products is acceptable. The whole lot of final products can be either rejected or accepted by a small sample collected. However, if statistically the manufacturer accepts a lot, which is supposed to be rejected, the consequence would be that customers will purchase defected merchandise and ruin the reputation of this manufacturer. If statistically the manufacturer rejects a lot, which is supposed to be accepted, good products can be discarded and manufacturing resources are wasted. Quality control is both an important area of expense and an important area of opportunities. Regarding expense, a typical factory spends about a quarter of its production budget just fixing and finding mistakes. And this cost does not reflect the true cost associated with this problem.

Computer Software for Quality Control

Computer software can relieve most of the tedious calculations formerly required to install and maintain a quality control system. Some popular packages, developed by TIME/WARE Corp, are listed with a brief description:

1. *ML105$* determines a sampling plan to fit combinations of AOPL (Average Outgoing Quality Level), lot size, etc., and randomly determines which parts to sample according to military standard.

2. *MLBIN$* evaluates multiple-level sampling plans where users inspect a number of parts from a large lot and accept, reject, or resample based on the number of defectives found (binomial distribution).

3. *OCBIN$* plots the OC (Operating Characteristic) curve. The user supplies the sampling size and the number of defectives required to reject the lot.

4. *CONLM$* determines confidence limits and sample statistics on a process average.

TOTAL QUALITY MANAGEMENT

With increased pressure from customers and competition, a new quality concept called *total quality management (TQM)* is emphasized across the industries. It has been touted as one of the few new management practices that will make companies competitive, particularly against the onslaught of Japanese competition. The shorthand "TQM" has come to mean a powerful solution to all that ails modern North American industry. It implies that if we will only pay supreme attention to the needs and desires of our customers, and if we deliver on those aspirations, we are bound to be successful. TQM focuses on awareness techniques for making products to the best of the organization's abilities. TQM theory can be described as a triangle, as shown in Figure 6-3.

Figure 6-3.
TQM THEORY

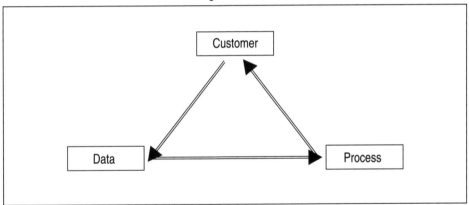

The focus is on the customer's requirements at the apex of the triangle. This in turn generates a process for achieving the requirements. The process is implemented and data is generated from which the effectiveness of the plan is evaluated. The results are then compared with the customer's requirements and the process is modified to improve results. TQM emphasizes a continuous improvement at all times. The modifications are implemented and the results are analyzed to see if they are in compliance with the customer's needs. In other words, TQM is "continuous improvements until perfection is achieved."

TQM is a quality revolution taking place in recent years. It consists of five principles:

- *Customer focus:* All efforts should be based on customers, including external customers and internal customers such as the accounting department within the company.

- *Continuous improvement:* TQM believes that quality can always be improved.

- *Everything TQM:* TQM includes everything the company produces, such as a product, a service, or how a customer service call is answered.

- *Accurate measurement:* TQM uses statistical techniques to measure every critical variable available and compares progress against benchmarks to identify problems.

- *Empowerment of employees:* TQM empowers everyone in the company to improve quality. Teamwork is heavily emphasized.

TQM represents a counterpoint of traditional management theories that emphasize cost reduction. The American auto industry is a classic case of what can go wrong when attention is focused on trying to keep the costs down to improve productivity without good quality management. As a matter of fact, productivity goes down when defects, recalls, and expensive repair of defective products are factored in.

LEADING-EDGE METHODS OF MANUFACTURING INTELLIGENCE

Expert Systems in Manufacturing

Expert systems (see Figure 6-4) use a rule base to generate decision suggestions. Users can input facts and preconditions so that the rules are triggered to provide results. Expert systems have been applied in many aspects of manufacturing. The fact is that much factory work has shifted to knowledge work such as planning, designing, and quality assurance from labor work, such as machining, assembling, and handling. As a matter of fact, knowledge work accounts for about two-thirds of total manufacturing cost. Robotics, expert systems, and other information systems can improve the productivity of labor work. For example, an expert system implemented at Northrop Corporation, a major producer of jet fighter planes, is responsible for the planning of manufacture and assembly of up to 20,000 parts that go into an aircraft. A parts designer is able to enter a description of the engineering drawing of a part, and the expert system tells him what materials and processes are required to manufacture it. This particular system actually improves the productivity of part design by a factor of 12 to 18. Without the help of an expert system, the same task would require several days instead of several hours.

An expert system is a computer system including computer hardware and software, which can perform reasoning using a knowledge base.

Figure 6-4.
EXPERT SYSTEM FRAMEWORK

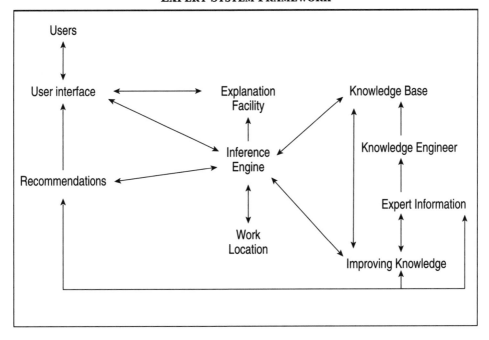

Expert systems are made up of a user's interface, a knowledge base, and an inference engine. The *user's interface* provides end-users with proper interactive channels so that they can interact with the system. A *knowledge base* contains a set of rules or cases to provide an expert system with the necessary conduct reasoning. An *inference engine* is the brain of an expert system; it receives the request from the user interface and conducts reasoning in the knowledge base. Different rules or cases can be triggered to conclude a solution. After several questioning/answering sessions, a conclusion or suggestion can be generated and provided to the end-user through the user interface.

Expert System Knowledge Bases

An expert system contains the subject knowledge of the human experts, called the knowledge base. There are two types of knowledge representations: deductive knowledge (rule-based) and inductive knowledge (case-based).

Rule-Based Expert Systems   The rule base of an expert system contains a set of production rules. Each rule has a typical IF-THEN clause. Expert system users provide facts or statements so that production rules can be triggered and the conclusion can be generated. Ford Motor Company uses an expert system to diagnose engine repair problems. Typically, Ford dealers call the help line in Ford headquarters to receive a suggestion when a complicated engine problem cannot be diagnosed. Today, dealers can access a company's expert systems and receive correct engine diagnosis within seconds. Expert systems can be used at any type of business domain and at any level in an organization. Examples are diagnosing illness, searching for oil, making soup, and analyzing computer systems. More applications and more users are expected in the future.

Case-Based Expert Systems   A case-based expert system uses an inductive method to conduct expert system reasoning. A case base consists of many historical cases, which have different results. The expert inference engine searches through the case base and finds the appropriate historical case, which matches the characteristics of the current problem. After a match has been found, the solution of a matched historical case is modified and used as the new suggestion for the current problem. Lockheed uses an expert system to speed the purchase of materials ranging from industrial coolant to satellite and rocket parts. The old MIS requested a purchase order to include more than 100 different forms, which were seldom completed by the purchaser. Lots of time was spent making corrections and changes to complete a purchase order. By using an expert system, less information was asked and the time required to finish a purchasing order reduced. One important issue of expert systems is the knowledge acquisition. Traditionally, interviewing experts in the field builds the knowledge base. More advanced technology allows intelligent software to "learn" knowledge from different problem domains. The knowledge learned by computer software is more accurate and reliable compared with that from human experts.

Benefits and Limitations of Expert Systems

For the past few years, the technology of expert systems has been successfully applied in thousands of organizations worldwide to problems ranging from cancer research to the analysis of computer configurations. Expert systems are popular for the following reasons:

- *Increased output and productivity:* Expert systems can work faster and more accurately than human experts. For example, a system called XCON by Digital Equipment Corporation is able to provide computer system configuration for potential buyers. This expert system increases fourfold the production preparation of minicomputers, which are customized for their clients.

- *Improved quality:* Expert systems provide advice or suggestions based on preprogrammed logistics, which are consistent and accurate. This reduces the number of mistakes made by human errors.

- *Capture of scarce expertise:* The scarcity of experience becomes evident when there are not enough experts for a task, when the expert is about to retire or leave the job, or when expertise is required over a broad geographic location.

- *Training:* Expert systems can be a very good training tool.

Robotics in Manufacturing

A robot with AI capability is an electromechanical manipulator able to respond to a change in its environment based on its perception of that environment. The sensory subsystem is programmed to "see" or "feel" its environment and respond to it. For example, an industrial robot can manufacture one of many parts in its repertoire and manipulate it to inspect it for defects, recognizing very small departures from established standards. Robots have been used extensively in Japan to improve the quality and reduce the cost of their products. They are reliable, consistent, accurate, and insensitive to hazardous environments.

A *robot* is a device that mimics human actions and appears to function with some degree of intelligence. Robots are commonly used in manufacturing and when it would be unsafe or unhealthful for a human to perform the same task. The major problem of controlling the physical actions of a mobile robot might not seem to require much intelligence. Even small children are able to navigate through their environment and to manipulate items such as playing with toys, eating with spoons, and turning on a TV. Although performed almost unconsciously by humans, these tasks require a machine to do many of the same abilities used in solving more intellectually demanding problems.

Research on robots or robotics has helped to develop many AI applications. It has led to several techniques for modeling "state of the world" and for describing the process of change from one world state to another. It has led to a better understanding of how to generate "action plans" in sequence and how to monitor the execution of these plans. One challenge is to develop methods for planning at high levels of abstraction, ignoring details, and then planning at lower levels when details become important.

Neural Networks in Manufacturing

The human is the most complex of all computing devices. The brain's powerful thinking, reasoning, creation, remembering, and problem-solving capabilities have inspired many scientists to attempt computer modeling of its operation. Some researchers have sought to create a computer model that matches the functionality of the brain in a very fundamental manner; the result has been neural computing.

The neuron is the fundamental cellular unit of the nervous system and the brain. Each neuron functions as a simple microprocessing unit, which receives and combines signals from many other neurons through input processes called dendrites. If the combined signal is strong enough, it activates the firing of the neuron, which produces an output signal; the path of the output signal is along a component of a cell called the axon. This simple transfer of information is chemical in nature, but has electrical side effects, which we can measure. The brain consists of hundreds of billions of neurons loosely interconnected. The axon (output path) of a neuron splits up and connects to dendrites (input path) of other neurons through a junction referred to as a synapse. The transmission across this junction is chemical in nature, and the amount of signal transferred depends on the amount of chemical (neurotransmitters) released by the axon and received by the dendrites. This synaptic efficiency is what is modified when the brain learns. The synapse and the processing of information in the neuron form the basic memory mechanism of the brain.

In an artificial neural network, the unit analogous to the biological neuron is referred to as a processing element. A *processing element* has many input paths and combines, usually by a simple summation, the values of these input paths. The result is an internal activity level for the processing element. The combined input is then modified by a transfer function, which can be a threshold function. This threshold function can pass information only if the combined activity level reaches a certain level, or it can be a continuous function of the combined input. The output path of a processing element can be connected to input paths of other processing elements through connection weights that correspond to the synaptic strength of neural connections. Since each connection has a corresponding weight, the signals on the input lines to a processing element are modified by these weights prior to being summed. Thus, the summation function is a weighted summation.

A *neural network* consists of many processing elements joined together in this manner. Processing elements are usually organized into groups called *layers,* or *slabs.* A typical network consists of a sequence of layers or slabs with full or random connections between successive layers. There are typically two layers with connections to the outside world: an *input buffer,* where data is presented to the network, and an *output buffer,* which holds the response of the network to an input. Layers distinct from the input and output buffers are called *hidden layers.* Applications of neural networks are language processing (text and speech), image processing, character recognition (handwriting recognition and pattern recognition), and financial and economic modeling.

7
DATABASE MANAGEMENT SYSTEMS

A *database* is a system in which data is organized in a certain way so that accurate and timely information can be retrieved. The information systems used to manage databases are called *database management systems (DBMS)*. A database management system is software that allows managers to create, maintain, and report the data and file relationships. A *file management system* is software that allows users to manipulate one file at a time. Database management systems offer many advantages over file management systems, such as:

- *Reduced data redundancy:* Data redundancy means the same data field appears in different tables sometimes in different format. For example, a customer's name, address, and phone number can be stored in both the checking account file and the receivables account file. This would cause problems in terms of maintenance and updating. It requires more time and money to maintain files with redundant records.

- *Improved data integrity:* Data integrity means that data is accurate, consistent, and up-to-date. If the same data is stored in different files, updating may not cover all data elements in different files. Some reports will be produced with erroneous information.

- *Improved data security:* Database management systems allow users to establish different levels of security over information in the database. This guarantees that data will be retrieved or updated only by authorized users. For example, the sales manager can read only employee payroll information, but not modify it. A nonmanagement employee may have no access privilege to the payroll data and can neither inquire nor modify the data.

- *Reduced development time:* Since database management systems organize data, a database administrator (DBA) can improve the efficiency and productivity of database development. For example, instead of creating a new file, the DBA can add new fields into existing files and still maintain data integrity.

FILES VERSUS DATABASES

A *database file* is a collection of related records that describe a subject by using a set of fields. Figure 7-1 shows a file with three records used to describe a student by using fields of "NAME," "GPA," and "MAJOR."

Figure 7-1.
A TYPICAL DATA FILE

STUDENT FILE		
Name	GPA	Major
Robert Smith	3.2	IS
Mary Lee	3.5	ACCT
Jim Shaw	2.9	IS

Most organizations have many files, which have the numbers of records from hundreds to hundreds of thousands. Files that are stored on secondary storage devices can be organized in several different ways, and there are advantages and disadvantages to each type of file organization.

THREE TYPES OF FILE ORGANIZATION

Three types of file organization are used on secondary storage devices: sequential, indexed-sequential, and direct file. Files stored on tape are processed as sequential files. Files on disk are usually direct or indexed-sequential.

Sequential File

Sequential files (see Figure 7-2) can be stored on a sequential access device such as tapes or a random access device such as a disk. In a sequential file, records are arranged one after another in a predetermined order. For example, an employee file can be organized by employees' ID numbers. If this file is stored on a disk or tape, the employee record with the smallest ID number would be the first record in the file.

Figure 7-2.
A SEQUENTIAL FILE

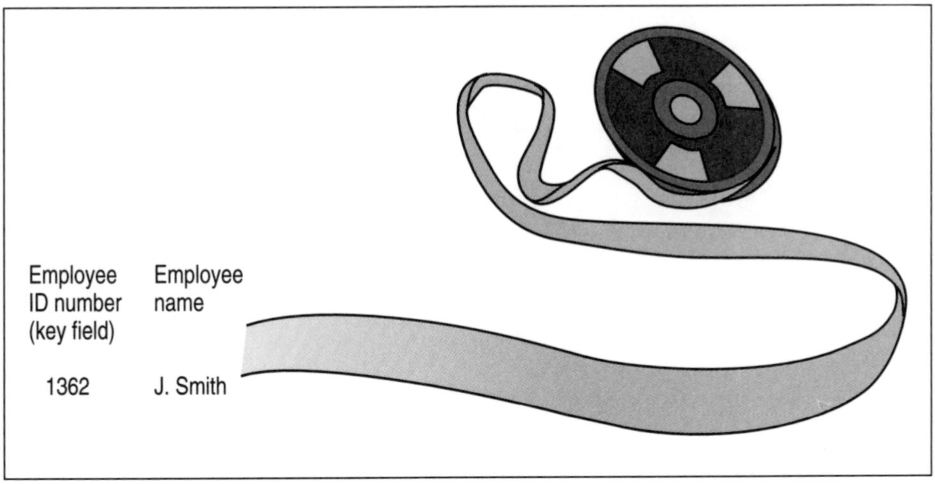

Indexed-Sequential Files

An indexed-sequential file (see Figure 7-3) allows both sequential and direct access to data records. Thus, files must be on a direct access storage device such as a disk. In indexed-sequential files, records are usually physically arranged on a storage medium by their primary key, just as they are with sequential files. The difference is that an index also exists for the file; it can be used to look up and directly access individual records. Files set up to allow this type of access are called *ISAM (indexed-sequential method)* files. Many database management systems (DBMS) use ISAM files because of their relative flexibility and simplicity. This is often the best type of file for business applications that demand both batch updating and on-line processing.

Figure 7-3.
AN INDEXED-SEQUENTIAL FILE

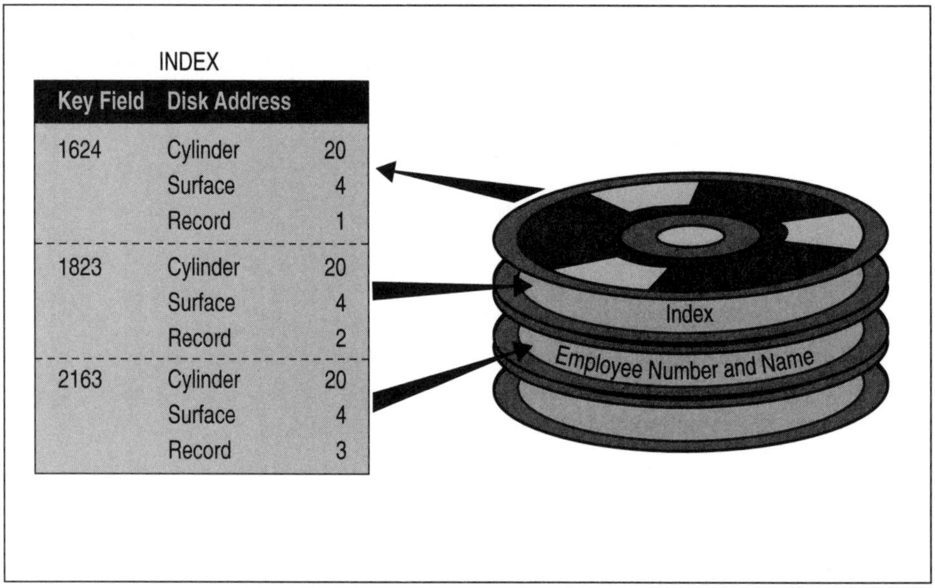

Direct Files

A direct file (see Figure 7-4) provides the fastest possible access to records. Direct file is typically the best when access time is critical and when batch processing is not necessary. A direct file uses a formula to transfer the primary key to the location of each record. This formula is called a *hashing algorithm*. Therefore, no index is needed to locate individual records. Many hashing algorithms have been developed. One popular procedure is to use prime numbers in the formula process. In general, the primary key value is divided by a prime number, which corresponds to the maximum number of storage locations allocated for the records of this file. The remainder obtained in this division is then used as the relative address of a record, but the relative address can be translated into a physical location on the storage medium.

Figure 7-4.
A DIRECT FILE

Key Value	Relative Address from Hashing	Relative Address after Collision
3428	33	33
3331	33	34

Relative record number 33

Relative Record Numbers

3428CHANG827.50   3331SAMS181.30

Relative record number 34

DIFFERENT TYPES OF DATA MODELS

Relational Databases

The relational database relates or connects data in different files through the use of a key field, or common data element (see Figure 7-5). In this arrangement, data elements are stored in different tables or files made up of rows and columns. In database terminology, tables are called *relations,* rows are called *tuples,* and columns are called *attributes.* In a table, a row resembles a record. For example, a student's GPA record has a field of "student name," a field of "GPA," a field of "address," and a field of "phone number." In this table, a student is described by a record or a combination of fields. The advantage of a relational database is that the managers do not have to be aware of any data structure or data pointer. Managers can easily add, update, delete, or create records using simple logic. However, a disadvantage is that some search commands in a relational database require more time to process compared with other database models.

Figure 7-5.
A RELATIONAL DATABASE

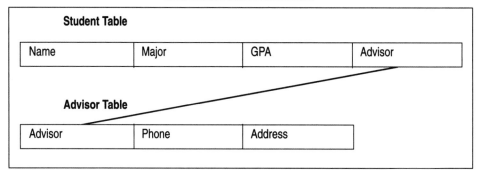

Hierarchical Databases

In a hierarchical database, fields and records are arranged in a family tree, with lower-level records subordinate to higher-level records (see Figure 7-6).

Figure 7-6.
A HIERARCHICAL DATABASE

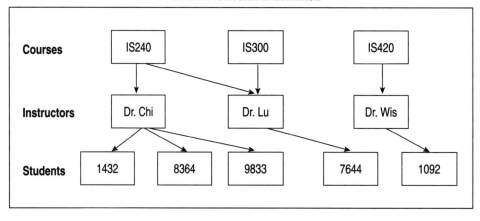

In a hierarchical database, a parent record may have more than one child, but a child always has only one parent. This is called a *one-to-many relationship*. To locate a particular record, you have to start at the top of the tree with a parent record and trace down the tree to the child. Hierarchical databases are the oldest of the four data models and are still used in some reservation systems. In addition, accessing records or updating records is very fast since the relationships have been predefined. The drawback of hierarchical data models is that the structure is rigid, and adding new records to the database may require that the entire database be redefined.

Network Databases

A *network database* (see Figure 7-7) is similar to a hierarchical database except that each child can have more than one parent record. In other words, a child record is referred to as a *member* and a parent record is referred to as an *owner*. The advantage of the network database is its ability to establish relationships between different branches of data records and thus offer increased access capability for the manager. However, like the hierarchical database, the data record relationships must be defined prior to the use of the database and must be redefined if records are added or updated.

Figure 7-7.
A NETWORK DATABASE

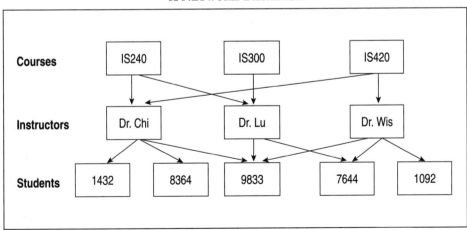

Object-Oriented Databases

An object-oriented database (see Figure 7-8) uses "objects" as elements within database files. An *object* consists of text, sound, images, and instructions on the action to be taken on the data. For example, traditional data models (hierarchical, network, and relational) can contain only numeric and text data of an instructor. An object-oriented database might also contain the instructor's picture and video. Moreover, the object would store operations, called *methods,* that perform actions on the data—for example, how to calculate this person's pension fund based on his/her age and contributions.

Figure 7-8.
AN OBJECT-ORIENTED DATABASE

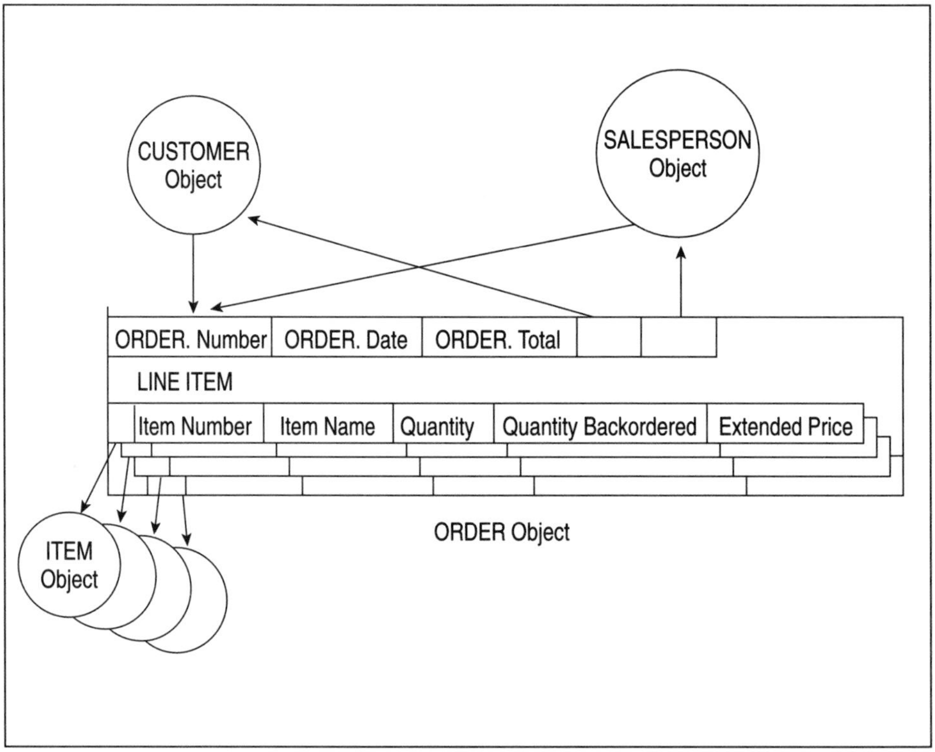

PRIMARY KEYS, SECONDARY KEYS, AND FOREIGN KEYS

In a database, data records are organized and identified by using the key field. A *key field* contains unique data used to identify a record so that it can be easily retrieved and processed. Three types of key fields are used for database management:

- *Primary keys:* The primary key can be a single field or a combination of several fields. It is the most important identifier to retrieve records. It is unique, and each table can have only one. For example, the social security number is a good primary key to identify each person, while age may not be useful since many people may have the same age.

- *Secondary keys:* Secondary keys can be any field or any combination of several fields. A secondary key does not have to be unique and can have many of them in a table. For example, we can use "major" as a secondary key to allocate students majoring in information systems.

- *Foreign keys:* The foreign key is the field or a combination of several fields that can be used to relate two tables. A foreign key must be a primary key in one table. This primary key can thus be connected to another table. For example, a student table contains social security number, major, and advisor's name. The advisor table has advisor's name, phone number, and address. The "advisor's name" is the foreign key to connect the student table with the advisor table (see Figure 7-9).

Figure 7-9.
KEY FIELDS

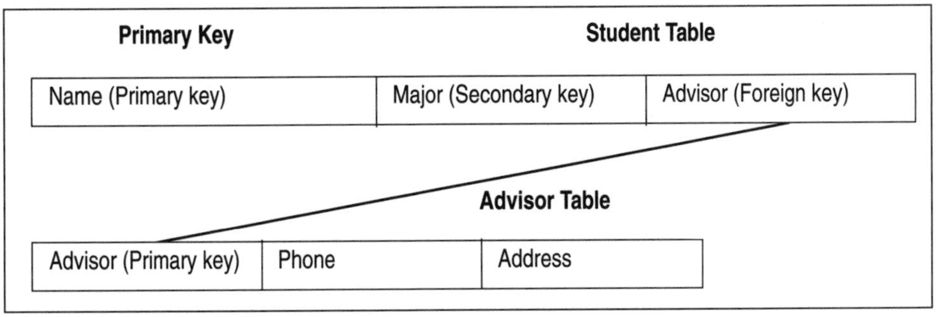

Primary Key	Student Table	
Name (Primary key)	Major (Secondary key)	Advisor (Foreign key)

Advisor Table		
Advisor (Primary key)	Phone	Address

TWO DIFFERENT QUERY LANGUAGES

What Is a Query Language?

A *query language* is an English-like language that allows managers to specify what data they are looking for, either on a printed report or on the screen. Generally speaking, there are two types of query language: structured query language and query by example.

- *Structured query language (SQL):* This is the most widely used database query language. In 1985, the American National Standards Institute formed a committee to develop industry standards for SQL. Today, most database management system support this standard. Figure 7-10 shows an example of SQL statements.

Figure 7-10.
STRUCTURED QUERY LANGUAGE

	SELECT name, gpa FROM student WHERE gpa >=3.0 ORDER BY name	

- *Query by example (QBE):* This type of language (see Figure 7-11) helps the manager construct a query by displaying a list of fields that are available in the files from which the query will be made.

DATABASE ENGINES AND FRONT-END TOOLS

Database Engines

Database engines are used to design, retrieve, and update data elements from the database. They are powerful and efficient in terms of database manipulation. However, they are not designed to provide a user interface for different applications. ORACLE is the largest database engine provider. Each complete package can cost buyers anywhere from $10,000 to $1 million. Other vendors are SYBSE, INFORIX, and the Microsoft SQL.

Figure 7-11.
QUERY BY EXAMPLE

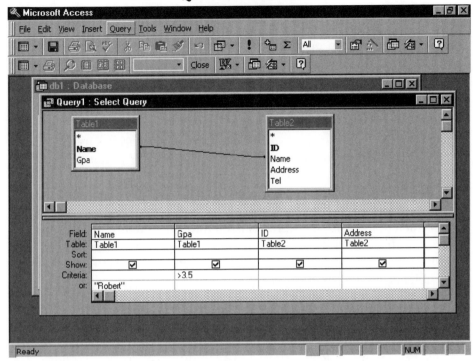

Database Front-End Tools

To provide a good user interface so that end-users can perform database functions easily and without intensive training, front-end tools are necessary to design user interfaces that can guide end-users to perform database functions. Two major front-end tools popular in database development are Visual Basic and Power Builder.

DATABASE DEVELOPMENT AND APPLICATIONS

Database Development Methodologies

Database design is an intuitive and artistic process. There is no strict algorithm for it. Typically, database design is an interactive process: During each iteration, the goal is to get closer to an acceptable design. Thus a design is developed and then reviewed. Defects in the design are identified, and the design is redone. This process is repeated until the development team and users are satisfied with what is available. A well-designed database enables managers to perform efficient and useful tasks. A poorly designed database may cost lots of money and time without any significant contribution to a company's operation. Database design procedures are therefore very important and crucial to the success of a database system. Procedures for database design are as follows:

- *Current system analysis and survey:* This process involves surveying and observing current manual data processes and the potential benefits from computerized database systems. Usually, both decision makers and process operators are interviewed to collect information of potential problems and opportunities. After the system analysis has been conducted, a feasibility report is prepared for evaluation. The suggestion of the feasibility report can be either positive or negative. The usual reason for a conclusion of infeasibility is financial or managerial problems.

- *Logical database design:* A logical database design specifies the logical format of the database. The records to be maintained, their contents, and their relationships are specified. It is sometimes called the *conceptual schema,* or the *logical schema.* A technique called *normalization* was developed for relational databases to improve the structure of files in a relational database. By using this method, data can be organized into the most efficient and logical file relationships.

- *Physical database design:* The logical schema is transformed into the particular data constructs that are available with the DBMS to be used. Whereas the logical design is DBMS-independent, the physical design is DBMS-dependent. Logical schema specifies general database design, which can be implemented in any database management software, while physical schema is designed based on real database management software and cannot be transferred from one to another.

- *Implementation:* After physical schema is designed, the database implementation is conducted. This process, which involves lots of coding and programming, can be done with a DBMS such as ORACLE, FOXBase, Microsoft SQL Server, and a front-end tool for user interface development such as Visual Basic or Power Builder.

- *Testing and debugging:* This process involves testing the system and making sure that it is ready to operate. In this stage, both program developers and end-users should get involved.

- *Training, evaluation, and documentation:* If both the end-user group and the development team are satisfied with the system, the training session should proceed. The purpose of the training session is to teach managers how to use this new system and perform simple troubleshooting functions. The development team should also prepare system documentation for the managers for reference purposes.

Database Tools

Data Dictionary A *data dictionary* stores the data definitions or a description of the structure of data used in the database. This information could be stored in a dictionary-like document or on a text file. Managers can check the data dictionary and retrieve necessary information about the properties and nature of the database. Some data dictionaries can also monitor the data being entered into the database management system to conform to the definition, such as field name, field size, and type of data (text, numeric, date, logic, and so on). The data dictionary can also help the database administrator and other database designers with security concerns, such as who has the right to access what kind of information.

Database Utilities The database needs to have certain maintenance to ensure that the data is properly organized. Database utility programs provide the DBA with functions that can fine-tune the database functionality, such as to remove redundant or unused records, assign priorities to different users, and monitor resource allocation. A good database utility program can improve the productivity and efficiency of a DBA.

Database Recovery A systems failure, computer malfunctioning, disk head crash, program bugs, and so on can cause a database management system crash. Unfortunately, when systems fail, business does not stop. Customers continue to buy and pay, return merchandise, and obtain servicing. Therefore, system failures must be recovered as soon as possible. Furthermore, transactions that were in processing when the failure occurred have to be recovered in such a way that their outputs are identical to what would have been produced. In other words, failure should be "transparent" in their effects on data. Recovering from a database system failure is getting more difficult due to the complexity of modern database management systems. It is impossible to simply fix the problem and resume program processing where it was interrupted. Even if no data is lost during a failure, the timing and scheduling of computer processing is too complex to be accurately recreated.

Some techniques have been developed to recover a system failure:

- Recovery via reprocessing

- Recovery via rollback/rollforward

- Transaction logging

- Write-ahead log

The details of these techniques are beyond the scope of this book. Readers can check database books for more information.

The Database Administrator

What Is a Database Administrator (DBA)?   The DBA is the person who manages all activities related to the database. Qualified DBAs should be able to understand the hardware configuration (such as the client-server environment) and take advantage of existing hardware capability to improve the performance of the database management system. They should have expertise in terms of database engine (such as SQL) and front-end tools (such as Visual Basic and Power Builder) to create a good user interface. DBAs should be able to do limited troubleshooting in both the application area and system level since a database crash may involve both application and system software.

Major Functions of a Database Administrator   The responsibilities of a DBA are the following:

- *Database design:* The database administrator helps determine the design of the database, including fields, tables, and key fields. Later, the DBA determines how resources are used on secondary storage devices, how files and records may be added and deleted, and how losses may be detected and remedied.

- *System backup and recovery:* Because loss of data or a crash in the database could vitally affect the organization, a database system must be able to recover if the system crashes. The DBA needs to make sure the system is regularly backed up and develop plans for recovering data should a failure occur.

- *End-user service and coordination:* A DBA should determine user access privileges and arrange resources allocation for different user groups. If users conflict with each other, the DBA should be able to coordinate usage for an optimal arrangement.

- *Database security:* The DBA can specify access privileges for users of a database management system to protect the database from unauthorized access and sabotage. For example, one kind of user is allowed to retrieve data, whereas another might have the right to update data and delete records.

- *Performance monitoring:* The database base system should maintain a certain standard of services for all users. The DBA monitors the system and uses different database tools to make sure that the system is set up to satisfy managers' performance requirements.

TYPES OF CLIENT-SERVER DATABASE SYSTEMS

Client-Server System

A *client-server system* consists of computers that are connected by a network in which some computers (called *clients*) process applications while other computers (called *servers*) provide services to the clients. Services include file storage, printing activities, Internet hosting, and many others.

A *client-server database system* is a client-server system in which at least one server stores and processes a database. The client computer executes application programs, which process the user interface, invoke application logic, and enforce some business rules. After the application programs collect the request from the end-user, they call the DBMS for database services. For relational databases, such service requests are generally represented in SQL. The DBMS processes the SQL statements and returns data and error messages to the application program on the client computer (see Figure 7-12).

Figure 7-12
END-USERS APPLICATION PROGRAM

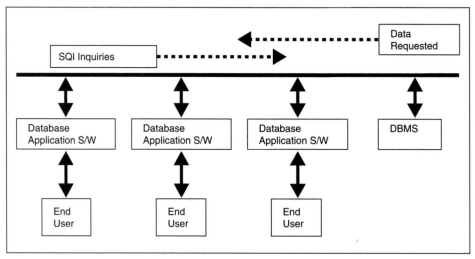

Open Database Connectivity

The open database connectivity (ODBC) is an interface by which application programs can access different databases in a DBMS-independent manner. In other words, any application programs that use the ODBC interface can process database engines such as ORACLE, SYBASE, or INFORMIX or any databases that are ODBC-compliant. ODBC was developed by a committee, which consisted of a group of industry experts in database management systems. In this ODBC standard, database standards are regulated so that data format in different database systems can be compatible. ODBC is important to client-server database architecture because it tends to have different application programs as well as database systems in a network. By an ODBC interface, all databases can be connected and data can be transferred.

DATA WAREHOUSE OVERVIEW

Data Warehouse Concept

The term "data warehouse" was first introduced by William Inmon, and proposed as a technology by IBM in 1991. A *data warehouse* is a place that stores enterprise data designed to facilitate management decisions. The major purpose of a data warehouse is to query a database source that is split over an entire enterprise. Thus, a data warehouse allows a user to access information from different databases. A data warehouse consists of data, tools, procedures, training, and personnel resources that make access to the data easier and more relevant to decision makers. Typically, there are two types of data warehouses. A traditional data warehouse uses metadata to create a common language for different data sources, enabling information sharing from a high-performance, central data warehouse. A virtual data warehouse does not have its information built from a central data menu. Instead, it has an easy-to-read front end that can query a database source split over the entire enterprise.

Applications for Data Warehouse

There are several components in the data warehouse:

- Metadata of data warehouse contents
- Warehouse database(s)
- Tools to extract data
- Tools to manage data
- Training courses

A typical data warehouse may contain a billion bytes of data in different databases with different formats. To be able to transfer data from one database to another so that all data elements are integrated within the data warehouse, programs are needed to reformat, integrate, and transfer data from one database management system to another. As a result, end-users can request data from the data warehouse without the knowledge of the data's type or format. Since the purpose of the data warehouse is to make organizational data more available, the warehouse must include tools not only to deliver the data to end-users but also to transform the data for decision makers for analysis, reporting, and query.

CONCLUSION

Information is the most valuable asset in a company and the database management system is one of the most important IS tools to manipulate the company's information. Understanding how data is organized and represented in database management systems becomes one of the most important concepts an executive should have in mind. By applying information technology properly, including database management systems, the manager can dramatically maximize productivity and reduce corporate costs and risks.

8
DATA COMMUNICATIONS: MEDIA AND DEVICES

Data communications has become more and more important in business. The ability to instantly communicate information is changing how people do business and interact with each other. New data communication technologies allow voice, image, and even video to be transmitted through the network. Many business applications are available because of new data communication technologies. Examples are electronic mail, voice mail, teleconferencing, fax, electronic data interchange (EDI), online services, and others. As a matter of fact, more and more new services will become available through the network because of the information superhighway.

DIGITAL VERSUS ANALOG SIGNALS

Digital signals are individual voltage pulses that represent the bits grouped together to form characters. This type of signal is usually used inside the computer to transmit data between electronic components and close-range devices. Digital signals have the characteristics of short-range transmission (at most several hundred feet) and are represented by on/off binary systems. Local area networks (LAN) usually use digital signals for transmission. This transmission is normally restricted to a certain area, such as a room or a building.

Analog signals are continuous electromagnetic waves. They are able to travel long distances, and most long-distance transmissions are carried out by analog signals. For example, voice transmission through the telephone lines and data transmission between computers uses analog signals.

187

DIGITAL VERSUS ANALOG DATA

Data can be defined as raw facts. To transfer data between devices, data must be represented in a certain format. There are generally two types of data representations: digital data and analog data. *Digital data* representation uses a binary system (i.e., 1 and 0) to represent anything. A number, a letter, an image, or even a video can be represented in a binary system. *Analog data* representation uses continuous signals. Voice, pictures, and video are normally represented in analog data representation. The videotape records video in analog signals and the audiocassette records sound signals in analog form. The same data or information can be represented by both digital and analog representations. For example, audiocassettes use analog representation to record voice, while compact disks have digital representation. In general, digital data representation is more accurate and durable for repetitive usage than analog data representation. However, digital data representations require more storage space for voice and video than analog representations.

DIGITAL VERSUS ANALOG TRANSMISSION

Digital transmission uses digital signals or analog signals to transmit information in digital format. All data or information must therefore be converted into digital representation prior to transmission. For example, an image can be converted into a digital file, and this digital file can be transmitted by analog signals, which carry this digital representation to the destination. Digital transmission uses repeaters instead of amplifiers for long-distance transmission. It is considered the best way for information transmission.

Analog transmission uses analog representation by analog signals. For example, a telephone conversation can be transmitted in analog representation and use analog transmission. Table 8-1 presents a comparison between digital transmission and analog transmission.

Table 8-1.
COMPARISON BETWEEN DIGITAL VS. ANALOG REPRESENTATION

	Digital Representation	*Analog Representation*
Digital Transmission	Integrated Services Digital Network (ISDN)	Not available
Analog Transmission	Using MODEM to transmit computer files	Traditional telephone calls

THREE TYPES OF WIRED COMMUNICATION MEDIA

There are three types of wired transmission media: twisted pair wire, coaxial cable, and fiber optical cable.

Twisted Pair Wire

Most telephone lines consist of cables made up of hundreds of copper wires called *twisted pair wire (TPW)*. TPW has been the standard transmission medium for years for both voice and data. However, it is being phased out by more technically advanced and reliable media (such as fiber optical cables).

Twisted pair wire consists of two or more strands of insulated copper wire, twisted around each other in pairs. The strands are then covered in another layer of plastic insulation. Since so much of the world is already served by twisted pair wire, it will no doubt continue to be used for years, both for voice messages and for transmitted computer data. However, it is relatively slow and does not protect well against electrical interference.

Coaxial Cable

Coaxial cable, commonly called "coax," consists of insulated copper wire wrapped in a solid or braided metal shield, then in an external cover. Coaxial cable has a larger bandwidth than TPW. *Bandwidth* is the capacity of the cable, expressed as the number of communications that can be transmitted at one time. A coaxial cable has about 80 times the transmission capacity of TPW. Coaxial cable is often used to link parts of a computer system in one building. In addition, coaxial cable is much better at resisting noise than twisted pair wiring.

Fiber Optical Cable

A *fiber optical cable (FOC)* consists of hundreds of thin strands of glass that transmit not electricity but rather pulsating beams of light. These strands, each as thin as a human hair, can transmit billions of pulses per second, each "on" pulse representing 1 bit. Signals, in the form of light waves, are transmitted through tubes of glass. When bundled together, fiber optical strands in a cable 0.12-inch thick can support a quarter to a half-million voice conversations at the same time.

In other words, fiber optical cable has the largest bandwidth of all three types of media. In general, FOC has 26,000 times the transmission capacity of TPW. In addition, compared with TPW and CC, FOCs are immune to electronic interference, which makes them more secure. They are also lighter and less expensive than coaxial cable and are more reliable at transmitting data.

WIRELESS COMMUNICATION MEDIA SYSTEMS

Major wireless transmission media are the microwave system and the satellite system, in addition to other systems, such as the Global Positioning System, pager, and mobile phone systems.

Microwave Systems

Microwaves are high-frequency radio waves that travel in straight lines through the air. (See Figure 8-1.) Because of the curve of the Earth, the signals must be regenerated and relayed through amplifiers or repeaters, which can be installed on towers, high buildings, and mountaintops. Satellites can also be used as microwave relay stations. Many of these rotate at a precise point and speed above the Earth, making them appear stationary, and can transmit signals as relay stations in the sky. The drawback is that bad weather can affect the quality of transmission.

Figure 8-1.
A MICROWAVE SYSTEM

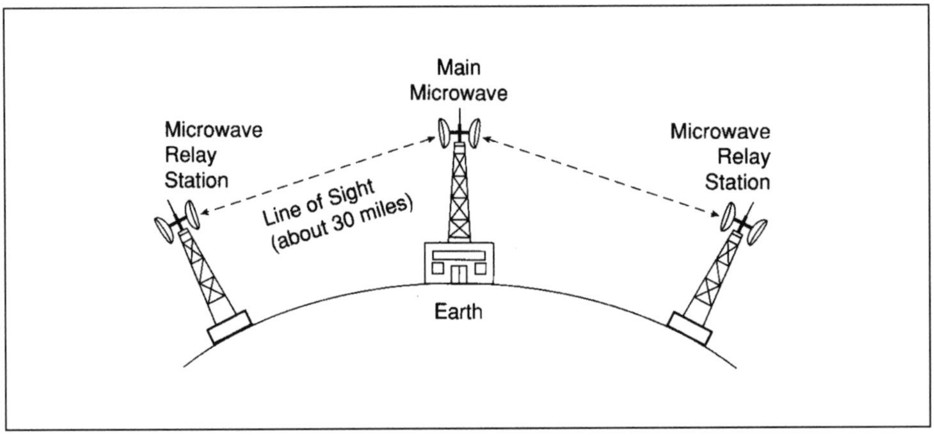

Satellite System

Satellite systems use a "sky station" to transmit signals between two locations on Earth. (See Figure 8-2.) Communication satellites are microwave relay stations in orbit around the Earth that are solar-powered. Typically the orbit is 22,300 miles above the Earth. Since the satellite travels at the same speed as the Earth, it appears to be stationary in space. When the satellite receives signals from one station on Earth, it transmits them to another station on Earth. Each satellite contains many communication channels and receives both analog and digital signals from Earth stations. Sometimes, it can take more than one satellite to deliver a message.

Figure 8-2.
A SATELLITE SYSTEM

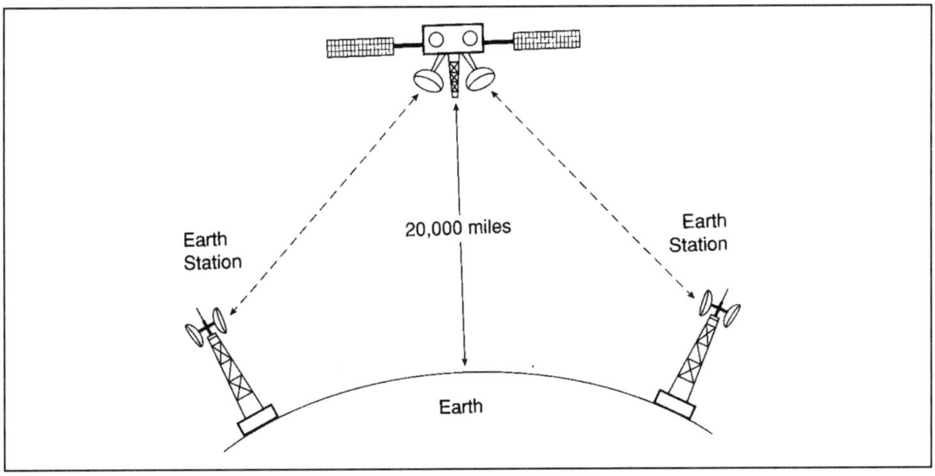

Global Positioning System

The original purpose of global positioning system (GPS) was for military. The project cost about $10 billion and consisted of 24 Earth-orbiting satellites that consistently transmit signals to identify Earth locations. A GPS receiver can then pick up the signals from four satellites, calculate the signals, and generate the longitude, latitude, and altitude within the accuracy of a few feet. Although the system was designed for military usage, business applications have been implemented. Examples are tracking a delivery truck and a salesperson's automobile.

Pagers and Cellular Phones

Pagers or beepers are designed to receive another party's phone number so that the page owner can call back immediately. This is a one-way communication device and does not provide response to the calling party. Paging services include SkyTel, PageNet, and EMBARC. Some pagers can transmit full-blown alphanumeric text and other data. Cellular phones are designed primarily for communicating by voice through a system of cells. Each cell is hexagonal in shape, usually eight miles or less in diameter, and is served by a transmitter-receiving tower. Calls are directly transmitted to a *mobile telephone switching office (MTSO)* and then connected to the regular telephone network. If the caller is moving from one cell to another, the ongoing call is "handed off" to another MTSO. Newer technologies allow digital signal to be transmitted by cellular phones.

MODEMS AND OTHER DEVICES

Current communication networks use voice-graded media. Digital signals, being voltage pulses, do not travel a long distance. To send digital signals from the computer into the networks, a special device is needed to convert digital signals into analog signals so that the analog signals can carry the information of digital signals and travel a long distance. Modems are used for this purpose. A modem can convert digital signals to analog signals when sending and convert analog signals to digital signals when receiving. In other words, computer digital signals can be converted into analog signals and transmitted through current telephone networks.

Internal Modems

The internal modem is designed to be installed in a computer system, usually occupying an expansion slot. The modem, in the form of a PC board, has a telephone jack used to connect to the telephone network. Most new computers come with an internal modem because of the popularity of the Internet.

External Modems   The external modem is portable. It usually has one RS232 serial port and a telephone jack. The RS232 port is connected to the computer system, while the telephone jack is connected to the telephone network. Since external modems are portable, different computer systems can use the same modem as long as they are equipped with one RS232 port.

Routers

Routers are digital switches used to connect the local area networks inside various organizations with the wide area networks of various network providers. This interconnection enables easy communication between separate networks across geographical distances. Another important function of routers is to provide security of the network. Since the popularity of Internet and electronic commerce, the router business has become a multibillion-dollar industry. The big players are Cisco, Bay Networks, and 3COM.

Multiplexor

The capacities of the communication media are generally greater than what is needed to maintain data transmission. Many individual transmissions can share a single physical channel through a variety of techniques collectively called *multiplexing*. The device that performs multiplexing is called a *multiplexor*. Just like modems, multiplexors are used in pairs, one multiplexor for each side.

There are two types of multiplexors: time division multiplexor and frequency division multiplexor. The *time division multiplexor* divides transmission time into many time slots and assigns each time slot to a device attached to the multiplexor. *Frequency division multiplexors* divide frequency into many channels and assign each channel to an individual device.

LOCAL AREA NETWORKS AND THEIR APPLICATIONS

A *local area network (LAN)* is a privately owned communications network that covers a limited geographic area such as a company computer laboratory, an executive's office, one building, or a group of buildings close together. The range is typically within a mile or so. The topologies of LANs are star, ring, bus, and hybrid.

Components of a LAN

A LAN consists of many workstations, each of which can be used as a server, a terminal, or a microcomputer. A *server* in a LAN stores network management software and performs management functions. There are different types of LAN servers depending on the major functions assigned in a client-server environment. A printer server provides printing services to other workstations, while a file server stores network and application software for the network. Other devices are a fax machine, a scanner, or a printer.

Network Interface Card

A *network interface card* is the interface between the network and the computer. This card provides the communication protocol recognized by the network architecture. For example, an Ethernet card is used to connect a PC with the network in a BUS network.

Network Operating System

A *network operating system (NOS)* is software that allows a user to manage the resources of a computer network. The NOS runs on the server computer in addition to the client operating systems, such as Windows or OS/2. The functions provided by NOS are:

- *Administration:* To add, delete, or organize client-users and perform maintenance tasks such as backup.
- *File management:* To store and transfer software to client computers.
- *Printer management:* To prioritize printing jobs and direct reports to specific printers on the network.
- *Network security:* To control the access and usage of the network.

Types of LANs

- *Peer-to-peer:* All workstations on the network have the same priority and equal status. Workstations can exchange data or information through the network.
- *Client-server:* Server computers are used to provide certain functions for other client computers. Each server computer is dedicated to a specific function.

WIDE AREA NETWORKS AND THEIR APPLICATIONS

Wide area networks (WANs) are communication networks covering a large geographical area. A WAN uses telephone lines, microwaves, satellites, or a combination of communication channels to transmit signals. A WAN that is limited to the area surrounding a city is referred to as a *metropolitan area network (MAN)*.

Integrated Services Digital Network

Integrated Services Digital Network (ISDN) is an international standard for the digital transmission of both voice and data. Using ISDN lines, data can be transmitted over one or more separate channels at up to 2.2 billion bits per second if fiber optical cables are used. This service, ranging from 64 to 128 kbps (Kilobaud Per Second), allows full-motion video images to be transmitted.

Leased Line Services

The connections in WANs can be leased lines. Telephone companies, both long-distance carriers (LDCs) and regional Bell operating companies (RBOCs), provide leased lines for data communications. Recently, cable system operators (CSOs) also joined this competition. This connection ranges from a 56 kbps to a 1.5 mbps (T1 line) connection to a very high T3 at 45 mbps.

Dial-Up Services

This is the most popular connection in WAN since it is the least expensive approach to connect to the WAN. The characteristics of this connection are temperate and low transmission speed.

BASIC NETWORK TOPOLOGIES

Generally speaking, three basic LAN topologies and a hybrid topology are recognized:

- *Star:* All microcomputers and other communication devices are connected to a central server. Electrical messages are routed through the central node to their destinations. The central node monitors the flow of traffic. (See Figure 8-3.)

Figure 8-3.
THE STAR NETWORK

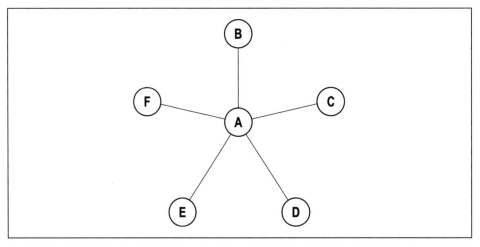

- *Ring:* All workstations are connected in a continuous loop. (See Figure 8-4.)A ring network uses a broadcast topology. Messages pass from node to node in one direction. The computer scans the message from the preceding node for an address that it recognizes. If the message contains the proper address, it is read. Otherwise, it is sent ahead to the next node.

Figure 8-4.
THE RING NETWORK

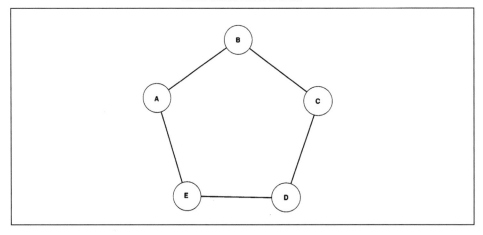

- *Bus:* The bus topology is a linear channel with many nodes connected. There is no central server. Each node transmits messages to all other devices. (See Figure 8-5.) If a node receives a message that was not addressed to it, this message is discarded. Otherwise it is read. Advantages of a bus are that it may be organized as a client-server or peer-to-peer network and it is easier to maintain than other networks. The bus topology is often called a *broadcast topology* since every message or set of data sent on the bus goes to every node.

Figure 8-5.
THE BUS NETWORK

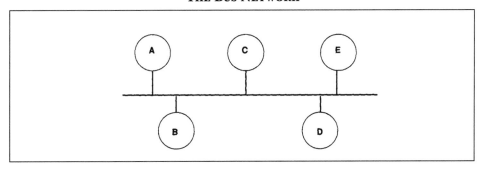

- *Hybrid:* Hybrid networks are combinations of star, ring, and bus networks. For example, a bus network may connect with a ring topology, which communicates with another star network.

Selection of the proper topology configuration depends on three primary criteria: the distance between points, the amount of time permissible for transmissions, and the amount of data to be transmitted from one point to another.

UNDERSTANDING THE INTERNET, INTRANET, AND ELECTRONIC COMMERCE

Internet

The Internet is an international network connecting approximately 36,000 smaller networks that link computers of commercial institutions and businesses. There are about 30 million Internet users and the number is increasing exponentially. The Internet is getting more and more popular because of its powerfulness and practicality. The potential utilization of the Internet for business is unlimited. The Internet is the largest and best-known wide area network in the world. Because of its tremendous size and number of users, most businesses have taken advantage of its powerful and convenient features for many business applications and opportunities.

The network infrastructure, however, is similar to that of WANs plus LANs. In fact, most of the Internet traffic travels on the same network used for local and long-distance calls, which consists of twisted pair wires, coaxial cables, fiber optical cables, and satellite systems. There are four levels of networks in Internet infrastructure: end-users, local access networks, regional networks, and backbone networks.

End-Users   End-users can be individuals connected to the Internet using a dial-up modem or parts of local area networks using routers to connect to the Internet.

- *Individual users:* This type of user uses either dial-up modem, ISDN, or leased line for connection.

- *LAN users:* This type of user is part of the LAN and uses LAN routers to connect to the Internet. The LAN router is therefore connected to the Internet by a leased line.

Local Access Networks   These networks are Internet service providers, Internet presence providers, university servers, or corporation servers that accept dial-up connections.

Regional Networks   These networks provide a bridge between local access networks and various backbone networks. A regional network may cover an area within a state or several states.

Backbone Networks   These networks carry Internet traffic between regional networks. Backbone networks are also linked internationally. For example, Mexico's networks are linked to the California Education and

Research Federation Network (CERFnet). A backbone network has a very high bandwidth made of fiber optical cables.

Intranet

Intranet is defined as an internal Internet. Using the same technology as Internet, Intranet takes advantage of all resources available on the Internet, but it provides a sense of security inside an organization. Using Intranet, paper memos can be eliminated by internal e-mails, meetings can be replaced by electronic conferences, and projects can be conducted on LANs. Intranets are internal corporate networks that use the infrastructure and standards of the Internet and the World Wide Web. In other words, it is a small version of the Internet that is developed and used by a corporation. Customers or employees can access the database or information in a company through web browsers to reduce operating costs. One of the greatest considerations of Intranet is security. That means unauthorized people can access a company's data through the Internet. To prevent this from happening, security software, called *firewalls,* has been developed. It blocks unauthorized traffic from entering the Intranet.

Electronic Commerce

Often called *electronic commerce,* business transactions can be made electronically. Consumers can browse the Internet virtual shopping mall and place orders for the company's merchandise. Investors can trade securities over the Internet. Telephone calls can also be connected via the Internet. Other services available on the Internet are:

- *Electronic mail:* E-mail can be sent anywhere in the world to users with Internet addresses.

- *File transfer and software downloads:* The Internet can transfer different files all over the world. Software can be downloaded from the Internet.

- *Database search:* The Internet can be used to access different databases.

- *Discussion and news group:* Thousands of discussion topics can be discussed in the bulletin board of the Internet. Information can be shared within this business group.

NETWORK SOFTWARE

Network System Software

Popular network system software for LANs are Novell's NetWare, Microsoft's Windows NT Server, and Apple's Apple Talk. Most network system software for WAN is custom-made and usually requires mainframe computers to operate.

Network Application Software

Most application software for individual computers has a network version. To share the same software on the network, the network version software (package) should be installed in the file server. This file server provides all the functions of the software including downloading the whole software to any client computer. A site license should be acquired so that all computers can access the software throughout the network regardless of the number of client computers. The restriction of a site license is that it is restricted in geographic location, such as within a company.

TELECONFERENCING AND COMPUTER CONFERENCING

Teleconferencing

Audio Conferencing   Audio conferencing is an extension of a conferencing call without the need for an operator to establish the connection between remote sites. Typically, audio conferencing occurs when meeting parties cannot physically get together in the same location. Audio conferencing allows attendants to communicate orally by speakerphones in different locations. All participants can hear one another. However, the remote participants cannot be seen.

Video Conferencing   Video conferencing is an extension of one-way closed-circuit TV. Typically, the participants can see and hear one another in a remote location. More than audio conferencing, video conferencing allows participants to view the accompanying body language. Currently, two types of video conferencing are available: full-motion and freeze-frame. Full-motion video conferencing is significantly more expensive than freeze-frame video conferencing since a real-time motion picture is transferred over the network. Freeze-frame sends periodic snap shots over the communication channel. Video conferencing allows participants to conduct meetings face-to-face without physically getting together. This dramatically reduces the cost for meetings.

Computer Conferencing

Computer conferencing provides not only audio and video effects, but also processing and storage capability. This capability provides participants with more power tools for decision making and problem analysis.

Electronic Bulletin Board   Electronic bulletin board is an extension of e-mail. A personal workstation is the means of access. To post messages on the electronic board, users send their messages to the e-mail address associated with the electronic bulletin board. The electronic bulletin board is public so that different issues and viewpoints can be discussed. This can further be developed as an online discussion forum or electronic chat room.

Computer Teleconferencing   Electronic bulletin boards are used in a highly unstructured manner. However, computer teleconferencing imposes a certain degree of structure to support remote and asynchronous communications. Teleconferencing allows participants to hear other participants' voices, view other participants' facial images, access different application software, and transfer image, video, and sound over the network. In terms of the time and location of different participants, there are four different scenarios:

1. *Same time, different location:* This type of computer teleconferencing allows participants to join the conference from different locations using LANs or WANs. However, all participants must participate in the conference at the same time. In other words, the conversation of the conference is real-time and results can be delivered right after the meeting. This type of computer teleconference requires high-speed transmission media so that video and images can be transferred real-time.

2. *Same time, same location:* The participants of the computer teleconference get together at the same time in the same location. This setting allows participants to exchange information and ideas without remote communication capacity. The results are similar to the previous one except that coordination is easier since all participants are in the same location and the oral communication can be used to assist the conference.

3. *Different time, same location:* This type of computer teleconferencing is the same as the previous one, except that participants can join the meeting at different times. This allows the meeting to be conducted over a certain time period. It provides a more flexible meeting schedule but restricts the online discussion and resolution.

4. *Different time, different location:* This type of computer teleconferencing allows participants to join the meeting at different times and locations. The transmission requirement is similar to that of the first type of computer teleconferencing, and this meeting is conducted in the same way as the third one. Since different participants can join the meeting at different locations and at different times, the coordination and management can be complicated. This issue is fully discussed in "group decision support systems" literature.

MULTIMEDIA AND MULTIMEDIA APPLICATIONS

Multimedia refers to technology that presents information in more than one medium, including text, graphics, animation, video, music, and voice.

Multimedia Components

A multimedia computer, which is able to deliver sound, video, image, and voice, requires a sound card. The sound card digitizes voice or sound into a computer data file. This data file can then be transmitted and converted back to sound or voice. In addition, a video capture card is also needed to convert a video from a regular video device, such as a VCR, to a digital file. This file can be converted back to a regular video. A digital camera can be useful when a picture is taken and needs to be transferred into a digital file. Scanning a picture through a scanner can do this. Since multi-media information (such as video) requires lots of storage space, a device called a CD-ROM is necessary. *CD-ROM* stands for *compact disk-read-only memory,* which is an optical disk format that is used to hold prerecorded text, graphics, and sound. Like a music CD, CD-ROM is a read-only disk. *Read-only* means the disk cannot be written on or erased by the user. A CD-ROM drive allows users to receive input information from a CD-ROM, which typically can store up to 650 megabytes of memory. At one time a CD-ROM drive was only a single-speed drive. Typically, a single-speed CD-ROM drive can access data at the speed of 150 kilobytes per second. That is to say a 12-speed can deliver data at the speed of 150 kilobytes $\times$ 12 = 1.8 megabytes per second. Other storage devices, such as an erasable optical disk, Easy drive, or Zip drive, are all designed to store large amounts of information.

Multimedia Applications

Multimedia provides business people with a better way to communicate. Managers can deliver a better presentation or lecture by including animation and voice. Productivity can therefore be improved by using multimedia. Some applications are discussed in the following sections.

Encyclopedias, Large Databases A large database that is not time-sensitive can be stored in a CD-ROM for later retrieval. For example, the encyclopedia and a collection of business articles can be stored on a CD-ROM.

Training A lecture can be given by interactive multimedia systems over the Internet. As a result, employees can go to virtual educational instruction on corporate business areas.

Presentations Presentation software is designed to include animation, voice, and pictures. By using these tools, presenters can more effectively deliver important messages than with traditional presentations.

Animation Corporate visual presenters use multimedia techniques for special effects to aid corporate employee learning. Presenters may use lots of multimedia techniques in the business education process.

DATA COMMUNICATIONS MANAGEMENT

Communication Hardware

Communication hardware determines the performance and capacity of data communication. In general, the performance is measured by *band-width,* which represents how many bits can be transferred in one second.

- *Broad-band:* A broad-band system can transmit signals in high capacity by creating multiple channels for data transmission. Media such as a fiber optical cable is a broad-band media.

- *Medium-band:* A medium-band media, such as some twisted pair wire and coaxial cables, can transmit signals by medium bandwidth. Multiple channels are available in medium-band media.

- *Base-band:* A base-band system allows basic communication requirements, including text or nongraphical file transfer. Twisted pair wire is a typical base-band media.

- *Network hub:* A network hub is used to connect all workstations in a network so that they can communicate.

Communication Software

Different kinds of communication software are available for data communication purposes:

- *Network operating system:* Network software is the most important software in terms of managing the entire network. Major functions are traffic management, security control, and communication management. A good network operating system can dramatically improve the performance of network operation. For example, Microsoft NT server and Novell Netware are popular network operating systems for LANs and UNIX. Other customized systems can be used to manage large-scale networks.

- *Web server software:* For host web sites, to be accessible from the network, a special software is needed. This software allows users to publish their web sites on the network, transfer files back and forth (FTP function), and monitor the performance of each site. Examples are Microsoft Internet Information Server and Netscape Commerce Server.

- *Network application software:* Generally speaking, application software can be either standalone or networked. If the software is designed for network use, the software should be installed in the network's file server. Other workstations, which are connected to this server, can use this software. Software licenses are usually purchased based on the number of workstations, which can share the software installed in the file server. Another alternative is to purchase a site license, which allows for an unlimited number of users in a certain area such as a university campus.

- *Network browser software:* To enable users to interact with the site and to view information, a software call browser must be available. User interactions include viewing, sending information, making transactions, or downloading software. Examples are Microsoft Internet Explorer and Netscape Navigator.

Network Manager

A good network manager must have the knowledge of both network software and hardware. The major duties of a network manager are to keep software and hardware functional and compatible with other networks, and to provide information and services to all users.

Software/Hardware Functionality   Many users share computer networks for different purposes. Physical as well as software damage may happen from time to time. To assure that all workstations are in good condition when needed, a security system, which protects both the hardware and software, is necessary. For example, users have to show their IDs to use the workstation and use correct user names and passwords to enter the system. Important or confidential files are write-protected and key configurations cannot be altered unless authorized.

Compatibility with Other Networks   Different network operating systems may be only partially compatible or incompatible. A network manager should be able to investigate compatibility issues before the system is installed. Sometimes the linkage between different networks can be achieved by using a gateway, a bridge, or a router. The installation of a bridge, a router, and a gateway can be very complicated and time-consuming since no two networks are identical. The transmission capacity and transmission media are important issues a network manager faces. Different application software requires different transmission capacities. For example, graphical design software requires more transmission capacity than word processing software. The number of users is also an important factor to determine how traffic should be handled.

Customer Services   A network manager should provide customer service when needed by end-users. Users may not have enough knowledge or background to diagnose the problems. The network manager must be capable of diagnosing the problem and providing a good solution. In addition, in the network environment, one user's mistake may affect other users. A prompt response is necessary to avoid other workstations being affected.

PLANNING FOR NETWORKS

Network Analysis

Before a network system is implemented, a detailed system survey should be conducted. What type of functions should be achieved? How many users will be using the network? How secure should the network be? How much traffic will the network carry? How much is budgeted? After answering all these questions, a clearer picture of the network can be generated.

Network Design

Network design should be based on the expectation and functionality of the network. For example, small retail stores using computers to manage inventory may require just a small LAN with several workstations. The file server would store the inventory management software to share with other workstations. However, a nationwide retail chain may require a data processing center with hundreds of high-performance workstations, which connect to different retail locations to retrieve data on a daily basis.

Centralized Processing versus Distributed Processing   *Centralized data processing* is used when data needs to be processed in one location. The computation power is focused on one powerful computer, typically a midrange or mainframe computer. Terminals are used as the input/output devices to collect data and display results for users. Since all data is forwarded to a centralized computer for processing, the central computer becomes essential to the whole system. Any interruption of the central computer can result in a systemwide breakdown. Also, since all terminals are connected to the central computer and some of them are in remote locations, the communication cost could be very high.

The distributed processing employs more than one computer system for processing. As a matter of fact, each computer in the network could, if so designed, process its own information locally. Therefore, the data processing workload can be spread over many workstations in the network. The communication cost can also be reduced since most information does not have to be transferred to a central computer for processing.

Choosing between centralized processing and distributed processing depends on the trade-off between the two types of system. Centralized systems have better systems and data security since all data processing power is controlled in one location. Distributed systems can be more reliable and economical because each workstation shares the workload. Furthermore, the communication cost can be reduced. More and more systems switch from centralized processing to distributed processing because of economic reasons.

Master-Slave Processing versus Client-Server Processing *Master-slave* processing uses a major computer to give commands to others for data processing. In consequence, the major computer becomes occupied with controlling and monitoring other computers. A *client-server* architecture uses a different philosophy to manage the computer resources. By specializing different computers with different tasks (called *server computers*), any other computers (called *client computers*) on the network can request services such as printing, file loading, web hosting, and database processing. Client computers therefore dedicate their processing capability to more tasks for the end-user. In the meantime, server computers are programmed and equipped with special functions for optimal processing efficiency.

Other Considerations Different communications media can determine the bandwidth, which affects the speed of the network. Proper equipment must be installed to be compatible with the current system. A server computer requires a large hard drive and a fast CPU for adequate service. Client computers require only what is needed for local application software. Bridges are needed (usually a specialized microcomputer) for connecting similar types of networks, while gateways are required to connect different types of networks. They all require professionals to develop and implement. Powerful printers can be installed for the whole network and many users can also share hard drives. It would be wise to stay on the same platform throughout the whole company. For example, it is difficult for a PC platform to communicate with a Mac platform since different operating systems are used.

Implementation and Expansion

Network implementation involves lots of detailed information from different products, for example, to install an Ethernet LAN, a network hub is required to connect all computers on the network. Each workstation is required to have an Ethernet card installed to provide network capability. The driver for an Ethernet should also be installed in the computer. Either coaxial cable or twisted pair wire is needed to connect workstations with the hub. After all the hardware is properly installed, server software should be installed in server computers. There will be lots of detailed fine-tuning to properly install all necessary components.

CORPORATE DATA MANAGEMENT IN A DISTRIBUTED ENVIRONMENT

Large corporations process a large volume of data on a daily basis. The data processed comes from geographically diverse locations, even international sources. The goal for a good management information system is to process data on a timely and efficient basis. To deliver timely information, more expensive online systems should be installed. This allows fast response and immediate results. To process data more efficiently, client-server architecture and distributed processing are appropriate. If the data processing requirement reaches a certain degree, an IS department is necessary. The functions of an IS department includes routing operation, development, and customer service and training.

- *Routing operation:* This involves daily IS operation including database maintenance, application installation and maintenance, data security enforcement, and hardware maintenance. Software engineers and hardware technicians are needed to accomplish this task.

- *Development:* This involves new software development, semicustomized software configuration, operating system reconfiguration, system integration, and long-term IS planning. System analysts and software engineers are needed for this function.

- *Customer service and training:* To fully implement an IS, training is extremely important. Without proper training, IS will not reach its designed goal. End-users may also resist the new system since they do not comprehend the functions available in the system. A complete training plan is necessary even before the system is designed. Customer service involves problem solving and consulting. To help users with computer problems, the IS department should provide good explanations so that similar problems will not occur again. Some problems occur because of the system itself, while others occur due to users' ignorance. If system errors occur, a warning signal should be delivered to all users to prevent more damage. If users' errors cause the problem, more training courses must be offered. With a well-designed training program and customer server, the learning curve of a newly implemented system can be shortened.

CONCLUSION

Data communications will continue to affect business life. Businesses are no longer limited to local information. With the help of data communication technologies, business managers are able to access different information from any corner of the world. With communication technologies rapidly changing, today's businesses are challenged to find ways to adapt the technology to provide better products and services. In addition, new business opportunities are created. For executives, the new technology offers increased access to worldwide information services and new opportunities for the business.

9 INFORMATION SYSTEMS DEVELOPMENT AND END-USER COMPUTING

SYSTEMS ANALYSIS AND DESIGN

Information systems development can be a complex task and involve many employees to work collaboratively. In this process, many existing small information systems may be combined into a large one so that all business functions can be integrated through information systems, or a new information system may be created from the ground up. Developing information systems within a planned framework often creates a better system and helps organizations avoid the necessity of patching together a collection of incompatible information systems. Therefore, the development of a successful information system is not a trivial task. It requires a thorough understanding of existing business processes, discipline, organizational policies, expertise in this field, a vision of the future, and good communication skills.

The rationale behind triggering the development of an information system could be to catch an opportunity or to solve a problem.

- *Catching an opportunity:* An *opportunity* is defined as a potential improvement in business such as the increase of sales, more efficient operations, or a gain in competitive advantages. Catching an opportunity is considered a proactive activity in business, while solving a problem is considered reactive.

211

- *Solving a problem:* A *problem* is defined as an undesired situation or unpredicted circumstances. For example, a business realizes that the cost of operations is not competitive anymore or the customer service does not meet the requirement level. A good information system can provide a solution that leads to the solution of a current problem.

THE SYSTEMS DEVELOPMENT LIFE CYCLE

The Systems Development Life Cycle (SDLC) consists of several distinct phases and subphases by different names. The SDLC approach assumes that the life of an information system starts with a need, followed by an assessment of the functions that the system will fulfill. It ends when the benefits of the system no longer outweigh its maintenance cost. A new system is then constructed for another life cycle. The SDLC includes five major phases (see Figure 9-1).

Figure 9-1.
FIVE STEPS OF THE SYSTEMS ANALYSIS PHASE

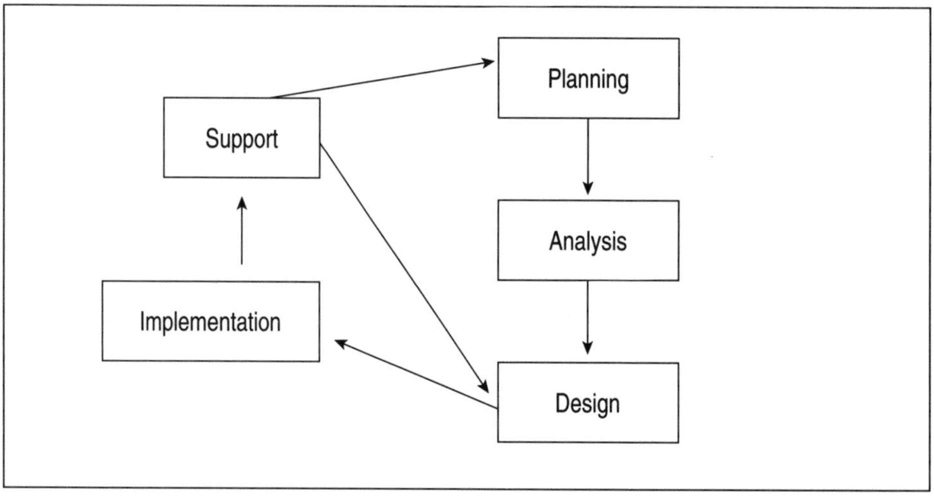

System Analysis

The purpose of system analysis is to establish in detail what the proposed system will do. This includes establishing the objectives of the new system and conducting an analysis of its costs and the benefits to be derived. Two steps are involved in this process: feasibility analysis and requirements analysis.

Feasibility Study Feasibility analysis consists of three steps: the technical feasibility study, the economic feasibility study, and the operational feasibility study. The *technical feasibility study* investigates whether the proposed system is technically feasible and whether the technology is sophisticated enough to accomplish the task. The *economic feasibility study* involves the financial status and the cost-benefit analysis of the proposed system. The potential benefits, including savings and extra revenue, must be greater than the potential cost, including maintenance. It does not make sense to build a system whose cost cannot cover its income. The *operational feasibility study* investigates whether the system is operational and the technology is available: Technology availability does not guarantee that the system will be operational. For example, running a system for 24 hours a day is possible technologically but infeasible due to budget constraints or government regulations. In general, a feasibility study consumes 5–10% of a project's resources. The question is, how much time will be spent on the development process?

Requirements Analysis The principal objective of requirements analysis is to produce the requirements specifications for the system, which specify what the system will do if implemented. The requirements can be used to establish understanding among future users, developers, and management, and they can serve as a contract among all parties.

A typical requirement analysis includes:

- What kind of output will the system produce? What input will be needed to generate this output?
- What volume of data will be handled? How many users can be served?
- What type of user interface will be provided?
- What kinds of obligations, in terms of usage and maintenance of the system, are required for users and developers?

System Analysis Alternatives To perform a good system analysis, information collection is an important step. There are different ways to collect information for the purpose of system analysis.

- *Collecting information from users:* Collecting information from users is usually by means of interviewing. The interview process should be planned in advance to make sure that managers from different levels can be questioned. Two types of questions are to be asked:

    Open-ended questions, such as, "How can this process be improved?" These give the interviewee the opportunity to find potential problems and create new solutions. The answer may be unorganized but could be very helpful in terms of finding possible opportunities.

    Closed-ended questions, such as, "Do you maintain an audit trail for this type of transaction?" These generally provide the interviewer with a short answer such as yes, no, or a brief response.

- *Collecting information from existing systems:* If the proposed system will replace the existing system or if it is similar to the existing system, the requirements for the proposed system may be derived from the existing one.

- *Collecting information from analyzing business functionality:* Decision analysis can help establish the information needs of an individual manager. This method consists of the following steps:

    Identify the key decision a manager makes.

    Identify the steps for the decision-making process.

    Identify the information needed for the decision making.

    Identify the input (usually the raw data) and output (usually the information) of the information systems.

System Design

Logical Design   The logical design is a translation of the user requirements into detailed functions of the system. The steps involved in logical design are as follows:

- The output of the proposed system and the input used to produce this output are identified.

- The components of the hardware and software are identified.

- The user interface is designed.

- The database management system is designed.

- The program that will compose the system is designed.

- The procedures to be employed in the operating system are specified.

- The controls that will be incorporated in the system are specified.

Physical Design The objective of *physical design* is to produce a complete specification of all system modules and their interfaces. The system's design must conform to the purpose, scale, and general concept of the system that management approved during the requirements analysis phase.

SYSTEM OUTPUT

When designing user output, consider six important factors:

1. *Content:* The actual pieces of data included among the outputs provided to users. For example, the content of a weekly report to a sales manager might consist of salesperson's name, sales calls made during the week, and the amount of each product sold to each major client category.

2. *Form:* How the content is presented to users. Content can be presented in various forms: quantitative, nonquantitative, text, graphics, audio, and video.

3. *Output volume:* "Volume" is commonly used in technology to measure the amount of activity taking place at a given time. The amount of data output required at any one time is known as output volume.

4. *Timeliness:* When users need outputs. Some outputs are required on a regular, periodic basic, perhaps daily, weekly, monthly, quarterly, or annually.

5. *Media:* The input/output medium is the physical substance or device used for input, storage, or output. The two most widely used media are paper and display. Paper involves printer or plotter hardware, whereas display involves a monitor or display terminal.

6. *Format:* The manner in which data are physically arranged. This arrangement is called output format when referring to data output on a printed report or on a display screen.

SYSTEM INPUT

User inputs should be designed next, after the outputs are designed. The input issues to consider are content, timeliness, media, format, and volume.

1. *Content:* The analyst should consider the types of data that need to be gathered to generate user outputs. Sometimes the data needed for a new system is not available within the organization—but a close substitute might be. For example, cost data can sometimes be cleverly manipulated into useful substitute information.

2. *Timeliness:* When inputs must enter the system is critical because outputs cannot be produced until certain inputs are available. Hence, a plan must be established regarding when different types of inputs will enter the system.

3. *Media:* The input media are the devices that enter the data, such as display workstations, magnetic tapes, magnetic disks, keyboards, optical character recognition (OCR), pen-based computers, and voice, to name a few.

4. *Format:* After the data content and the media requirements are determined, input formats are considered. When specifying record formats, for instance, the type and length of each data field, as well as any other special characteristics, must be defined.

5. *Input volume:* Input volume relates to the amount of data that must be entered in the computer system at any one time. In some decision support systems and many real-time transaction-processing systems, input volume is light. In batch-oriented transaction-processing systems, input volume can be heavy.

DETERMINING PROCESSING REQUIREMENTS

This determination helps the project team decide which types of application software products are needed and consequently the degree of processing the system needs to handle. This leads the system developers to decisions regarding the systems software and computer hardware that will most effectively get outputs to users.

USER INTERFACE

User interface design is the specification of a conversation between the system user and the computer. This conversation generally results in either input or output—possibly both. There are several types of user interface styles. Traditionally these styles were viewed as alternatives. However, with recent movements toward designing systems with graphical user interfaces, a blending of all styles can be found.

1. *Menu selection:* The more traditional user interaction dialogue strategy is menu selection. This strategy presents a list of alternatives or options to the user. The system user selects the desired alternative or option by keying in the number or letter that is associated with that option.

2. *Menu bars:* Menu bars are used to display horizontally across the top of the screen or window a series of choices from which the user can select.

3. *Pull-down menus:* Pull-down menus provide a vertical list of choices to the user. A pull-down menu is made available once the user selects a choice from a menu bar. The choices are typically organized from top to bottom according to the frequency in which they are chosen.

4. *Cascading menus:* This type of menu must be requested by the user from another higher-level menu.

5. *Iconic menus:* An iconic menu uses graphic representations for menu options. Iconic menus offer the advantage of easy recognition. The use of graphic images helps the user to memorize and recognize the functions available within an application. Instead of menus, some traditional applications were designed using a dialogue around an instruction set (also called a *command language interface*). Because the user must learn the syntax of the instructions set, this is suitable only for dedicated users.

6. *Question-answer dialogue:* Question-answer dialogue strategy is a style that was primarily used to supplement either menu-driven or syntax-driven dialogues. The simplest questions involve yes and no answers. Question-answer dialogue is difficult because you must try to consider everything that the system user might do wrong!

7. *Direct manipulation:* The newest and most popular of the user interface styles allows direct manipulation of graphical objects appearing on a screen. Essentially, this user interface style focuses on using icons, or small graphic images, to suggest functions to the user. A trash-can icon, for instance, might symbolize a delete command.

Acquisition

At the end of the design phase, the firm has a reasonably good idea of the types of hardware, software, and services it needs for the system being developed. These physical items are identified after the logical design of the system model is finished.

The Vendor Marketplace

Today, thousands of technology-related vendors exist, and a single organization might buy from hundreds of companies before meeting its full set of processing needs. The technology industry can be broken down into three primary market segments: hardware, software, and services.

- *Hardware:* The hardware segment of the computer industry consists of firms that make computer units (that is, system units), peripheral devices, and/or communications devices. Some firms primarily produce mainframes, others mini, and still others micros. Some firms have products in all three markets, and many make peripherals as well as computer units. Several of these firms produce software as well. It is possible to lease computer hardware (enter into a contract with a vendor to possess and use a computer system over a specified time period for a specified payment) or to buy it.

- *Software:* Unlike hardware, software is usually licensed (rather than leased or purchased). Its use may be licensed on a single-payment basis (the standard practice for microcomputer software) or on a monthly basis (common for mainframe software). Such licensing agreements give the organization the right to use the software.

- *Services:* Many firms in the computer industry supply services, including providing software and hardware maintenance, creating and maintaining banks of financial data that other companies can access, providing capability on a communications network, allowing remote access to computing facilities, performing data processing and system integration (system development), giving advice, developing programs or applications, educating, and so on. The availability of such services has given many companies the option of outsourcing their information-processing activities, that is, contracting with another firm to provide the information-processing services that were previously provided in-house.

THE REQUEST FOR PROPOSAL (RFP)

Firms may approach vendors to acquire hardware, software, or services in various ways. One method is to send vendors a document called a *request for proposal (RFP)*. This document outlines the firm's system needs and requests that interested vendors submit a formal proposal detailing how they will satisfy those needs.

- *Evaluating vendor proposals:* The proposals or bids are evaluated and a selection is made. Two useful procedures to aid in this process are the vendor rating system and the benchmark test.

  In a *vendor rating system,* vendors are quantitatively scored with respect to how well their systems stack up against a specific set of criteria.

  In a *benchmark test,* one or more programs (or sets of data) are prepared by the potential buyer and then processed under the hardware or software of the vendors being considered. The collection of programs and data submitted by the potential buyer is called a *benchmark.* The benchmark should reflect the type of work that the vendor's hardware and software will actually perform, thereby providing a realistic indication of how well that hardware will do when used for real applications.

- *Contracting with vendors:* After a vendor is chosen, a contract is signed. A *contract* is a document, enforceable in a court of law, that defines such items as the basic agreement, the parties to the agreement, the goods, services, and monies exchanged, the continuing expectations, and the course of action if either of the parties fails to live up to expectations.

- *Construction:* Once the software development tools are chosen, the construction of the system begins. System construction is predominantly programming by translating input, output, and processes into programs. After the program module is completed, it is tested by means of walk-through and simulation. In a *walk-through,* system analysts follow the logic of the program and compare it with what they know the result should be. In *simulation,* the team runs the program with the data. After the modules of the application are completed and tested, the modules are integrated into one coherent program.

- *System testing:* It is critical to test the entire integrated system. System testing consists of runs for the purpose of finding errors. The system is checked against the system requirements originally defined in the analysis phase, by running typical data through the system. The quality of the output is examined, and processing times are measured to ensure that the original requirements are met. This is a crucial step in the development effort, since many unforeseen impediments can be detected and fixed before the system is introduced for daily use.

Implementation

Implementation, also called *delivery,* consists of two steps: training and conversion.

Training Staffs must be trained in one of several ways, such as class training, which takes advantage of the economical use of instructors, or on-the-job training, by which people learn by doing. Training can be achieved by using multimedia technology and other training software, in which employees can train themselves and learn the system at their own pace.

Conversion Conversion takes place when an operation switches from the old system to the new system. There are the broad ranges of activities that prepare the intended users for work with the new system and for "owning" it. The operators need time to get used to new systems and a lot of effort to test the system. In this stage, services to other departments and to customers may be delayed, and data may be lost.

EXPLORING THE PROTOTYPING ALTERNATIVE

A *prototype* is an original information system that serves as a model for the production of other information systems with similar goals and functionality. In the manufacturing industry, a prototype refers to an actual physical product that is later mass-produced for marketing. IS prototyping is different from manufacturing prototyping in how it is produced. IS prototyping tends to use a more interactive approach than a systematic approach. The users and developers are consistently interacting, revising, and testing the prototype system until it evolves into an acceptable application. This approach is totally different from the traditional step-by-step analysis and development process.

The purpose of prototyping is to develop a system from a working model as quickly as possible. This working model is then revised and tweaked, as developers and users work together. A typical development process consists of the following steps:

- Quick development of a working model.

- Test by users, with feedback and suggestions.

- Modification of the system based on the feedback and suggestions.

Studies have shown that prototyping has become a popular approach to system development since it requires fewer staff than the traditional approach. This implies that prototyping costs less than the traditional approach. Prototyping also significantly shortens the time required to complete the system development process. However, the risk is that, since the analysis phase is reduced to a minimum level to save time and cost, incompatibilities and other unforeseen mishaps may occur.

The documentation process can be complicated when the system is complete.

Knowing When to Prototype

Prototyping is an efficient approach to development in two situations. The first is when the system is small in scale, because the risk involved in the lack of thorough analysis is minimal. If the development takes longer than planned, the overall cost is still likely to be smaller than if a full SDLC were performed. The second is when the system deals with unstructured problems; it leads to de facto prototyping. The developer interviews the experts and builds a crude system; then the experts try to improve it. If users cannot specify all the requirements at the start of the project, the developers have no choice but prototype, and the users can communicate their requirements as the development proceeds.

Knowing When Not to Prototype

Prototype is not recommended if a system is large or complex because it requires a significant investment of resources. A system failure could entail great financial loss. Prototyping should be avoided when the system is designed to interface with other systems. The requirements and integration must be analyzed carefully to reduce the risk of damage to the existing system. For example, a payroll system or a large order-entry system is rarely prototyped.

OUTSOURCING OPTIONS

A company no longer has to develop its own information system, because a lot of companies specializing in IS services provide expertise and economies of scale that no single company can achieve. However, in regard to whether to develop a system in-house or to outsource its development, top managers should ask basic questions: What are the core business competencies? What are the specialties that the company should continue to do by itself? What does the company do outside of its specialty that could be done better by an organization that specializes in that area?

Many companies realize that IT is not among their core competencies and should not be a focus of their efforts. With this change in business operations, outsourcing has come to mean two different things:

1. A short-term contractual relationship with a service firm to develop a specific application for the organization.
2. A long-term contractual relationship with a service firm to take over all or some of the IS functions.

The advantages of outsourcing are as follows:

- *Improved cost clarity:* The client knows exactly what the cost of the IS functions will be over the period of the contract.
- *Reduced license and maintenance fees.*
- *User concentration on core business:* Outside experts manage IT, freeing executives from managing an IS business, so that they can concentrate on the company's main business.

INTEGRATING END-USER COMPUTING

The End-User Environment

End-users are persons who need the outputs produced by application software to perform their jobs. *End-user computing (EUC)* is the involvement of end-users, such as employees, managers, or executives, in the development and use of the information system. As the field of end-user computing evolves, more end-users are becoming directly involved in satisfying their own data and information needs.

Factors Encouraging End-User Computing

A complete list of the applications that motivate end-users to employ computing resources or to acquire their own computing resources would be extensive.

Many end-users' applications fall into one or more of eight areas:

1. *Data entry:* Data entry refers to entering data into the computer system. Many data-entry operations are part of transaction-processing operations. In this case, the entry application was probably developed by computer professionals and not by end-users.

2. *Document processing:* Document processing includes such activities as the preparation of memos, letters, and other types of correspondence, as well as such tasks as electronic document management and routing. Document routing is often performed by electronic mail and the image processing system.

3. *Data management:* Data management refers to the set of computing and development activities involved with maintaining large computerized banks of data. It refers to the types of activities that comprise data management, as well as the file and database management software used to implement these activities.

4. *Extract reports:* Extract reports are business reports that use data extracted from files or databases. A user can create a report that consists only of selected records from a file. A user can also do arithmetic on report records and sort records in various ways.

5. *Display retrieval:* Preparing extract reports normally involves permanent hardcopy output, formatting information into a report style, and completeness attributed to the report. Display retrieval, on the other hand, involves temporarily summoning only a few pieces of output to the display screen.

6. *Schedules and lists:* Schedules and lists consist of outputs as budgets, profit-and-loss statements, and annuities.

7. *Analysis:* Analysis involves drawing conclusions from a set of data. Analysis can be performed by end-users in numerous ways, such as sensitivity analysis or artistical analysis.

8. *Presentation:* Many end-users need to put information into a highly presentable form. For instance, presentations made at a meeting often require that information be shown in an easily understood or graphical format.

Managing End-User Computing

According to Thomas Gerrity and John Rockart, three principal approaches to management of end-user computing (EUC) exist.

Monopolist Approach   End-user development is often perceived as a threat to the power of an IS department. As end-users acquire their own systems, they depend less on the resources of the IS department to meet their needs. The IS department has thwarted the onrush of end-user computing by convincing management that computer professionals should control all information processing. The monopolist approach was the strategy for an IS department attempting to retain its power.

Laissez-Faire Approach   The laissez-faire approach is in direct contrast to the monopolist approach. In this approach, end-user computing should be left completely to the discretion of the end-users themselves. Unfortunately, this approach can easily lead to chaos. End-user computing costs, which may already be substantial, can zoom out of control. As each user group does what it wants, the proliferation of technologies can make systems integration a nightmare.

Information Center Approach   The newest, and often the most sensible, approach to the management of EUC is the information center. This approach enables users to retain the authority to care for their own need (most end-users operate under normal budgetary constraints and are motivated to spend funds wisely) and, if properly managed, provides some control over the unbridled proliferation of end-user systems.

Advantages and Problems

Increased Individual Performance   Perhaps the single most important benefit of EUC is increased individual performance from the viewpoints of both effectiveness and efficiency. Most people agree that decision support system (DSS) tools in the hands of informed managers usually make those managers much more effective.

Easier and More Direct Implementation   With end-user development, it is more likely that the final system will be exactly what the end-user wants and expects.

Technological Literacy   As users become more sophisticated with end-user tools, it is likely that benefits will accrue that management never expected.

Competitive Advantage   Numerous examples exist in which companies employed end-user technologies to establish a competitive advantage. In these instances, benefits to the organization may include shifting inventory carrying costs to the supplier, greater control over suppliers, increased ordering efficiency, enhanced quality of incoming supplies, and easier shopping for the best price.

Reducing the Applications Backlog   As end-users become capable of meeting their own computing needs, both the visible and invisible applications backlogs may lessen.

Challenges and Problems   From a management perspective, three of the most critical challenges associated with end-user computing and development are cost control, product control, and data control.

Problems Arising from EUC

1. The cost of EUC often cannot be effectively measured.

2. Many end-user–related costs are not formally justified in any way.

3. Some end-user computing costs are not optimized at the enterprise level.

4. End-users often buy products that are incompatible with those bought by other end-users, with whom someday they might have to integrate applications.

5. End-users often solve the wrong problems or apply the wrong tools and models.

6. The information center staff often does not follow up properly after initial end-user needs appear to be satisfied.

7. End-users typically do not apply rigorous data integrity or accuracy controls, making the results they get from their systems less reliable than those obtained from formal systems.

8. End-users typically have little security or backup on their systems.

9. Some end-users get carried away with their computer systems, using them inefficiently or ineffectively, to the detriment of their main job functions.

10. End-users are typically deficient at documentation and setting up audit trails.

11. End-users often fail to upgrade their systems.

TOOLS FOR SYSTEMS DEVELOPMENT

Computer-Aided Systems Engineering Technology

Computer-aided systems engineering (CASE) is the application of computer technology to systems development activities, techniques, and methodologies. CASE *tools* are programs (software) that automate or support one or more phases of a system development life cycle. The technology is intended to accelerate the process of developing systems and to improve the quality of the resulting systems.

The History and Evolution of CASE Technology

The history of CASE dates back to the early to mid-1970s. The ISDOS project, under the direction of Dr. Daniel Teichrowe at the University of Michigan, developed a language called *Problem Statement Language (PSL)* for describing user problems and solution requirements for an information system into a computerized dictionary. A companion product, called *Problem Statement Analyzer (PSA),* was created to analyze the problem and requirements statement for completeness and consistency. The real breakthrough came with the advent of the IBM Personal Computer. Not long thereafter, in 1984, an upstart company called Index Technology (now known as INTERSOLV) created a PC software tool called Excelerator. Its success established the CASE acronym and industry. Today, hundreds of CASE products are available to various systems developers. It is important to realize that modern CASE technology is still very young, but the technology is improving at a staggering rate. New tools are emerging monthly. The best existing products are improving annually.

The Framework of the CASE Tool

CASE framework is based on the following popular terminology:

- The term *upper-CASE* describes tools that automate or support the "upper," or front-end, phases of the systems development life cycle: systems planning, systems analysis, and general systems.

- The term *lower-CASE* describes tools that automate or support the "lower," or back-end, phases of the life cycle: detailed systems design, systems implementation, and systems support.

- The term *cross life cycle CASE* refers to tools that support activities across the entire life cycle. This includes activities such as project management and estimation.

CASE Tools for Systems Planning (Upper-CASE) Upper-CASE tools for systems planning are intended to help analysts and consultants capture, store, organize, and analyze models of the business. These models and their evaluation help the information systems planners define and prioritize:

- Business strategies that are being (or will be) implemented.
- Complementary information systems and information technology strategies to be implemented.
- Databases that need to be developed.
- Networks that need to be developed.
- Applications that need to be developed around the databases and networks.

CASE Tools for Systems Analysis and Design (Upper-CASE) Upper-CASE tools for systems analysis and design are intended to help systems analysts better express users' requirements, propose design solutions, and analyze the information for consistency, completeness, and integrity. This information helps analysts:

- Define project scope and system boundaries.
- Model and describe the current information system (if required in the methodology).
- Model and describe the users' business requirements for a new information system.
- Prototype requirements for the purpose of discovery or verification.
- Design a computer-based information system that will fulfill users' business requirements.
- Prototype specific design components (such as screens and reports) for the purpose of verification and ease of use.

CASE Tools for Systems Design and Implementation (Lower-CASE) Lower-CASE tools for detailed design and systems implementation are intended to help designers and programmers more quickly generate applications software. This includes:

- Helping programmers more quickly test and debug their program code.
- Helping programmers or analysts to automatically generate a program code from analysis and design specifications.

- Helping designers and programmers to design and automatically generate special or detailed system design components like screens and databases.

- Automatically generating complete application code from analysis and design specifications.

CASE Tools for Systems Support (More Lower-CASE)   Lower-CASE tools support the maintenance activities for production information systems. For systems support, these tools are intended to help analysts, designers, and programmers react to inevitable, ever-changing business and technical environments, including:

- Helping programmers restructure existing or old program code to be more maintainable.

- Helping programmers and analysts react to changing user requirements.

- Helping analysts and programmers reengineer programs to accommodate newer technology (such as changing the "preferred" database management system).

- Helping analysts and programmers determine when the costs of maintaining a system exceed the benefits of maintaining the system. (In other words, "Is it time to start over?")

- Helping analysts recover any reusable information from obsolete programs as a preface to taking that information back to upper-CASE tools and redeveloping a major, new information system.

CASE Tools that Support Cross Life Cycle Activities   A wide variety of CASE tools support activities across the entire system development life cycle.

Project management is one cross life cycle activity common to most projects. A wide variety of project management software packages exist because numerous professions use them. Project management tools help managers plan, schedule, report on, and manage their projects and resources. But some project management tools have crossed into CASE by virtue of their interfaces to other CASE tools.

One growing category of cross life cycle CASE technology is that of *process managers*. Process management software provides the necessary online guidance and expertise. The best process managers, such as Rapid System Development's Hyper Analyst, are actually capable of invoking (starting) CASE tools at appropriate times in the methodology.

Another category of cross life cycle CASE is *estimation*. Attempting to accurately assess the size of a project (or system) and then estimate the time and cost to complete the project is very difficult. But now how do you estimate size and cost? Function points is a formal, mathematically based technique.

Yet another cross life cycle activity is *documentation*. The deployment of CASE technology creates a wealth of documentation. Tools like KnowledgeWare's ADW/DOC allows you to design a custom work product or deliverable, and then automatically retrieves the appropriate diagrams, specifications, or information. It can even incorporate word processing and spreadsheet files.

The Architecture of the CASE Tool

The center of CASE tool architecture is a database called a *repository,* which is a developer's database. Here the developers can store diagrams, descriptions, specifications, applications programs, and any other working byproducts of systems development. Synonyms include design database, dictionary, and encyclopedia. Most first-generation CASE tools had standalone, proprietary repositories. A CASE tool could only read and write from its own repository. Second-generation CASE tools were frequently built around a shared repository. These tools not only share a repository; they make the workbenches highly dependent on one another.

Facilities and Functions

To use a repository, we obviously need input and output facilities:

- *Graphic facilities* are used to diagram or model information systems using various techniques.

- *Description facilities* are used to record, delete, edit, and output non-graphical information and specifications.

- *Prototyping facilities* are used to analyze or design components such as inputs, outputs, screens, or forms.

- *Inquiry and reporting facilities* are used to extract information and specifications out of the repository. They can support simple inquiries such as, "Tell me about the input called ORDER," or more complex inquiries such as, "Provide me a listing of every input or file that contains any field that includes a two-character date field."

- *Quality assurance facilities* analyze graphs, descriptions, and/or prototypes for consistency, completeness, and conformance to generally accepted "rules" of systems development.

- *Decision support facilities* analyze information in the repository to provide support for decisions.

- *Documentation facilities* are used to assemble graphs, repository descriptions, prototypes, and quality assurance reports into formal documents or deliverables that can be reviewed by project participants.

- *Transform facilities* automate or assist the transformation of something into another form.

- *Generators* automatically translate user requirements and/or technical designs into working applications and programs.

- *Data-sharing facilities* provide export and import repository information between different local repositories of the same CASE tool.

- *Security and version control facilities* maintain the integrity of repository information.

- *Housekeeping facilities* establish user accounts, project directories, user privileges, tool defaults and preferences, backup and recovery, and so forth.

The Benefits of the CASE Tool

- *Increased productivity:* CASE automates many of the most tedious clerical activities of developers. It reduces the time needed to complete many tasks, especially those involving diagramming and associated specifications.

- *Improved quality:* CASE can eliminate or substantially reduce omissions and defects that would prove very costly to correct during systems implementation or support.

- *Better documentation:* An early benefit of CASE is higher-quality documentation. CASE tools also make it easier to maintain documentation.

- *Reduced lifetime maintenance:* The net benefit of higher-quality systems and better documentation should be reduced costs and effort required for maintaining systems. This, in turn, creates more time and resources for new systems development.

10

INFORMATION SYSTEMS AND DECISION SUPPORT

WHAT IS AN INFORMATION SYSTEM?

An information system comprises computer-based processing and/or manual procedures that provide useful, complete, and timely information. This information must support management decision making in a rapidly changing business environment. The IS must supply managers with information quickly, accurately, and completely. Information systems are not new; only computerization of them is new. Before computers, information system techniques existed to supply information for functional purposes. The scope and purpose of IS is better understood if each part of the term is defined. (See Figure 10-1.)

Management

Management has been defined in a variety of ways, but for our purposes it comprises the processes or activities that describe what managers do in the operation of their organization: plan, organize, coordinate, and control operations. They *plan* by setting strategies and goals and selecting the best course of action to achieve the plan. They *organize* the tasks necessary for the operational plan, set these tasks up into homogeneous groups, and delegate authority. They *control* the performance of the work by setting performance standards and avoiding deviations from standard.

Figure 10-1.
THE MEANING OF AN INFORMATION SYSTEM (IS)

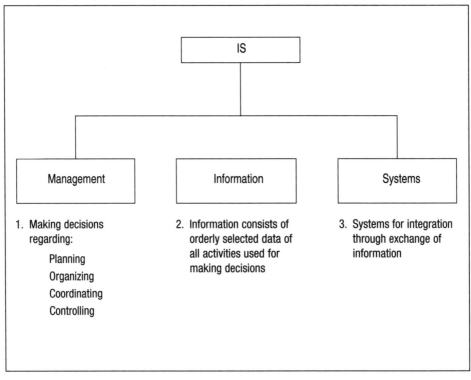

Because *decision making* is such a fundamental prerequisite to each of the foregoing processes, the job of an IS becomes that of facilitating decisions necessary for planning, organizing, and controlling the work and the functions of the business.

In general, the work that management performs can be classified as planning, organization and coordination, controlling, and decision making.

- *Planning:* The planning function of management involves the selection of long- and short-term objectives and the drawing up of strategic plans to achieve those objectives. For example, the vice president of marketing must consider numerous factors when planning short-term ad campaigns and promotional activities aimed at opening up new long-term markets.

- *Organizing and coordinating:* In performing the organization and coordination function, management must decide how best to put together the firm's resources in order to carry out established plans. For example, top management must decide on the type and number of divisions and departments in the company and evaluate the effectiveness of the organizational structure. Furthermore, managers must identify the personnel needs of the company and select the personnel, as well as training staff.

- *Controlling:* Controlling entails the implementation of a decision method and the use of feedback so that the firm's goals and specific strategic plans are optimally obtained. This includes supervising, guiding, and counseling employees to keep them motivated and working productively toward the accomplishment of organization objectives.

- *Decision making:* Decision making is the purposeful selection from a set of alternatives in light of a given objective. Each primary management function involves making decisions, and information is required to make sound decisions. Decisions may be classified as short-term or long-term. Depending on the level of management, decisions can be operational, tactical, or strategic.

Information

Data must be distinguished from information, and this distinction is clear and important for our purposes. Data consists of facts and figures that are not currently being used in a decision process, and it usually takes the form of historical records that are recorded and filed without immediate intent to retrieve for decision making. An example is one of the supporting documents, ledgers, and other records that comprise the source material for profit-and-loss statements. Such material would be of historical interest only to an external auditor.

Information consists of data that has been retrieved, processed, or otherwise used for informative or inference purposes, for arguments, or for forecasting or decision making. An example is any of the supporting documents previously mentioned, but in this case the data could be used by an internal auditor, by the management services department of an external auditor, or by internal management for profit planning and control or for other decision-making purposes.

Systems

A *system* can be described simply as a set of elements joined together for a common objective. A *subsystem* is part of a larger system. All systems are parts of larger systems. For our purposes the organization is the system and the parts (divisions, departments, functions, units, etc.) are the subsystems. While we have achieved a very high degree of automation and joining together of subsystems in scientific, mechanical, and manufacturing operations, we have barely scratched the surface of applying systems principles for organizational or business systems. The concept of synergism has not generally been applied to business organizations, particularly as it applies to the integration of the subsystems through information interchange. Marketing, production/operations, and finance are frequently on diverse paths and working at cross-purposes. The systems concept of IS is therefore one of optimizing the output of the organization by connecting the operating subsystems through the medium of information exchange.

CLASSIFYING INFORMATION SYSTEMS BY TYPE OF OUTPUT

Another way of classifying ISs depends on the format of the output desired by the users of the information system. Three distinctions are made:

1. *ISs that generate reports:* These reports can be income statements, balance sheets, cash flow reports, accounts receivable statements, inventory status reports, production efficiency reports, or any reports on situations of interest to the decision maker. The reports can be historical or refer to current status.

2. *ISs that answer "what-if" kinds of questions asked by management:* These information systems take the information stored in the database and reply to questions asked by management. These questions are in the form of, "What would result if this or that happened?" The information system thus uses its stored information, its comparison and calculation capabilities, and a set of programs especially written for this situation to provide management with the consequences of an action under consideration.

   It works like this. The vice president for human resources of an airline wonders what pilot recruiting levels would be necessary if the company changed its retirement age from 65 to 62 at the same time that the Civil Aeronautics Board (CAB) reduced the maximum number of hours a pilot can fly monthly from 80 to 75. The vice president uses a what-if information system approach to answer her question. The computer indicates that monthly recruiting levels would have to be increased from 110 to 185 pilots to meet these two conditions. She realizes that doing so is not feasible and now "asks" the system the what-if question with the retirement age changed to 63. The reply is now 142 pilots a month recruited. She feels this is an attainable recruiting target. Some what-if systems print out entire financial statements reflecting the financial consequences of actions that are being contemplated. Figure 10-2 depicts a what-if scheme.

Figure 10-2.
"WHAT-IF" IS

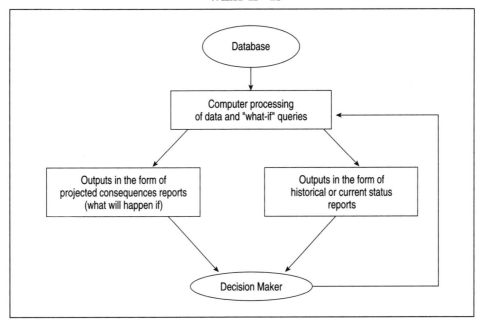

What-if information systems combine models (to be discussed later), software enabling the decision maker to make various inputs to those models and receive the outputs, and report-generating capability. These systems are generally run on a real-time system, which can be online and which can also run on a timesharing basis.

3. *ISs that support decision making (decision support systems):* These advanced systems attempt to integrate the decision maker, the database, and the models used. A decision support system (DSS) requires a very comprehensive database, together with the ability to manage that database, to provide outputs to the decision maker, and to update whatever permanent models are stored in the system. It requires extensive hardware and software. Two features distinguish DSS from other information systems: (1) They actually make a recommended decision instead of merely supplying additional information to the decision maker, and (2) they "build in" the decision maker as an integral part of the system (the software accommodates the person as part of the decision process). Figure 10-3 illustrates a DSS management information system.

Figure 10-3.
DECISION MAKER'S "WHAT-IF" QUESTIONS

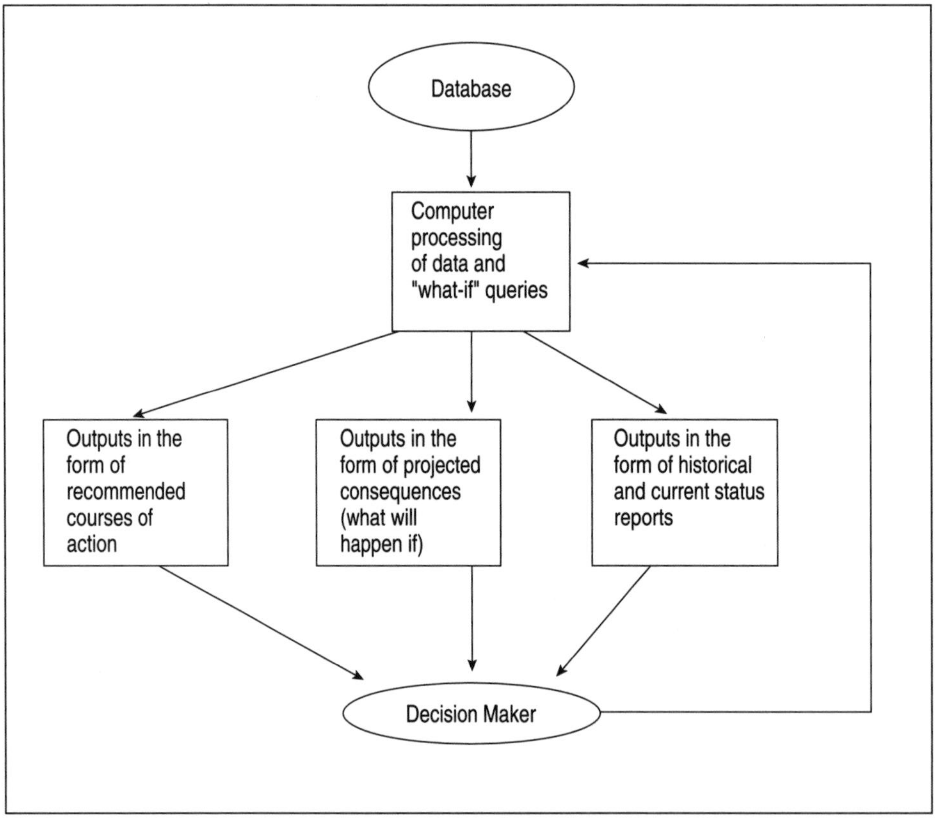

INFORMATION SYSTEMS AND ORGANIZATIONAL LEVELS

An information system should produce useful, accurate, and timely information to management on three levels: low level (operational), middle level (tactical), and top level (strategic). Lower managers make day-to-day operational decisions that affect a relatively narrow time frame and that involve details. These decisions are structured. Middle managers are involved in more tactical decisions that cover a broader range of time and involve more experience. Middle managers use summary reports, exception reports, periodic reports, on-demand reports, and event-initiated reports to make semi-structured decisions. Top management deals with decisions that are strategic and long-term in nature.

The primary objective of the IS is to satisfy the needs at the various levels. Generally the information needs to be (1) more summarized and relevant to the specific decisions that need to be made than an organization's information normally is and (2) available soon enough to be of value in the decision-making process. The information flows up and down through the three levels of management and is made available in various types of reports.

LEVELS OF MANAGEMENT: WHAT KINDS OF DECISIONS ARE MADE?

Each level of management can be differentiated by the types of decisions made, the time frame considered in the decisions, and the types of report information needed to make decisions (see Table 10-1).

Lower Management

The largest level of management, lower (operational) management, deals mostly with decisions that cover a relatively narrow time frame. Lower management, also called supervisory management, actualizes the plans of middle management and controls daily operations—the day-to-day activities that keep the organization humming. Examples of lower-level managers are the warehouse manager in charge of inventory restocking and the materials manager responsible for seeing that all necessary materials are on hand in

Table 10-1.
A COMPARISON OF THE ISs AT THE OPERATIONAL,
TACTICAL, AND STRATEGIC LEVELS

Characteristic	*Operational*	*Tactical*	*Strategic*
Frequency	Regular, repetitive	Mostly regular	Often ad hoc (as needed)
Dependability of results	Expected results	Some surprises may occur	Results often contain surprises
Time period covered	Past	Comparative	Future
Level of data	Very detailed	Summaries of data	Summaries of data
Source of data	Internal	Internal and external	Internal and external
Nature of data	Highly structured	Some unstructured data	Highly unstructured (semistructured)
Accuracy	Highly accurate data	Some subjective data	Highly subjective data
Typical user	First-line supervisors	Middle managers	Top management
Level of decision	Task-oriented	Control and resource allocation oriented	Goal-oriented

Source: Adapted from R. Schultheis and M. Sumner, *Management Information Systems: The Manager's View,* 2nd ed. (Homewood, IL: Richard D. Irwin, 1992), p. 329.

manufacturing to meet production needs. Most decisions at this level require easily defined information about current status and activities within the basic business functions—for example, the information needed to decide whether to restock inventory. This information is generally given in detailed reports that contain specific information about routine activities. These reports are structured; so their form can usually be predetermined. Daily business operations data is readily available, and its processing can be easily computerized. Managers at this level typically make *structured decisions,* which are predictable decisions that can be made by following a well-defined set of predetermined, routine procedures. For example, a clothing store floor manager's decision to accept your credit card to pay for some new clothes is a structured decision based on several well-defined criteria:

1. Does the customer have satisfactory identification?

2. Is the card current or expired?

3. Is the card number on the store's list of stolen or lost cards?

4. Is the amount of purchase under the cardholder's credit limit?

Middle Management

The middle level of management deals with decisions that cover a somewhat broader range of time and involve more experience. Some common titles of middle managers are plant manager, division manager, sales manager, branch manager, and director of personnel. The information that middle managers need involves review, summarization, and analysis of historical data to help plan and control operations and implement policy that has been formulated by upper management. This information is usually given to middle managers in two forms: (1) *summary reports,* which show totals and trends, such as total sales by office, by product, by salesperson, and total overall sales, and (2) *exception reports,* which show out-of-the-ordinary data, such as inventory reports that list only items numbering fewer than 10 in stock.

These reports may be regularly scheduled (periodic reports), requested on a case-by-case basis (on-demand reports), or generated only when certain conditions exist (event-initiated reports). *Periodic reports* are produced at predetermined times—daily, weekly, monthly, quarterly, or annually. They commonly include payroll reports, inventory status reports, sales reports, income statements, and balance sheets. *On-demand reports* are usually requested by a manager when information is needed for a particular problem. For example, if a customer wants to establish a large charge account, a manager might request a special report on the customer's payment and order history. *Event-initiated reports* usually result from a change in conditions that requires immediate attention, such as an out-of-stock report or a report on an equipment breakdown.

Managers at the middle level of management are often referred to as tactical decision makers who generally deal with semistructured decisions. A *semistructured decision* is a decision that includes some structure procedures and some procedures that do not follow a predetermined set of procedures. In most cases, a semistructured decision is complex, requiring detailed analysis and extensive computations. Examples of semistructured decisions include deciding how many units of a specific product should be kept in inventory, whether or not to purchase a larger computer system, from what source to purchase personal computers, and whether to purchase a multiuser minicomputer system. At least some of the information requirements at this level can be met through computer-based data processing.

Top Management

The top level of management deals with the broadest type of decisions and covers the widest time frame. Typical titles of managers at this level are chief executive officer (CEO), chief operating officer (COO), chief financial officer (CFO), treasurer, controller, chief information officer (CIO), executive vice president, and senior partner. Top managers include only a few powerful people who are in charge of the four basic functions of a business: marketing, accounting and finance, production, and research and development. Decisions made at this level are unpredictable, long-range, and related to the future, not just past and/or current activities. Therefore, they demand the most experience and judgment.

A company's IS must be able to supply information to top management as needed in periodic reports, event-initiated reports, and on-demand reports. The information must show how all the company's operations and departments are related to and affected by one another. The major decisions made at this level tend to be directed toward (1) strategic planning, such as how growth should be financed and which new markets should be tackled first; (2) allocation of resources, such as deciding whether to build or lease office space and whether to spend more money on advertising or the hiring of new staff members; and (3) policy formulation, such as determining the company's policy on hiring minorities and providing employee incentives. Managers at this level are often called strategic decision makers. Examples of unstructured decisions include deciding five-year goals for the company, evaluating future financial resources, and deciding how to react to the actions of competitors.

At the higher levels of management, much of the data required to make decisions comes from outside the organization (for example, financial information about other competitors).

Table 10-2 shows the decision areas that the three levels of management deal with in a consumer product business and a bank.

Table 10-2.
THREE MANAGERIAL LEVELS AND INFORMATION NEEDS

Consumer product business	
Strategic	Competitive
Planning	Industry statistics
Tactical	Sales analysis by customer
	Reorder analysis of new products
	Sales analysis by product line
	Production planning
Operational	Bill of materials
	Manufacturing specifications
	Product specifications
	Order processing
	Online order inquiry
	Finished goods inventory
	Accounts receivable
	General ledger

Bank	
Strategic	Market forecast
Planning	New product development
	Financial forecast
Tactical	Branch profitability
	Product profitability
Operational	Loan billing
	Accounting systems
	Policy issuance and maintenance

MODELING A REAL-LIFE SYSTEM

Many information systems are model-based. The real world is complex, dynamic, and expensive to deal with. For this reason, we use models instead of real-life systems. A *model* is an abstraction of a real-life system that is used to simulate reality. Especially in a computing environment we live in, managers and decision makers find the use of models easy and less expensive to understand what is happening and to make better decisions.

There are many different types of models. They are:

1. Narrative
2. Physical
3. Graphical
4. Mathematical

Narrative Models

A *narrative model* is either a written or an oral narrative that represents a topic or subject. In an organization, reports, documents, and conversations concerning a system are all important narratives. Examples include: a salesperson's verbal description of a product's competition to a sales manager and a written report describing the function of a new piece of manufacturing equipment.

Physical Models

The fashion model is an example of *physical models,* as are dolls and model airplanes. Many physical models are computer-designed or constructed. An aerospace engineer may develop a physical model of a shuttle to gain important information about how a large-scale shuttle might perform in space. A marketing department may develop a prototype of a new product.

Graphical Models

A *graphical model* is a pictorial representation of reality. Lines, charts, figures, diagrams, illustrations, and pictures are all types of graphical models. These are used often in developing computer programs. *Flowcharts* show how computer programs are to be developed. A graph that shows budget and financial projections and a break-even chart are good examples of graphic models. The break-even chart depicts the point at which sales revenues and costs are equal, as shown in Figure 10-4.

Figure 10-4.
BREAK-EVEN CHART

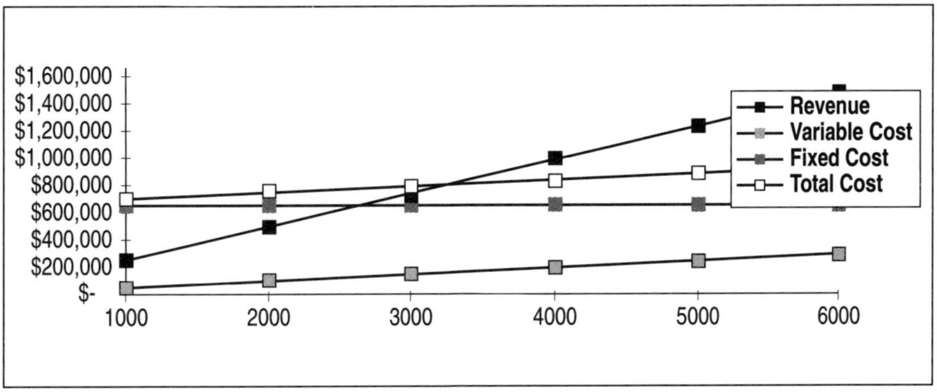

Mathematical Models

A *mathematical model* is a quantitative representation of reality. These models are most popular for decision making in all areas of business. Any mathematical formula or equation is a model that can be used for simulation or what-if analysis. Once they are properly constructed, management can experiment with mathematical models just as physical scientists do a controlled experiment in their laboratory. In a sense, mathematical models are the managers' laboratory. For example, the formula used to compute the break-even point in Figure 10-4 is simply:

$$X_{be} = \frac{FC}{(P - V)}$$

where X_{be} = break-even point, P = price or average revenue per unit, V = unit variable cost, and FC = total fixed costs.

USING THE MODEL BASE TO MAKE DECISIONS

The purpose of the model base in an IS is to give decision makers access to a variety of models and to assist them in the decision-making process. The model base can include *model management software (MMS)* that coordinates the use of models in an IS. Depending on the needs of the decision maker, one or more of these models can be used.

Financial Models

Financial models provide cash flow, internal rate of return, and other investment analysis. Spreadsheet programs such as Excel are often used for this purpose. In addition, more sophisticated financial planning and modeling programs such as *Interactive Financial Planning System (IFPS)* can be employed. Some organizations develop customized financial models to handle the unique situations and problems faced by the organization. However, as spreadsheet packages continue to increase in power, the need for sophisticated financial modeling packages may decrease.

Statistical Models

Statistical models can provide summary statistics, trend projections, hypothesis testing, and more. Many software packages, including *Statistical Packages for Social Scientists (SPSS)*, *Statistical Analysis System (SAS)*, and *MINITAB*, provide outstanding statistical analysis for organizations of all sizes. These statistical programs can calculate means, variances, correlation coefficients, and regression analysis; they can do hypotheses testing, etc. Many packages also have graphics output capability.

Example 1: The Use of SPSS for Windows for Regression Analysis Cypress Consumer Products Corporation wishes to develop a forecasting model for its dryer sales by using multiple regression analysis. The marketing department prepared the following sample data.

Month	Sales of Washers (x_1)	Disposable Income (x_2)	Savings (x_3)	Sales of Dryers (y)
January	$45,000	$16,000	$71,000	$29,000
February	42,000	14,000	70,000	24,000
March	44,000	15,000	72,000	27,000
April	45,000	13,000	71,000	25,000
May	43,000	13,000	75,000	26,000
June	46,000	14,000	74,000	28,000
July	44,000	16,000	76,000	30,000
August	45,000	16,000	69,000	28,000
September	44,000	15,000	74,000	28,000
October	43,000	15,000	73,000	27,000

SPSS for Windows was employed to develop the regression model. Figure 10-5 presents the regression output results using three explanatory variables.

Figure 10-5.
REGRESSION OUTPUT RESULTS

****MULTIPLE REGRESSION****

Listwise Deletion of Missing Data

Equation Number 1   Dependent Variable   SALESDRY

Block Number 1. Method: Enter SALESWAS INCOME SAVINGS

Variable(s) Entered on Step Number

1. SAVINGS
2. SALESWAS
3. INCOME

Multiple R	.99167
R Square	.98340
Adjusted R Square	.97511
Standard Error	.28613

Analysis of Variance

	DF	Sum of Squares	Mean Square
Regression	3	29.10878	9.70293
Residual	6	.49122	.08187

F = 118.51727   Signif F = .0000

———————————— Variables in the Equation ————————————

Variable	B	SE B	Beta	Tolerance	VIF	T
SALESWAS	.596972	.081124	.394097	.964339	1.037	7.359
INCOME	1.176838	.084074	.752425	.957217	1.045	13.998
SAVINGS	.405109	.042234	.507753	.987080	1.013	9.592
(Constant)	−45.796348	4.877651				−9.389

Durbin-Watson Test = 2.09377

Optimization Models

Optimization models refer to techniques for establishing complex sets of mathematical equations and inequalities that represent objectives and constraints. These models are "prescriptive" in that they try to provide the best possible solution to the problem at hand. They include mathematical programming such as linear programming (LP) and goal programming (GP) models.

Linear programming (LP) is a mathematical technique designed to determine an optimal decision (or an optimal plan) chosen from a large number of possible decisions. The optimal decision is the one that meets the specified objective of the company, subject to various restrictions or constraints. It concerns itself with the problem of allocating scarce resources among competing activities in an optimal manner. The optimal decision yields the highest profit, contribution margin (CM), revenue, or lowest cost. A linear programming model consists of two important ingredients:

1. *Objective function:* The company must define the specific objective to be achieved.

2. *Constraints:* Constraints are in the form of restrictions on the availability of resources or meeting minimum requirements. As the name linear programming indicates, both the objective function and constraints must be in linear form.

For example, a firm wishes to find an optimal product mix. The optimal mix is the one that maximizes its total CM within the allowed budget and production capacity. Or the firm wants to determine a least-cost combination of input materials while meeting production requirements, employing production capacities, and using available employees.

The applications of LP are numerous. They include:

1. Selecting least-cost mix of ingredients for manufactured products.

2. Developing an optimal budget.

3. Determining an optimal investment portfolio (or asset allocation).

4. Allocating an advertising budget to a variety of media.

5. Scheduling jobs to machines.

6. Determining a least-cost shipping pattern.

7. Scheduling flights.

8. Blending gasoline optionally.

9. Allocating optimally the workforce.

10. Selecting the best warehouse location to minimize shipping costs.

FORMULATION OF LP

To formulate an LP problem, certain steps are followed:

1. Define what are called the *decision variables* for which you are trying to solve.

2. Express the objective function and constraints in terms of these decision variables. All the expressions must be in linear form.

Example 2: The Optimal Product Mix The JKS Furniture Manufacturing Company produces two products: desks and tables. Both products require time in two processing departments: assembly department and finishing department. Data on the two products are as follows:

PRODUCTS AVAILABLE

Processing	*Desk*	*Table*	*Hours*
Assembly	2	4	100
Finishing	3	2	90
Contribution margin per unit	$25	$40	

The company wants to find the most profitable mix of these two products.

Step 1: Define the decision variables as follows:

A = Number of units of desk to be produced

B = Number of units of table to be produced

Step 2: The objective function to maximize total contribution margin (CM) is expressed as:

Total $CM = 25A + 40B$

Then formulate the constraints as inequalities:

$2A + 4B \leq 100$ (assembly constraint)

$3A + 2B \leq 90$ (finishing constraint)

In addition, implicit in any LP formulation are the constraints that restrict A and B to be nonnegative:

$A, B \geq 0$

Our LP model is:

Maximize: Total $CM = 25A + 40B$

Subject to: $2A + 4B \leq 100$

$\qquad\qquad 3A + 2B \leq 90$

$\qquad\qquad\quad A, B \geq 0$

Use of Computer LP Software   We can use a computer LP software package, such as *LINDO (Linear Interactive and Discrete Optimization)* and *What's Best!*, to quickly solve an LP problem.

Figure 10-6 shows a LINDO output by an LP program for our LP model in Example 2. The printout shows the following optimal solution:

A = 20 units

B = 15 units

CM = $1,100

Shadow prices are:

Assembly capacity = $8.75

Finishing capacity = $2.50

Decision Analysis Models

Decisions are made under certainty or under uncertainty. Decision making under *certainty* means that, for each decision, there is only one event and therefore only one outcome for each action. Decision making under *uncertainty*, which is more common in reality, involves several events for each

Figure 10-6.
LINDO COMPUTER PRINTOUT FOR LP

** INFORMATION ENTERED **

NUMBER OF CONSTRAINTS	2
NUMBER OF VARIABLES	2
NUMBER OF <= CONSTRAINTS	2
NUMBER OF = CONSTRAINTS	0
NUMBER OF >= CONSTRAINTS	0

MAXIMIZATION PROBLEM

25 A   + 40 B

SUBJECT TO

2 A   + 4 B   < = 100
3 A   + 2 B   < = 90

** RESULTS **

VARIABLE	VALUE	ORIGINAL COEFF.	COEFF. SENS.
A	20	25	0
B	15	40	0

Solution:
A = 20, B = 15

CONSTRAINT NUMBER	ORIGINAL RHS	SLACK OR SURPLUS	SHADOW PRICE
1	100	0	8.75

(shadow price of the assembly capacity)

OBJECTIVE FUNCTION VALUE: 1100 = CM

SENSITIVITY ANALYSIS

OBJECTIVE FUNCTION COEFFICIENTS

VARIABLE	LOWER LIMIT	ORIGINAL COEFFICIENT	UPPER LIMIT
A	20	25	60
B	16.67	40	50

RIGHT HAND SIDE

CONSTRAINT NUMBER	LOWER LIMIT	ORIGINAL VALUE	UPPER LIMIT
1	60	100	180
2	50	90	150

action with its probability of occurrence. When decisions are made in a world of uncertainty, it is often helpful to make the computations of: (1) expected value, (2) standard deviation, and (3) coefficient of variation.

Standard Deviation The *standard deviation* measures the tendency of data to be spread out. Cost analysts and managerial accountants can make important inferences from past data with this measure. The standard deviation, denoted with the Greek letter σ (sigma), is defined as follows:

$$\sigma = \sqrt{\frac{\Sigma(x-\bar{x})^2}{n-1}}$$

where x is the mean (arithmetic average).

The standard deviation can be used to measure the variation of such items as the expected contribution margin (CM) or expected variable manufacturing costs. It can also be used to assess the risk associated with investment projects.

Example 3: Quarterly Returns on Stock One and one-half years of quarterly returns are listed below for United Motors stock.

Time Period	x	(x − x̄)	(x − x̄)²
1	10%	0	0
2	15	5	25
3	20	10	100
4	5	−5	25
5	−10	−20	400
6	20	10	100
	60		650

From this table, note that:

$x = 60 / 6 = 10\%$

$$\sigma = \sqrt{\frac{\Sigma(x-\bar{x})^2}{n-1}} = \sqrt{\frac{650}{(6-1)}} = 130 = 11.40\%$$

The United Motors stock has returned on the average 10% over the last six quarters and the variability about its average return was 11.40%. The high standard deviation (11.40%) relative to the average return of 10% indicates that the stock is very risky.

Although statistics such as expected value and standard deviation are essential for choosing the best course of action under uncertainty, the decision problem can best be approached using what is called decision theory. *Decision theory* is a systematic approach to making decisions especially under uncertainty. Decision theory utilizes an organized approach such as a decision matrix (or payoff table).

DECISION MATRIX

A decision matrix is characterized by:

1. The *row* representing a set of alternative courses of action available to the decision maker.

2. The *column* representing the state of nature or conditions that are likely to occur and the decision maker has no control over.

3. The *entries* in the body of the table representing the outcome of the decision, known as payoffs, which may be in the form of costs, revenues, profits, or cash flows. By computing the expected value of each action, we can pick the best one.

Example 4: Daily Demand for a Product   Assume the following probability distribution of daily demand for a product:

Daily demand	0	1	2	3
Probability	.2	.3	.3	.2

Also assume that unit cost = $3, selling price = $5 (i.e., profit on sold unit = $2), and salvage value on unsold units = $2 (i.e., loss on unsold unit = $1). We can stock either 0, 1, 2, or 3 units. The question is, "How many units should be stocked each day?" Assume that units from one day cannot be sold the next day. Then the payoff table can be constructed as follows:

	Demand	State of Nature				Expected value
		0	1	2	3	
Stock (probability)		(.2)	(.3)	(.3)	(.2)	
	0	$0	0	0	0	$0
Actions	1	−1	2	2	2	1.40
	2	−2	1*	4	4	1.90**
	3	−3	0	3	6	1.50

* Profit for (stock 2, demand 1) equals (number of units sold)(profit per unit) − (number of units unsold)(loss per unit) = (1)($5 − 3) − (1)($3 − 2) = $1.

** Expected value for (stock 2) is: −2(.2) + 1(.3) + 4(.3) + 4(.2) = $1.90.

The optimal stock action is the one with the highest expected monetary value, i.e., stock 2 units.

DECISION TREE

Decision tree is another approach used in decision making under uncertainty. It is a pictorial representation of a decision situation.

As in the case of the decision matrix approach discussed, it shows decision alternatives, the states of nature, the probabilities attached to the states of nature, and the conditional benefits and losses. The decision tree approach is most useful in a sequential decision situation.

Example 5: Introduction of a New Product XYZ Corporation wishes to introduce one of two products to the market this year. The probabilities and present values (PV) of projected cash inflows are given below:

Product	Initial Investment	PV of Cash Inflows	Probabilities
A	$225,000		1.00
		$450,000	0.40
		200,000	0.50
		−100,000	0.10
B	80,000		1.00
		320,000	0.20
		100,000	0.60
		−150,000	0.20

A decision tree analyzing the two products is given in Figure 10-7.

Figure 10-7.
DECISION TREE

	Initial Investment (1)	Probability (2)	PV of Cash Inflows (3)	PV of Cash Inflows (2) X (3) = (4)
		0.40	$450,000	$180,000
	$225,000	0.50	$200,000	100,000
Product A		0.10	–$100,000	–10,000
			Expected PV of Cash Inflows	$270,000
Choice A or B				
Product B		0.20	$320,000	$64,000
	$80,000	0.60	$100,000	60,000
		0.20	–$150,000	–30,000
			Expected PV of Cash Inflows	$94,000

For product A:
Expected NPV = expected PV – I = $270,000 – $225,000 = $45,000

For product B:
Expected NPV = $94,000 – $80,000 = $14,000

Based on the expected NPV, choose product A over product B; however, this analysis fails to recognize the risk factor in project analysis.

Graphical Models

Graphical modeling programs are software packages that assist decision makers in designing, developing, and using graphic displays of data and information. Numerous personal computer programs that can perform this type of analysis are available on the market. In addition, sophisticated graphic design and analysis, such as computer-assisted design (CAD), is widely available.

Project Planning and Management Models

Project planning and management models are used to navigate and coordinate large projects, as well as to discover critical paths that could delay or jeopardize an entire project if they are not completed in a timely and cost-effective fashion. Some of these programs, such as *Microsoft Project,* can also determine the best way to speed up a project by effectively using additional resources, including cash, labor, and equipment. Project management allows decision makers to keep tight control over projects of all sizes and types.

Program Evaluation and Review Technique (PERT) is a useful management tool for planning, scheduling, costing, coordinating, and controlling complex projects such as:

- Formulation of a master budget
- Construction of buildings
- Installation of computers
- Scheduling the closing of books
- Assembly of a machine
- Research and development activities

Questions to be answered by PERT include:

- When will the project be finished?
- What is the probability that the project will be completed by any given time?

Simulation Models

The primary use of a simulation model is to respond to what-if questions. These descriptive models can produce large amounts of detailed output because they work by mimicking many parts of the real world. One major weakness is that no automatic searching or optimizing is done by the model. (Any such features must be built on top of the simulation model and must be used as a submodel.) In such cases, the simulation may have to be performed many, many times while a search for the best decision parameters is under way. This can be quite expensive if the simulation is complex.

Two major issues in simulation modeling are how long a simulation run must proceed to achieve *steady state* (typical behavior) and how many different runs must be performed to achieve statistical significance. Inside most simulation models is a pseudorandom number generator. This is a mathematical subroutine that produces numbers that appear to be random. These random numbers are manipulated further to represent parts of the model that are not deterministic. Examples might include the arrival of customers at a ticket counter or the time of failure of an electronic circuit component. These random number generators can be "seeded" with special input parameters to make them produce different streams of random values. Repeating runs with different seed values provides a set of outputs that has a statistical distribution to be analyzed.

Many commercial software packages are available that can be used to build simulation models. Some of these are general-purpose simulation languages that have general but powerful features, such as waiting lines and resource pools, that ease the modeling task. At the other extreme are tailored simulation models (such as oil refinery models) that are already built but afford the user the ability to specify input parameters to describe the precise configuration under study. Between these extremes are simulation languages that are suited for a large class of models, such as networks, that are formalized so that many problems can be represented.

Example 6: Waiting Lines During lunch hour, customers arrive at a fast-food restaurant at a rate of three per minute. They require 1.5 minutes to place an order and pay the bill before going to pick up the food. How many cash register stations are needed to ensure that the number of customers waiting in line does not exceed six and that the waiting time does not occur more than 30% of the time during the lunch-hour rush?

A simulation language such as SLAM II can be used to simulate the sequence of the operation in this problem. The language consists of symbols that can be composed on a computer terminal screen into a diagram like this:

The first circle represents customer arrivals. The second circle represents the queue, or waiting line. The last circle represents departures from the system.

A random normal probability distribution was chosen to model the customer arrivals. The mean, or average, time between arrivals is set at 20 seconds, and the standard deviation is set to 5 seconds. The simulation model was run for 3,600 seconds for each experiment. The number of servers was changed between runs. The service time was represented by an exponential distribution with a mean of 90 seconds.

The simulation software generates random numbers using mathematical formulas and then computes when customers arrive, how long they require service, and so forth. A clock is simulated to keep track of what should happen next. These performance statistics are collected and reported.

Statistics describing the queue are produced automatically by the simulation software package. Table 10-3 shows that five servers are needed to ensure that the queue will be no longer than six persons for 70% of the time. The table serves as a tool for establishing optimal staffing levels for a fast-food restaurant. A thorough analysis would involve making more runs to confirm that these statistics still hold true when different random numbers are used and longer periods of simulation are tried.

Table 10-3.
PERCENT OF TIME THAT QUEUE LENGTH IS NO MORE THAN 6

Number of Servers	0	1	2	3	4	5	6	7
4	14	20	24	27	27	28	31	36
5	46	55	60	63	64	68	73	76

Financial Information Systems and Packages

Finance has been an important functional area for virtually all types of organizations. The finance area monitors cash flow and profitability. Well-conceived financial information systems are capable of providing financial managers with timely information, which is vital to success in today's competitive global economy. History has witnessed the results of poor financial decisions. Banks and savings institutions have gone into bankruptcy because of bad decisions and unfavorable economic conditions. Companies with too much debt and leverage have also gone bankrupt. On the contrary, good financial decisions have resulted in growing and prosperous organizations.

A financial information system provides financial information to all financial managers within an organization. Specifically, the financial IS assists financial managers in performing their responsibilities, which include:

- *Financial analysis and planning:* Analyzing historical and current financial activity and determining the proper amount of funds to employ in the firm; that is, designating the size of the firm and its rate of growth.

- *Investment decisions:* Allocating funds to specific assets. The financial manager makes decisions regarding the mix and type of assets acquired, as well as modifying or replacing assets.

- *Financing and capital structure decisions:* Projecting future financial needs and raising funds on favorable terms; that is, determining the nature of the company's liabilities. For instance, should funds be obtained from short-term or long-term sources?

- *Management of financial resources:* Monitoring and controlling the use of funds over time and managing cash, receivables, and inventory to accomplish higher returns without undue risk.

Figure 10-8 shows the inputs, function-specific subsystems, and outputs of a financial IS.

Figure 10-8.
OVERVIEW OF A FINANCIAL IS

Inputs	Subsystems	Outputs
Strategic goals	Financial forecasting	Financial forecasts
Transaction processing system	Financial data from departments (profit/loss and costing)	Funds management
Internal accounting		Financial budget, planning, and control
External sources	Financial intelligence	

INPUTS TO THE FINANCIAL INFORMATION SYSTEM

Decisions supported by the financial IS require diverse information needs. The sources, both internal and external, are:

1. *Corporate strategic goals and policies:* The strategic plan covers major financial goals and targets. Earnings growth, loan ratios, and expected returns are some of the measures that can be incorporated in the strategic plan. The plan often projects financial needs three to five years down the road. More specific information needs, such as expected financing needs, the return on investment (ROI) for various projects, and desired debt-to-equity ratios, evolve directly from the strategic plan.

2. *The transaction-processing system:* Important financial information is captured by a number of internal accounting systems. One is the *order entry system,* which enters the orders into the accounting system. Another is the *billing system,* which sends bills or invoices to customers. A third is the *accounts receivable system,* which collects the funds. Other key financial information is also collected from almost every transaction processing application: payroll, inventory control, accounts payable, and general ledger. Many financial reports are based on payroll costs, the investment in inventory, total sales over time, the amount of money paid to suppliers, the total amount owed to the company from customers, and detailed accounting data.

3. *External sources:* Information from and about the competition can be critical to financial decision making. Annual reports and financial statements from competitors and general news items and reports can be incorporated into IS reports to provide units of measure or a basis of comparison.

   Government agencies also provide important economic and financial information. Inflation, consumer price indexes, new housing starts, and leading economic indicators can help a company plan for future economic conditions. In addition, important tax laws and financial reporting requirements can be reflected in the financial IS.

FINANCIAL INFORMATION SYSTEM SUBSYSTEMS AND OUTPUTS

Financial decisions are typically based on information generated from the accounting system. Depending on the organization and its needs, the financial IS can include both internal and external systems that assist in acquiring, using, and controlling cash, funds, and other financial resources. The financial subsystems, discussed in the following sections, include financial forecasting, profit/loss and costing, and financial intelligence systems. Each subsystem interacts with the transaction processing system in a specialized, functionally oriented way, and has informational outputs that assist financial managers in making better decisions. The outputs are financial forecasts, management of funds reports, financial budgets, and performance reports such as variance analysis used for control purposes.

Financial Forecasting

Financial forecasting, the process of making predictions on the future growth of products or the organization as a whole, is based on projected business activity. For example, the expected sales of goods and services can be converted into expected revenues and costs. The sales price per unit and production cost factors can be multiplied by the number of units expected to be sold to arrive at a forecasted value for revenues and costs. Fixed costs, such as insurance, rent, and office overhead, are estimated and used to determine expected net profits on a monthly, quarterly, or yearly basis. These estimates are then incorporated into the financial IS. The financial forecasting subsystem relies on input from another functional subsystem (namely, the marketing forecasting system) to determine projected revenues.

Having an estimate of future cash flows can be one of the first steps for sound financial management. Financial managers and executives use this valuable information to project future cash needs. For instance, an organization's managers will know in advance that, in some months, additional cash might be required, while in other months excess cash will have to be invested. Improperly managed cash flow is one of the major causes of business failure and bankruptcy. Financial forecasting can help financial executives avoid cash-flow problems by predicting cash-flow needs.

Profit/Loss and Cost Systems

Two specialized financial functional systems are profit/loss and cost systems. Revenue and expense data for various departments is captured by the transaction processing system (TPS) and becomes a primary internal source of financial information. Many departments within an organization are *profit centers,* which means they track total expenses, revenues, and net profits. An investment division of a large insurance or credit card company is an example of a profit center. Other departments may be *revenue centers,* which are divisions within the company that primarily track sales or revenues, such as a marketing or sales department. Still other departments may be *cost centers,* which are divisions within a company that do not directly generate revenue, such as manufacturing or research and development. These units incur costs with little or no revenues. Data on profit, revenue, and cost centers is gathered (mostly through the TPS but sometimes through other channels), summarized, and reported by the financial IS.

Financial Intelligence

Financial intelligence is responsible for gathering data and information from stockholders, the financial community, and the government. Since the financial function controls the money flow through the firm, information is needed to expedite this flow. The day-to-day flow of money from customers and to vendors is controlled by the internal accounting subsystem. The financial intelligence subsystem is concerned with flows other than those involved in daily operations. This system seeks to identify the best sources of additional capital and the best investment of surplus funds.

Most of the information flows from the firm to the stockholders in the form of annual and quarterly reports. Stockholders have an opportunity to communicate information (complaints, suggestions, ideas, etc.) to the firm through the stockholder relations department. Also, once a year an annual stockholders meeting is held at which stockholders can learn firsthand what the firm is doing. Very often, stockholders use these meetings as an opportunity to communicate directly with top management. Information gathered informally from stockholders is seldom entered into the computerized system, but it is disseminated by verbal communication and written memo to key executives in the firm.

The relationship between the firm and the financial community also receives attention from financial management. There should be a balanced flow of money through the firm, but this equilibrium is not always achieved. At times additional funds are needed or investments of surplus funds are desired. It is the responsibility of the financial intelligence subsystem to compile information on the sources of funds and investment opportunities. An important indirect environmental effect influences this money flow through the firm. The federal government controls the money market of the country through the Federal Reserve System. There are various means of releasing the controls to expedite the money flow and of tightening the controls to reduce the flow.

The firm therefore must gather information from both financial institutions and the Federal Reserve System. This information permits the firm to remain current on national monetary policies and trends and possibly to anticipate future changes. A variety of publications can be used for this purpose. They are prepared by both the financial institutions and the government. Two examples are the *Monthly Economic Letter,* prepared by the City Bank of New York, and the *Federal Reserve Bulletin,* prepared by the Federal Reserve System.

In addition to the need to acquire funds, the firm frequently must invest surplus funds on either a short- or long-term basis. These funds can be invested in a number of different ways—in United States Treasury securities, commercial paper, or certificates of deposit (CDs). Since the terms and rates of return for some of these vary over time, it is necessary to monitor these investment opportunities continually so that the optimum ones can be used when needed.

Gathering information from the financial environment is the responsibility of the financial intelligence subsystem. As with the other two functional intelligence subsystems, the information is usually handled outside the computer system. This subsystem is one area where computer use could improve.

Two major financial dailies are worth mentioning as a great source of financial intelligence: *The Wall Street Journal (WSJ)* and *Investor's Business Daily (IBD).* The *WSJ* contains news of happenings throughout the business community. It provides especially informative descriptions of the economic environment in which businesses operate. Simply by reading a periodical such as the *WSJ,* you can keep up with many of the important environmental influences that shape a manager's decision strategy.

Each day the front page contains a "What's News" section in columns 2 and 3. The "Business and Finance" column offers a distillation of the day's major corporate, industrial, and economic news. The "World-Wide" column captures the day's domestic and international news developments. "Special Reports" appears in column 5 each day. On Monday, "The Outlook" provides an economic overview, analyzing the economy from every conceivable angle. On Tuesday, the "Labor Letter" addresses work news of all kinds—government, management, unions, labor relations, and

personnel. Wednesday brings the "Tax Report," which alerts readers to new
tax trends. The "Business Bulletin" appears each Thursday and tries to spot
emerging trends. The idea is to make information available while managers can still act on it. Finally, every Friday brings the "Washington Wire,"
providing an interpretation of government policy and its possible impact
on business.

Published by William O'Neil & Co., Inc., *Investor's Business Daily* reports
daily coverage of: (1) "The Top Story," the most important news event of the
day; (2) "The Economy"—sophisticated analysis of current economic topics
and government economic reports; (3) "National Issues/Business," a major
national and business issue of our time; (4) "Leaders & Success," profiles of
successful people and companies; (5) "Investor's Corner," coverage of a
wide variety of personal finance topics including investment ideas; and (6)
"Today's News Digest," 35–40 brief but important news items of the day.

Funds Management

Funds management is another critical function of the financial IS.
Companies that do not manage and use funds effectively produce lower
profits or face possible bankruptcy. Outputs from the funds management
subsystem, when combined with other aspects of the financial IS, can locate
serious cash-flow problems and help the company increase returns. Internal
uses of funds include additional inventory, new plants and equipment, the
acquisition of other companies, new computer systems, marketing and
advertising, raw materials, and investments in new products. External uses
of funds are typically investment-related. On occasion, a company might
have excess cash from sales that is placed into an external investment.
Current profitability is only one important factor in predicting corporate
success; current and future cash flows are also essential. In fact, it is possible
for a profitable company to have a cash crisis; for example, a company with
significant credit sales but a very long collection period may show a profit
without actually having the cash from those sales.

Financial managers are responsible for planning how and when cash
will be used and obtained. When planned expenditures require more cash
than planned activities are likely to produce, financial managers must
decide what to do. They may decide to obtain debt or equity funds or to dis-
pose of some fixed assets or a whole business segment. Alternatively, they
may decide to cut back on planned activities by modifying operational

plans, such as ending a special advertising campaign or delaying new acquisitions, or to revise planned payments to financing sources, such as bondholders or stockholders. Whatever is decided, the financial manager's goal is to balance the cash available and the needs for cash over both the short and the long term.

Evaluating the statement of cash flows is essential if you are to appraise accurately an entity's cash flows from operating, investing, and financing activities and its liquidity and solvency positions. Inadequacy in cash flow has possible serious implications, including declining profitability, greater financial risk, and even possible bankruptcy.

Financial management also involves decisions relating to sources of financing for, and use of financial resources within, an organization. Virtually all activities and decisions within an organization are reflected in financial information. One useful application of a real-time system of financial information involves inquiry processing. An online financial information system makes possible immediate responses to inquiries concerning comparisons of current expenditure with budgeted expenditure, up-to-date calculations of profit center contribution, or information required for audit investigation.

For example, the fund management subsystem can prepare a report showing cash flow for the next twelve-month period. The report can be printed by a mathematical model that uses the sales forecast plus expense projections as the basis for the calculation.

Another application of real-time systems to financial management with great potential is the area of computer models for financial planning, which is discussed later.

Financial Budgeting, Planning, and Control

More and more companies are developing computer-based models for financial planning and budgeting, using powerful, yet easy-to-use, financial modeling languages such as *Up Your Cash Flow* and *Comshare's Interactive Financial Planning System (IFPS)* (discussed and illustrated in a later chapter). The models help not only to build a budget for profit planning but answer a variety of what-if scenarios. The resultant calculations provide a basis for choice among alternatives under conditions of uncertainty. Furthermore, budget modeling can also be accomplished using spreadsheet programs such as Microsoft's Excel.

In this section we illustrate the use of spreadsheet software such as *Excel* and standalone packages such as *Up Your Cash Flow* to develop a financial model. For illustrative purposes, we will present:

1. Three examples of projecting an income statement.
2. Forecasting financial distress with *Z*-score.
3. Forecasting external financing needs—the percent-of-sales method.

Example 7: Income Statement
Given:

Sales for first month = $60,000

Cost of sales = 42% of sales, all variable

Operating expenses = $10,000 fixed plus 5% of sales

Taxes = 30% of net income

Sales increase by 5% each month

Based on this information:

1. Figure 10-9 presents a spreadsheet for the contribution income statement for the next 12 months and in total.
2. Figure 10-10 shows the same spreadsheet, assuming that sales increase by 10% and operating expenses = $10,000 plus 10% of sales. This is an example of what-if scenarios.

Example 8: Projection of Net Income
Delta Gamma Company wishes to prepare a three-year projection of net income using the following information:

1. 2000 base year amounts are as follows:

Sales revenues	$4,500,000
Cost of sales	2,900,000
Selling and administrative expenses	800,000
Net income before taxes	800,000

Figure 10-9.
CONTRIBUTION INCOME STATEMENT

	1	2	3	4	5	6	7	8	9	10	11	12	Total	Percent
Sales	$60,000	$63,000	$66,150	$69,458	$72,930	$76,577	$80,406	$84,426	$88,647	$93,080	$97,734	$102,620	$955,028	100%
Less: VC														
Cost of sales	$25,200	$26,460	$27,783	$29,172	$30,631	$32,162	$33,770	$35,459	$37,232	$39,093	$41,048	$43,101	$401,112	42%
Operating ex.	$3,000	$3,150	$3,308	$3,473	$3,647	$3,829	$4,020	$4,221	$4,432	$4,654	$4,887	$5,131	$47,751	5%
CM	$31,800	$33,390	$35,060	$36,812	$38,653	$40,586	$42,615	$44,746	$46,983	$49,332	$51,799	$54,389	$506,165	53%
Less: FC														
Op. expenses	$10,000	$10,000	$10,000	$10,000	$10,000	$10,000	$10,000	$10,000	$10,000	$10,000	$10,000	$10,000	$120,000	13%
Net income	$21,800	$23,390	$25,060	$26,812	$28,653	$30,586	$32,615	$34,746	$36,983	$39,332	$41,799	$44,389	$386,165	40%
Less: Tax	$6,540	$7,017	$7,518	$8,044	$8,596	$9,176	$9,785	$10,424	$11,095	$11,800	$12,540	$13,317	$115,849	12%
NI after tax	$15,260	$16,373	$17,542	$18,769	$20,057	$21,410	$22,831	$24,322	$25,888	$27,533	$29,259	$31,072	$270,315	28%

Figure 10-10.
CONTRIBUTION INCOME STATEMENT—WHAT-IF SCENARIOS

	1	2	3	4	5	6	7	8	9	10	11	12	Total	Percent
Sales	$60,000	$66,000	$72,680	$79,860	$87,846	$96,631	$106,294	$116,923	$128,615	$141,477	$155,625	$171,187	$1,283,057	100%
Less: VC														
Cost of sales	$25,200	$27,720	$30,492	$33,541	$36,895	$40,585	$44,643	$49,108	$54,018	$59,420	$65,362	$71,899	$538,884	42%
Operating ex.	$6,000	$6,600	$7,260	$7,986	$8,785	$9,663	$10,629	$11,692	$12,862	$14,148	$15,562	$17,119	$64,153	5%
CM	$28,800	$31,680	$34,848	$38,333	$42,166	$46,383	$51,021	$56,123	$61,735	$67,909	$74,700	$82,170	$615,867	48%
Less: FC														
Op. expenses	$10,000	$10,000	$10,000	$10,000	$10,000	$10,000	$10,000	$10,000	$10,000	$10,000	$10,000	$10,000	$120,000	9%
Net income	$18,800	$21,680	$24,848	$28,333	$32,166	$36,383	$41,021	$46,123	$51,735	$57,909	$64,700	$72,170	$495,867	39%
Less: Tax	$5,640	$6,504	$7,454	$8,500	$9,650	$10,915	$12,306	$13,837	$15,521	$17,373	$19,410	$21,651	$148,760	12%
NI after tax	$13,160	$15,176	$17,394	$19,833	$22,516	$25,468	$28,715	$32,286	$36,215	$40,536	$45,290	$50,519	$347,107	27%

2. Use the following assumptions:

    Sales revenues increase by 6% in 2001, 7% in 2002, and 8% in 2003.

    Cost of sales increase by 5% each year.

    Selling and administrative expenses increase only 1% in 2001 and will remain at the 2001 level thereafter.

    The income tax rate = 46%.

Figure 10-11 presents a spreadsheet for the income statement for the next three years.

Figure 10-11.
INCOME STATEMENT—DELTA GAMMA COMPANY
THREE-YEAR INCOME PROJECTIONS (2000–2003)

	2000	2001	2002	2003
Sales	$4,500,000	$4,770,000	$5,103,900	$5,512,212
Cost of sales	$2,900,000	$3,045,000	$3,197,250	$3,357,113
	$1,600,000	$1,725,000	$1,906,650	$2,155,100
Selling and administrative expense	$800,000	$808,000	$808,000	$808,000
Earnings before tax	$800,000	$917,000	$1,098,650	$1,347,100
Tax	$368,000	$421,820	$505,379	$619,666
Earnings after tax	$432,000	$495,180	$593,271	$727,434

Example 9: Developing a Budget Based on specific assumptions (see Figure 10-12), develop a budget using *Up Your Cash Flow* (Figure 10-13).

A budget is a tool for both planning and control. At the beginning of the period, the budget is a plan or standard; at the end of the period, it serves as a control device to help management measure its performance against the plan so that future performance may be improved. Each month, each manager with budget responsibilities receives a report showing actual expenditures compared with the budget figures and the appropriate variances, so that unusual variances can be addressed and properly rewarded or penalized.

In addition to the budget, the financial control system generates a number of *performance measures* or *ratios* that enable managers on all levels to compare their performance with benchmarks such as standards or targets. There

Figure 10-12.
BUDGET ASSUMPTIONS

Category	Assumptions
Sales:	alternative 1 from book Up Your Cash Flow
Cost of goods sold:	Use 45% of sales
Advertising:	59% of sales
Automobile:	Company has 4 autos @ 1500 each 4 x 1500 = -6000 ÷ 12 1500 per month
Bad debts:	Maintain @ 29% of sales —— I hope
Business promotion:	Prior year was $65,000. 10% increase equals $71,500 ÷ 12
Collection costs:	Use 1000 per month
Continuing education:	$10,000 for year = ÷ 12
Depreciation:	$84,000 for year—Use 7000 per month
Donations:	$10,000 for year = ÷ 12
Insurance-general:	agent said $24,000, use 2000 per month
Insurance-group:	15 employees @ 1500 ea. = 22,500 ÷ 12 = month #
Insurance-life:	600 per month
Interest:	expect to borrow 250 m @ 15% = 37,500 ÷ 12 = 3125 per month + other borrowings
Office supplies:	2% of sales—and keep it there please!
Rent:	4000 per month
Repairs and maintenance:	Use 400 per month
Salaries:	Schedule the payroll per month
Taxes and license:	Prior year was 1.5% of sales—use same this year
Taxes, payroll:	20% of monthly payroll
Telephone-utilities:	$29,000 last year. Use 33,000 ÷ 12 Travel—use $1000 per month.

Figure 10-13. Budget

	Jan.	Feb.	Mar.	Apr.	May	Jun.	Jul.	Aug.	Sep.	Oct.	Nov.	Dec.	Total
Sales	$129,030	$129,030	$129,030	$129,030	$192,610	$192,610	$162,690	$129,030	$192,610	$129,030	$162,690	$192,610	$1,870,000
Cost of Sales @ 45%	58,063	58,063	58,063	58,063	86,675	86,675	73,211	58,063	86,675	58,063	73,211	86,675	841,500
Gross profit	70,967	70,967	70,967	70,967	105,935	105,935	89,479	70,967	105,935	70,967	89,479	105,935	1,028,500
Advertising @ 5%	6,450	6,450	6,450	6,450	9,600	9,600	8,100	6,450	9,600	6,450	8,100	10,050	93,750
Automobile	500	500	500	500	500	500	500	500	500	500	500	500	6,000
Bad debts @ 2%	2,580	2,580	2,580	2,580	3,840	3,840	3,240	2,580	3,840	2,580	3,240	3,920	37,400
Business promotions	5,958	5,958	5,958	5,958	5,958	5,958	5,958	5,958	5,958	5,958	5,958	5,962	71,500
Collection costs	1,000	1,000	1,000	1,000	1,000	1,000	1,000	1,000	1,000	1,000	1,000	1,000	12,000
Continuing education	1,000	1,000	1,000	1,000	1,000	1,000	1,000	1,000	1,000	1,000	1,000	1,000	12,000
Depreciation	7,000	7,000	7,000	7,000	7,000	7,000	7,000	7,000	7,000	7,000	7,000	7,000	84,000
Donations	833	833	833	833	833	833	833	833	833	833	833	833	10,000
Dues & subscriptions	833	833	833	833	833	833	833	833	833	833	833	833	10,000
Insurance—general	2,000	2,000	2,000	2,000	2,000	2,000	2,000	2,000	2,000	2,000	2,000	2,000	24,000
Insurance—group	1,875	1,875	1,875	1,875	1,875	1,875	1,875	1,875	1,875	1,875	1,875	1,875	22,500
Insurance—life	600	600	600	600	600	600	600	600	600	600	600	600	7,200
Interest	3,125	3,125	3,125	3,125	4,375	4,375	4,375	4,450	4,450	4,450	4,450	4,450	47,875
Legal & accounting	1,000	1,000	1,000	1,000	1,000	1,000	1,000	1,000	1,000	1,000	1,000	1,000	12,000
Office supplies @ 2%	2,580	2,580	2,580	2,580	3,840	3,840	3,240	2,580	3,840	2,580	3,240	3,920	37,400
Rent	4,000	4,000	4,000	4,000	4,000	4,000	4,000	4,000	4,000	4,000	4,000	4,000	8,000
Repairs	400	400	400	400	400	400	400	400	400	400	400	400	4,800
Salaries	21,000	21,000	21,000	21,000	21,000	21,000	24,833	24,833	24,833	24,833	24,833	24,835	275,000
Taxes & license @ 1.5%	1,935	1,935	1,935	1,935	2,880	2,880	2,430	1,935	2,880	1,935	2,430	2,890	28,000
Taxes, payroll	4,200	4,200	4,200	4,200	4,200	4,200	4,966	4,966	4,966	4,966	4,966	4,970	55,000
Telephone—utilities	2,750	2,750	2,750	2,750	2,750	2,750	2,750	2,750	2,750	2,750	2,750	2,750	33,000
Travel	1,000	1,000	1,000	1,000	1,000	1,000	1,000	1,000	1,000	1,000	1,000	1,000	12,000
Profit	$(1,652)	$(1,652)	$(1,652)	$(1,652)	$25,451	$25,451	$7,546	$(7,576)	$20,777	$(7,576)	$7,471	$20,139	$85,075

are quite a few financial or operational ratios. A couple of ratios are given as an example. One popular ratio is the *current ratio,* which measures a firm's ability to pay short-term bills.

$$\text{Current ratio} = \frac{\text{Current assets}}{\text{Current liabilities}}$$

Another popular ratio is the *debt ratio,* which reveals the amount of money a company owes to its creditors. Excessive debt means greater risk to the company. The debt ratio is:

$$\text{Debt ratio} = \frac{\text{Total liabilities}}{\text{Total assets}}$$

FORECASTING FINANCIAL DISTRESS WITH Z-SCORE

There has recently been an increasing number of bankruptcies. Will your company go bankrupt? Will your major customers or suppliers go bankrupt? What warning signs exist and what can be done to avoid corporate failure?

How to Use Prediction Models

Prediction models can help in a number of ways: In merger analysis, it can help to identify potential problems with a merger candidate. Bankers and other business concerns can use it to determine whether to give a new loan (credit) or extend the old one. Investors can use it to screen out stocks of companies that are risky. Internal auditors can use such a model to assess the financial health of the company. Those investing in or extending credit to a company may sue for losses incurred. The model can help as evidence in a lawsuit.

Financial managers, investment bankers, financial analysts, security analysts, and auditors use early warning systems to detect the likelihood of bankruptcy. But their system is primarily based on financial ratios of one type or the other as an indication of a company's financial strength. Each ratio (or set of ratios) is examined independently of others. Plus, it is up to the professional judgment of a financial analyst to decide what the ratios are really telling.

To overcome the shortcomings of financial ratio analysis, it is necessary to combine mutually exclusive ratios into a group to develop a meaningful predictive model. Regression analysis and multiple discriminant analysis (MDA) are two statistical techniques that have been used thus far.

Z-Score Model

This section describes the Z-score predictive model that uses a combination of several financial ratios to predict the likelihood of future bankruptcy. Edward Altman developed a bankruptcy prediction model that produces a Z-score as follows:

$$Z = 1.2 \times X1 + 1.4 \times X2 + 3.3 \times X3 + 0.6 \times X4 + 0.999 \times X5$$

where

X1 = Working capital/Total assets

X2 = Retained earnings/Total assets

X3 = Earnings before interest and taxes (EBIT)/Total assets

X4 = Market value of equity/Book value of debt (Net worth for privately held firms)

X5 = Sales/Total assets

Altman established the following guideline for classifying firms:

Z-Score	Probability of Failure
1.8 or less	Very high
3.0 or higher	Unlikely
1.81–2.99	Not sure

The Z-score is known to be about 90% accurate in forecasting business failure one year in the future and about 80% accurate in forecasting it two years in the future. There are more updated versions of Altman's model.

Example 10: Assessing Financial Stability Navistar International (formerly International Harvester) continues to struggle in the heavy and medium truck industry, and is selected for illustrative purposes. Figure 10-14 shows the 19-year financial history and the Z-scores of Navistar. Figure 10-15 presents the corresponding graph.

Figure 10-14.
FINANCIAL HISTORY AND THE Z-SCORES

NAVISTAR INTERNATIONAL—NAV (NYSE)   Z-SCORE—PREDICTION OF FINANCIAL DISTRESS

| Year | Balance Sheet | | | | | | Income Statement | | Stock Data | Calculations | | | | | Z-Score | Misc. Graph Value | | |
	Current Assets (CA)	Total Assets (TA)	Current Liability (CL)	Total Liability (TL)	Retained Earnings (RE)	Working Capital (WC)	SALES	EBIT	Market Value or Net worth (MKT-NW)	WC/TA (X1)	RE/TA (X2)	EBIT/TA (X3)	MKT-NW/TL (X4)	Sales/TA (X5)		Top Gray	Bottom Gray	Year
1979	3266	5247	1873	3048	1505	1393	8426	719	1122	0.2655	0.2868	0.1370	0.3681	1.6059	3.00	2.99	1.81	1979
1980	3427	5843	2433	3947	1024	994	6000	-402	1147	0.1701	0.1753	-0.0688	0.2906	1.0269	1.42	2.99	1.81	1980
1981	2672	5346	1808	3864	600	864	7018	-16	376	0.1616	0.1122	-0.0030	0.0973	1.3128	1.71	2.99	1.81	1981
1982	1656	3699	1135	3665	-1078	521	4322	-1274	151	0.1408	-0.2914	-0.3444	0.0412	1.1684	-0.18	2.99	1.81	1982
1983	1388	3362	1367	3119	-1487	21	3600	-231	835	0.0062	-0.4423	-0.0687	0.2677	1.0708	0.39	2.99	1.81	1983
1984	1412	3249	1257	2947	-1537	155	4861	120	575	0.0477	-0.4731	0.0369	0.1951	1.4962	1.13	2.99	1.81	1984
1985	1101	2406	988	2364	-1894	113	3508	247	570	0.0470	-0.7872	0.1027	0.2411	1.4580	0.89	2.99	1.81	1985
1986	698	1925	797	1809	-1889	-99	3357	163	441	-0.0514	-0.9813	0.0847	0.2438	1.7439	0.73	2.99	1.81	1986
1987	785	1902	836	1259	-1743	-51	3530	219	1011	-0.0268	-0.9164	0.1151	0.8030	1.8559	1.40	2.99	1.81	1987
1988	1280	4037	1126	1580	150	154	4082	451	1016	0.0381	0.0372	0.1117	0.6430	1.0111	1.86	2.99	1.82	1988
1989	986	3609	761	1257	175	225	4241	303	1269	0.0623	0.0485	0.0840	1.0095	1.1751	2.20	2.99	1.81	1989
1990	2663	3795	1579	2980	81	1084	3854	111	563	0.2856	0.0213	0.0292	0.1889	1.0155	1.60	2.99	1.81	1990
1991	2286	3443	1145	2866	332	1141	3259	232	667	0.3314	0.0964	0.0674	0.2326	0.9466	1.84	2.99	1.81	1991
1992	2472	3627	1152	3289	93	1320	3875	-145	572	0.3639	0.0256	-0.0400	0.1738	1.0684	1.51	2.99	1.81	1992
1993	2672	5060	1338	4285	-1588	1334	4696	-441	1765	0.2636	-0.3138	-0.0872	0.4119	0.9281	0.76	2.99	1.81	1993
1994	2870	5056	1810	4239	-1538	1060	5337	158	1469	0.2097	-0.3042	0.0313	0.3466	1.0556	1.19	2.99	1.81	1994
1995	3310	5566	1111	4696	-1478	2199	6342	262	966	0.3951	-0.2655	0.0471	0.2057	1.1394	1.52	2.99	1.81	1995
1996	2999	5326	820	4410	-1431	2179	5754	105	738	0.4091	-0.2687	0.0197	0.1673	1.0804	1.36	2.99	1.81	1996
1997	3203	5516	1267	4496	-1301	1936	6371	242	1374	0.3510	-0.2359	0.0439	0.3055	1.1550	1.57	2.99	1.81	1997

Note: (1) To calculate Z-score for private firms, enter Net Worth in the MKT-NW column. (For public-held companies, enter Market Value of Equity).

(2) EBIT = Earnings before interest and taxes

Figure 10-15.
Z-SCORE GRAPH

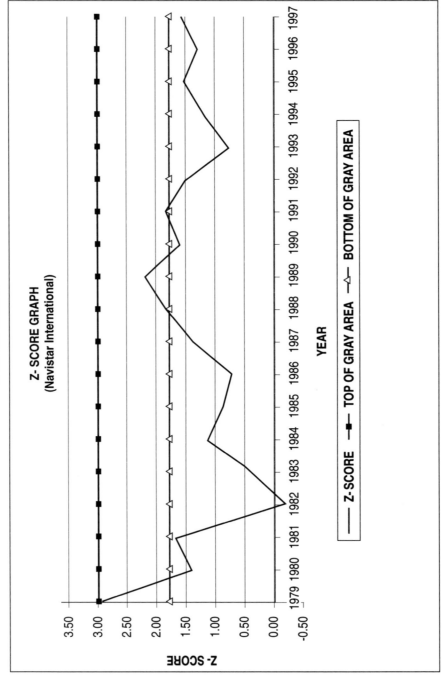

Z- SCORE GRAPH
(Navistar International)

The graph shows that Navistar International performed at the edge of the ignorance zone ("unsure area") for the year 1979. Since 1980, though, the company started signaling a sign of failure. However, by selling stock and assets, the firm managed to survive. Since 1983, the company showed an improvement in its Z-scores, although it continually scored in the danger zone. Note that the 1994 Z-score of 1.19 is in the high probability range of <1.81. However, the 1995–1997 increase in Z-scores over 1993 and 1994 may indicate that Navistar is improving its financial position and becoming a more viable business.

More Applications of the Z-Score

Various groups of business people can take advantage of this tool for their own purposes, such as for:

1. *Merger analysis:* The Z-score can help identify potential problems with a merger candidate.

2. *Loan credit analysis:* Bankers and lenders can use it to determine if they should extend a loan. Other creditors such as vendors have used it to determine whether to extend credit.

3. *Investment analysis:* The Z-score model can help an investor in selecting stocks of potentially troubled companies.

4. *Auditing analysis:* Internal auditors are able to use this technique to assess whether the company will continue as a going concern.

5. *Legal analysis:* Those investing or giving credit to the company may sue for losses incurred. The Z-score can help in their defense.

Words of Caution

The Z-score offers an excellent measure for predicting a firm's insolvency, but, like any other tool, it must be used with care and skill. The Z-score of a firm should be looked on not for just one or two years but for a number of years. Also, it should not be used as a sole basis of evaluation.

The Z-score can be used to compare the economic health of different firms. Here again extreme care should be exercised. Firms to be compared must belong to the same market. Also, Z-scores of the same periods are to be compared. For further reference, see Charles W. Kyd, "Forecasting Bankruptcy with Z Scores," *Lotus*, September 1985, pp. 43–47 and Jae K. Shim, "Bankruptcy Prediction: Do It Yourself," *Journal of Business Forecasting*, Winter 1992.

FORECASTING EXTERNAL FINANCING NEEDS— THE PERCENT-OF-SALES METHOD

Percentage of sales is the most widely used method for projecting the company's financing needs. Financial officers need to determine the next year's fund requirements, a portion of which has to be raised externally. Thus they have a head start on arranging a least-cost financing plan.

This method involves estimating the various expenses, assets, and liabilities for a future period as a percent of the sales forecast and then using these percentages, together with the projected sales, to construct pro forma balance sheets.

Basically, forecasts of future sales and their related expenses provide the firm with the information needed to project its future needs for financing.

The basic steps in projecting financing needs are:

1. Project the firm's sales. The sales forecast is the initial most important step. Most other forecasts (budgets) follow the sales forecast.

2. Project additional variables, such as expenses.

3. Estimate the level of investment in current and fixed assets that are required to support the projected sales.

4. Calculate the firm's financing needs.

Example 11: Developing a Pro Forma Balance Sheet and Determining the Amount of External Financing Needed   Assume that sales for 20X1 = $20, projected sales for 20X2 = $24, net income = 5% of sales, and the dividend payout ratio = 40%.

The steps for the computations are outlined as follows:

Step 1. Express the balance sheet items that vary directly with sales as a percentage of sales. Any item such as long-term debt that does not vary directly with sales is designated "n.a." (not applicable).

Step 2. Multiply these percentages by the 20X2 projected sales = $2.4, to obtain the projected amounts shown in the last column.

Step 3. Simply insert figures for long-term debt, common stock, and paid-in-capital from the 20X1 balance sheet.

Step 4. Compute 20X2 retained earnings as shown in note b.

Step 5. Sum the asset accounts, obtaining a total projected assets of $7.2, and also add the projected liabilities and equity to obtain $7.12, the total financing provided. Since liabilities and equity must total $7.2, but only $7.12 is projected, we have a shortfall of $0.08 "external financing needed."

Figure 10-16 presents the projected balance sheet.

Figure 10-16.
PROJECTED BALANCE SHEET (IN MILLIONS OF DOLLARS)

	Present (20X1)	*% of Sales* (20X1 Sales = $20)	*Projected* (20X2 Sales = $24)	
Assets				
Current assets	2	10	2.4	
Fixed assets	4	20	4.8	
Total assets	6		7.2	
Liabilities and Stockholders' Equity				
Current liabilities	2	10	2.4	
Long-term debt	2.5	n.a.	2.5	
Total liabilities	4.5		4.9	
Common stock	0.1	n.a.	0.1	
Paid-in-Capital	0.2	n.a.	0.2	
Retained earnings	1.2		1.92 [a]	
Total equity	1.5		2.22	
Total liabilities and stockholders' equity	6		7.12	Total financing provided
			0.08 [b]	External financing needed
			7.2	Total

[a] 20X2 retained earnings = 20X1 retained earnings + projected net income − cash dividends paid
= $1.2 + 5% ($24) − 40% [5%($24)]
= $1.2 + $1.2 − $0.48 = $2.4 − $0.48 = $1.92

[b] External financing needed = projected total assets − (projected total liabilities + projected equity)
= $7.2 − ($4.9 + $2.22) = $7.2 − $7.12 = $0.08

The major advantage of the percent-of-sales method of financial forecasting is that it is simple and inexpensive to use. To obtain a more precise projection of the firm's future financing needs, however, the preparation of a cash budget is required. One important assumption behind the use of the method is that the firm is operating at full capacity. This means that the company does not have sufficient productive capacity to absorb a projected increase in sales and thus requires additional investment in assets.

FINANCIAL MODELING LANGUAGES

Remember that financial models are essentially used to generate pro forma financial statements and financial ratios. These are the basic tools for budgeting and profit planning. Also, the financial model is a technique for risk analysis and what-if experiments. The financial model is also needed for day-to-day operational and tactical decisions for immediate planning problems. For these purposes, the use of computers is essential. In recent years, spreadsheet software and computer-based financial modeling software have been developed and utilized for budgeting and planning in an effort to speed up the budgeting process and allow CFOs to investigate the effects of changes in budget assumptions and scenarios.

These languages do not require any knowledge of computer programming. They are all English-like languages. Among the well-known system packages are IFPS, SIMPLAN, EXPRESS, Encore! Plus, Venture, Cashe™, and MicroFCS.

FINANCIAL ANALYSIS WITH SPREADSHEETS

Companies—whether large or small, profit-oriented or nonprofit, employing one hundred or ten thousand, etc.—live or die by the extent of their powers in financial planning. There are other important contributing factors to success in business, but nothing can send a company into the abyss of Chapter 11 bankruptcy faster than a few major ill-fated financial decisions.

Financial analysis is employed in an effort to be more scientific about coming to a good financial decision. Questions must be asked about the company and accurate answers found to gain insight that will assist in determining the most prudent use of precious resources for some period in the future. The questions stem from numerous aspects of the business. Some are straightforward and easily answered: Are profits greater this year than last? Other questions are not so easily answered: Will an increase in advertising expenditures lead to increased profits? Would a price cut be more appropriate? Would some combination of the two be best?

Spreadsheet programs are ideally suited for performing financial analyses because they possess the capacity to hold and process complex formulas and functions while making modification and manipulation of one or more variables or functions an easy operation. With a microcomputer, software, and some training and practice, you can master rather complex financial analysis techniques.

OTHER FINANCIAL MANAGEMENT SOFTWARE

More and more financial software—client-server and Windows-based—are clouding the market. A few popular ones are summarized in the following sections.

Commander FDC and Commander Budget

Comshare's integrated suite of Windows-based, client-server financial and managerial applications for statutory consolidations, enterprise budgeting, and management reporting are built around a central financial database and share the same core technology. Commander FDC and Commander Budget provide specialized application interfaces to the financial database, which holds historic, actual, budget, and forecast data. Commander FDC is designed for use by finance professionals involved in the monthly closing process. Commander Budget is designed to meet the needs of all business professionals involved in the budgeting process, from cost center managers to budget administrators. With either application, anyone familiar with Excel or Lotus 1-2-3 can easily do reporting and data entry. Additional modules for what-if analysis, exception detection, and executive reporting from the financial database round out Comshare's financial management applications.

Cashe™

Cashe™, by Business Matters Incorporated, is a new approach to financial forecasting and business modeling for people who make decisions that affect the overall financial position of their organizations. Cashe™ gives you a disciplined way of capturing and modifying your business assumptions so that financial forecasts can be reviewed, updated, and compared easily. Cashe™'s power comes from its built-in content and knowledge, which allow you to forecast your business's financial performance accurately without having to worry about formulas or accounting rules. Working on the business information you provide, Cashe™'s self-adjusting model ensures accuracy by automatically reflecting any changes you make throughout the entire model. Cashe™ is not intended to replace your spreadsheet but to work with it, allowing you to import and export all your financial models. The result is that with Cashe™ you forecast more accurately, more comprehensively, and more often.

QL Financials

QL Financials, by Microcompass Systems, Ltd., delivers true client-server financial management with many advanced features in a full Windows environment. It is a fully integrated suite of functionally rich modules, including general ledger, budget management, cash book/treasury management, accounts payable, accounts receivable, sales ordering/invoicing, fixed assets, requisitioning/purchase ordering, inventory management, and system integration. QL is written in Uniface Version 6, the world's leading 4GL development environment, and has been designed to meet the needs of both public and private sectors at departmental and corporate levels. Written to full TICKIT standards, QL offers multicurrency and multilingual functionality in a complete desktop environment.

POPULAR BUDGETING AND PLANNING SOFTWARE

In addition to specialized budgeting and financial modeling software discussed previously, a variety of programs are designed specifically for budgeting and *decision support systems (DSS)* software. Some are stand-alone packages, others are templates, and still others are spreadsheet add-ins.

Budget Express

Budget Express, an add-in, "understands" the structure of financial worksheets and concepts such as months, quarters, years, totals, and subtotals, speeding up budget and forecast preparation. The program creates column headers for months, automatically totals columns and rows, and calculates quarterly and yearly summaries. And for sophisticated what-if analyses, just specify the goal and Budget Express displays the current and target values as the user makes changes.

ProPlans

ProPlans, a template, creates financial plans automatically and accurately—and slices months from the annual planning and reporting process. The user just enters your forecast data and assumptions into easy-to-follow, comprehensive data-entry screens, and ProPlans automatically creates the detailed financials for the next year: income statement, balance sheet, cash flow statement, and ratio reports.

Profit Planner

This program provides titles and amounts for revenues, cost of sales, expenses, assets, liabilities, and equity in a ready-to-use 1-2-3 template. Financial tables are automatically generated on screen. It presents results in 13 different table formats, including a pro forma earnings statement, balance sheet, and cash flow statement. Profit Planner even compares earnings statement, balance sheet, and ratios against industry averages.

Up Your Cash Flow

The stand-alone program generates cash flow and profit-and-loss forecasts, detailed sales by product/product line and payroll by employee forecasts, monthly balance sheets, bar graphs, ratio and breakeven analyses, and more.

Cash Collector

Cash Collector, a stand-alone, assists in reviewing and aging receivables: Nothing "falls through the cracks." When collection action is required, the user clicks through menu-driven screens to automatically generate letters and other professionally written collection documents (all included) that are proven to pull in the payments.

Cash Flow Analysis

This stand-alone software provides projections of cash inflow and cash outflow. The user inputs data into eight categories: sales, cost of sales, general and administrative expense, long-term debt, other cash receipts, inventory buildup/reduction, capital expenditures (acquisition of long-term assets such as store furniture), and income tax. The program allows changes in assumptions and scenarios, and provides a complete array of reports.

Quicken

Quicken is a stand-alone program that is fast, easy to use, and inexpensive. This accounting and budgeting program helps manage the business, particularly cash flow. Users record bills as postdated transactions when they arrive; the program's Billminder feature automatically reminds users when bills are due. Then, it can print checks for due bills with a few keystrokes. Similarly, users can record invoices and track aged receivables. Together, these features help you maximize cash on hand.

CapPLANS

This template evaluates profitability based on net preset value (NPV), internal rate of return (IRR), and payout period. Choose among five depreciation methods, including Modified Accelerated Cost Recovery System (MACRS), and run up to four sensitivity analyses. Project profitability can be extended to over a 15-year horizon. In addition to a complete report of the analysis, CapPLANS generates a concise, four-page executive summary. Users can add ready-made graphs to illustrate profitability clearly.

Project Evaluation Toolkit

Project Evaluation Tookit, a template, calculates the dollar value of a project based on six valuation methods, including discounted cash flow and affect on the corporate balance sheet. Users can assess intangibles such as impact on corporate strategy, investors, or labor relations. Scenario planning shows the effects of changing start dates, sales forecasts, and other critical variables.

@Risk

How will a new competitor affect market share? @RISK, an add-in, calculates the likelihood of changes and events that affect the bottom line. First use @RISK's familiar @ functions to define the risk in the worksheet.

Then let @RISK run thousands of what-if tests using Monte Carlo simulation. The result is a clear, colorful graph that shows the likelihood of every possible bottom-line value. @RISK lets users view the model's results from hundreds or even thousands of what-if scenarios. The software furnishes answers to questions like, "What's the chance of a negative result?" "What's the chance of a result over one million?" At a glance users know whether the risk is acceptable, or if they need to make a contingency plan.

CFO Spreadsheet Applications

These ready-to-use spreadsheet templates offer easy ways to make many financial decisions. They are divided into four modules: cash management, tax strategies, capital budgeting, and advanced topics.

What's Best!

If you have limited resources—for example, people, inventory, materials, time, or cash—then What's Best! shows how to allocate these resources to maximize or minimize a given objective, such as profit or cost. What's Best! uses proven methods—linear programming (LP), integer programming, and nonlinear programming—to help the firm achieve its goals. This product can solve a variety of business problems that cut across every industry at every level of decision making. This stand-alone program also has sensitivity analysis, extensive error handling, full solution report capabilities, and user interface via Excel or Lotus.

Inventory Analyst

Inventory Analyst, a template, tells precisely how much inventory to order and when to order it. Users can choose from four ordering methods: economic order quantity (EOQ), fixed order quantity, fixed months requirements, and level load by work days. Inventory Analyst ensures enough stock to get through an ordering period. Users load up to 48 months' worth of inventory history, and Inventory Analyst makes the forecast based on one of three forecasting methods: time series, exponential smoothing, or moving averages. It explains which method is best for the firm. Inventory Analyst also adjusts the forecast for seasonality.

PrecisionTree

PrecisionTree, an Excel add-in, helps create decision trees and identify the best course of action using proven decision-analysis techniques. Users clarify options and rewards, describe uncertainty quantitatively, weigh multiple objectives simultaneously, and define their attitudes about risk in the spreadsheet. PrecisionTree can also combine decision analysis with Monte Carlo simulation for risk-analysis capabilities.

SIMUL8

SIMUL8 is a full-features, stand-alone simulation package. Fully integrated with Excel, it uses easy-to-enter graphics to represent both the objects in the system—such as machines and workers—and the process flows that describe their interaction. It is a powerful tool for many business processes, such as invoice and order flow, hospital process design, and any other situations where flows and processes can be redesigned and optimized.

Optima!

Optima! is a stand-alone Windows-based application designed to model and simulate business processes. It layouts the structure of the business (or a process within the business), define how processes work, then tries various what-if scenarios to determine how to improve things. It takes flowcharting to the next level by bringing simulation to charts. The program can be used for business process reengineering (BPR), ISO 9000 registration, total quality management (TQM), process improvement, and more.

MARKETING INFORMATION SYSTEMS AND PACKAGES

The internal accounting information system is the primary source of marketing information in most business organizations and provides two basic types of information to management: information generated from processing sales orders, and cost report and analyses. Profitability analysis is generated from sales data records, together with product cost data. Sales data processing also includes analysis of sales trend. In addition to the accounting and marketing departments, other departments within the company may contribute to the flow of information to marketing personnel. For example, the production or engineering department may provide information relating to product quality or design, which is useful to product planning or to sales staff. The economics department may provide useful analysis of the economy or of the field within which the firm operates. The personnel department may provide information relating to potential marketing department employees. While information from all the sources may be important, it is generally not so regular or so voluminous as the information provided by the accounting department. The information needs of marketers, in the order of importance, are shown in the survey results in Figure 10-17.

Figure 10-17.
INFORMATION NEEDS OF MARKETING MANAGERS

Rank	Main Information Needs
1	Improving new product development
2	Improving the use of market information
3	Measuring and managing brand equity
4	Market orientation and bottom line
5	Market segmentation and implementation
6	Identifying, anticipating, and responding to competitors
7	Studying buyer behavior
8	Strategic new product issues
9	Integrating marketing mix
10	Service quality/performance links

Source: J. Honomichi, "Time Is Ripe to Overhaul Traditional Marketing Research Departments," *Marketing News* 27, No. 12 (June 7, 1993), pp. H34–39.

A marketing IS supports managerial activity in the areas of product development, marketing mix, distribution, pricing decisions, promotional effectiveness, and sales forecasting. Recall that an IS is made up of three sets of activities: information collection, information analysis, and information dissemination. A marketing IS is no exception.

Figure 10-18 shows the inputs, subsystems, and outputs of a typical marketing IS.

Figure 10-18.
AN OVERVIEW OF A MARKETING IS

Inputs	Subsystems	Outputs
Strategic plan	Product development	Product development reports
Transaction processing system	Marketing research	Marketing research reports
Internal sources	Promotion and advertising system	Locational analysis
External sources:	Pricing system	Supply-and-demand analysis
Competition	Place planning system	Sales by product
The market		Sales by salesperson
		Sales by customer

INPUTS TO THE MARKETING INFORMATION SYSTEMS

Among the other functional areas, the marketing IS relies more heavily on external sources of data. These sources include commercial intelligence, competition, customers, trade shows, trade journals and magazines, and other publications. There are also important internal company information sources. An overview of these inputs is presented in the following sections.

The Corporate Strategic Plan or Policies   Marketing depends on the company's strategic plan for sales goals and projections. For instance, a strategic plan might show that sales are expected to grow by a stable 5% for the next three years. A marketing IS report for this company might detail current sales performance in terms of this strategic target. In addition to sales projections, the strategic plan can spell out detailed information about anticipated needs for the sales force, pricing, distribution channels, promotion, and new product features. The strategic plan can provide a framework in which to integrate marketing information and make appropriate marketing decisions.

The Transaction Processing System (TPS)   The TPS encompasses a huge amount of sales and marketing data on products or services, customers, and the sales force. Technology is revolutionizing the selling process. Most firms collect an abundance of information on a regular basis that can also be used in making marketing decisions. Sales data on products can expose which products are selling at high volumes, which ones are slow sellers, and how much they are contributing to profits. The marketing IS might synthesize this information in such a way as to be useful in formulating promotional plans. It can also be used to activate product development decisions. Analysis of sales by customers may display which customers are contributing to profits. This data can also be disseminated to determine the products that specific customers are buying to help the sales force with their promotional efforts. The performance of the sales force can also be monitored from data captured in the TPS, which can help develop bonus and incentive programs to reward well-performing salespeople.

Internal Company Information   Internal company information includes routinely collected accounting records, such as daily sales receipts, weekly expense records and profit statements, production and shipment schedules, inventory records, orders, monthly credit statements, and quarterly and biennial reports. Field salespeople are increasingly likely to have portable personal computers, pagers, and personal digital assistants (PDAs) to log in data for immediate transmission back to the company or customers, and to receive information from the company and customers. Technology is revolutionizing the selling process. Most companies collect an abundance of information on a regular basis that can also be used in making marketing decisions.

External Sources: The Competition and the Market   In most marketing decisions it is important to determine what is happening in the business's external environment, particularly anything that involves the competition, the economy, the market, and consumers. External information can be obtained from many sources. Some of the most commonly used sources are commercial intelligence, trade shows, trade journals, the government, private publications, commercial data suppliers, and the popular press.

Many companies purchase their competition's products and then perform "autopsies" to find out what makes them tick so that they can improve on them. Marketing managers attend trade shows and read trade journals to keep an eye on the competition.

Figure 10-19 lists some trade journals and publications. Information can be purchased from information brokers—individuals and companies who help businesses by electronically searching information bases for useful data. Valuable information can be obtained by training salespeople to listen to and observe customers, suppliers, members of the distribution system, and the competition, and then contributing this intelligence to the IS. The intent should be to obtain usable *marketing intelligence* (information that is available to the public), not to conduct *industrial espionage* (stealing information not available to the public). The latter is unethical and illegal. Marketers should be savvy enough to realize that as they are collecting information about their competition, the competition is probably collecting information about them.

An additional external source of important information for the marketing IS is the market for a company's products. A large amount of useful data can be obtained from the TPS for markets already being served by the company, but insights into buyer behaviors and preferences in new markets can be obtained only from sources outside the firm.

The Internet may become the ultimate information source for both the competition and the market. It already provides access to information provided by government (.gov), for-profit business (.com), nonprofits (.org), universities (.edu), and individuals.

MARKETING INFORMATION SYSTEMS SUBSYSTEMS AND OUTPUTS

Subsystems for the marketing IS include forecasting, marketing research, product, place, promotion, and price subsystems. These subsystems and

Figure 10-19.
TRADE JOURNALS AND PUBLICATIONS

Air Conditioning, Heating &
  Refrigeration News

Airline Executive

American Banker

American Druggist

American Gas Association Monthly

Automotive Industries

Aviation Week & Space Technology

The Banker

Best's Industry Report

Broadcasting

Brewers Digest

Chain Store Age Executive

Chemical Week

Computer Decisions

Computers and People

Credit and Financial Management

Datamation

Drug & Cosmetic Industry

Electronic News

Fleet Owner

Food Management

Food Processing

Forest Industries

Fuel Oil & Oil Heat
  and Solar Systems

Housing

Industry Week

Iron Age

Journal of Retailing

Labor Law Journal

Leather and Shoes

Merchandising

Modern Plastics

National Petroleum News

Oil and Gas Journal

Paper Trade Journal

PC World

Personnel

Pipeline & Gas Journal

Polk's National New Car Sales

Printer's Ink

Progressive Grocer

Public Utilities Fortnightly

Pulp & Paper

Quick Frozen Foods

Television Digest

Textile World

Transportation Journal

Ward's Auto World

World Oil

their outputs help marketing managers and executives increase sales, reduce marketing expenses, and develop plans for future products and services to meet the changing needs of customers.

Forecasting

Forecasts are needed for marketing, production, purchasing, manpower, and financial planning. Further, top management needs forecasts for planning and implementing long-term strategic objectives and planning for capital expenditures. Based on the firm's projected sales, the production function determines the machine, personnel, and material resources needed to produce its products or services. Marketing managers use sales forecasts to (1) determine optimal sales force allocations, (2) set sales goals, and (3) plan promotions and advertising. Other things—such as market share, prices, and trends in new product development—are required. As soon as the company makes sure that it has enough capacity, the production plan is developed. If the company does not have enough capacity, it will require planning and budgeting decisions for capital spending for capacity expansion. Production planners need forecasts to schedule production activities, order materials, establish inventory levels, and plan shipments. Other areas that need forecasts include material requirements (purchasing and procurement), labor scheduling, equipment purchases, maintenance requirements, and plant capacity planning. The personnel department requires a number of forecasts in planning for human resources in the business. Workers must be hired and trained, and these personnel must be provided with benefits that are competitive with those available in the firm's labor market. Also, trends that affect such variables as labor turnover, retirement age, absenteeism, and tardiness need to be forecast as input for planning and decision making in this function. On this basis, financial managers must estimate the future cash inflow and outflow. They must plan cash and borrowing needs for the company's future operations. Forecasts of cash flows and the rates of expenses and revenues are needed to maintain corporate liquidity and operating efficiency. In planning for capital investments, predictions about future economic activity are required so that returns or cash inflows accruing from the investment may be estimated. Many forecasting methods are in use, one of which is regression analysis. It is illustrated in the following paragraphs, using Excel.

Example 12: Developing a Sales Forecasting Model A firm wishes to develop a sales forecasting model by relating sales to price and advertising.

Month	Sales (Y)	Advertising (X1)	Price (X2)
1	25	4	75
2	26	5	82
3	32	6	94
4	30	6	95
5	32	7	98
6	37	7	110
7	38	8	110
8	41	8	99
9	46	9	95
10	48	10	97

SUMMARY OUTPUT

Regression Statistics

Multiple R	0.97366474
R square.	0.94802302
Adjusted R square	0.93317246
Standard error	2.0400664
Observations.	10

ANALYSIS OF VARIANCE

	df	SS	MS	F	Significance F
Regression	2	531.37	265.68	63.84	3.20
Residual	7	29.13	4.16		
Total	9	560.50			

	Coefficients	Standard Error	t Stat
Intercept	10.17	6.25	1.63
X Variable 1	4.42	0.48	9.19
X Variable 2	−0.06	0.08	−0.72

Using Regression on Excel   To utilize Excel for regression analysis, the following procedure needs to be followed:

1. Click the Tools menu.
2. Click Data Analysis.
3. Click Regression.

Marketing Research

Marketing research is essentially a twofold activity that involves (1) collecting current data describing all phases of the marketing operations, and (2) presenting the findings to marketing managers in a form suitable for decision making. The focus is on the timeliness of the information. The goal of marketing research is to conduct a systematic, objective, bias-free inquiry of the market and customer preferences. A variety of tools such as surveys, questionnaires, pilot studies, and in-depth interviews are used for marketing research. Marketing research can identify the features that customers really want in a product or from a service. Important attributes of products or services—style, color, size, appearance, and general fit—can be investigated through the use of marketing research.

Marketing research broadly encompasses advertising research and consumer behavior research. *Advertising research* is research on such advertising issues as ad and copy effectiveness, recall, and media choice. *Consumer behavior research* answers questions about consumers and their brand selection behaviors and preferences in the marketplace. Research results are used to make marketing mix decisions and for pricing, distribution channels, guarantees and warranties, and customer service. Inexpensive software and statistical analysis software is used to analyze the data collected from marketing research endeavors. These software packages can determine trends, test hypotheses, compute statistical values, and more. This data is then often input into the marketing IS so that marketing managers can be better informed and can better make their planning and resource allocation decisions.

Product Development

Product development is one of "the four Ps" in the marketing mix—product, place, promotion, and price, each of which is explained later.

Product development involves the transformation of raw materials into finished goods and services, and focuses primarily on the physical attributes of the product. Many factors, including materials, labor skills, plant capacity, and technical factors are important in product development decisions. In many cases, a computer program for mathematical programming and simulations can be utilized to analyze these various factors and to select the appropriate mix of labor, materials, plant and equipment, and engineering designs. Make-or-outsource decisions can also be made with the assistance of computer software. A framework, called the *product life cycle,* guides the manager in making product development decisions. It takes into account four stages in the life cycle: introduction, growth, maturity, and decline.

Place Planning

Place planning involves planning on the means of physically distributing the product to the customer. It includes production, transportation, storage, and distribution on both the wholesale and retail levels. Where to deliver the product to the customer and how to get the product to this location are the principal concerns of place analysis subsystems. Typically, a distribution chain starts at the manufacturing plant and ends at the final consumer. In the middle is a network of wholesale and retail outlets employed to efficiently and effectively bring goods and services to the final consumer. But where are the best places to locate manufacturing facilities, wholesale outlets, and retail distribution points? Factors such as manufacturing costs, transportation costs, labor costs, and localized demand levels become factors that are critical to answering this issue.

Today, marketing IS subsystems can analyze these factors and determine the least-cost placement of manufacturing facilities, wholesale operations, and retail outlets. The purpose of these locational analysis programs is to minimize total costs while satisfying product demand. Digital maps combined with customer database information in computer mapping software can be used to pinpoint locations for new retail outlets. For example, Yamaha Motor Corporation, USA has made decisions as to where to locate the dealership by blending computer graphics with behavioral demographics. Behavioral demographics link psychological, life-style, and family-expenditure data to geographic locations, often by ZIP Code.

Promotion Planning

One of the most important functions of any marketing effort is promotion. Promotion is concerned with all the means of marketing the sale of the product, including advertising and personal selling. Product success is a direct function of the types of advertising and sales promotion done. The size of the promotions budget and the allocation of this budget to various promotional mixes are important factors in deciding the type of campaigns that will be launched. Television coverage, newspaper ads and coverage, promotional brochures and literature, and training programs for salespeople are all components of these promotional and advertising mixes. Because of the time and scheduling savings they offer, computer software is widely used to establish the original budget and to monitor expenditures and the overall effectiveness of various promotional campaigns.

Promotional effectiveness can be monitored either through the TPS or through a specialized functional system focusing exclusively on sales activity. For example, a significant proportion of many marketing managers' compensation is determined by the results of their promotional campaigns through specialized sales activity subsystems. Such systems often use data from retail outlet bar code scanners to compile information on how effective certain promotions were within the promotional period. Without such sales activity, the time delay between wholesale shipments and retail sales would prevent the promotion's effectiveness from being accurately measured.

Example 13: Use of Linear Programming to Determine Optimal Media   The management of an electric products company decided to spend up to $1 million on the advertising of its women's electric razors. The advertising budget is to be spent in twelve consumer magazines with full-page, full-color advertisements. Let Xi be the number of dollars spent on advertising in magazine *i*. Management is advised by an advertising agency that an appropriate goal is to *maximize* the number of effective exposures given the advertising budget. Management wants to assure that no more than twelve insertions are made in any one magazine and that the number of insertions in *Mademoiselle* and *Ladies Home Journal* is less than or equal to 7 and 2, respectively. Suppose also that management wishes to specify minimum expenditures in certain of the magazines, say, $X2 \geq 17{,}810$, $X3 \geq 67{,}200$, $X5 \geq 42{,}840$, and $X10 \geq 32{,}550$. Finally, management desires an expenditure of no more than $320,000 in four of the magazines, say, 3, 9, 10, 12. Table 10-4 presents the number of exposures and cost for each advertising media.

Table 10-4.
EXPOSURES AND COST PER MEDIA

Media	Effective Readings per Dollar Spent	Cost of One Full-Page, Full-Color advertisement
1. Cosmopolitan	158	$5,500
2. Mademoiselle	263	5,950
3. Family Circle	106	33,600
4. Good Housekeeping	108	27,400
5. McCall's	65	42,840
6. Modern Romance	176	3,275
7. Modern Screen	285	3,415
8. Motion Picture	86	2,248
9. True Confessions	120	25,253
10. Women's Day	51	32,550
11. Seventeen	190	8,850
12. Ladies Home Journal	101	35,000

The LP model is:

Maximize $158 X1 + 263 X2 + 106 X3 + 108 X4 + 65 X5 + 176 X6 + 285 X7 + 86 X8 + 120 X9 + 51 X10 + 190 X11 + 101 X12$

Subject to

(1) $0 \leq Xi \leq 12$ (i = 1, 2, 3, . . . ,12)

(2) $X2 \leq 7, X12 \leq 2$

(3) $5950 X2 \geq 17,810, 33,600 X3 \geq 67,200,$
$42,840 X5 \geq 42,840$
$32,550 X10 \geq 32,550$

(4) $33,600 X3 + 25,253 X9 + 32,550 X10 + 35,000 X12 \leq 320,000$

The LINDO input and output follow:

MAX 158 X1 + 263 X2 + 106 X3 + 108 X4 + 65 X5 + 176 X6 + 285 X7
+ 86 X8 + 120 X9 + 51 X10 + 190 X11 + 101 X12

SUBJECT TO
  2)   X1 <= 12
  3)   X2 <= 12
  4)   X3 <= 12
  5)   X4 <= 12
  6)   X5 <= 12
  7)   X6 <= 12
  8)   X7 <= 12
  9)   X8 <= 12
 10)   X9 <= 12
 11)   X10 <= 12
 12)   X11 <= 12
 13)   X12 <= 12
 14)   X2 <= 7
 15)   X12 <= 2
 16)   5950 X2 >= 17810
 17)   33600 X3 >= 67200
 18)   42480 X5 >= 42480
 19)   32550 X10 >=32550
 20)   33600 X3 + 25253 X9 + 32550 X10 + 35000 X12 <=t 320000
END
LP OPTIMUM FOUND AT STEP 14

OBJECTIVE FUNCTION VALUE

         1)   15966.6100

VARIABLE	VALUE	REDUCED COST
X1	12.000000	.000000
X2	7.000000	.000000
X3	2.000000	.000000
X4	12.000000	.000000
X5	12.000000	.000000
X6	12.000000	.000000
X7	12.000000	.000000
X8	12.000000	.000000
X9	8.721736	.000000
X10	1.000000	.000000
X11	12.000000	.000000
X12	.000000	65.316860

Pricing

Pricing is an important managerial decision with a long-term effect on the sales and profitability of the firm. In most instances—especially in the field of durable consumer goods such as audio–video equipment, automobiles, etc.—the scope for product differentiation allows competing firms considerable leeway in setting the prices of their products. Three popular pricing approaches are: a cost-based pricing policy, a return-on-investment (ROI)–based pricing policy, and a demand-based pricing policy. The IS can support the manager in all three pricing policies. With the cost-based approach, the accounting system can provide accurate product cost data on which to base a decision. With the other approaches, the IS enables the manager to engage in what-if modeling to determine the price level that maximizes contribution to profits but retards competitive activity.

A major factor in determining pricing policy is an analysis of the demand curve, which attempts to determine the relationship between price and sales. Most companies try to develop pricing policies that will maximize total sales revenues. This is usually a function of price elasticity. If the product is highly price-sensitive, a reduction in price can generate a substantial increase in sales, which can result in higher revenues. The price of a product that is relatively insensitive to price can be substantially increased without a large reduction in demand. Figure 10-20 shows the relationships between price elasticity (e_p) and sales revenue (S), which can aid a firm in setting its price.

Figure 10-20.
RELATIONSHIP BETWEEN PRICE ELASTICITY AND SALES REVENUE

Price	$e_p > 1$	$e_p = 1$	$e_p < 1$
Price rises	S falls	No change	S rises
Price falls	S rises	No change	S falls

Computer programs exist that help determine price elasticity and various pricing policies. Typically, marketing managers, with the aid of computer software for spreadsheets and statistical packages, can develop what-if scenarios in which they can alter factors to see price changes on future demand and total revenues.

Sales Analysis

Sales analysis assists managers in identifying the products, sales personnel, and customers that are contributing to profits and those that are not. Several reports can be generated to help marketing managers make good sales decisions. The *sales-by-product* report lists all major products and their sales for a period of time, such as a month. This report shows which products are doing well and which ones need improvement or should be discarded altogether. The *sales-by-salesperson* report lists total sales for each salesperson for each week or month. This report can be subdivided by product to show which products are being sold by each salesperson. The *sales-by-customer* report is a useful way to identify high- and low-volume customers.

POPULAR FORECASTING
AND STATISTICAL SOFTWARE

Numerous computer programs are used for forecasting purposes. They are broadly divided into two major categories: forecasting software and general-purpose statistical software. Some programs are stand-alone, while others are spreadsheet add-ins or templates. A brief summary of some popular programs follows.

Sales & Market Forecasting Toolkit

This is a Lotus 1-2-3 template that produces sales and market forecasts, even for new products with limited historical data. It features eight powerful methods for accurate forecasts and spreadsheet models, complete with ready-to-use graphs. The Sales & Market Forecasting Toolkit offers a variety of forecasting methods to generate accurate business forecasts, even in new or changing markets with limited historical data. The forecasting methods include:

- Customer poll
- Whole market penetration
- Chain method
- Strategic modeling
- Moving averages, exponential smoothing, and linear regressions

The customer poll method helps build a forecast from the ground up, by summing the individual components such as products, stores, or customers. Whole market penetration, market share, and the chain method are top–down forecasting methods used to predict sales for new products and markets lacking sales data. The strategic modeling method develops a forecast by projecting the impact of changes to pricing and advertising expenditures. Statistical forecasting methods include exponential smoothing, moving averages, and linear regression.

You can use the built-in macros to enter data into your forecast automatically. For example, enter values for the first and last months of a 12-month forecast. The compounded-growth-rate macro will automatically compute and enter values for the other ten months.

Forecast! GFX

Forecast! GFX is a stand-alone forecasting system that can perform five types of time-series analysis: seasonal adjustment, linear and nonlinear trend analysis, moving-average analysis, exponential smoothing, and decomposition. Trend analysis supports linear, exponential, hyperbolic, S-curve, and polynomial trends. Hyperbolic trend models are used to analyze data that indicate a decline toward a limit, such as the output of an oil well or the price of a particular model of personal computer. Forecast! GFX can perform multiple-regression analysis with up to ten independent variables.

ForeCalc

ForeCalc, a Lotus add-in, uses nine forecasting techniques and includes both automatic and manual modes, and eliminates the need to export or reenter data.

It can be used in either automatic or manual mode. In automatic mode, the user highlights the historical data in the spreadsheet, such as sales, expenses, or net income; then ForeCalc tests several exponential-smoothing models and picks the one that best fits the data.

Forecast results can be transferred to the spreadsheet with upper and lower confidence limits. ForeCalc generates a line graph showing the original data, the forecasted values, and confidence limits.

ForeCalc can automatically choose the most accurate forecasting technique:

- Simple one-parameter smoothing
- Holt's two-parameter smoothing
- Winters's three-parameter smoothing
- Trendless seasonal models
- Dampened versions of Holt's and Winters's smoothing

ForeCalc's manual mode lets you select the type of trend and seasonality, yielding nine possible model combinations. You can vary the type of trend (constant, linear, or dampened), as well as the seasonality (nonseasonal, additive, or multiplicative).

StatPlan IV

StatPlan IV is a stand-alone program for those who understand how to apply statistics to business analysis. Users can apply it to market analysis, trend forecasting, and statistical modeling.

StatPlan IV lets you analyze data by range, mean, median, standard deviation, skewdness, kurtosis, correlation analysis, one- or two-way analysis of variance (ANOVA), cross tabulations, and *t*-test.

The forecasting methods include multiple regression, stepwise multiple regression, polynomial regression, bivariate curve fitting, autocorrelation analysis, trend and cycle analysis, and exponential smoothing.

The data can be displayed in X-Y plots, histograms, time-series graphs, autocorrelation plots, actual versus forecast plots, or frequency and percentile tables.

Geneva Statistical Forecasting

Geneva Statistical Forecasting, a stand-alone program, can batch-process forecasts for thousands of data series, provided the series are all measured in the same time units (days, weeks, months, and so on). The software automatically tries out as many as nine different forecasting methods, including six linear and nonlinear regressions and three exponential-smoothing techniques, before picking the one that best fits the historical data.

The program incorporates provisions that simplify and accelerate the process of reforecasting data items. Once users complete the initial forecast, they can save a data file that records the forecasting method assigned to each line item. When it is time to update the data, simply retrieve the file and reforecast, using the same methods as before.

SmartForecasts

SmartForecasts, a stand-alone forecasting program, automatically chooses the right statistical method, lets users manually adjust forecasts to reflect their business judgment, and produces forecast results.

SmartForecasts combines the benefits of statistical and judgmental forecasting. It can determine which statistical method gives the most accurate forecast, and it handles all the math. Forecasts can be modified using the program's EYEBALL utility. You may need to adjust a sales forecast to reflect an anticipated increase in advertising or a decrease in price. SmartForecasts summarizes data with descriptive statistics, plots the distribution of data values with histograms, plots variables in a scattergram, and identifies leading indicators.

Users can forecast using single- and double-exponential smoothing, as well as simple and linear moving averages. It even builds seasonality into forecasts using Winters' exponential smoothing, or users can eliminate seasonality by using times-series decomposition and seasonal adjustment.

In addition, SmartForecasts features simultaneous multiseries forecasting of up to 60 variables and 150 data points per variable, offers multivariate regression to let you relate business variables, and has an Undo command for mistakes.

Tomorrow

Tomorrow, a stand-alone forecasting software, uses an optimized combination of linear regression, single exponential smoothing, adaptive rate response single exponential smoothing, Brown's one-parameter double exponential smoothing, Holt's two-parameter exponential smoothing, Brown's one-parameter triple exponential smoothing, and Gardner's three-parameter damped trend.

Some of the main features include:

- There is no need to reformat your existing spreadsheets. Tomorrow recognizes and forecasts formula cells (containing totals and subtotals, for example). It handles both horizontally and vertically oriented spreadsheets. It accepts historical data in up to thirty separate ranges.

- Users can specify seasonality manually or lets the program calculate seasonality automatically.

- Users can do several forecasts of different time-series (for example, sales data from different regions) at once.

- The program recognizes and forecasts time series headings (names of months, etc.).

- Forecasts optionally become a normal part of your spreadsheet.

- The undo command restores the original spreadsheet.

- The browse feature allows users to look at any part of the spreadsheet (including the forecast) without leaving TOMORROW.

- The program checks for and prevents accidental overlaying of non-empty or protected cells.

- An optional annotation mode labels forecast cells, calculates MAPE, and, when seasonality is automatically determined, describes the seasonality.

- Comprehensive, context-sensitive, on-line help is available.

Forecast Pro

Forecast Pro is a stand-alone statistical forecasting package available for either Windows or DOS. It uses artificial intelligence. A built-in expert system examines your data. Then it guides you to proven forecasting methods, including moving averages, exponential smoothing, Box-Jenkins, and dynamic regression—whichever method suits the data best. Forecast Pro provides a neat diagnostic summary that shows why the chosen technique is the best. Forecast Pro accepts a variety of different formats, which makes it easier for users to feed in the data and get the forecasting done.

MicroTSP

MicroTSP is a stand-alone software that provides the tools most frequently used in practical econometric and forecasting work. Its features include:

- Descriptive statistics
- A wide range of single-equation estimation techniques, including ordinary least squares (multiple regression), two-stage least squares, nonlinear least squares, and probit and logit

Its forecasting tools include:

- Exponential smoothing, including single-exponential, double-exponential, and Winters's smoothing
- Box-Jenkins methodology

Sibyl/Runner

Sibyl/Runner is an interactive, stand-alone forecasting system. In addition to allowing the usage of all major forecasting methods, the package permits analysis of the data, suggests available forecasting methods, compares results, and provides several accuracy measures in such a way that it is easier for the user to select an appropriate method and forecast needed data under different economic and environmental conditions. For details, see S. Makridakis, R. Hodgsdon, and S. Wheelwright, "An Interactive Forecasting System," *American Statistician,* November 1974.

Other Forecasting Software

There are many other forecasting software, such as Autocast II, 4 Cast, and Trendsetter Expert Version.

General-Purpose Statistical Software

Numerous statistical programs are widely in use that can be utilized to build a forecasting model. Some of the more popular ones include:

- Systat
- SAS Application System

- Statgraphics

- SPSS

- PC-90

- Minitab

- RATS

- BMD

Today's managers have powerful tools at hand to simplify the forecasting process and increase its accuracy. Several forecasting models are available, and the automated versions of these should be considered by any manager who is regularly called on to provide forecasts. A personal computer with a spreadsheet is a good beginning, but the stand-alone packages currently available provide the most accurate forecasts and are the easiest to use. In addition, they make several forecasting models available and can automatically select the best one for a particular data set.

USING DECISION SUPPORT SYSTEMS

The manager who uses information systems helps distinguish them. Transaction processing systems (TPSs) are used at the operational level of an organization such as by clerks or secretaries. Executive information systems (EISs) are used specifically by personnel at the senior management level such as vice presidents or presidents of an organization. Decision support systems (DSSs) are used by middle management such as managers of the accounting department. Expert systems (ESs) are used by personnel at all levels of an organization.

Another factor in distinguishing information systems is function. Transaction-processing systems were established to computerize manual systems. Executive information systems (EISs) were designed to aid senior managers in decision making. Decision support systems were designed to aid middle managers in decision making. Expert systems were designed to aid all personnel in decision making.

The final distinguishing factor of information systems consists of the attributes of the system. Transaction processing systems are used to handle day-to-day transactions such as the accounts payable system. Executive information system attributes include visual summaries of the forecasts and budgets of an organization. Decision support system attributes include visual displays of the sales, income, or interest estimates for the day, month, or year. Expert system attributes include systems that assess bad debt or authorize credit.

A DSS is an interactive information technology-based system that assists managers in making many complex decisions, such as decisions needed to solve poorly defined or semistructured problems. Instead of replacing managers in the decision process, the DSS supports them in their application of the decision process. In other words, it is an automated assistant that extends the mental capabilities of the manager. Most authorities view the DSS as an integral part of the IS, in that its primary purpose is to provide decision-making information to managerial decision makers. A DSS allows the manager to change assumptions concerning expected future conditions and to observe the effects on the relevant criteria. As a result of these direct benefits, a DSS enables the manager to gain a better understanding of the key factors affecting the decision. It enables the manager to evaluate a large number of alternative courses of action within a reasonably short time frame.

A DSS summarizes or compares data from either or both internal and external sources. Internal sources include data from an organization's database such as sales, manufacturing, or financial data. Data from external sources include information on interest rates, population trends, new housing construction, or raw material pricing.

DSSs often include query languages, statistical analysis capabilities, spreadsheets, and graphics to help the user evaluate the decision data. More advanced decision support systems include capabilities that allow users to create a model of the variables affecting a decision. With a model, users can ask what-if questions by changing one or more of the variables and seeing the projected results. A simple model for determining the best product price includes factors for the expected sales volume at each price level. Many people use electronic spreadsheets for simple modeling tasks. A DSS is sometimes combined with executive information systems (EISs). DSS applications used in business include systems that estimate profitability, plan monthly operations, determine the source and application of funds, and schedule staff. Table 10-5 presents the characteristics of a decision support system.

Table 10-5.
CHARACTERISTICS OF DSS

Graphical
Large database
Integrates many sources of data
Report and presentation flexibility
Geared toward individual decision-making styles
Modular format
Optimization and heuristic approach
What-if and simulation
Goal-seeking and impact analysis
Performs statistical and analytical analysis

DSS DEVELOPMENT TOOLS

DSS development tools include:

- *IFPS/Plus (Interactive Financial Planning System),* developed by Comshare, is a modeling language that allows model building for what-if, impact, and goal-seeking analyses. The program contains spreadsheet analysis, word processing abilities, and a convenient report writer.

- *EIS Micro-Workstation,* developed by Boeing computer services, is an integrated software package that includes database systems, modeling, statistical analysis, forecasting, graphics, and report writing.

- *Encore,* developed by Ferox Microsystems, has good financial modeling abilities. It can assist with cash-flow analysis, financial planning, and budget development and analysis. Word processing capabilities, graphics features, and forecasting and investment analysis are also available.

- *Microforesight* provides sophisticated modeling abilities. It can analyze risk and determine how sensitive results are to certain decision or model parameters. Forecasting and statistical analysis are also available. This package can support goal seeking, thus allowing a decision maker to determine the inputs required to obtain certain goals, such as profitability levels, rate of return targets, or cost targets.

- *Pro*Fas,* developed by Decision Support Technology, is a DSS package to assist with fixed asset management. It allows managers to compare various depreciation models, using what-if analysis capabilities.

- *CFO Advisor* is a DSS software package that performs financial analysis and allows managers to analyze the impact of financial changes on future financial outcomes.
- *Precalc,* developed at INSEAD in France, helps decision makers choose from various options in the presence of multiple criteria in the decision. It is an interactive, menu-driven package with graphical capabilities.
- *Commander™ Decision,* developed by Comshare, is decision support software that allows decision makers flexible access to the information they need when they need it. Decision is designed for line managers, middle managers, directors, executives, analysts, and those who need to work hands-on with business information to make good business decisions. Decision is especially designed for analysis applications: Users gain insight by investigating plans and results by product, by market, by version, by region, and so on.
- *Fiscal,* developed by Lingo Computer Design Inc., is "Groupware for Decision Support," moving decision support beyond spreadsheets. Fiscal supplies a complete architecture for rapidly implementing and managing major decision support systems. It can be used to extend the functionality of any major client-server application or database by supplying full decision support functionality for that application. Some of the industry uses include financial services, insurance, mutual funds, pension funds, telecommunications, management consulting, utilities, oil and gas, healthcare, and manufacturing. Fiscal's architecture is a top–down approach to decision support and data warehousing, which ensures that the system will meet the business needs of end-users.

INTERACTIVE FINANCIAL PLANNING SYSTEM

IFPS/Plus is a multipurpose, interactive financial modeling that supports and facilitates the building, solving, and asking of what-if questions. It is a powerful modeling and analysis tool designed to handle large, complicated problems with lots of data. It is unsurpassed for corporatewide applications, especially those that get their data directly from the enterprise's relational database. Originally marketed by Execucom in the 1970s, IFPS is currently used by more than 600 businesses. The data and models created through IFPS/Plus can be shared throughout the organization because the model logic is self-documenting. The capabilities of the program include the ability to explain, perform spreadsheet-type editing, produce reports, and built-in business functions. Some of the capabilities of the system are forecasting, linear regression, and automatic extrapolation. The applications may range from EIS information generation to inventory management and distribution.

The output from an IFPS model is in the format of a spreadsheet, that is, a matrix or table in which:

- The rows represent user-specified variables such as market share, sales, growth in sales, unit price, gross margin, variable cost, contribution margin, fixed cost, net income, net present value, internal rate of return, and earnings per share.

- The columns designate a sequence of user-specified time periods such as month, quarter, year, total, percentages, or divisions.

- The entries in the body of the table display the values taken by the model variable over time or by segments of the firm such as divisions, product lines, sales territories, and departments.

Key features of IFPS include:

- Like other special-purpose modeling languages, provides an English-like modeling language. Without an extensive knowledge of computer programming, financial officers can build their own financial models and use them for what-if scenarios and managerial decisions.

- Has a collection of built-in financial functions that perform calculations such as net present value (NPV), internal rate of return (IRR), loan amortization schedules, and depreciation alternatives.

- Has built-in mathematical and statistical functions such as linear regression, linear interpolation, polynomial autocorrelation, and moving-average functions.

- Supports use of leading and/or lagged variables commonly used in financial modeling. For example, cash collections lag behind credit sales of prior periods.

- Supports deterministic and probabilistic modeling, offering a variety of functions for sampling from probability distributions such as uniform, normal, bivariate normal, and user-described empirical distributions.

- Is nonprocedural. The relationships, logic, and data used to calculate the various values in the output do not have to be arranged in any particular top-to-bottom order. IFPS automatically detects and solves a system of two or more linear or nonlinear equations.

- Has extensive editing capabilities that include adding statements to and deleting statements from a model, making changes in existing statements, and making copies of parts or all of a model.

IFPS also supports sensitivity analysis by providing the following solution options:

- *What-if:* The IFPS lets users specify one or more changes in the relationships, logic, data, and/or parameter values in the existing model and recalculates the model to show the impact on the performance measures.

- *Goal-seeking:* IFPS can determine what change would have to take place in the value of a specified variable in a particular time period to achieve a specified value for another variable. For example, the financial officer can ask the system to answer the question, "What would the unit sales price have to be for the project to achieve a target return on investment of 20%?"

- *Sensitivity:* This command is employed to determine the effect of a specified variable on one or more other variables. The command is similar to the What-if command but it produces a convenient, model-produced tabular summary for each new alternative value of the specified variable.

- *Analyze:* This command examines in detail the variables and their values that have contributed to the value of a specified variable.

- *Impact:* The command is used to determine the effect on a specified variable of a series of percentage changes in one or more variables.

- *IFPS/Optimum:* The routine is employed to answer questions of "what is the best" type rather than "what-if."

Other features of IFPS include:

- Routine graphic output
- Interactive color graphics

- Data files that contain both data and relationships
- A consolidation capability that lets the financial officer produce composite reports from two or more models
- Extraction of data from existing non-IFPS data files and placing them in IFPS-compatible data files
- Operating on all major computer mainframes and microcomputers

As of late 1998, the current version of IFPF/Plus is 5.1.1, which introduces Visual IFPS. This is a Microsoft Windows application that acts as the client in the client-server application. The application runs on the PC and is connected to the IFPS/Plus running on the server. In other words, IFPS/Plus can access and take the data from the organization's main database and send the results directly to the user. The user is not inundated with all the data, just presented with the results. This keeps the network from getting bogged down. Thus, the user has the power of the server on a PC and all the benefit of IFPS/Plus.

Prospective users of IFPS/Plus are encouraged to refer to the following sources from Comshare (3001 S. State St., P.O. Box 1588, Ann Arbor, MI 48106):

- IFPS Cases and Models, 1979
- IFPS Tutorial, 1980
- IFPS User's Manual, 1984
- IFPS/Personal User's Manual, 1984
- IFPS University Seminar, 1984
- Comprehensive Fundamentals of IFPS, 1984
- Papers available from the Comshare University Support Programs

RATIONALE FOR USING PALISADE'S DECISIONTOOLS SUITE

Palisade's DecisionTools Suite is a DSS tool in the area of risk and decision analysis. It includes such programs as @RISK, @RISK for Project, TopRank, PrecisionTree, BestFit, and RISKview. These programs analyze risk, run Monte Carlo simulations, perform sensitivity analyses, and fit data to distributions.

- *@RISK* is a risk analysis and simulation add-in for Microsoft Excel and Lotus 1-2-3. Replace values in your spreadsheet with @RISK distributions to represent uncertainty, then simulate your model using powerful Monte Carlo simulation methods. @RISK recalculates your spreadsheet hundreds (or thousands) of times. The results: distributions of possible outcome values! Results are displayed graphically and through detailed statistical reports.

- *@RISK for Project* adds the same powerful Monte Carlo techniques to your Microsoft Project models, allowing users to answer questions such as, "What is the chance the project will be completed on schedule?"

- *TopRank* is a what-if analysis add-in for either Microsoft Excel or Lotus 1-2-3 for Windows. Users take any spreadsheet model and select the cells that hold your results. TopRank automatically determines which spreadsheet values affect results the most. TopRank then ranks the values in order of importance. The results can be displayed in Tornado, Spider, and Sensitivity high-resolution graphs, allowing the user to easily understand the outcome at a glance. TopRank works easily and effectively with @RISK, by identifying the critical cells users should concentrate on when running Monte Carlo simulations.

- *PrecisionTree* is a powerful, innovative decision analysis tool. Users enter decision trees and influence diagrams directly into their spreadsheet models. Detail all available decision options and identify the optimal decision. The decision analysis factors in your attitudes toward risk, and the uncertainty is present in your model. Sensitivity analysis identifies the critical factors affecting the decision. It is a real plus for outlining all available options for a decision or for identifying and presenting the best course of action.

- *BestFit* is the distribution fitting solution for Windows. BestFit takes data sets (up to 30,000 data points or pairs) and finds the distribution that best fits the data. It accepts three types of data from text files: direct entry, cut and paste, or direct link to data within Excel or Lotus 1-2-3 spreadsheets. BestFit tests up to 26 distribution types using advanced optimization algorithms. The results are displayed graphically and through an expanded report that includes goodness-of-fit statistics. BestFit distributions can be used directly in @RISK for Excel, Lotus 1-2-3, and Microsoft Project models.

- *RISKview* is the distribution viewing companion to @RISK, @RISK for Project, or BestFit. It is a powerful tool for viewing, assessing, and creating probability distributions.

INCORPORATING PRACTICAL DSS APPLICATIONS

There are many DSS practical applications:

- Hewlett-Packard developed *Quality Decision Management* to perform production and quality-control functions. It can help with raw material inspection, product testing, and statistical analysis.
- *Manufacturing Decision Support System (MDSS)*, developed at Purdue University to support decisions in automated manufacturing facilities, is especially useful for CAD/CAM operations.
- RCA has developed a DSS to deal with personnel problems and issues. The system, called *Industrial Relations Information Systems (IRIS)*, can handle problems that may not be anticipated or that may occur once, and can assist in difficult labor negotiations.
- The Great Eastern Bank Trust Division developed a DSS, called *On-line Portfolio Management (OPM)*, that can be used for portfolio and investment management. The DSS permits display and analysis of various investments and securities.
- *RealPlan,* a DSS to assist with commercial real estate decisions, is useful for various decision aspects of purchasing, renovating, and selling property.
- *EPLAN (Energy Pion)* is a DSS being developed by the National Audubon Society to analyze the impact of U.S. energy policy on the environment.
- The *Transportation Evacuation Decision Support System (TEDSS)* is a DSS used in nuclear plants in Virginia. It analyzes and develops evacuation plans to assist managers in crisis management decisions regarding evaluation times and routes and the allocation of shelter resources.
- The U.S. Army has developed an enlisted-manpower DSS to help with recruitment, training, education, reclassification, and promotion decisions. It encompasses simulation and optimization to model personnel needs and requirements. It interacts with an online database and other statistical analysis software packages.

- *Voyage Profitability Estimator* has been utilized by a shipping firm to compute the income from decisions affecting charter rates to be charged for trips. The system saves time and makes it possible to evaluate trade-offs between speed and fuel usage. The analysis involves ship and voyage characteristics such as tonnage, rate of fuel consumption, and port cost.

- *Monthly Plan Calculations* serves as a corporate budgeting tool to measure the levels of manpower needed to perform various functions, to calculate costs, and in general to evaluate the adequacy of proposed operational plans. Using simple formulas, this system calculates the cost of materials and inventory, among other items, based on input that consists of monthly production and shipment plans. Typically, the system is used iteratively in an attempt to generate a plan that is sufficiently profitable and that meets the company's goal of maintaining reasonable level production in spite of the seasonal nature of the product.

- *Source and Application of Funds* is an online budget of source and applications of funds used for operational decision making and financial planning in an insurance company to provide monthly cash flow figures. The DSS "output" is used at weekly meetings of an investment committee to help in allocating funds across investment areas and to minimize the amount of cash left idle in banks.

- *Interactive Audit Staff Scheduling Systems* is an integer programming model designed by Balachandran and Zoltners to assist companies in scheduling their audit staff in an optimal and effective manner. The computerized management support system for scheduling staff to an audit can include the basic model along with a judgmental scheduling system and a scheduling information database. Motivation, morale, turnover, and productivity of the audit staff can all be affected by scheduling. In the scheduling process, the audit firm needs to consider its audit philosophy, objectives, staff size, rotational plans, and auditor evaluation. Many feasible audit staff schedules may fill these needs, but the firm needs to select the schedule that best meets its own objectives.

GROUP DECISION SUPPORT SYSTEM ANALYSIS

The DSS approach has resulted in better individual decision making. However, many DSS approaches and techniques are not suitable for a group decision-making environment. Although many workers and some managers are not involved in many committee meetings and group decision-making sessions, tactical and strategic-level managers can spend more than half of their decision-making time in a group setting. Indeed, some top-level managers and executives can spend 80% or more of their decision-making time in groups, which means they need effective approaches to assist with group decision making.

A group decision support system (GDSS) consists of all hardware, software, people, databases, and procedures needed to provide effective support in group decision-making settings.

Characteristics of GDSS

GDSS has many characteristics that make it more suitable for group decision making than traditional DSS:

- *Special design:* The GDSS approach acknowledges that special procedures, devices, and approaches are needed in group decision-making settings. Software packages called *groupware,* such as Novell Netware and Microsoft Windows NT Server, allow two or more individuals in the group to effectively work together to use word processing, database, spreadsheet, and related software packages.

- *Suppression of negative group behavior:* One aspect of any GDSS is the suppression or elimination of group behavior that is counterproductive or harmful to effective decision making.

- *Support of positive group behavior:* A number of positive, highly effective group decision-making approaches have resulted in superior overall decision making.

Components and Structure of GDSS

In addition to groupware to facilitate group member communications, GDSS contains most of the elements found in a traditional DSS:

- Data management
- User interface
- Model management system
- Knowledge management system
- Groupware

GDSS Alternatives

Group decision support systems can take a number of alternative network configurations, depending on the needs of the group, the decision to be supported, and the geographical location of group members.

- The *local area network (LAN)* is used when group members are located in the same building or geographical area and when group decision making is frequent. In these cases, the technology and equipment of the GDSS approach is placed directly into the offices of group members. Usually this is accomplished via a local area network.

- The *wide area network (WAN)* allows decisions makers located throughout the country or the world to be linked electronically. All group members are at geographically dispersed locations.

BENEFITS OF EXECUTIVE INFORMATION SYSTEMS AND EXECUTIVE SUPPORT SYSTEMS

An *executive information system (EIS)* is a DSS made specially for top managers and specifically supports strategic decision making. It differs from the typical DSS in that it does not answer what-if scenarios for the executive, but gives rapid access to real-time information and direct access to management reports. It displays technology since it does not have any type of analysis capabilities for the user, offering no diagnosis or explanation of information. The information that is presented tends to be static since changing external conditions are not factored into the data.

An EIS draws on data not only from systems internal to the organization but also from those outside, such as news services and market research databases. The EIS user interface often uses a mouse or a touch screen to help executives unfamiliar with using a keyboard. One leading system uses a remote control device similar to those used to control a television set. An EIS might allow senior executives to call up predefined reports for their personal computers, whether desktops or laptops. They might, for instance, call up sales figures in many forms—by region, by week, by fiscal year, by projected increases. In contrast, an *executive support system (ESS)* is a comprehensive support system that goes beyond EIS to include capabilities for analyzing data and doing what-if scenarios.

Because top managers may not be familiar with (or comfortable with) computer systems, the EIS features make them easier for executives to use. Another aspect of the EIS user interface is the graphic presentation of user information. The EIS relies heavily on graphic presentation of both the processing options and data. Again, this is designed to make the system easier to use.

Because executives focus on strategic issues, the EIS often has access to external databases such as the Dow Jones News/Retrieval service. Such external sources of information can provide current information on interest rates, commodity prices, and other leading economic indicators.

Table 10-6 presents the attributes of an executive information system.

Table 10-6.
CHARACTERISTICS OF AN EXECUTIVE INFORMATION SYSTEM (EIS)

Graphical
Easy-to-use interface
Broad, aggregated perspective
Different data sources
Optionally expand to detail level
Provide context
Timeliness crucial

A popular EIS software is *Xecutive Pulse,* developed by Megatrend Systems, Inc. It is a Windows-based executive information system. The software interfaces with many popular LAN-based accounting applications. It provides decision makers with easy access to financial and sales information including trend analysis using drill-down and drill-across technology. Hundreds of charts, graphs, and views are available with a mouse click. The system extracts data from accounting history files, builds a database, and stores up to three years of information for each accounting period. Users can drill down through five organizational levels, compare actual versus history and actual versus budget, and display report or graphic results. Xecutive Pulse features extensive sales, cash flow, and human resource analysis, plus daily trends for accounts receivable, accounts payable, margins, sales, and inventory.

Comshare's *Commander OLAP* is another popular client-server software product for EIS and DSS applications like sales reporting and analysis, product profitability reporting, P&L analysis and reporting, enterprise budget reporting, critical success factor and key performance indicator reporting, and performance analysis and reporting. It transforms existing corporate data into usable information for management decision making.

Limitations of Current EIS

Although they offer great promise, many EISs have not been successfully implemented and many executives have stopped using them. A common reason cited in several failed attempts is the mistake of not modifying the system to the specific needs of the individual executives who use the system. For example, many executives prefer to have information presented in a particular sequence with the option of seeing different levels of supporting detailed information such as cost data on a spreadsheet. The desired sequence and level of detail varies for each executive. It appears that an EIS must be tailored to the executives' requirements or the executives will continue to manage with information they have obtained through previous methods. This limitation can be corrected by tailoring the software based on the particular needs of the managers within the specific company. After the software has been appropriately modified, it will have significant practical applications.

PRACTICAL EIS APPLICATIONS

There are many EIS applications for managers, including measuring productivity and making product-costing decisions.

EIS in Measuring Productivity   This application bears on management's concern over productivity. Management may use both internal and external information extracted from the EIS to show how productivity in an organization has declined in recent years. Financial data can be retrieved from the EIS database to demonstrate how increases in unit labor costs over time have been primarily responsible for significant increases in the product's unit cost and have been damaging to the company's competitiveness by forcing increases in the product's selling price. Executives can also compare company sales (internal data) to industry sales trends (external data) from the EIS to project market share changes in response to changes in selling price.

External information may also be extracted from the EIS database to indicate how competitors achieve greater efficiency by using less labor and more advanced technology to manufacture a quality product and a materially lower unit cost. As a result, management may demonstrate that the competition is able to sell greater quantities of their products at lower prices. This information may provide justification for closing the unprofitable plant and opening a modern facility that will enable a company to be more competitive in the industry.

EIS in Product-Costing Decisions   Resolving the conflict between profitability in the short run and increasing market share in the long run requires a mix of both external and internal data for a rational decision. Executives need information on product demand and elasticity, competing products and strategies, the economy and other factors such as the cost of manufacturing the product and trade-offs that exist relative to different product quality levels under different cost assumptions. Some questions executives may raise are:

- What is the current level of quality and how does the level differ from the desired level?

- What is the current full cost of producing a unit and how does the amount differ from the full cost at the desired level of quality?

- What costs are variable over different levels of product quality?

- What costs are controllable relative to producing and selling the products?

EIS can provide data for solutions to some of these questions by computation. Many internal decisions depend on assumptions and measurements that require judgment and that may be subject to different interpretations. In product-costing decisions, issues involving appropriate cost and product quality trade-offs are equally subjective and unlikely to have a unique interpretation.

11

ARTIFICIAL INTELLIGENCE AND EXPERT SYSTEMS*

Artificial intelligence (AI) is the application of human reasoning techniques to machines. Artificial intelligence systems use sophisticated computer hardware and software to simulate the functions of the human mind. The commercial application of AI technology has experienced rapid growth in the past decade. The technologies used in AI applications include expert/knowledge systems, neural networks, case-based reasoning, pattern matching, machine learning, fuzzy logic, and others. Among different AI applications, *expert systems (ES)* are the most promising applications of artificial intelligence and have received the most attention from the commercial world. The problem domains covered by expert systems range through medicine, engineering, finance, and science, and they cover tasks such as diagnosis, design, problem solving, planning, repair, searching, interpreting, training, monitoring, and control, to mention a few.

Expert systems are computer programs exhibiting behavior characteristics of experts. Expert systems involve the creation of computer software that emulates the way people solve problems. Like a human expert, an expert system gives advice by drawing on its own store of knowledge and by requesting information specific to the problem at hand. Expert systems are not exactly the same thing as decision support systems. A DSS is computer-based software that assists decision makers by providing data and models. It performs primarily semistructured tasks whereas an expert system is more appropriate for unstructured tasks. Decision support systems can be interactive just like

*This chapter was coauthored by Roberta M. Siegel, a computer consultant.

319

expert systems. But, because of the way decision support systems process information, they typically cannot be used for unstructured decisions that involve nonquantitative data. Unlike expert systems, decision support systems do not make decisions but merely attempt to improve and enhance decisions by providing indirect support without automating the whole decision process.

Some general characteristics indicate whether a given business application is likely to be a good candidate for the development of an expert system, such as an application that requires the use of expert knowledge, judgment, and experience. The business problem must have a heuristic nature and must be defined clearly. The area of expertise required for the application must be well-defined and recognized professionally, and the organization developing the expert system must be able to recruit an expert who is willing to cooperate with the expert system's development team. The size and complexity of the application must be manageable in the context of organizational resources, available technical skills, and management support.

MECHANICS OF EXPERT SYSTEMS

An expert system, sometimes called a *knowledge system,* is a set of computer programs that performs a task at the level of a human expert. Expert systems are created on the basis of knowledge collected on specific topics from human experts, and they imitate the reasoning process of a human being. Expert systems have emerged from the field of artificial intelligence, which is the branch of computer science attempting to create computer systems that simulate human reasoning and sensation. We describe artificial intelligence in more detail later in the chapter.

Expert systems are used by management and nonmanagement personnel to solve specific problems, such as how to reduce production costs, improve workers' productivity, or reduce environmental impact. It is a computer program that, based on methodically using a narrowly defined domain of knowledge that is built into the program, comes up with a solution to a problem in much the same way as an expert would. The key to the definition is that the domain must be narrowly defined. An expert system cannot (at this point) be developed to give useful answers about all questions; it is limited, as a human expert is limited to a particular field. For example, one expert system would not tell the controller both whether to lease or buy a piece of equipment based on the tax differences and also whether a pending business combination needs to be treated as a pooling or as a purchase.

Why Expert Systems?

Companies are building expert systems for many reasons. One major reason is to preserve expertise. Expert systems capture and store tremendous amounts of experts' knowledge and expertise, which in turn is made available for people with less experience. Other reasons include:

- Improving productivity
- Making expertise portable
- Obtaining otherwise unavailable expert advice
- Enhancing the public image of the company

How Expert Systems Work

Expert systems are usually considered to have six major components. The relationships of these components are illustrated in Figure 11-1. Based on the relationships in the figure, expert systems must work interactively with system users in assisting them in making better decisions. The system interacts with the user by continuously asking for information until it is ready to make a decision. Once the system has sufficient information, an answer or result is returned to the user. *Note:* Not only must the system assist in making the decision itself, it must also provide the user with the logic it employed to reach its decision.

The inference engine processes the data that the user inputs to find matches with the knowledge base, where the expert's information is stored. The user interface allows the user to communicate with the program. The explanation facility shows the user how each decision was derived.

Expert systems are only as good as their programming. If the information in the knowledge base is incorrect or if the inference engine is not designed properly, the results will be useless. GIGO holds true: garbage in, garbage out.

The process of converting expert advice to coded rule sets and constructing a knowledge base is known as *knowledge engineering.* Such efforts typically require close collaboration between human experts in the application of interest and knowledge engineers familiar with the construction process. Management support and involvement have been key factors in the successful delivery of a viable system.

Figure 11-1.
EXPERT SYSTEM RELATIONSHIPS

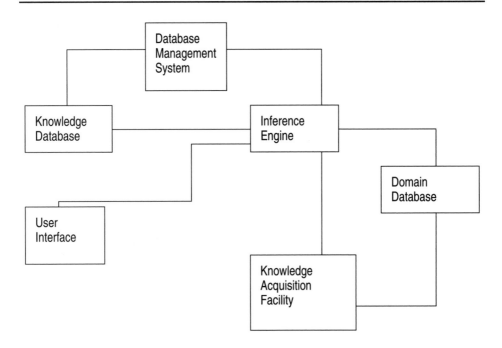

1. *Knowledge database* contains the rules and cases used when making decisions.
2. *Domain database* is the set of facts and information relevant to the domain (area of interest).
3. *Database management system* controls input and management of both the knowledge and domain databases.
4. *Inference engine* contains the inference strategies and controls used by experts to manipulate knowledge and domain databases. It is the brain of the expert system. It receives the request from the user interface and conducts reasoning in the knowledge base.
5. *User interface* consists of the explanatory features, online help facilities, debugging tools, modifications systems, and other tools designed to assist the user in effectively utilizing the system.
6. *Knowledge acquisition facility* allows for interactive processing between the system and the user—how the system acquires "knowledge" from human experts in the form of rules and facts. More advance technology allows intelligent software to "learn" knowledge from different problem domains. The knowledge learned by computer software is more accurate and reliable compared with that of human experts.

Expert Systems (ES) Tools

The construction of viable expert systems depends on powerful development tools. Many ES tools exist in the market today and they vary widely in their functionality and hardware support requirements. One may start by using a general-purpose AI programming language, such as Lisp or Prolog, to design and program various parts of ES from scratch. On the other end of the spectrum, one can work with a large hybrid development environment that provides an ES shell, user interface builder, and other helpful facilities. The rest of this section provides a general overview and comparison of some popular commercial tools.

Languages for Expert System Development

The most basic ES development tool is a general-purpose programming language. Lisp has been and continues to be the most widely used language for ES development. It provides many features that ease the task of building any symbolic processing system. Moreover, Lisp is becoming more popular for conventional programming, particularly with the advent of Common Lisp and Lisp development environment, which provide GUI support.

Prolog is another symbolic, general-purpose programming language. Prolog is gaining in popularity, although its use as an ES development language has been far less extensive than that of Lisp.

Conventional programming languages, such as C and C++, have also been used to develop expert systems. Because of the efficiency and popularity of C language, many developers use Lisp to develop prototype systems and use C language to construct a final delivery system.

Using a general-purpose programming language gives the expert system developers more flexibility in terms of adapting the system to suit the problem domain. On the other hand, such languages are more difficult to apply because they give little or no guidance as to how knowledge should be represented or how mechanisms for accessing the knowledge base should be designed.

Expert System Shells and Products

An alternative to using a programming language in developing ES is to use an ES-specific tool, often referred to as an *ES shell*. An ES shell contains all the essential elements of an expert system except the domain-specific knowledge. The knowledge representation method and inference engine are built-in features that can be applied to the construction of ES for similar domains. For an ES shell to be successful, the domain characteristics must match those expected by the shell's internal model.

An ES shell is essentially a collection of software packages and tools used to design, develop, implement, and maintain expert systems. Expert system shells exist in many different forms. A number of off-the-shelf expert system shells are complete and ready to run. The user enters the appropriate data or parameters, and the expert system provides output to the problem or situation. Some of the expert system shells include Level 5, VP-Expert, and Windows Expert Systems. Other shells are described in Table 11-1.

Table 11-1.
POPULAR ES SHELLS

1st-Class Fusion offers a direct, easy-to-use link to the knowledge base. It also offers a visual rule tree, which graphically shows how rules are related.

Financial Advisor is an ES shell that can analyze capital investments in fixed assets, such as equipment and facilities.

Knowledgepro is a high-level language that combines functions of expert systems and hypertext. It allows the setup of classic if-then rules, and can read database and spreadsheet files.

Leonardo is an ES shell that employs an object-oriented language used to develop an expert system called COMSTRAT, which marketing managers can use to help analyze the position of their companies and products relative to their competition.

Personal Consultant (PC) Easy is a shell used to route vehicles in warehouses and manufacturing plants.

Furthermore, a number of other tools make the development of expert systems easier and faster. These products help capture *if-then* rules for the rule base, assist in using tools such as spreadsheets and programming languages, interface with traditional database packages, and generate the inference engine.

Once developed, an expert system can be run by people with virtually no computer experience. The expert system asks the user a series of questions. Subsequent questions are often based on answers to previous questions. After the user answers the system-generated questions, the expert system generates conclusions. Many expert systems have word processing capabilities that can generate letters asking users for additional information.

APPLICATIONS OF EXPERT SYSTEMS

The use of expert systems is on the rise. Sales of expert system shells are increasing at about 20 percent per year, with about 60 percent of the sales for use on IBM PCs or compatibles. One of the main challenges to the development and use of expert systems is to integrate expert system concepts and functions into existing applications, including transaction processing. The applications of expert systems are many and varied, including security, capacity planning for information systems, military analysis, construction of maps, and law enforcement.

A number of expert systems have been in existence for several years or more. A few of these systems are:

1. *CoverStory* is an expert system that extracts marketing information from a database and automatically writes marketing reports.
2. Westinghouse Electric has an expert system called *Intelligent Scheduling and Information System (ISIS-11)* for scheduling complex factory orders.
3. *CARGEX-Cargo Expert System* is used by Lufthansa, the German airline, to help determine the best shipping routes.
4. NCR Corporation has an expert system for communications. The system allows the collection and encoding of an expert's knowledge into a form that can be used by a personal computer. The overall emphasis of the product is to allow more efficient analysis of difficulties regarding data communications.
5. *ACE* is an expert system used by AT&T to analyze the maintenance of telephone networks.
6. General Electric has an expert system called *DELTA* that assists in engine repair.
7. *XCON (Expert VAX System Configuration)* is an expert system developed by Digital Equipment Corporation (DEC) to help in configuring and organizing minicomputer systems. The system uses thousands of rules and helps DEC get the correct minicomputer system to customers.

8. *Authorizer's Assistant (AA)* is an ES developed by American Express for credit authorization. It is used to weed out bad credit risks and reduce losses.

9. *Watchdog Investment Monitoring System* is an ES developed by Washington Square Advisors, the investment management subsidiary of Northwestern National Life Insurance Company. It is used to analyze potential and existing corporate bonds to enhance clients' revenue. The analysis includes a change in financial ratios as an indicator of past performance and predictor of future financial directions.

10. *Escape* is an expert system by Ford Motor Company for claim authorization and processing.

11. *Auditor,* developed by C. Duncan (University of Illinois), is an expert system to aid internal auditors in analyzing a company's allowance for bad debts.

12. *TICOM,* developed by A. Baily and M. Gagle (University of Minnesota), is an expert system to evaluate internal control systems.

13. *Financial Advisor,* developed by MIT Sloan School of Management, provides expert advice on projects, products, and mergers and acquisitions.

14. *Plan Power,* developed by Applied Expert Systems, is an expert system that takes into account a company's financial situation, then matches needs with the most appropriate financial products and services. The system runs scenario spreadsheets showing the income tax situation, cash flows, net worth, and other critical factors based on alternative decisions.

15. *GURU,* developed by Micro Data Base Systems, is an expert system shell and spreadsheet providing management advice and financial analysis.

16. Peat Marwick is using the advice of an expert system to bring more consistency and precision to the auditing of commercial bank loans. This allows them to assess a company's provision for bad debts.

17. *XSEL,* Digital Equipment Corp's sales support expert system, reduced a three-hour system configuration/alternative generation task to 15 minutes and reduced the number of nonmanufacturable systems specified from 30 to 1 percent, all of which Digital claims is worth $70 million per year.

18. Canon's Optex camera lens design system has made scarce, highly skilled lens designers twelve times more productive.

19. The British National Health Services' PC-based *Performance Analyst System* reduced the time required for an evaluation task from two hours to nine minutes—a factor of 80 in productivity gain.

FUNCTIONAL AREA APPLICATIONS

In addition to the preceding applications, expert systems are used in accounting systems, capital resource planning, loan applications, strategic marketing, and developing strategic objectives for the organization.

Accounting Systems

Internal accounting systems are an ideal area for expert systems applications. Expert systems can be developed to analyze cash flows, accounts payable, accounts receivable, and the appropriate use of general ledger entries. The knowledge base can include information from accounting organizations, such as the American Institute of Certified Public Accountants (AICPA). Current tax laws, Securities and Exchange Commission requirements, and generally accepted accounting practices can also be entered into the knowledge base. The inference engine for the accounting expert system can assist in many important decisions, including financial accounting approaches, the management of cash flows, and other related accounting practices.

Four areas of accounting in which expert systems can be used are accounting standards, taxation, management and control, and auditing.

1. *Accounting standards:* An expert system applies standards in a consistent manner when preparing accounts or performing audits. This task would probably be performed more often by external auditors than by internal auditors.

2. *Taxation:* This area is restricted by a complex set of rules and procedures. Expert systems make compliance with these rules much easier since all rules can be programmed into the computer. Tax planning is an area that has also benefited. More on this is explained later.

3. *Management and control:* Expert systems are used to supplement information systems, providing decision models used for planning and control. As with any new management system the internal auditor should evaluate the potential benefits and control areas. Furthermore, the auditor must periodically evaluate established expert systems to determine whether the systems continue to meet the objectives they were designed to meet.

4. *Auditing:* Expert systems can choose an audit program, choose test sample, determine the level of error, perform an analytical review, and then make a judgment based on the findings.

   Expert systems can also assist in:

   - Preparing working papers
   - Maintaining the ledger
   - Preparing financial statements
   - Planning budgets and forecasts
   - Preparing and analyzing payroll
   - Analyzing revenue by volume, price, and product-service mix
   - Analyzing expenses
   - Specifying costs in terms of volume, price, and category
   - Converting from cash to accrual basis
   - Aging accounts receivable
   - Analyzing financial statements
   - Other financial aspects of the business

Currently, there are only a few tax expert systems available due to two primary factors. First, if the information in the knowledge base is incorrect and bad decisions are made based on the system, the developer could be sued. Second, many expert systems are developed by large firms who want to protect their investment. It is not difficult to develop an expert system using a shell. The reasons may include: the Tax Code is under constant revision (more change implies higher cost to maintain the expert system), tax practitioners do not believe in the benefits of expert systems, existing CD-ROM tax databases provide a lot of information, and tax-only expert systems are not sufficient to do business planning (more support is needed to make planning decisions).

There are examples of programs used in tax. *ExpeTAX,* developed by Coopers and Lybrand, is used in tax planning and tax accrual. It uses a question-and-answer format to run a maze of three thousand rules and outlines a client's best tax options. For example, it identifies the differences between book and tax values. *Taxadvisor* is used for estate planning. *Corptax* examines the tax consequences for stock redemptions. CCH Inc. introduced *CCH Tax Assistant,* which, while not termed an expert system by CCH, performs in many ways like an expert system. Tax Assistant accepts user-entered information while making decisions. The software can reduce the time spent by accountants calculating and generating reports. In addition, lower-level accountants can complete more difficult research tasks using the software.

Some believe that expert systems are the future in tax accounting, Expert systems could be used for compliance work, such as to determine whether an activity is passive. In addition, they could be used for identifying problems and for planning purposes, for example, to determine whether a company is a personal holding company and how to avoid the associated penalty.

Capital Expenditures Planning

Capital investment planning involves making long-term planning decisions for alternative investment opportunities. In order to grow, the company may have to make many investment decisions. Examples of capital budgeting applications are product line selection, keeping or selling a business segment, leasing or buying, and which asset to invest in. Resource commitments may also be evaluated in the form of new product development, market research, introduction of a computer, refunding of long-term debt, and so on.

Expert systems may also be used in mergers and acquisitions analysis in the form of buying another company to add a new product line. *CashValue* is a commercially available expert system in capital projects planning.

Analysis of Credit and Loan Applications

A major part of any lending institution is making sound, profitable loans to business. A large number of risky loans can result in large financial losses and potential bankruptcy for the institution. Reliable loans to companies with little chance of defaults can substantially increase a bank's overall profitability. Due to the high degree of analytical skills and experience involved, the analysis of loan applications is quite appropriate for computerized expert systems. Extending loans and lines of credit to businesses involve several key considerations, one of which is *management attitudes and style.* Does management have the ability to grow in adverse as well as in good times? How will management use the proceeds of the loan? Are there any potential problems with the company or management?

The loan analysis expert system can either accept or reject the application for loans and credit. The acceptance can also be conditioned on some criteria. For example, the loan can be made only if the company receiving the funds agrees to make certain changes in its operation, management style, marketing strategy, and so forth. The expert system can also identify questionable loans in terms of default risk. The result could be a higher interest rate, a lower loan amount, an altered repayment structure, or higher collateral requirements.

GMAC invested millions of dollars in its *Analyst* system, which evaluates the credit worthiness of GM's 10,000 domestic dealerships. The system is deployed in over 300 networked sites across the United States and pays back over $2 million a year.

Marketing Applications

Marketing expert systems can be developed to allow marketing managers to make strategic marketing-related decision-making and planning activities. Establishing sales and profit goals, products and services to focus on, and prospective customer profiles are examples.

The marketing expert system requires a knowledge base covering relevant data on customers, the overall market structure, diverse internal and external factors, and the competition. Once the overall strategic marketing plan has been mapped out, the expert system can explore specific goals. The types of marketing mix—that is, what products and services to be produced, promotional efforts, pricing considerations, and the distribution system—are resolved at this level. The product quality, style, packaging, warranties, customer services offered, features and options, and return policies are analyzed. Pricing policy decisions are equally important. The list price, discounts, and credit terms are determined as a part of price analysis. Advertising, the role of sales representatives, direct marketing, publicity, the use of marketing research firms, and using professional marketing companies are important decisions for promotion. Finally, the distribution channel of delivering products and services to customers is examined.

Forecasting is a critical activity for numerous organizations. It is often costly and complex for reasons that include a multiplicity of forecasting methods and combinations, the absence of an overall best forecasting method, and the context dependence of applicable methods, based on available models, data characteristics, and the environment. In recent years AI-based techniques have been developed to support various operations management activities. One AI technique, namely *rule induction,* can be used to improve forecasting accuracy. Specifically, the proposed methodology involves training a rule induction-based ES with a set of time series data (the training set). Inputs to the ES include selected time-series features and, for each time-series, the most accurate forecasting method from those available. Subsequently, the ES is used to recommend the most accurate forecasting method for a new set of time series (the testing set).

Applications in Production, Operations, and Business Process Reengineering

Production scheduling involves the allocation of raw materials and machinery among various product lines. The Goodyear Tire & Rubber Co. plant in Houston, Texas developed an expert system, *The Manager for Interactive Modeling Interfaces (MIMI),* to improve production scheduling. Within two years, the plant had cut its inventory and operating costs, increased plant capacity, improved delivery performance, and reduced transportation costs. MIMI integrates an expert system with simulation capabilities, allowing the plant to create an exact scheduling model for the plant. An ES is also used to build design and configuration systems that support the reuse and modification of standard designs. Two notable examples are Nippon Steel's *QDES* and Lockheed's *Clavier.*

Computer companies such as Digital Equipment Corporation (DEC) are using expert systems to help configure computer systems. Digital Equipment Corporation is also utilizing expert systems to act as a sales assistant and to help perform scheduling functions. Aerospace firms such as Boeing and Lockheed have developed expert systems for navigation control, planning and scheduling functions, fault diagnosis, and training functions. Boeing has even developed a workstation called *Aquinas* to help perform knowledge acquisition and knowledge base development.

Compaq Computer's *SMART* system is an integrated call-tracking and problem-resolution system that contains hundreds of cases related to diagnostic problems arising in the use of Compaq products. The system is in use by Compaq's Customer Service Department in handling calls to the central toll-free number. Incoming customer problems are presented to SMART, which retrieves the most similar cases from its case base and presents them to the customer service analyst, who then uses them to resolve the problem. Evaluation of the initial version of SMART indicated the percentage of customer problems resolved on the first call rose from 50 percent without the system to 87 percent with the use of the system. According to Compaq, the system paid for itself within a year. SMART runs on PCs running the Microsoft Windows operating environment.

Oil companies such as Schlumberger-Doll and Amoco have developed expert systems to help with mineral exploration and identification of faults in the oil-refining process. Airline companies have used expert systems for assigning planes to gates at selected major airports. Telecommunications firms are using expert systems on a daily basis to identify telephone cable and switch maintenance problems and to provide online assistance to network analysts and operators. Trucking companies are using expert systems for resource allocation and scheduling functions. Financial institutions and investment firms use some expert systems for providing financial and estate planning advice. Insurance companies are using expert systems for assisting underwriters in questioning clients on life insurance.

ES can be used to detect and analyze various patterns of variation that can occur in manufacturing quality control charts. The expert system looks for the following six potential patterns of variation: (1) trend, (2) cycle, (3) mixture, (4) shift, (5) stratification, and (6) systematic. Statistical significance tests as interpretive rules are used to determine the pattern of variation. Once the pattern is identified, the expert system supplies the user with possible causes for the out-of-control condition. The magnitude of the out-of-control condition and where it starts and stops are also provided.

Many production/operations activities such as facilities layout design, product planning and design, process selection, and CAD/CAM are also being made in conjunction with ES methodology. Most successful manufacturers improve their designs and processes continually. This is possible with systems that manage design and manufacturing data effectively. Giddings & Lewis's Assembly Automation Division decided to have its process planners build on the company's knowledge base instead of creating new plans for each order. Management saw cultivating such a knowledge base as an expedient way to reduce time to market and respond to customer demands for installing automated custom assembly lines, such as the body line at the

Saturn plant and the chassis line for the new Ford Explorer, in six months instead of the usual nine to eighteen months.

ES applications are also found in business process reengineering. One such example is the *Prism* telex classification system developed by Cognitive Systems, Inc. Prism is used in several banks to route incoming international telex communications to appropriate recipients, a task relying on the accurate classification of the telex to determine the appropriate routing. Prism increased classification accuracy from 75 to 90 percent and reduced the average time taken to route a telex from several minutes (from human telex operators) to 30 seconds. Prism also demonstrated improvements in accuracy and speed over a previous rule-based implementation of the same type of system. Prism runs on Macintosh-11 workstations. Another example of business process reengineering is NEC Corporation's *SQUAD* system. SQUAD is an ambitious long-term effort to provide a corporatewide system for the capture and distribution of software quality-control knowledge. Some 3,000 cases per year have been added to the system since 1982, and the developers estimate the productivity savings due to the use of SQUAD at over $100 million per year. SQUAD runs on UNIX workstations.

APPLICATIONS IN FINANCE

Banking

Banks have become big-time converts because ES and AI are saving them a bundle. Among MasterCard International Inc.'s member institutions, for example, ES programs that are designed to nip credit card fraud in the bud prevented the loss of an estimated $50 million in one 18-month period. Other companies joining the bandwagon are Citibank and Deere & Co.

Insurance

- *Underwriting:* Expert systems can increase the consistency of applying company standards in evaluating various risks (fire, flood, theft, and so on).

- *Claims processing:* Fraud detection is particularly difficult in medical insurance due to the complexity of claims. Expert systems can substantially reduce labor cost by quickly evaluating claims and improving the detection of suspicious information.

- *Reserving:* Deciding how much reserve to set aside for future claims and ongoing payout is similar to factory inventory schedules. In many ways, ES can provide the means to consistently allocate resources to meet uncertain demands.

Portfolio Management

- *Security selection:* With over 100,000 stocks and bonds to choose from, selecting the right securities is a substantial challenge. Too much information is available than can be intelligently digested. ES analyzes data and provides recommendations. For example, Unitek Technologies' *Expert Strategist* performs financial statement analysis.

- *Consistent application of constraints:* Managers of multiple portfolios must consistently apply multiple constraints on different portfolios. The constraints include compliance with legal SEC rules, clients' guidelines, consistency across related accounts, etc. ES helps financial professionals in applying different portfolio designs under multiple constraints.

- *Hedge advisor:* The number of financial instruments available and the complexity of their relationships are increasing rapidly. These instruments vary in margin, liquidity, and price. They can be combined to create "synthetic securities," thereby hedging against market risk. ES helps the process of creating "synthetic securities."

Trading Advisor

- *Real-time data feed:* Timely information is critical in any trading application. Expert systems integrate real-time multiple external/internal data sources, and provide timely information.

- *Trading rules and rule generators:* The conventional knowledge-engineering approach to rule writing is replaced by rule generators. A rule-generator ES recognizes data patterns and generates immediate hypothesis (trading rules) that lead to trading recommendations.

- *Critics and neural nets:* Critic ES review and evaluate system-recommended trades, process explanations of those trades, and find out culprits and heroes.

The Global Financial Market

- *Financial statement advice for multinational companies:* Multinational firms have unique problems with regard to reporting and legal requirements. These firms must deal with inconsistencies, such as varying reporting formats, regulatory requirements, and account types. These problems can be solved by ES.

- *24-hour trading programs:* Individual human traders cannot work for 24 hours, but ES can. With traderless expert systems, smaller companies can have a better chance of entering global markets and foreign exchange trading.

- *Hedges:* In the international security markets, many different types of hedges are possible, including interest rate swaps, currency swaps, options, and futures. ES can take advantage of those hedges.

- *Arbitrage:* ES quickly identify and evaluate arbitrage opportunities, and triggers transactions.

BENEFITS AND DISADVANTAGES OF EXPERT SYSTEMS

Expert systems offer the following benefits:

- Increased output and productivity as well as better accuracy, quality, and reliability

- Tutorial function, since they distill expertise into clearly defined rules

- Capture of scarce expertise

- Knowledge sharing (The system is available to provide second opinions within the domain, as well as provide what-if analysis where results are sought on variable changes.)

- A shorter decision time (Routine decisions are rapidly made by the system.)

- Enhancement of problem-solving capabilities

- More secure systems than an expert employee, who may be hired by a competitor

- Reduced errors

- Decreased personnel required
- Reduced training time
- Improved decisions
- Retention of volatile or portable knowledge
- Improved customer service

The drawbacks to expert systems are that:

- They fail to adapt to a continually changing environment.
- They are usually confined to a very narrow domain and may have difficulty coping with broad discipline knowledge decisions.

THE APPLICATIONS OF ARTIFICIAL INTELLIGENCE

Besides expert systems, these are the major AI applications.

Fuzzy Logic

Fuzzy logic deals with uncertainty. This technique, which uses the mathematical theory of fuzzy sets, simulates the process of normal human reasoning by allowing the computer to behave less precisely and logically than conventional computers. Fuzzy logic is a type of mathematics. It deals with nonprecise values with a certain degree of uncertainty. This technology allows logistics to be utilized by nonprecise information.

Applications of fuzzy logic have been in controllers of appliances such as rice cookers, VCRs, air conditioners, and cameras. In these products fuzzy logic is used to make continuous small adjustments instead of merely switching a feature on or off. Fuzzy logic can be advantageous because it:

- Provides flexibility
- Gives you options
- Gives you imagination
- Is forgiving
- Allows for observation

For example, fuzzy logic is being used extensively in consumer products whose input is provided by sensors rather than by people. It is believed that fuzzy logic will become a valuable component in the next generation of computer systems. In such systems, each of the central technology building blocks can be used in series or in parallel.

As another example, a fuzzy reasoning model was constructed and applied to contract decision making in Hong Kong. According to professional experience, six inputs are identified as essential factors determining contract choice: (1) the scale of the project, (2) the nature of the works to be carried out, (3) the characteristics of the client, (4) the time constraint, (5) the source of materials for construction, and (6) the characteristics of the building design. These factors determine whether the contract to be chosen should be in the form of a simple quotation, a lump sum contract on drawings and specifications, a schedule of rates, a management contract, a lump sum contract in standard form without quantities, or one with quantities. Many decision rules are then constructed based on expert opinions.

Automatic Programming

Automatic programming is described as a "super-compiler," or a program that could take in a very high-level description of what the program is to accomplish and produce a program in a specific programming language. One of the important contributions of research in automatic programming has been the notion of debugging as a problem-solving strategy. It has been found that it is often much more efficient to produce an inexpensive, errorful solution to a programming or robot control problem and then modify it, than to insist on a first solution completely free of defects.

Natural Language Processing

Natural language technology gives computer users the ability to communicate with computers in their native language. This technology allows for a conversational type of interface, in contrast to using a programming language of computer jargon, syntax, and commands. Limited success in this area is typified by current systems that can recognize and interpret written sentences. Although this ability can be used to great advantage with some applications, a general natural language processing (NGP) system is not yet possible. There are two types of natural language processing:

- *Natural language understanding:* This process investigates methods of allowing the computer to comprehend instructions given in ordinary English so that the computer can understand people more easily.

- *Natural language generation:* This process allows computers to produce ordinary English language so that people can understand computers more easily.

Intelligent Agent

An *intelligent agent* is defined as software that can perform intelligent functions. This technology is one of the fastest growing areas of research and new application development on the Internet today. The key attributes of intelligent agents are:

- *Autonomy:* The intelligent agent must have the capability to take actions leading to the completion of tasks or objectives, without trigger or impetus from the end-user. The agent must have an element of independence. Much like human agents, they take our direction, interests, wants, and desires as input and perform actions to achieve goals.

- *Communication ability:* Intelligent agents should access information from the environment about the current "state" in the course of achieving their objectives. This requires the ability to communicate with the repositories of this information.

- *Capability for cooperation:* Intelligent agents must have a collaborative "spirit" to work with other agents for complex problem domains that require multiagent efforts.

- *Capability for reasoning:* Intelligent agents should be able to conduct reasoning based on an existing knowledge base including rule-based, case-based, and artificial evolution-based systems. Rule-based reasoning is the use of a set of user preconditions to evaluate conditions in the external environment. Case-based reasoning is drawing suggestions or conclusions based on prior scenarios and resulting actions, from which they deduce their future moves. In artificial evolution based-reasoning, agents are able to acquire new knowledge each time problems are solved.

- *Adaptive behavior:* An intelligent agent must have some mechanism for accessing the current state of its external domain so that the agent can improve or adjust itself for further actions.

Intelligent Computer-Aided Instruction

Intelligent computer-aided instruction (ICAI) refers to machines that can tutor humans so that information can be passed. Computer-assisted instruction (CAI), which has been in use for several decades, brings the power of the computer to bear on the educational process. Now AI technologies are applied to the development of intelligent computer-assisted instruction systems in an attempt to create computerized tutors that shape their teaching techniques to fit the learning patterns of individual employees.

MECHANICS OF NEURAL NETWORKS

Expert systems typically require huge databases of information gathered from recognized experts in a given field. The system then asks questions of the user and deduces an answer based on the responses given and the information in the database. These answers are not necessarily right, but should be logical conclusions based on the information provided.

Neural networks (NNs) are a developing technology in which computers try to learn from the database and the operator what the right answer is to a question. The system gets positive or negative response to output from the operator and stores that data so that it will make a better decision the next time. While still in its infancy, this technology shows promise for use in fraud detection, economic forecasting, and risk appraisals.

The idea behind this software is to convert the order-taking computer into a "thinking" problem solver. This would allow computers to take over some of the more mundane decision-making jobs of accountants, such as determining if a lease is operating or capital. Neural networks are software programs that simulate human intelligence. They are designed to learn from experience. For example, each time a neural network program makes the right decision (which is predetermined by a human instructor) on recognizing a number or sequence-of-action pattern, the programmer reinforces the program with a confirmation message that is stored. In the event of a wrong decision, a negative message is reinforced. Thus, it gradually builds experimental knowledge in that subject.

Today most neural networks take the form of mathematical simulations embedded in software that runs on ordinary microprocessors. Future developments will include the emergence of network chips that will dramatically increase both the speed of operations and their work applications.

These chips will be used to mimic decision operations and carry them out the way humans do.

Neural Network Applications in Business

Currently a neural computer network is being employed at the Mellon Bank's Visa and MasterCard operation in Wilmington, Delaware which daily tracks 1.2 million accounts. One of the functions of this operation's computer is to scan customer purchases and look for spending patterns that may indicate stolen credit cards. The neural network compares purchases with customer behaviors. It also generates data without being told to do so because the system has been programmed to take the initiative and think like a human.

One way in which neural networks will help accountants is in internal audits. Complex pattern recognition tasks performed by NNs include forecasting earnings and detecting fraud. The ability to forecast a company's earnings may be useful in planning an audit or assisting management in developing an operating strategy. While many types of NNs exist, those useful to financial managers can be classified in four categories: prediction networks, classification networks, data-filtering networks, and optimization networks. NNs are much more tolerant of perfections in the input data than conventional computers and are much more efficient at solving pattern recognition problems. NNs also overcome many of the limitations of expert systems, including the necessity to extract knowledge from experts and the inability to learn. Ernst & Young in Dallas is working on an application that would allow financial managers to improve their handling of working capital.

Neural networks are beginning to be helpful in many business problems when information is not easy to quantify. They are being used in the management of portfolios. A portfolio manager must continuously scan for nonperforming stocks, while on the other side stock analysts are looking for undervalued stocks. Neural networks are particularly good for problems when deductive reasoning gives mixed results. The inductive reasoning of neural networks can do a better job. A large store of historical information about good and bad investments can be analyzed for relationships that may be quite subtle. Shearson–Lehman is using neural networks to predict stock patterns.

Further, neural networks appear to be a useful tool in bankruptcy prediction. They can use some of the tools already in place to improve prediction. If the ratios chosen for the Z-Score model (discussed in Chapter 10) are used but the neural network is allowed to form its own functions, the predictive abilities of the Z-score formula can be much improved. This is of significant value to managers, creditors, and investors since misclassification, particularly of a firm that is going bankrupt, has huge monetary implications. The *Neural Bankruptcy Prediction Program,* developed in 1995 by Dorsey, Edmister, and Johnson, is a good example. This DOS-based software is available and can be downloaded from the University of Missouri Business School's Internet web page (www.bus.olemiss.edu/johnson/compress/compute.htm). The following example illustrates an application of this program.

Example 1 A set of financial data was obtained from America Online's "Financial Reports" database. Each corporation's 1994 (one year prior to the insolvency) financial reports are shown here. Then the following 18 ratios required by the Neural Network Bankruptcy Prediction Program were calculated (see Table 11-2):

Table 11-2.
DATA SET RATIO DEFINITIONS

Ratio	Definition
CASH/TA	Cash/Total assets
CASH/TS	Cash/Net sales
CF/TD	Cash flow operations income/Total liabilities
CA/CL	Total current assets/Total current liabilities
CA/TA	Total current assets/Total assets
CA/TS	Total current assets/Net sales
EBIT/TA	(Interest expense + Income before tax)/Total assets
LOG (INT+15)	LOG (Interest expense + Income before tax)/(Total assets + 15)
LOG (TA)	LOG (Total assets)
MVE/TK	Shareholder's equity/(Total assets − Total current liabilities)
NI/TA	Net income/Total assets
QA/CL	(Total current assets − Inventories)/Total current liabilities
QA/TA	(Total current assets − Inventories)/Total assets
QA/TS	(Total current assets − Inventories)/Net sales
RE/TA	Retained earnings/Total assets
TD/TA	Total liabilities/Total assets
WK/TA	(Total assets/Net sales)/(Working capital/Total assets)
WK/TS	1/(Net sales/Working capital)

Table 11-2 (continued)
RESULTS OF 1994 DATA ANALYSIS FOR A SELECTED GROUP OF FIRMS

Year	Company	Bankrupt (1-yes/0-no)	Value	Insolvency Predicted (1-yes/0-no)	Error
1994	Apparel Ventures Inc.	0	0.38085095	0	
1994	Apple Computer Inc.	0	0.00267937	0	
1994	Biscayne Apparel Inc.	0	0.43153563	1	
1994	Epitope Inc.	0	0.18238553	0	
1994	Montgomery Ward Holding Co.	0	0.06268501	0	30%
1994	Schwerman Trucking Co.	0	0.57828138	1	
1994	Signal Apparel Co.	0	0.37081639	0	
1994	Southern Pacific Transportation	0	−0.3514775	0	
1994	Time Warner Inc.	0	0.57828138	1	
1994	Warner Insurance Services	0	−0.1020344	0	
1994	Baldwin Builders	1	0.57828138	1	
1994	Bradlees Inc.	1	1.00828347	1	
1994	Burlington Motor Holdings	1	1.00828347	1	
1994	Clothestime Inc.	1	0.43153563	1	
1994	Dow Corning	1	0.65517535	1	0%
1994	Edison Brothers Stores	1	0.61124180	1	
1994	Freymiller Trucking Co.	1	1.00828347	1	
1994	Lamonts Apparel Inc.	1	1.28955072	1	
1994	Plaid Clothing Group Inc.	1	1.28955072	1	
1994	Smith Corona Co.	1	0.43153563	1	

Companies with values over 0.4 (the threshold value) are predicted as insolvent. Three of ten solvent companies (as of early 1998) received values over 0.4, indicating bankruptcy. Although those companies did not go bankrupt in 1995, they can be considered as "high-risk." The results of the insolvent companies' analysis was rather impressive; all of the insolvent corporations are recognized.

The foregoing analysis confirms that the Neural Network Bankruptcy Prediction Program is a reliable tool for screening financially distressed large companies. Despite the small sample size, 100-percent accuracy in predicting insolvency was remarkable. The program is a relatively simple and easy process for analyzing data and interpreting the results. It holds promise even to those who are not proficient in mathematics.

Further, the program allows the user to import data from a Compact Disc (CD.) This CD contains all public corporations' 10K reports and is available to financial analysts. The program calculates in ratios after drawing data from the CD. This eliminates the time and effort in collecting data and calculating ratios. A high accuracy rate may make the program a useful decision-making tool for purchasing and selling bonds. It may also be a valuable tool in screening large corporations or financial institutions when:

- Lending money
- Contracting to supply or to receive products and services
- Leasing property
- Purchasing stocks

Because many financially distressed corporations and financial institutions are in active operation, it is a good idea to analyze their likeliness of going bankrupt before one decides to do business with them.

Popular Neural Network Software

The following is a list of popular neural network software.

VENDORS AND PRODUCTS

AL WARE INC.
3659 Green Road
Beachwood, Ohio 44122
(216) 421-2380
Products: Unix computer system
VMS computer system

CALIFORNIA SCIENTIFIC SOFTWARE
10024 Newtown Road
Nevada City, California 95959
(800) 284-8112
Products: BrainMaker
BrainMaker Plus
Condensed Version

HNC SOFTWARE, INC.
5930 Cornerstone Court West
San Diego, California 92121-3728
(619) 546-8877
Products: Explore Net 3000
           Knowledge Net

NEURAL SYSTEMS, INC.
2827 West 43rd Avenue
Vancouver, British Columbia V6N 3HG
Canada
(604) 263-3667
Product: Genesis

NEURAL WARE, INC.
220 Park West Drive
Pittsburgh, Pennsylvania 15275
(800) 635-2442
Products: Neural Works Professional, II/Plus
           Neural Works Explorer

SCIENTIFIC CONSULTANT SERVICES, INC.
20 Stagecoach Road
Selden, New York 11784
(516) 696-3333
Product: N-Train

TRIANT TECHNOLOGIES
20 Townsite Road, 2nd Floor
Nanainmo, British Columbia V9S 5T7
Canada
(800) 633-8611
Products: ModelWare
           ModelWare Professional

Table 11-3 lists commercially available AI, ES, and neural network software products, describes their major features, gives their prices, and provides developers' names, addresses, and telephone number.

Table 11-3.
ARTIFICIAL INTELLIGENCE SOFTWARE

(in alphabetical order by developer's name)

VENDOR

AI Ware
3659 Green Road
Beachwood, Ohio 44122
Tel: (216) 514-9700
Fax: (216) 514-9030
e-mail: ai-sales@aiware.com

PRODUCT AND DESCRIPTION

a. *Business Advisor* is a complete business forecasting and optimization decision support system providing solutions to business problems. It utilizes neural networks and fuzzy logic in modeling. The software tells the business person how to achieve his objectives for any one or combination of outputs. It identifies the values of the inputs or outputs to achieve an optimized condition based upon the established constraints and priorities. Relationship patterns are uncovered between business and operating strategies. Business models relate to how you perform your tasks, procedures, policies, and operating conditions, and uncover their effects on profitability and operating strategies. The business models enable you to anticipate problems so you can make more efficient use of resources and time. It aids in selecting financial opportunities and lowering risk. It improves decision making by simulating decision choices and appraising each one based on your goals and constraints. Sensitivity analysis identifies relative effects of varying inputs. There are multi-objective features and import/export capabilities with Microsoft Office. *Business Advisor* has many business applications including fraud detection, risk management, forecasting revenue and costs (including by area or product), budgeting, bankruptcy prediction, valuing securities, estimating production yields, maximizing rate of return on investments, resource requirement planning, lost sales evaluation, demographic appraisal, fault detection in machinery and products, quality appraisal and improvement, site selection, optimizing product/service mix, analyzing survey responses, predicting personnel staffing levels, and pinpointing sales prospects.

Price: $9,995

b. *Process Advisor* is a process monitoring and optimization system. It develops process models considering such factors as manufacturing costs, age of machinery, raw material levels, operating characteristics, quality levels, and by-products. The relationship modeling helps predict quality upstream, formulate improved operating strategies, anticipate preventive maintenance needs, and make better use of equipment. The system aids in feature-based design and manufacturing problem solving, lowering costs, reducing environmental impact, improving efficiency and productivity, improving preventive maintenance scheduling, and reducing energy consumption. *Process Advisor* can detect data patterns preceding mechanical problems and by so doing avoiding unnecessary repairs and downtime. The user may run process simulations for pilot projects or new production strategies. Process models help understand relationships and trade-offs, and to anticipate changes.

Price: $10,000

Table 11-3 (continued)

c. *CAD/CHEM* is a formulation modeling and multi-objective optimization system using intuitive neural networks, sensitivity analysis, data clustering, and fuzzy objective functions. It allows you to choose between design trade-offs and sees the effects of changes in formulation. *CAD/CHEM* aids in making better products faster, shortens the time to market, integrates the product development process, improves processing efficiency and performance, and optimizes product quality at lower costs. It improves responsiveness to customer demands, costs, resource constraints, and environmental regulations.

Price: $4,995

VENDOR

Acquired Intelligence Inc.
1095 McKenzie Ave., Ste. 205
Victoria, British Columbia
Canada V8P 2L5
Tel: (250) 479-8646
Fax: (205) 479-0764
WWW Site: http://www.com/ai/acquire/price.htm

PRODUCT AND DESCRIPTION

Acquire is an expert-based knowledge acquisition system having business applications.

Price: $995

VENDOR

BioCamp Systems, Inc.
4018 148th Ave., N.E.
Redmond, Washington 98052
Tel: (800) 716-6770
Fax: (425) 869-6850
WWW Site: http://www.bio-comp.com

PRODUCT AND DESCRIPTION

Neuro Genetic and Trade is neural network software to discover and model the hidden and important relationships in such data as sales figures, financial market information, marketing research survey information, customer profiles, and demographic information. The software can detect fraud for auditor attention, evaluate processing costs and quality, forecast product/service demand, explain consumer behavior, aid in materials management, prepare forecasts, and optimize investment management.

Price: 16 inputs $295, 32 inputs $395, 64 inputs $595, etc.

Table 11-3 (continued)

VENDOR

California Scientific Software
10024 Newton Road
Nevada City, California 95959
Tel: (800) 284-8112
Fax: (916) 478-9041
e-mail: sales@calsci.com
WWW Site: http://www.calsci.com

PRODUCT AND DESCRIPTION

Brain Maker Professional is neural network simulation software used in solving business problems, financial forecasts of revenue and costs, conducts manufacturing analysis (e.g., safety, production yields, quality), evaluates processing costs, analyzes loan applications, performs investment analysis, predicts current prices, predicts corporate bond ratings, predicts the S&P 500 index, appraises real estate, and performs marketing analysis. The software shows the relationship between two types of data, recognizes patterns, performs sensitivity analysis, and generates financial indicators.

Price: $795

VENDOR

Elf Software Company
210 W. 101st Street
New York, New York 10025
Tel: (212) 316-9078.

PRODUCT AND DESCRIPTION

Access Elf is query interface software to access Microsoft databases.

Price: $49

VENDOR

HNC Software Inc.
5930 Cornerstone Court West
San Diego, California 92121-3728
Tel: (619) 546-8877
Fax: (619) 452-6524

PRODUCT AND DESCRIPTION

a. *Falcon Payment Card Fraud Detection System* is neural network software that audits and detects fraudulent transactions by customer accounts of card-issuing banks and other financial institutions. The system monitors and scores card transactions for fraud. Different score thresholds may be assigned to different

Table 11-3 (continued)

sets of credit cards. Fraud analysts use the system to identify potential problems (e.g., fraudulent transactions in a particular ZIP Code). The neural network-based models determine the probability of fraud with each transaction by comparing it with the cardholder's known purchase patterns. If necessary, the transaction may be blocked.

Price: Varies from $250,000–$600,000 per installation plus $.02 per account per month

b. *Capstone Application Decision Processing System* is software that books new payment card accounts both efficiently and profitably. It is capable of processing approximately 10,000 applications per hour with real-time credit pulls and high-speed network access for analyst workstations. The system is an intelligent neural network with user-definable rules, and the ability to incorporate traditional score cards. It has an expert rules base letting each issuer specify the decision flow that meets its needs. The system identifies and refuses poor applications.

Price: Varies from $250,000–$600,000 per installation plus $.02 per account per month

VENDOR

IBM
Department AC 297, AS/400
P.O. Box 16848
Atlanta, Georgia 30321-0848
Tel: (800) IBM-CALL
Fax: (800) 2 IBM-FAX

PRODUCT AND DESCRIPTION

a. *Knowledge Tool for AS/400* is a troubleshooting knowledge expert-base application software performing risk analysis and capacity planning.

Price: Ranging from $685 to $4,205 depending on product group purchased

b. *The Integrated Reasoning Sheel for OS/2 Release 3* is an expert system shell providing for the development of knowledge-based applications in a workstation environment. It facilitates the management of performance and growth of the business. The shell creates application solutions to business problems, improves operations, and has productivity enhancements. The shell enables large amounts of data to be analyzed quickly, resulting in recommendations to increase the responsiveness of the company.

Price: Basic license $8,190 (one-time charge with receipt of enhancements at no additional charge); additional license $7,875

c. *Neural Network Utility Product Family* is neural network software used to identify financial trends and patterns to guide business operations. It discovers relationships in large sets of financial data to make predictions about new data. It incorporates rules and guidelines for better decision making. The software can detect fraud, assess (score) risk, perform portfolio management, and test products.

Price: Ranging from $495 to $4,995 depending on product group purchased

Table 11-3 (continued)

VENDOR

Level 5 Research
1335 Gateway Drive, Ste. 2005
Melbourne, Florida 32901
Tel: (800) 444-4303
Tel: (407) 729-6004
Fax: (407) 727-7615
WWW site: http://www.L5R.com

PRODUCT AND DESCRIPTION

a. *Level 5 Object Professional Release 3.0 for Microsoft Windows* is a knowledge-based expert system development shell tool. *Object* is the basis to build an intelligent business support system. It shows object relationships within the company and can represent complex data structures (e.g, linked lists, queues, and trees). It aids in budgeting, scheduling of resources and activities, planning shipments, making manufacturing decisions, and managing inventory (including on-line stock reporting). *Object* allows for targeted trouble shooting and corrective action to solve business problems. It allows for the tracking and following up of opportunities from initial identification to final contract. Different types of reports may be created using various selection criteria in extracting information from a database. It increases corporate productivity at all levels of the organization. Motorola uses this system.

Price: $2,995

b. *Level 5 Quest* is a fuzzy logic base query environment search engine. It scores and ranks results of a search based on their relevance and importance to the business. *Quest* provides an array of match methods using artificial intelligence.

Price: $96

VENDOR

Multi Logic
1720 Louisiana Blvd., N.E., Ste. 312
Albuquerque, New Mexico 87110
Tel: (800) 676-8356
Fax: (800) 256-8356
WWW Site: http://www.exsysinfo.com/products/prices.htm

PRODUCT AND DESCRIPTION

Multi Logic Exsys Professional is a knowledge-based neural network development tool used in business for financial modeling and allocation of corporate resources to improve the rate of return.

Price: $2,900

Table 11-3 (continued)

VENDOR

Neural Ware Inc.
202 Park West Drive
Pittsburgh, Pennsylvania 15275
Tel: (800) 635-2442
Fax: (412) 787-8220
WWW Site: http://www.neuralware.com

PRODUCT AND DESCRIPTION

Neural Works Predict is a neural network product used to solve prediction, modeling, and classification problems. It can be used to identify credit card and insurance fraud, loan analysis, investment analysis, financial forecasting, database marketing including market segmentation, process modeling, risk management, evaluating new customers for credit purposes, predicting future warranty claims, industrial inspection and quality control, and rate bonds. It has features of sensitivity analysis, case-based reasoning, and explanation.

Price: $1,995

VENDOR

Scientific Consultant Services, Inc.
20 Stagecoach Road
Selden, New York 11784
Tel: (516) 696-3333

PRODUCT AND DESCRIPTION

a. *N-Train: Neural Network System* is neural network software aiding in solving business problems such as evaluating credit risk, trading in the financial markets, controlling manufacturing processes, and detecting and analyzing signals of difficulties arising. The system is useful in business decision making, pattern recognition of accounts, classification of financial data, and forecasting. Acceptable error measurements may be selected.

Price: $747 (4 add-on modules are available at an additional total cost of $299)

b. *Trading Systems for Trade Station* are rule-based expert systems for investment portfolio selection. They include technical analysis of stocks and commodities and incorporate consideration of foreign currencies.

Price: $240 per system (minimum order of 5 systems for $1,200)

c. *The Trading Simulator* is a simulation of trading accounts and portfolios. It can simulate systems over multiple contracts.

Price: $495

Table 11-3 (continued)

VENDOR

Sterling Wentworth Corp.
57 West 200 South, Ste. 500
Salt Lake City, Utah 84101
Tel: (800) 752-6637 / Fax: (801) 355-9792

PRODUCT AND DESCRIPTION

Expert Series is expert system software used in personal financial planning for clients. It performs portfolio management, data management, risk analysis and management, estate planning, retirement planning, income tax planning, and cash flow analysis.

Price: $1,695

VENDOR

Texas Instruments Corp.
P.O. Box 660246
Mail Station 8671
Dallas, Texas 75266
Tel: (800) 336-5236

PRODUCT AND DESCRIPTION

Capital Investment Expert System is artificial intelligence software that analyzes, manages, and reports on the purchase of machinery and equipment. It includes cash flow analysis, legal aspects (e.g., conformity to environmental regulations), and installation considerations. The expert system recommends if the fixed assets should be bought or not and why. The software results in buying only financially and operationally feasible equipment.

Price: Varies with application

VENDOR

Triant Technologies
20 Townsite Road, 2nd Floor
Nanainmo, British Columbia, Canada V9S 5T7
Tel: (800) 663-8611 / Fax: (604) 754-2388
e-mail: mail@triant.com

PRODUCT AND DESCRIPTION

Model Ware is an expert system involving predictive modeling. It can be used in credit analysis, forecasting stock and commodity prices, detecting faults in the manufacturing process, simulation, quality control, customer retention analysis, financial securities trading analysis, and production and inventory planning. It includes graphic capabilities. *Model Ware* can predict up to 150 variables simultaneously.

Price: $595

12

AUDITING INFORMATION TECHNOLOGY*

Information technology (IT) techniques have had an enormous impact on information management and auditing. IT auditors are a source of invaluable assistance to an organization (see Appendix E). They provide special skills and have a thorough understanding of computer technology.

TWO TYPES OF AUDITORS

There are two types of auditors: internal auditors and external auditors. Both internal and external auditors perform an independent appraisal function. *Internal auditors,* however, work for a given organization and its management. *External auditors* are not employed by the organization. External auditors are typically certified public accountants (CPAs) and are not working under the management of an organization. CPAs are generally hired to perform an independent audit of an organization's financial statements. Their primary purpose in an audit is to ascertain the reliability of financial statements.

Internal auditors' scope is generally broader. Internal auditors are concerned with safeguarding their organizations' assets as well as promoting operational efficiency. Internal auditors are also concerned with ensuring

---

*This chapter was coauthored by Uzma Qureshi, EDP Auditor, Higher Education Services Corporation of New York.

that their companies have adequate internal controls and that the procedures used are cost-efficient as well as cost-effective. Internal auditors typically report to top management or the audit committee.

Both internal and external auditors perform IT auditing. The IT auditor has technical expertise not only in auditing but also in computer technology. IT auditors help an organization assess the risks related to the use of computer technology. They also help by recommending appropriate controls, which tend to be more complex than controls in manual systems. Specialized computer audit techniques must be used in highly complex automated environments.

IT auditors frequently review planned enhancements to computer systems. They also evaluate and review systems under development. The purpose of the IT auditors' review is to ensure that systems meet quality criteria and contain adequate controls. Participation in the development process avoids the need to modify systems after they have been implemented. Modification afterward tends to be difficult and expensive—sometimes even impossible. The review should include determining whether there is compliance with the organization's system development methodology.

While IT auditors may review and evaluate systems, they should take care to remain independent and objective. The IT auditor must not assume any operational responsibility for system development.

IT auditors' responsibilities include audits of data centers, which are an important part of any organization. An audit of a data center generally entails a review of:

- The organizational structure of the data center
- Systems development standards
- The efficiency and effectiveness of operating and administrative procedures
- Library control procedures for programs and data
- Networks
- Backups
- Contingency planning
- Security
- Personnel practices

External auditors, in consultation with IT auditors, often review application systems. Programmed control procedures such as edit checks and exception reporting are especially important. Other controls that auditors consider include:

- Segregation of duties
- Management approval of transactions
- Timely completion of job duties

The IT auditor is also responsible for determining whether adequate controls exist:

- To ensure that transactions are processed accurately, completely, and with management's authorization
- To prevent and detect errors and omissions

IT auditors often provide assistance to external auditors and operational internal auditors. Assistance to internal auditors typically includes:

- Collecting, extracting, and analyzing data
- Reviewing and testing internal controls
- Investigating exceptions

Audit efficiency can be enhanced by coordinating IT auditors' and external auditors' activities. IT auditors might be called on to train and guide non-IT auditors in IT procedures and methods. IT auditors might manage the computer system during audit processing.

ACCEPTING FINANCIAL AUDIT ENGAGEMENTS

The decision to accept or continue with a client is based on several factors:

- The auditor must evaluate the integrity of management. There is a greater likelihood of errors and irregularities when management lacks integrity.

- The auditor should identify any unusual risks or special circumstances in accepting the engagement. For example, the auditor should consider the client's financial stability.

- The auditor should assess the CPA firm's ability to competently perform the audit. This involves determining if the CPA firm has individuals with appropriate technical background. This also involves considering the need for consultants and specialists.

- The auditor should consider whether the professional standards for independence are satisfied.

- An engagement letter should be prepared by the auditor and accepted by the client. It should include, among other things, information about the scope of the audit as well as audit fees. The engagement letter is a legal contract between the auditor and the client. It should be renewed each year.

PERFORMING AUDIT TESTS

In both manual and automated systems, auditors generally conduct two types of tests: test of controls and substantive tests.

Test of Controls

The auditor first reviews internal controls to determine if they have been designed properly. If so, the next step is to do a test of controls, primarily to ensure that controls are functioning as designed and planned.

The auditors' reliance on the controls determines the extent of substantive procedures required. When testing controls, the auditor typically performs procedures such as:

- Observation
- Inquiry
- Reperformance

The auditor typically does not test all the controls. The importance of the controls with respect to overall objectives is the primary factor used to select controls. Any problem discovered by the auditor during evaluation and testing is reported to management.

Controls can be tested either around the computer or through the computer. Testing *around the computer* involves the auditor using a black box approach. It is similar to testing controls in a manual system. Auditors use this approach to avoid reliance on complex computer programs. Auditors also test around the computer when they would rather use manual auditing procedures with which they are familiar. The main disadvantage of auditing around the computer is that the capabilities of the computer are not used in extracting and analyzing the data.

Testing *through the computer,* using computer-assisted audit techniques, results in significant cost savings. Testing through the computer is especially useful when the transaction trail is not visible or when a large number of records needs to be tested. Testing through the computer is necessary when significant controls are programmed into the computer application.

Three commonly used *computer-assisted audit techniques (CAATs)* are: parallel simulation, test data, and integrated test facility.

- *Parallel simulation:* Actual company data is reprocessed by the auditor using a controlled software program. This technique does not affect the client's actual data files.

- *Test data:* The auditor prepares dummy transactions that are processed by the client's computer program. The test data contain both valid and invalid conditions. Output from the processing is examined to determine if the controls are operating effectively.

- *Integrated test facility (ITF):* A subsystem with dummy master files is created. Sometimes dummy records are appended to existing files. Specially coded test data, along with actual data, are introduced into the computer system. The test data include valid and invalid transactions, including all types of errors and exceptions. Test data are processed subject to programmed controls just like actual data. Separate output is produced for the dummy files in the subsystem and the results are compared with those expected by the auditor. The main disadvantage of ITF is the possibility of introducing errors into the client data. Moreover, modifications to clients' programs are typically required to process the dummy data.

Substantive Tests

Substantive tests are performed to determine if errors exist in account balances. Substantive tests consist of either tests of details of balances or analytical reviews. Examples of procedures used in substantive testing include:

- Observation
- Confirmation
- Inspection
- Vouching
- Reperformance
- Reconciliation
- Ratio analysis
- Regression analysis

UNDERSTANDING THE SCOPE OF MATERIALITY

Materiality affects the quantity of evidence required by the auditor. The Financial Accounting Standards Board (FASB) defines materiality in *Statement of Financial Accounting Concepts (SFAC) No. 2* as:

> The magnitude of an omission or misstatement of accounting information that, in the light of surrounding circumstances, makes it probable that the judgment of a reasonable person relying on the information would have been changed or influenced by the omission or misstatement.

While there are no official guidelines or quantitative measures of materiality, the following are often used in practice:

- 5–10 percent of net income
- 1 percent of stockholders' equity
- ½–1 percent of total assets
- ½–1 percent of gross revenue

PREPARING FOR AUDIT RISKS

Audit risk must be considered in planning an audit. *Audit risk* is defined by SAS No. 47, *Audit Risk and Materiality in Conducting and Audit,* as ". . . the risk that the auditor may unknowingly fail to appropriately modify his or her opinion on financial statements that are materially misstated." The three components of audit risk (AR) are: inherent risk (IR), control risk (CR), and detection risk (DR):

- *Inherent risk* refers to susceptibility to material misstatements in the absence of an internal control structure. Inherent risk is greater for some types of assertions than others. Cash, for example, is more susceptible to misappropriation than plant assets and therefore has a higher inherent risk.

- *Control risk* depends on the effectiveness of the client's internal control structure. Control risk is the risk that a material misstatement will not be detected or prevented by the client's internal control structure. Control risk can never be zero since internal controls can never provide complete assurance that material errors or irregularities will be prevented or detected.

- *Detection risk* is the risk that the auditor will fail to detect a material misstatement in an assertion. It is a function of the effectiveness of audit procedures. The level of detection risk can be changed by varying the nature, timing, and extent of substantive testing. For example, detection risk can be lowered by using more effective audit procedures. Detection risk can also be lowered by performing the substantive tests closer to the balance sheet date.

The Audit Risk Model

The relationship among the components is represented by the following model:

$$AR = IR \times CR \times DR$$

At a given level of audit risk, there exists an inverse relationship between the assessed level of inherent and control risks and the level of acceptable detection risk. In other words, the higher the assessed level of inherent and control risk, the lower is the acceptable level of detection risk.

TYPES OF AUDIT SOFTWARE AVAILABLE

It is now virtually impossible for auditors to perform their tests using manual methods. Computer-assisted audit techniques (CAAT) have been developed to assist auditors in testing computer-based systems. Audit software enables auditors to test and access a large amount of electronically stored data (see Appendix F). Query languages can be used to create ad hoc reports and perform a variety of computer-assisted audit techniques.

Audit software allows the auditor to examine all the data; the auditor does not have to sample the data. Data files can be read quickly and accurately. Freed from certain routine activities, the auditor can devote time to items that require attention. Over a period of time, auditors will see productivity gains and significant cost savings. Audit software functions include:

- Recalculation

- Data extraction from computer files

- Appraising reasonableness (e.g., accuracy of sales discounts) and trends, including aging analysis

- Data analysis and reporting

- Comparing financial data on different files for consistency

- Checking for duplicate invoices or payments

- Statistical sampling and analysis

- Field comparison to determine errors or inconsistencies

- Exception reporting (e.g., excessive inventory balances, unusual employee salary)

- Fraud detection

When auditing computer-based systems, the IT auditor should consider the following:

- The audit trail is maintained so that transactions can be traced and vouched through the system.

- Personnel are trained in the proper operation of the computer system.

- Appropriate steps are taken to obtain authorization before a system override.

Generalized Audit Software

Generalized audit software can easily be used in different computer systems. It can identify errors keyed into accounting software. It tends to be more cost-effective than custom software. Generalized audit software provides cost savings because most audits involve similar activities such as:

- Recalculating balances
- Analyzing data for unusual or erroneous values
- Selecting a sample
- Stratifying data
- Analyzing or comparing data stored in two or more separate, but logically related data files
- Testing transactions
- Generating and formatting reports

Examples of commonly used generalized audit software packages are:

ACL SOFTWARE
575 Richards Street
Vancouver, British Columbia
Canada V6B 2Z5
Phone: 888-669-4225
Fax: 604-669-3562
Web Page: www.acl.com

Interactive Data Extraction and Analysis (IDEA)
Audimation Services, Inc.
16151 Cairnway, Suite 100
Houston, Texas 77084
Phone: 888-641-2800
Fax: 281-345-2399
Web Page: www.cica.ca

Custom Audit Software

A packaged audit program may not meet the company's needs. In this case, customized audit software may be the answer. Customization should be considered if there are highly complicated applications, if excessive restrictions and limitations exist with the "canned" programs, and if "tailored" applications are required.

Industry-Specific Audit Software

Some audit techniques are industry-specific. Specialized audit software is available for industries such as banking, healthcare, entertainment, insurance, etc.

IMPLEMENTING CONTINUOUS AUDITING

Continuous auditing involves using certain audit procedures to capture and analyze data in real time. Any deviations from normal are reported for investigation. Continuous auditing is used to obtain reasonable assurance that account balances are free of material misstatements. Effective continuous auditing greatly reduces the need for year-end substantive testing.

Several factors affect the selection of audit areas that are conducive to continuous auditing. Audit areas where the assessed risk is high or areas that require a lot of audit hours should be considered for continuous auditing. The volume of transactions and the nature of the audit environment should be considered.

Continuous auditing reports deviations from expectations. Hence, expectations must be developed before continuous auditing can be implemented. The following factors should be considered in developing expectations:

- Inherent risk
- Existing controls
- Industry norms
- The business environment

Continuous auditing software is needed to capture data from key transactions. There are three ways of capturing such data:

- External audit software can be executed frequently, such as daily. The audit software queries and extracts data from different applications. This approach approximates continuous auditing.
- Audit procedure code can be embedded in the application program code to capture and test the data. This technique results in the immediate testing of data but it tends to be complex. Additional resources are needed to create and maintain a specialized audit procedure code.
- Front-loaded software resides in the user's computer and captures key transactions during the input process. Both hardware and software tools are needed to capture and test data using this technique.

VARIOUS APPLICATION CONTROLS

Application controls should exist over *input, processing,* and *output.* The purpose of these controls is to provide reasonable assurance that data is recorded, processed, and reported properly.

Input Controls

Most EDP errors occur at the time of input. Properly designed input controls provide reasonable assurance that the inputted data was authorized and converted to electronic format. Transactions should be approved and authorized by management. The authorization may be specific or general. Specific authorization may be evidenced by a signature or stamp on the source document.

Controls over converting data to electronic format include verification controls, edit controls, and control totals.

- *Verification controls* involve some or all of the input data being rekeyed from the source documents by a second individual for comparison purposes.

- *Edit controls* include limit check, valid character check, sign check, missing data check, check digit, and valid code check.

- *Control totals,* or *batch totals,* include hash totals (hash total is the sum of some numeric representation of the characters in a program), financial totals, and record counts.

Input errors should be logged for control purposes and corrected by those responsible for the mistake.

Processing Controls

Processing controls provide reasonable assurance that transactions were processed as intended. Processing controls are typically coded into the application and keep the data from being lost, duplicated, or altered during processing. Processing controls include:

- Limit and reasonableness checks
- Control totals
- File identification labels
- Process tracing
- Sequence checks

Output Controls

Output controls provide reasonable assurance that the results of processing are correct and only the authorized personnel receive the output reports. Output controls include:

- Scanning for completeness and reasonableness
- Comparing output data with source documents
- Reconciling output totals with input and processing control totals

AUDITING THE INFORMATION TECHNOLOGY FUNCTION

Since the IT function is a major cost center in most organizations, improving controls over the function can help the entire organization. An operational audit of IT can help improve its efficiency, effectiveness, and reliability. While a review of the IT function should be based on the needs of management, it typically includes such areas as:

- IT operations and management
- IT facilities
- User services
- Technical development
- Contingency planning

A review of the IT function should be performed periodically based on the needs of the organization. An operational review should generally be performed if the department is incurring excessive expenditures and frequently goes over budget. A review is also advisable if the users frequently complain about IT and the user needs are not met by the department. For example, users might complain about computer errors and nonresponse. Excessive staff turnover may also indicate problems.

13

ELECTRONIC COMMERCE

WHAT IS ELECTRONIC COMMERCE?

The term "electronic commerce" emerged only a few years ago when business people started to understand the powerful tool of the Internet. However, electronic commerce goes beyond simply "doing business electronically." Doing business electronically means that many conventional business processes, such as advertising and product ordering, are being digitized and conducted on the Internet. Beyond the basic idea of electronic commerce of "letting business people conduct business transactions over the Internet," new products have been released from their physical constraints and are being converted into digital products that can be delivered via the global network and paid for using digital currency. With digitization and digital payment systems, the electronic marketplace becomes a separate and independent market needing no physical presence for stores, products, sellers, or buyers. For example, a corporate buyer can browse the Internet, look at the merchandise on the Internet, and place an order. This transaction can be completed by sending a company's purchase order number to the vendor and receiving a confirmation number without a physical location.

The advantage of electronic commerce is that business transactions can be very efficient and fast. Entrepreneurs can use the Internet as the marketplace rather than huge retail channels (see Figure 13-1). However, other issues need to be researched, such as how to police the transactions

---

*This chapter was coauthored by Roberta M. Siegel, a computer consultant.

over the network, how to certify the accuracy of each transaction, and how to prevent transaction fraud.

Figure 13-1.
THE INTERNET

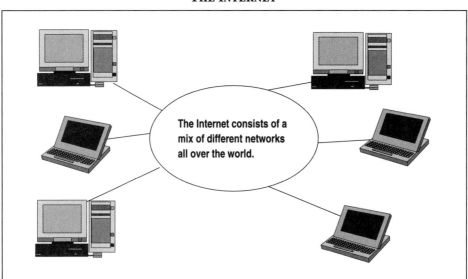

The Internet consists of a mix of different networks all over the world.

Electronic Commerce Examples

Recently, more and more businesses use electronic commerce technologies for within-business, business-to-business, and business-to-consumers transactions. Electronic commerce technologies are also used in nonbusiness activities such as communication (sending e-mail), paying taxes over the Internet, managing personal finance, and searching for information.

Most good examples of electronic commerce involve new technology and innovative ideas. For example, Mobil (*www.mobil.com*) as well as Chevron (*www.chevron.com*) gas stations developed a key sensor, by which customers can get credit card approval and activate a gas pump by moving the key across the sensor. Customer preferences can also be recorded in the device so that a cup of coffee or donuts can be delivered to their cars while they are pumping gas. Best Buy (*www.bestbuy.com*) also installed kiosks in their stores that offer access to the company's full inventory of products and enable customers to order and pay for products to be delivered. In addition, many personal services are moving from telephone to the Internet, with easy customization for product selection, payment, and delivery. For example, many grocery shopping web sites allow customers to order groceries on the Internet.

Other typical electronic commerce applications include:

- Shopping for merchandise
- Paying for goods and services
- Online financial services
- Customer service
- Online help
- Internet electronic mail and messaging
- Online search for documents, projects, and peer knowledge
- Supply chain management for inventory, distribution, and warehousing
- Tracking orders and shipments

Although the way each application operates is different, all these are not really a separate application, but rather one aspect of the whole electronic commerce process. For example, inventory and supply chain management is tied to production as well as to the demand data collected from consumers ordering via web stores. The business potential of electronic commerce is the capability to innovate and integrate business and marketing processes. The optimal goal of electronic commerce is to achieve transaction efficiency and customer satisfaction.

Electronic Commerce of Digital Products

A market is composed of three components: players, products, and processes. Market *players* are sellers, buyers, intermediaries, and other third parties, such as governments and consumer advocacy groups. *Products* are the commodities to be exchanged. The interactions between market agents regarding products and other market activities are *processes*, which include product selection, production, market research, product search, ordering, paying, delivery, and consumption. These three components could be in the form of digital format (online) or in the form of physical format (offline). A traditional commerce has three components in physical format, while the core of electronic commerce has three components in digital format (see Figure 13-2). A business transaction may have both physical and digital components. For example, buying a book on the Internet has the following characteristics: The players and processes are digital, and the products are physical.

Figure 13-2.
COMPARISON BETWEEN E-COMMERCE AND TRADITIONAL COMMERCE

Market Components	Traditional Commerce	Electronic Commerce
Market players	Physical (a shopper in the department store)	Digital (an online shopper)
Products	Physical (a printed magazine)	Digital (an online magazine)
Processes	Physical (Buying books in a bookstore)	Digital (Buying books on the network)

Market activities—from production, through distribution, to consumption—can occur online, bypassing all paper-based transactions and traditional communication media. This represents the future of electronic commerce. Although not all market components can be converted into digital format, most components can be more efficient if digital format is partially implemented. For example, a car with a smart device to display driving direction is both physical and digital.

THE INFRASTRUCTURE OF ELECTRONIC COMMERCE

The network infrastructure of the Internet is similar to that of a telephone network. Most of the Internet traffic travels on the same network used for local and long-distance calls. The media used in the telephone network consists of copper wires, coaxial cables, fiber-optical cables, and wireless and satellite systems.

The Information Superhighway

The term "information superhighway" has roared into the business world's consciousness in recent years. It is, in fact, a vision or a metaphor for a fusion of the two-way wired and wireless capabilities of telephone and networked computers with cable TV's capability to transmit hundreds of programs, images, multimedia and other types of information. The information superhighway, after its completion, will link all business around the globe. Today, this information superhighway remains a vision, much like today's interstate highway system was a vision in the 1950s. However, it is believed that by the early twenty-first century most of the country will be linked by the information superhighway.

Networks in Different Levels

There are four levels of networks in this traffic distribution system: users' networks, Internet access networks, regional networks, and backbone networks.

Users' Networks A *user's network* is the network of consumers or business that has an individual computer system or a computer network consisting of computer systems, modems, and other equipment. It connects to the Internet either directly through a leased line, such as an ISDN line or T1 line, or a dial-up line by using a telephone line. The dial-up connection can establish only a temporary connection to the network.

Internet Access Networks The *Internet access networks* provide connections between the user's network and Internet service providers, and the company servers that accept remote dial-up connections. These networks can be of different types:

- A dial-up connection using telephone lines
- A dial-up connection using ISDN (integrated services digital network) lines
- Lease-line connection using ISDN lines
- Lease-line connection using T1 lines

Dial-up lines are normally used for residential users, while lease lines are good for business users who require large volume of traffic and 24-hour connections.

Regional Networks   *Regional networks* provide bridges between Internet access networks and backbone networks. A regional network may cover an area within a state or several states, receiving messages and sending messages via the backbone networks. Examples are the California Education and Research Federation Network (CERFnet), the Southern Universities Research Association (SURAnet), THEnet of Texas, and NYSERnet of New York.

Backbone Networks   *Backbone networks* carry major Internet traffic between regional networks or direct the traffic to other backbone networks if the current connection does not exist. A backbone network has a very high bandwidth due to the transmission media used. It often can send hundreds of megabits per second. These networks are used to connect the regional network between countries or even between continents. For examples, EBONE connects most European countries (see Figure 13-3).

Figure 13-3.
NETWORKS IN DIFFERENT LEVELS

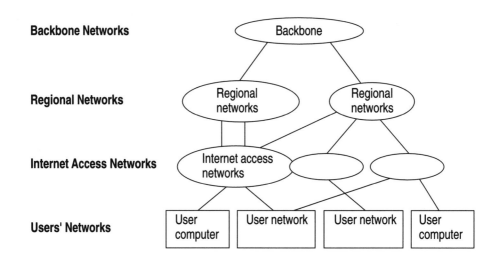

Traffic Control on the Internet

The traffic of the Internet is controlled by a set of protocols called *Transmission Control Protocol/Internet Protocol (TCP/IP)*. These protocols, along with other protocols, regulate how information is transferred through the Internet.

Packet Switching versus Circuit Switching *Circuit switching* is the method to establish a connection for telephone calls. In other words, when a telephone call is connected, a physical link is established between the sender and the receiver. During the conversation, the circuit becomes connected until one party hangs up. *Packet switching* uses a different method to make the connection. When a message or datum is ready to be sent, it is broken into many packets. Each packet can be delivered by different routes depending on which routes are available. To assure that each package is delivered to the right place, it contains necessary information such as the address for the destination, called an *IP address*. The method can reduce the traffic on the network and improve the performance of data communications.

Internet Protocol Address Just like telephone numbers, each computer that is connected to the Internet has a unique Internet protocol (IP) address. One IP address consists of 32 bits and is divided into four 8-bit segments, which are separated by a period. For example, "126.78.231.4" is an IP address that can uniquely identify a computer on the Internet. By typing in this address, users can access the site. If the Internet connection is temporarily set up, such as America Online users, the Internet server will temporarily assign an IP address for you.

Since the IP address is very hard to remember, a *domain name* corresponding to each address is used to reduce the complexity. A domain name consists of two levels: *top-level domain names* are classifications of different purposes of the usage. For example, "edu" stands for educational institute and "gov" stands for governments. Other top-level domain names include countries such as "us" (USA), "cn" (CHINA), and "mx" (MEXICO). The *lower-level domain name* is a unique name, which identifies the server. For example, IBM and FORD are lower-level domain names. The combination of the top-level domain name and the lower-level domain name can therefore identify the type of business and its country. For example, *www.ibm.com* represents that IBM is a commercial entity (.com), or *www.csulb.edu* states that "csulb" is an educational institute. Unlike the IP address, there is no limit to the number of possible domain names. A single server may have several domain names as long as there is a way to map between domain names and their corresponding IP addresses. Such a database is kept in the DNS server, or name server, accessible by a router. In other words, after a user types in the domain name, it is transferred to a corresponding IP address and the server with that IP address is accessed.

The coordinator of domain names is known as the Internet Network Information Center, or InterNIC. This organization regulates the way domain names are used (see Figure 13-4).

Figure 13-4.
THE COMPONENTS OF A DOMAIN NAME

Internet Computer Suffix	Organization Type	Domain Name	Entity
.com	Commercial organization	www.ibm.com	IBM Corporation
.edu	Academic institution	www.csulb.edu	California State University at Long Beach
.gov	Government agency	www.irs.gov	Internal Revenue Service
.org	Nonprofit organization	www.acm.org	Association for Computing Machinery
.net	Internet service provider	www.aol.net	America Online
	All Other Countries		
.cn	China	www.aaa.com.cn	
.au	Australia		
.jp	Japan		
.uk	United Kingdom		

Network Publishing

The Internet information superhighway provides a vehicle to carry information in terms of text, voice, image, video, and animation to different destinations connected to the network. This information is stored in server computers all over the Internet. These server computers equipped with

Internet server software "publish" information on the net. Thus, they enable network publishing in the World Wide Web. The web allows businesses to have presence on the network and to develop content in the form of HyperText Markup Language (HTML) and other tools such as VB script, Java script, Java, and others.

Business Service Infrastructure

The Internet allows business transactions, including buying and selling, to be conducted on the network online commerce, in which the buyer sends payment for goods or services electronically to the seller. The type of payment could be in the form of electronic check, digital cash, or credit card number. A transaction is then settled when the payment and remittance information are authenticated by the seller and accepted as valid.

To assure the safety of online commerce, the Internet infrastructure must provide *encryption* (to make sure that the information delivered is not intercepted by other parties) and *authentication* (to make sure that customers are who they say they are). In addition to these services, which prevent faulty transactions, the Internet infrastructure should provide services such as transaction escrow services, currency exchange, billing, online brokerage, and online investment management.

BUSINESS APPLICATIONS IN E-COMMERCE

Customer Electronic Commerce

Customer e-commerce can be classified as transaction-oriented and information-oriented.

Transaction-Oriented E-Commerce   *Transaction-oriented* e-commerce enables consumers to perform online transactions on the network so that the vendor can deliver goods or services through the Internet or other means. Transaction-oriented e-commerce focuses on the business transaction over the network. Users can access the web site to make purchases, transfer funds from one account to another, and invest in the stock market over the network. This type of transaction requires a database as the back-end mechanism so that the information collected from the user can be entered into the database, which can be used later for further processing. This technique allows users from all over the world to make transactions.

Information-Oriented E-Commerce   *Information-oriented* e-commerce allows users to retrieve and exchange information on the net. Such applications include chat room applications, e-mail, news groups, net meetings, and other online information services. Organizations may post or publish corporate policies, product specifications, employee information, etc.

Business-to-Business Electronic Commerce (Extranet)

This type of EC application, also called *Extranet,* consists of transactions between business entities. The Extranet serves as a bridge between the public Internet and the private Intranet. It is classified as vendor management e-commerce and distribution management e-commerce. *Vendor management* e-commerce creates alliances with vendors by processing purchase orders, accounts payable, and merchandise received. All these processes can be more efficient and accurate if proper e-commerce applications are employed. *Distribution management* e-commerce applications can be used to process merchandise delivery service for different retail channels. Operations include accounts receivable, inventory control, product pricing, and distribution management.

The Extranet allows the connection of multiple organizations such as suppliers, distributors, contractors, customers, and trusted others behind virtual firewalls. These organizations can partner and share the network for transactions. Extranets are a critical link between the extremes of the Internet and Intranet. Extranets enable commerce through the web at a low cost and allow companies to maintain one-to-one relationships with their customers, members, staffs, and others.

Extranets are powerful. They support and streamline business processes across collaborating companies. Efficiencies are achieved through economies of scale and other returns on investment for collaborating companies. Extranets are flexible, scalable, portable, and extendible. They may be used for integration across distributed, cross-platform, and heterogeneous system environments. Extranets significantly reduce barriers to cross-organizational networking.

Vendor Management   EC applications can have alliances with vendors by connecting the vendor's computer systems with a firm's. This approach allows vendors to transfer payments or invoices over the Internet, which makes purchasing more efficient and accurate. In other words, this approach integrates a company's computer system with the vendor's by Internet technology.

Distribution Management   Electronic commerce applications can also be used to process merchandise delivery services.

Intranet Commerce

Intranet commerce consists of employee communications and electronic publishing. Employee communications enable employees in the same organizations to communicate using e-mail, video conferencing, and electronic bulletin boards. The major benefits are a reduction in the cost of meetings, time savings for memo writing, and improved efficiency and effectiveness in communications. Electronic publishing allows organizations to post or publish corporate policies, product or service specifications, investment information, and other company information requiring printing and distribution. Savings can be achieved by reducing printing cost, distribution cost, and updating costs. The information can also be delivered faster and more accurately.

Intranet users are able to access the Internet, but firewalls keep outsiders from accessing private and confidential data. Intranets use low-cost Internet tools, are easy to install, and provide flexibility. Intranet applications are scalable—they can start small and grow. This feature allows many businesses to "try out" an Intranet pilot, that is, publish a limited amount of content on a single platform and evaluate the results. If the pilot succeeds, additional content can be migrated to the Intranet server.

Employee Communications   These applications enable employees in the same organizations to communicate using e-mail, video conferencing, and electronic bulletin board. The major benefits are reduced meeting costs, presentation costs, and preparation costs, along with more efficient, effective, and less costly communications.

Electronic Publishing   These applications are for information involving printing and distribution. Savings can be achieved by reducing the printing cost, distributions cost, and update cost. The information can be delivered faster and more accurately. Animation can be added to different destinations connected to the network. This information is stored in server computers all over the Intranet. The information published is available for corporate staff. Since the Intranet contains information about the company that is confidential to some users, different levels of security can be set up for different users by entering user names and passwords.

E-Commerce Examples

Marketing and Advertising   The internet supports marketing, advertising, and sales in a variety of ways. For example, potential customers might access a company's web site before taking the time to make a phone call or otherwise find product information. Such customers find it easier to view corporate information online. To meet these customers' needs, marketing and sales departments utilize the web to deliver both corporate and product messages, display product and service descriptions, advertise their products and services, offer downloadable software for potential customers, and advertise special discounts and promotions. The web site can therefore save the cost of making catalogs, manuals, and brochures. Online advertisements have full-color graphics, artwork, and text.

The web also provides a convenient sales medium. Direct mail and other companies have started to place catalogs online, offering potential customers full-color graphics and pictures plus easy ordering procedures. People wanting to purchase items online can do so easily, perhaps to avoid the Christmas crowds of shoppers. From toy stores to clothing stores, hobby shops, or sports stores, users can find all they need on the web. Like any other paper catalogs, online catalogs offer full-color pictures and text on the latest products. Once the item is selected, the user can simply fill out the online purchase form, submit the form with a credit card number, and click the submit button. After the order has been processed, usually within seconds, a receipt is sent back to the customer and shortly thereafter the product is shipped.

Technical Support   Technical and customer support is fundamental to gaining new customers and retaining existing customers. Without good service, people go elsewhere to purchase products and do business. Since increasing numbers of individuals have Internet access, many companies offer technical online support. Technical support includes e-mail, online discussion forums, news groups, online questionnaires, product upgrades, and service patch downloads for software debugging.

For example, a company's customer support can offer a newsgroup for each one of their products and services. This allows both the customers and the support department to talk about the latest offering, current problems, how to solve technical problems, and upcoming company offerings. The newsgroup environment allows the customer to freely express opinions and share feedback with companies. Given this information, decision makers can act more rapidly on customer demands, advice, and complaints. Posting lists of *frequently asked questions (FAQs)* also helps customers who come across problems that need to be addressed immediately. In this case, customers do not have to talk to the company's sales representative and wait on hold for several minutes or receive the salesperson's voice mail. If FAQs are posted interactively, this creates a discussion forum in which users can exchange their opinions freely. By doing so, technical problems can be solved by allowing users to exchange ideas.

INTERNET SERVICE PROVIDER AND OTHER SERVICES

The original goal of the Internet was to connect military computers with redundant communication routes during a war. This network ensures that communications can be carried on even if part of the network is not functional. Since 1991, the National Science Foundation eased the restriction of accessing the Internet, and commercial access became available. Since then, the traffic and activities on the Internet have grown exponentially. Companies and individuals can access the Internet through many service providers. The service providers can provide simple access, value-added service, or presence on the Internet.

Internet Access Providers

Internet access providers enable customers to connect to the regional network, which is then connected to the backbone network of the Internet. Generally speaking, the Internet access provider does not provide any information on the network; the major focus is on connectivity to the Internet. Companies such as MCI, AT&T, GTE, and Pacific Bell provide access to the Internet by connecting the telephone network to the modem of users. Users of Internet access providers pay a flat fee for unlimited usage.

Internet Service Provider

Internet service providers provide Internet access as well as other information such as news, sports, discussion forum, travel service, and online shopping (value added). Users can go either to a provider's network or to the Internet for different purposes. The provider's network is usually better organized and indexed, while the information on the Internet is not managed. Users pay a flat fee for unlimited usage or a lower fee for limited usage plus an hourly charge if the user exceeds the maximum usage. Such companies are America Online, Prodigy, Microsoft Network, and CompuServe.

Internet Presence Providers

Internet presence providers provide Internet presence by hosting the user's web pages on the Internet. Some companies provide an Internet mall with spaces for various vendors to sell their products. Vendors pay a fee plus the traffic charge and receive a space for an electronic store, which is actually disk space where the store's web site is saved. Therefore, online transactions can be made on the network.

WEB PAGE DESIGN TECHNOLOGIES

To design web pages on the Internet, proper tools are required. HyperText Markup Language (HTML) is designed to implement home page design. This language requires certain programming training and many people may not like to learn a new language. Recently, more Internet development tools have been developed. Microsoft FrontPage is a tool that provides users with a graphical user interface (GUI) and a word processing type of user-friendliness. Netscape also provides Internet development tools. In addition, Java by Sun Microcomputers provides sophisticated functions for Internet application development.

Using Text Editor

Any text editor such as Notepad, Word, or WordPerfect may be used to code HTML. The code in HTML can then be published on the web server.

HTML HTML is a relatively easy-to-learn programming language. However, the design of advanced features such as tables and frames are time-consuming to write. In HTML, every file consists of many tags that format elements of an HTML document: string of text, graphics, animation, and music. Elements are formatted by providing an opening tag and a closing tag for the particular instruction. Tags are combinations of letters surrounded by "<>". For example:

<h1> This is the Title </h1>

represents the way that "This is the Title" will be displayed on the web site.

The use of HTML is recommended in developing Intranets and Extranets because it is easier to program than Windows environments such as Motif of Microsoft Windows. HTML is a good integrating tool for database applications and information systems. It facilitates the use of hyperlinks and search engines, enabling the easy sharing of identical information among different responsibility segments of the company. Intranet data usually goes from back-end sources (e.g., mainframe host) to the web server to users (e.g., customers) in HTML format.

Using WYSIWYG Web Editor

Microsoft Office 97, Front Page, and Netscape Communicator are tools used to design a web page in the WYSIWYG environment. Users do not need to have any knowledge in HTML to design a web page. All design tools are displayed in icons and easy to use. After users finish the design work, the editor generates the HTML code.

Graphical Design Tools

Adobe Photoshop is a popular software for image processing. A company's logo, a picture, or a background pattern can be designed by this tool. The finished product can then be included in the web page.

Common Gateway Interface Tool

The availability of hypertext and graphics is essential for business to be conducted successfully on the web. Other features, such as interactivity with a database, become more important as more business is conducted on the web. The technology referred to as *common gateway interface (CGI)* allows a computer that is accessing a web site to have some similar functions, such as a client might have with a server. The user can fill out a form online and submit the data into a database that resides on a server; then the CGI program can separate the data from the web page and run a program on the server to update the database for later retrieval. The CGI program may also provide immediate feedback to the user by creating and transmitting a revised HTML page (see Figure 13-5).

Figure 13-5.
CGI PROCESS FLOW

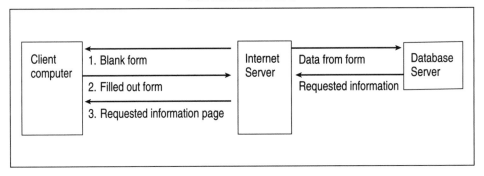

CGI can be implemented in different languages such as Java Script, VB Script, and Perl.

THE INTERNET AND INTRANET

The Internet

What Is the Internet? In 1969, the U.S. Department of Defense's Advanced Research Projects Agency (ARPA) wanted to establish a communications network that would operate in case of a nuclear strike, as an alternative to telephone, radio, and television, all of which might quickly become nonfunctional in a military crisis. The most important feature of ARPAnet is that it has no central point for controlling communications. One message can be transmitted to another location through any possible routes so that in case one route is destroyed, the message can still be transmitted. ARPAnet's computers exchange information in the form of digitized data, operating according to standards agreed upon by all participants, with no one person, institution, or organization in charge. Since the ARPAnet uses open system design, this network had a dramatic growth in the last several years and that became the Internet.

Today, the Internet is a network of networks with hundreds of thousands of servers. Tens of millions of people take for granted that, with a simple phone call via their modems, they can access a huge number of files of all types from all Internet servers, do research, purchase merchandise, and participate in discussion forums with someone in another country.

The Internet Infrastructure   Physically, the Internet is a network of communications media to which hundreds of thousands of computers are connected. Within all the connections, the major lines of communication are the backbone networks. Servers—computers that are connected to the network and perform certain functions—link *clients* or *user computers* (computers that are connected to the network but do not perform as servers). In May 1993, one hundred servers were on the Internet. After two years, there were 22,000 and by 1997 there were about 100,000 servers in the Internet. Today, it is estimated that over 100 million user computers are on the Internet.

The Internet is not owned by anyone or any organization. No one can decide who has the privilege to connect to which user or how the resources can be used. However, to connect to the Internet, an *Internet service provider (ISP)* must be available. In general, a fee is charged to connect to the Internet.

Doing Business on the Internet   The Internet became a popular place for shopping, entertaining, and information retrieval due to its convenience. Almost any information can be retrieved from the network. For example, the menu of a restaurant in France may be available on the web site of gourmet cooking and restaurants. A book with a specific title can be found by a library search system, and a retailer's address and phone number can be found from the Internet yellow pages.

Intranet

Intranet is defined as an enterprise-owned network that uses an Internet interface for information exchange and sharing. In other words, Intranet is a private, small-scale version of the Internet. It is mainly designed to perform functionality within the enterprise by using a common infrastructure of the Internet. The designer of the Intranet uses the same tools to build web sites and pages, and the users can use the same browser to access the information on the Intranet. In fact, many of today's Intranets do not require any additional hardware; the existing LANs and other intraorganizational networks are used for telecommunications, but the web applications, such as server programs and browsers, add to these networks all the advanced features that the Internet provides (see Figure 13-6).

Figure 13-6.
HOW THE INTERNET IS CONNECTED TO AN INTRANET

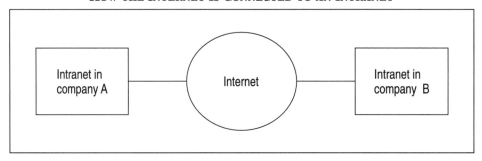

Intranet and Its Popularity More and more U.S. companies use the Intranet as a major tool to communicate within the company. In 1996, approximately 25 percent of American companies had Intranet, and another 40 percent were planning to adopt it (see Figure 13-7). Today, Intranets have already been established by at least two-thirds of the *Fortune* 500 companies.

Figure 13-7.
THE PERCENTAGE OF INTRANETS

Status	Percentage (%)
Plan to have or are constructing an Intranet	40
Do not have a plan for an Intranet	38
Have a plan for an Intranet	22

Source: Forrester Research, Inc., quoted in *Fortune,* July 22, 1996, advertisement section.

The number of Intranet servers has outpaced the installation of Internet servers. Figure 13-8 displays the potential of both the Internet and Intranet enhanced productivity for a business. Table 13-1 presents practical applications of intranets and extranets.

Figure 13-8.
The Percentage of Servers Installed

Server Installation	Percentage (%)
Internet	45
Intranet	55

Source: Forrester Research, Inc., quoted in *Fortune,* July 22, 1996, advertisement section.

Table 13-1.
Practical Applications of Intranets/Extranets

- Providing managers with accounting, audit, and tax information
- Providing marketing and sales information to current and prospective customers
- Furnishing information to salespersons in the field and managers at different branches
- Furnishing resource needs and reports to suppliers
- Communicating corporate information to employees such as company policies and forms, operating instructions, job documents, business plans, and newsletters
- Assisting in employee training and development
- Transferring information to government agencies (e.g., Department of Commerce, SEC, IRS)
- Furnishing current and prospective investors with profitability, growth, and market value statistics
- Providing lenders and creditors with useful liquidity and solvency ratios
- Providing project, proposal, and scheduling data to participating companies in joint ventures
- Providing press releases and product/service announcements
- Giving legal information to outsider attorneys involved in litigation matters
- Providing trade associations with input for their surveys
- Furnishing information to outside consultants (e.g., investment management advisors, pension planners)
- Providing insurance companies with information to draft or modify insurance coverage
- Furnishing economic statistics about the company to economic advisors
- Facilitating database queries and document requests
- Providing spreadsheets, database reports, tables, checklists, and graphs to interested parties
- Displaying e-mail

Source: Joel Siegel, Stephen Hartman, and Anique Qureshi, "The Intranet and Extranet," *The CPA Journal,* February 1998, p. 72.

ELECTRONIC COMMERCE TECHNOLOGIES

Web Servers

A *web server* is a computer that hosts all web sites so that other users can access the information through the Internet. Information in the web paradigm is provided or published on a web server. Web servers are principally used to maintain a directory of web pages. A web server could use the Unix system as its operating system, called a Unix server, or the Microsoft Windows NT operating system as an NT server. The major responsibility of a server is to respond to requests from clients' or users' computers via a browser. Essentially, web servers release information to the users when the users send requests through the browser. If the web server breaks down, web pages and all applications will not be available to users. Vendors of web server software are presented in Table 13-2.

Table 13-2.
VENDORS OF WEB SERVER SOFTWARE

Vendor	Telephone No.	Name
IBM	(800) 426-2255	Internet Connection Server for MVS
Microsoft	(800) 426-9400	Internet Information Server (comes with Microsoft's NT Server)
Netscape	(415) 528-2555	Fast Track and Commerce Server for Windows NT
Lotus	(800) 828-7086	Internotes Web Publisher
CompuServe	(800) 848-8199	Spry Web Server for Windows NT
Quarterdeck	(800) 683-6696	Web Server and Web Star for Windows 95/NT

Web Browsers

A *web browser* is the vehicle that allows users to browse the World Wide Web. Users simply type in the address of a specific web server's web page (the URL) in the designated retrieve area, and the web browser locates the web server to request the web page addressed. The web browser then waits, usually only seconds, until the request information is sent back from the web server. The user can then view the information through the web browser.

Among many browsers available in the market, two of them account for 90 percent of the browser market. They are Netscape Communicator and Microsoft Internet Explorer browsers. All of them offer a suite of functions that assists the user's everyday needs, including a bookmark catalog for organizing the addresses of frequently visited web sites, e-mail, a newsreader, and setup scripts for Internet service providers. Web browsers allow one to access corporate information over the existing network. Employees in different divisions of the company located in different geographic areas can access and use centralized or scattered information. Along with the growth of the web, browser usage has risen dramatically. According to CyberAtlas, web servers currently number more than 1.5 million, up from 130 in 1993 (*Source:* Information Data Corporation).

Universal Resource Locator

URL stands for *Universal Resource Locator.* The purpose of URL is to provide an address so that information can be located on the Internet. The URL guides a browser request to the appropriate server through the various components in the address. The following URL: *http://www.csulb.edu* can retrieve information from the web site of California State University at Long Beach. The "http:" indicates that the browser is sending a request via the *HyperText Transfer Protocol (HTTP),* the protocol of the web. HTTP allows the transfer of a network request to a web server. However, if "ftp" is used, *File Transfer Protocol* will be applied instead. The "ftp" allows data or program files to be transferred between computers. The second part of the URL string is a double forward slash "//"; this indicates that a machine name follows. The third part of the URL string indicates the type of host machine sought. Any remote web server is identified with the now nearly ubiquitous "www" identification.

Search Engines

Web browsers and servers allow users to locate information worldwide. However, finding a particular piece of information can be very difficult. Many companies recognize this and have responded by developing search sites and search engines. The better-known search sites include Lycos, Yahoo, InfoSeek, and AltaVista. Users connect to a search site the same way they connect to any other site. Once the search site is connected, users simply type the key words that pertain to the subject of interest and the search engine locates hundreds of sites about the topic. Search engines typically display a 50- to 100-word description about each site to assist users in narrowing their search. Some search engines even provide special local search engines focused on specific areas or countries, such as Yahoo LA or Yahoo Japan.

THE FUTURE OF ELECTRONIC COMMERCE

The information superhighway will provide ever better transmission media, and lead to a business environment in which a virtual economy is driven by new, networked, distributed, online technologies. The future is not easy to predict, even for experts who are in the process of changing technology and market processes, but Table 13-3 gives us a glimpse.

Table 13-3.
"EXPERT" PREDICTIONS THROUGH TIME

(Selected quotes from the "Internet Grapevine: Wet Blankets Throughout History.")

1859: "Drill for oil? You mean drill into the ground to try and find oil? You're crazy!"—*Drillers whom Edwin L. Drake tried to enlist in his project to drill for oil*

1876: "This 'telephone' has too many shortcomings to be seriously considered as a means of communication. The device is inherently of no value to us."—*Western Union internal memo*

1920: "The wireless music box has no imaginable commercial value. Who would pay for a message sent to nobody in particular?"—*David Sarnoff's associates in response to his urgings for investment in the radio*

1943: "I think there is a world market for maybe five computers."—*Thomas Watson, chairman of IBM*

1949: "Computers in the future may weigh no more than 1.5 tons."—*Popular Mechanics, forecasting the relentless march of science*

1968: "But what . . . is it good for?"—*Engineer at the Advanced Computing Systems Division of IBM, commenting on the microchip*

1977: "There is no reason anyone would want a computer in their home."—*A top executive of Digital Equipment Corp.*

Source: Adopted from S. Choi, D. Stahl and A. Whinston, *The Economics of Electronic Commerce,* 1997, Technical Macmillan Publishing.

14

SPECIAL ISSUES IN DOING BUSINESS ON THE WEB*

Technology plays a vital role in retail business, improving efficiency and allowing retailers to provide higher value and greater convenience to their customers. Perhaps the most exciting new technology with the potential to make a significant impact on the industry is the Internet. The Internet allows retailers to reach both their customers and suppliers and provides another medium for retailers to expand internationally at a relatively low cost. Predictions of sales over the Internet are wide-ranging—from a low of $7 billion to a high of $16 billion by the year 2000.

Specialized online retailers—such as CDNow, a music store, PC makers such as Dell, and various flower and gift stores—are thriving, proving that Internet retailing can work when properly done. The "best-of-breed" stores dominate each category; these specialized companies are able to out-innovate their competitors and retain customers.

Some business retailers such as Amazon.com and Virtual Vineyards have moved aggressively onto the Internet. Amazon.com is an online bookstore offering millions of titles. Amazon's low distribution costs allow it to pass a significant discount to its customers.

Virtual Vineyards, a specialty retailer which opened in 1994, offers hard-to-find wines and gourmet foods. The company reports that its "online shop" is visited by over 100,000 people each month. In addition to selling rare wines, fine foods, and gifts, Virtual Vineyards provides customers with

*The authors gratefully acknowledge the research assistance of Jinhee Park, Rakesh Patel, Sushmita Pathak, and Hoi Shun Wong.

wine selections from nationally known wine experts, and gives them advice on matching food and wine.

Many retailers, however, are proceeding cautiously, using the Internet as a means to advertise their merchandise and providing a toll-free telephone number for customer orders. Retailers are reluctant to devote more resources to the Internet until they feel more confident of consumer interest.

Surveys indicate that most Americans would not give out their credit card number online. In response, MasterCard and Visa are jointly developing Secure Electronic Transfer (SET) technology. SET would make credit card transactions significantly safer. SET encrypts the consumers' credit card numbers. Even the merchants are not able to see the credit card numbers. This prevents unscrupulous merchants from selling a product over the Internet solely to collect credit card numbers. As technology improves and consumers become more comfortable with the Internet, it is likely that privacy/encryption issues will not be a serious barrier to Internet commerce.

Internet speed is also an issue. Some analysts argue that consumers do not have the patience to wait for images to download for viewing. However, with increased competition in the communications industry, consumers will benefit from faster and more affordable access to the Internet. With time, the Internet will become an additional medium through which business will be transacted both domestically and internationally.

Selling merchandise over the Internet reaches not only domestic consumers but also international consumers. A resident from a foreign country can just as easily browse the books at Amazon.com as a U.S. citizen. However, the Internet is much more expensive to log onto in foreign countries than it is in America. For example, Europeans pay one and a half times as much to connect to the Internet and pay an additional 30 cents for each minute of connection. Clearly the cost of connecting to the Internet must decrease in Europe before it is profitable for American retailers to use the Internet to sell their merchandise to this market. Analysts believe that connection charges will decrease when the deregulation of Europe's telecommunication companies occurs in 1999. It is expected that the number of users of the Internet—both business and individual—will increase to 35 million in the year 2000 from the 9 million users today. Internet sales in Europe are expected to increase to $3 billion in the year 2000 from today's $500 million.

The home shopping industry is expanding overseas and firms are marketing internationally over the Internet. For example, the home shopping industry has entered into an agreement with the Chinese government. They announced the creation of ChinaWeb, a web site dedicated to promoting business and commerce with China through the Internet. Home shopping channels have also entered Australia, Canada, Hong Kong, India, and Japan. It is likely that the $8 billion global home shopping market will continue to steadily increase over the next few years. International marketing over the Internet is beginning to evolve, though significant infrastructure and regulatory barriers remain. It appears, however, that with the rapid expansion of the Internet domestically and internationally, commercial web sites will become a profitable distribution channel for businesses.

The future of retailing on the Internet promises to greatly benefit consumers. Firms are developing search engines that will be able to find merchandise on the Internet at the lowest price. This will put pressure on retailers to cut their margins. Some analysts believe that retail prices will drop by 30 percent over the next ten to fifteen years, as a result of consumers being more informed about prices.

Another developing technology that will greatly assist consumers in making purchases over the Internet is 3-D imaging. Instead of just reading a description and looking at a photograph, a consumer will be able to visually inspect the product at virtually any angle.

ELECTRONIC DATA INTERCHANGE

Some analysts are predicting that the real breakthrough for retailers on the Internet will be in the cost savings realized through electronic data interchange (EDI). Today, many large retailers communicate electronically through *value-added networks (VANS)*. Using VANS to conduct business-to-business transactions improves cycle times, reduces errors, and provides significant cost savings. However, VANS are proprietary and, therefore, relatively expensive. In contrast, the Internet provides a relatively low-cost method for retailers to communicate, without diminishing any of the benefits from VANS. Experts estimate that the use of the Internet for EDI will reduce the cost of transmitting data by as much as 90 percent.

Electronic data interchange is defined as the application-to-application transfer of business documents between computers. Many businesses choose EDI as a fast, inexpensive, and safe method of sending purchase orders, invoices, shipping notices, and other frequently used business documents. There are other different types of EDI. These include person-to-application transfer, application-to-person transfer, person-to-person transfer. The uses for these kinds of EDI are for product registration, retail orders, information updates, product information, text messaging, image transmission, etc. The technologies they use include web browser, electronic mail, and fax.

EDI is quite different from sending electronic mail messages or sharing files through a network, a modem, or a bulletin board. The straight transfer of computer files requires that the computer applications of both the sender and receiver (referred to as *trading partners*) agree upon the format of the document. The sender must use an application that creates a file format identical to the computer application of the receiver. In using EDI, however, the trading partners do not need to have identical document processing systems. When the sender sends a document, the EDI translation software converts the proprietary format into an agreed-upon standard. When the receiver gets the document, receiver's EDI translation software automatically changes the standard format into the proprietary format of his or her document processing software.

Unlike Internet commerce, which is built on free-form documents and open networks, EDI is built using well-established standards using private networks. Recently, there has been a move to transfer EDI documents through the Internet, making EDI more affordable for smaller businesses.

EDI has been under development in the United States in one form or another since the mid-1960s. In 1968, a group of railroad companies concerned with the quality of intercompany exchanges of transportation data formed an organization to study the problem and to do something to improve it. This organization was the Transportation Data Coordinating Committee (TDCC). At about the same time, individual companies such as General Motors, Super Valu, Sears, and K-Mart were also addressing the inefficiencies of intercorporate document movement by using their own electronic systems with their major trading partners. The problem lay in the fact that each system was specific to that company with no standard except in a proprietary sense.

It was no later than the 1970s, when Super Valu, a large American grocery chain that had to deal with its large "within-the-company" EDI issues, recognized the needs for industry-specific standards. They felt that, between available levels of technology and the extent of its own needs, a universal standard was not necessary and impractical. In 1973, the Transportation Data Coordinating Committee decided to develop a set of standards for EDI between companies. This resulted in the first interindustry EDI standard in 1975 covering air, motor, ocean, rail, and some banking applications.

To transfer the company's data electronically, a Mapper, a Translator, a Communication Tool, and membership with a value-added network are needed. These tools reorganize the data into a structured format that the other trading partner can use.

The use of value-added networks is just like a post office, that is, it electronically stores and forwards data. The trading partners themselves do not need to have modem connections to send the EDI data. The sender's computer can simply call the VAN and put all the EDI data that has to be sent in the VAN. The VAN will then transmit the data to the other trading partner's computer system.

The introduction of integrated EDI makes its use even more advantageous. Integrated EDI means that, instead of retyping or reprinting data such as purchase orders, order entry forms and inventory data, users automatically send the data for these documents into the company's computer system. The wonderful thing about integrated EDI is that, once all the bits and pieces are in place and data is exchanged back and forth, the process is invisible to the end-user. The real value of integrated EDI is the increase in a company's productivity. It reduces the cycle time of data interchange, eliminates paperwork, reduces postage costs, and improves accuracy. A company can easily implement just-in-time inventory data and provide enhanced, faster, and more efficient customer service.

With this kind of paperless way of processing information, certain kinds of controls are necessary. Audit techniques can no longer be paper-based. With a lack of paper-based documents, controls must be in place to ensure the completeness, accuracy, and authorization of financial statements.

Computer tests should be used to ensure that electronic records are correct. For example, tests could be performed to check whether the number sequence continuity of the sales invoice is maintained. If not, the computer can trace the gaps and generate a variance report for the auditor. The auditor, however, cannot rely on the computer test all the time. Sometimes, the information stored in the computer is available only for a limited time. In such cases, the auditor has to consider the timeliness of retrieving the relevant information.

On occasion, there is a need for joint control. The auditor needs to ensure that the computer program is properly written and unauthorized alternations have not been made. The auditor must make sure that individuals can access areas only for which they have authorization. Passwords should not be easy to guess and should be changed periodically. Passwords should also be changed whenever the employee leaves the company.

CPA WEBTRUST

Growing global electronic commerce has provided consumers with the opportunity to buy different types of products online. The proliferation of commerce on the web is advantageous and should be encouraged. However, many customers are afraid of transacting online because of security reasons.

To give consumers confidence in transacting online, the American Institute of Certified Public Accountants (AICPA) and the Canadian Institute of Chartered Accountants (CICA) have jointly developed the *WebTrust program.* It is a type of electronic seal that provides certain assurances. A Certified Public Accountant (CPA) who is a member either of the AICPA [or a Chartered Accountant (CA)] or of the CICA is able to perform a WebTrust examination. The WebTrust seal on a web site indicates that a CPA (or CA in Canada) has evaluated the web site's business practices and controls and the site meets all the WebTrust criteria. After issuing the initial WebTrust seal, the CPA must perform an update at least quarterly to make sure that all guidelines for authenticity, security, and privacy have been followed by the web site.

Three sets of principles were established by the two institutes to ensure that electronic commerce transactions and the personal information exchanged between businesses and consumers remains confidential and secure. WebTrust principles address three broad categories:

- *Business practices disclosure:* The web site operator is required to disclose its business practices for electronic transactions. The operator must make sure that the transactions are in fact processed in accordance with its disclosed practices.

- *Transaction integrity:* The web site operator has to maintain effective controls to provide reasonable assurance that the customers' orders placed using electronic commerce were completed and billed as agreed.

- *Information protection:* The web site operator has to maintain effective controls to provide reasonable assurance that the information received in an electronic transaction is kept private. In other words, information received must be protected from uses not related to the business.

Before a company can start using the WebTrust seal, it has to demonstrate over a period of at least two or three months (typically three months) that it actually executed transactions in accordance with its disclosed business practices. The business should have in place reasonable policy controls to ensure that customer information obtained through electronic transactions is protected from misuse. For example, encryption should be used to protect private customer information, such as credit card numbers and other personal and financial information, that is transmitted to the business entity.

If a web site meets all of the prescribed business practices and control criteria, the CPA issues a report indicating that the company's site complies with all the standard requirements, and the site is granted the WebTrust seal. Consumers can learn about the company and the WebTrust principles and criteria by just clicking on the WebTrust seal.

WebTrust seal is supported technically by VeriSign, Inc. *VeriSign* is a leading Internet Certification Authority. It is a trusted third party that authenticates, issues, and manages digital certificates on the Internet. Without such technical support, it would have been easy for an unscrupulous merchant to forge the WebTrust seal. VeriSign also provides the encryption necessary to ensure confidentiality in an electronic transaction.

All web sites that have the WebTrust seal are linked to an online listing. This allows consumers to easily locate other web sites that have received the WebTrust seal. The WebTrust seal is revocable if the entity at any time stops complying with the WebTrust criteria.

TAXATION OF ELECTRONIC COMMERCE

The Internet offers a new way of conducting commerce. It has enormous commercial potential because it allows for rapid cost-efficient distribution of information anywhere in the world. As electronic commerce is beginning to grow, so is the debate over how to tax it. It appears that tax policy will play a significant role in determining how successful the Internet's commercial development will be. If governments decide to impose new taxes and regulations on the Internet, the Internet's extraordinary commercial potential may not be realized.

Given the enormous commercial potential, state and local governments are looking for ways to tax both Internet service providers, such as America Online, and the transactions that take place in cyberspace. Virtually every type of commerce in the United States is subject to some form of taxation at the federal, state, or local level. At this time, the U.S. federal government has taken a stance not to enact federal taxes, but some state and local governments are currently imposing or planning to impose taxes on Internet commerce. State tax officials are looking at existing tax laws to determine how goods and services purchased across state borders can be taxed. The total revenues are staggering. According to the Census Bureau, general sales taxes bring in a third of all state tax revenue.

However, due to the decentralized nature of the Internet, problems exist as to how Internet sales transactions should be taxed. It is not easy to collect on sales in cyberspace. Our world has been defined by city, state, and country boundaries, which we have used to tax commerce. Such boundaries, however, are difficult to define in cyberspace. The concept of physical space does not apply to the Internet. Questions arise:

- Where exactly is the Internet located?
- Which state can levy a tax on a transaction that travels through more than a dozen individual states?
- What can and should be taxed over the Internet—goods and services sold over the Internet or the online services themselves?
- What level or levels of government can impose taxes?

Such questions cannot be answered by current tax policies, which are geared toward addressing traditional commerce, not electronic commerce. Currently, there is no uniform taxation of the information "content" that crosses the Internet and other forms of electronic commerce. However, there is widespread sales taxation of the "transmission" component of electronic commerce—the interstate and intrastate telecommunications, including local telephone, cellular phone, satellite transmission, or cable transmission. Approximately 80 percent of the states tax intrastate telecommunications and 40 percent of the states tax interstate telecommunications. The charges are for transmission of information, not for the information content. Still, which activities are considered "transmissions"? Telephone calls and cellular communications can be classified as "transmissions." However, what about certain "enhanced services," such as Internet access, e-mail, electronic bulletin boards, packet switching, and ATM transactions? Are these "transmissions" and hence subject to the telecommunications sales tax? These "enhanced services" involve additional "linkage" or value-added, such as the temporary storage of messages on a computer server. Many states don't have a clear stance on whether such value-added services are included within the definition of "telecommunications" and, in these states, businesses must guess which activities are included in that definition.

Under federal regulatory definitions, a basic transmission service is a transmission between or among points without change in the form or content of the information sent and received. Examples include local exchange and local phone calls. However, an *enhanced* service is any service offered over a telecommunications network in which computers process and manipulate data. Under the narrow definition of telecommunications, states impose a sales or use tax on basic transmission services only. Some jurisdictions are attempting to expand this definition into a broader definition of telecommunications in order to apply taxes to a wider range of value-added or enhanced information services. Florida, for instance, is seeking to impose taxes on providers of services such as Internet, computer bulletin boards, and electronic mail. However, states that utilize a broader definition of "transmission" may have difficulty concluding which enhanced services can be classified as taxable or nontaxable. New York, for instance, currently treats e-mail and computer bulletin boards as subject to its sales and use taxes, but has yet to decide on the taxation of Internet access services.

There are problems with utilizing a broader definition of transmission activities. One is that the inclusion of enhanced services makes the sales and use tax rules more difficult to enforce. Another problem is created by the common practice of online companies' "bundling," or packaging together, transmission services such as e-mail with information services such as software downloads. Usually, with bundled taxable and nontaxable services, the nontaxable services are taxed as well. Another problem is that, while local or regional phone calls are clearly within the definition of intrastate telecommunications, there is uncertainty whether e-mail or Internet access charges are within the definition. Inherently, such transactions can involve intrastate or interstate communications.

Currently, 25 percent of the states impose a broad-based sales and use tax on online content transferred by means of electronic commerce. There are different approaches to taxing electronically transmitted information. Certain states treat the electronic transmission of information content as a taxable "information service," "electronic information service," or "computer service." For instance, Washington, D.C. treats the electronic transmission of information content as a taxable information service. Ohio treats the electronic transmission of information content as a taxable electronic information service. In other states, such transmissions are treated as taxable computer services. For instance, Connecticut imposes a sales tax on computer services that provide computer time, storing and filing information, retrieving or providing access to information. Moreover, in certain states (such as Texas and Illinois), the electronic transmission of information content is treated as a sale of tangible personal property, or as a lease of tangible personal property if the information is accessed from a computer in that state. Thus, there is considerable variation in how the electronic transmission of information content is taxed, and this can lead to confusion in determining which services are taxable.

Only 25 percent of the states impose a broad-based sales tax on numerous categories of online content, such as electronic information or computer services. Yet approximately 50 percent of the states impose a sales tax on specific categories of online content, such as the electronic transmission of canned software (sold electronically over telecommunications networks) or cable television. More states generally tax these specific types of electronic commerce. However, a particular transaction may qualify for an exemption from sales or use tax, depending on the state. For instance, in New York, although the electronic transmission of information content is a taxable information service, the sales tax is not imposed if the information furnished is personal or individual in nature.

Even if the transaction is otherwise subject to a sales or use tax, if the seller has no "nexus" with the taxing jurisdiction, then the seller has no obligation to collect or forward the tax. Normally a state can impose taxes on interstate transactions only if the seller has "sufficient nexus." In other words, a seller must collect sales tax from a buyer if the seller has a significant physical presence ("nexus") in the same jurisdiction where the buyer takes delivery.

Currently, nexus claims by states are being expanded. To establish nexus, the rules require activities such as owning, leasing, using, or maintaining real or tangible personal property in a jurisdiction or having employees in the state. However, various state interpretations of these rules have been stretched to include factors such as interest in intangible property (e.g., software license), use of a collection agency, utilization of the public telephone system, etc.

Two court cases have essentially set the stage for future state actions in this area. In a 1992 decision called *Quill Corp. v. North Dakota,* the U.S. Supreme Court held that the mail order stationery and paper products company Quill was not obligated to collect sales taxes from transactions to consumers buying its products in other states unless it could be proved that the company had nexus—some sort of physical presence—in the buyers' states, such as a sales force working on its behalf or property used for its business. Thus, a computer sold by a company in New York to anyone in any other state would escape sales taxation unless the company had nexus in any of those states. The Quill decision holds that a sales presence is required for nexus to exist, and with it the responsibility to collect sales taxes. In *Geoffrey, Inc. v. South Carolina Tax Commission,* the South Carolina Supreme Court ruled in 1993 that the physical presence test for substantial nexus in the state is necessary only for sales and use taxes. A company's licensing of an intangible asset for use in the state could form the basis of "economic" nexus and could become the justification for imposing an income tax, as opposed to sales or use tax.

If the concept of nexus was applied to transactions made over the Internet, establishing this nexus would be very difficult and tricky. The seller may have no idea of the buyer's location and thus whether sales tax is due. Moreover, the location of the seller may be even tougher to determine.

Because of the intangible nature of Internet commerce, there are currently no uniform set of tax rules and regulations. The taxation of electronic commerce varies from state to state; so determining what's taxable and who is responsible for paying those taxes becomes very complex. Depending on what state you're in, electronic commerce may be taxed as a telecommunications service, a computer service, an information service, or some combination. Consequently, state and local attempts to tax such intangible electronic commerce would result in a confusing and overlapping set of tax laws. As a result, double taxation as well as multiple reporting and compliance problems would be inevitable. The state and local tax laws governing electronic commerce are ambiguous. This ambiguity may already be inhibiting a business's involvement in electronic commerce. Many businesses may not know if their companies are even subject to sales and transactions taxes for the sale of products and services over the Internet.

In spite of the confusion surrounding taxation of Internet commerce, state and local authorities are scrambling to tax as much of the Internet transactions as possible as they see their taxable base decreasing. To address this, on March 13, 1997, Senator Ron Wyden and Representative Christopher Cox introduced the Internet Tax Freedom Act. This bill is an attempt to give a "time-out" for at least six years on state and local Internet taxes until governments come up with a consistent and uniform set of rules regarding Internet taxation. The bill would impose a moratorium on state and local taxes on electronic commerce, though it would exempt certain taxes, including most sales taxes, that are already in place. The bill also calls on the administration to develop a comprehensive plan to address the issue and to seek trade agreements that make all Internet activity internationally free of taxes, tariffs, and trade barriers. The aim of the Internet Tax Freedom Act is to provide time to clarify questions relating to tax liability.

Under the bill, Internet access services cannot be classified and taxed as a telecommunications service. The taxes imposed on the underlying phone service is not affected. There are differences between information services, such as the Internet, and telecommunications services. One important difference is that the Internet service providers often do not know or cannot determine the origin or destination of the service being rendered to the end-user, thus making it difficult to apply a telecommunications tax that distinguishes between interstate and intrastate transactions. Normal business taxes and property taxes will not be affected by the bill. While Internet access cannot be taxed as an information service, information services offered over the Internet would be subject to taxes if the provider of the services meets rules requiring nexus.

Although the Internet Tax Freedom Act seems like a good policy, critics of the bill maintain that it would create a tax haven or exemption for commerce that is conducted electronically. Some claim that the bill provides an advantage to businesses that engage in electronic commerce. However, the bill protects consumers as well as sellers of all sizes. There would be no advantage created for one type of commerce because the bill would simply prohibit taxation of economic activity that is electronic. Moreover, the bill would help small and independent businesses cut costs and be able to reach a wider market.

Electronic commerce is a new medium that is changing traditional relationships between the buyer and seller and traditional approaches to the taxation of goods and services. Inevitably, taxing authorities are testing new ways to prevent the loss of tax revenue. However, imposing discriminatory taxes on electronic commerce will stifle the development of this new medium before it even gets a chance to develop and prosper. The Internet Tax Freedom Act would allow for the development of uniform and consistent rules and regulations pertaining to electronic commerce.

15

LEGAL AND ETHICAL CONSIDERATIONS*

Information technology has revolutionized the ability and speed at which we can collect, process, monitor, manipulate, distribute, receive, and access information. This ability has conferred valuable benefits on society and the business world. However, along with the benefits come potential negative consequences. The potential consequences have given rise to many societal, business, and management issues. Many of these issues may be social or ethical in nature, but may also carry serious legal consequences. These issues will affect society, as well as the relationships between businesses and their customers, and employers and employees. Because business liabilities may arise, it is imperative that information managers be cognizant of the ethical and regulatory environment.

Among the legal and social issues we must be prepared to address are: Who owns the information, data, or processes? Who has access to the information, and how and when can that information be used? Who is responsible for the accuracy of that information, and what are the consequences that flow from errors? Every time individuals make a credit card purchase, deposit, or withdraw money from a bank account, register to vote, or file an income tax return, data is being collected on them. The collection and dissemination of data on individuals raises questions on privacy. In addition, there is the responsibility and an interest in making sure that all matters are

*This chapter was coauthored by Joyce O. Moy, J.D., a practicing attorney and adjunct professor of law at Queens College. She is a consultant to companies on legal matters.

401

recorded accurately. All of us have heard the horror stories of mistakes on credit reports and other documents and the ensuing harm to individuals. Computer-related mistakes and waste must be avoided to prevent costly damage to reputations and profitability.

These issues are not always easy to sort out. While something may be perfectly legal, it may also be socially unacceptable or even unethical. For example, while it does not violate any law for an employee to use an employer-provided computer to access the Internet, viewing inappropriate material may be socially and ethically unacceptable. Monitoring of these activities by the employer may be absolutely necessary, but certainly has an effect on the employee's sense of privacy and creates questions of ethical propriety. Often, managers have to balance legal issues against questions of social responsibility and ethics.

This chapter provides an overview of some of the legal and ethical questions with which information systems managers should have familiarity. These areas include intellectual property rights, such as patents, copyrights and trademarks, trade secrets, basic contract negotiation, and issues in granting or using software licensing rights.

In the area of ethical issues, this chapter discusses the issues of computer waste, privacy (including the monitoring of employee activities), unauthorized use and access to information, and potential legal implications of not handling these matters correctly. Specific computer crime legislation is also discussed.

ETHICAL RAMIFICATIONS

Ethics are essentially the guiding principles that help individuals decide between right and wrong. The question of what is right or wrong may be viewed from several perspectives. From the perspective of the individual, we may decide that what is best for that person is right. From the prospective of law and what promotes the health and good of human beings, what is right may be the authority to which we are willing to submit. Others may say that ethical behavior requires that we do what is best for the greatest number of people, and others may say that what is ethical is the moral rule adopted by the most people. Although ethics and law are not the same thing, they do overlap, and many unethical behaviors are illegal.

THE SCOPE OF INTELLECTUAL PROPERTY LAW

The aim of the legal system, at least with respect to computer technology, should be to promote and encourage innovation. Restraints should be imposed only when mandated by clear, countervailing policies. Innovation is greatly affected by copyright, patent, and trade secret laws. The creative or innovative individual or organization is granted the exclusive right to use and distribute the product.

There exists a split in the computer industry about the effect of intellectual property laws on the economic environment. Some believe that the software industry will benefit if there are strong intellectual property protections. Others argue that an unregulated and open market increases competition and results in greater innovation.

Technology offers tremendous opportunities to expand and to improve efficiency and productivity. But the benefits from the use and application of this technology require an understanding of potential legal pitfalls to which businesses may be subject, if there is not a sufficient understanding of the laws governing the rights and obligations accompanying this use.

Information technology is changing so rapidly that an entirely new area of computer law is developing with each new technological advance and application. However, the traditional areas of intellectual property that cover the products of the intellectual and creative processes of the mind are expanding as well to cover these changes. Intellectual property law includes patents, copyrights, and trademarks (among other things), which give the creator or owner certain rights in the intangible property, to the exclusion of others. In other words, intellectual property laws answer the question of who owns the information.

The application of traditional patent, copyright, and trademark law to computer software is further complicated by the fact that this technology may possess characteristics protected in part by each of the three areas. Thus all three of these areas apply. The failure to observe or assert intellectual property rights may result in severe legal and financial consequences such as the loss of beneficial rights or in liability for infringing on the rights of another, as in infringement on the patent, copyright, or trademark owned by another.

Questions on intellectual property rights are encountered in the overall planning of a business operation and in the daily course of business of an information systems manager. Who owns the rights to the custom software and hardware designs developed by outside consultants hired by the business? What rights does a user have with respect to prepackaged or licensed software? What are the responsibilities and rights of a business that has access to or is provided with proprietary data? What are the responsibilities of an employer for the acts of employees who have access to use this information? Managers must have some knowledge of the law in these areas.

Patents

Granted by the federal government, patents give the inventor of an invention, discovery, or design (that is original, novel, and not obvious) the exclusive right to manufacture, use, and sell the invention for seventeen years. Patents are also available for not so obvious and ornamental designs for manufacturing such as a design for a car. Anyone making, using, or selling the invention without the patent holder's consent commits the tort of patent infringement. The application process for a patent is expensive and time-consuming. This often discourages inventors of software because the changes in technology are taking place at such a speed that the value of the software on the market may be substantially diminished by the time the patent is approved.

Patent laws have generally been used to protect hardware technology. Lately, however, patents have also been used to protect software. To obtain protection under patent law, there are substantially higher requirements for inventiveness and disclosure. However, an inventor's rights under the patent law are significantly stronger than an author's rights under the copyright law.

A patent holder can stop others not only from copying, but also from using, the patented process or object. No one else may make, use, or sell the invention for twenty years from the time a patent application is filed.

If two inventors are working on an identical invention and one inventor files the application for the patent first, he may prevent the other from using the invention. It does not matter that the two inventors developed and derived their invention independently. The first to file gets exclusive rights.

To obtain a patent, the inventor must undergo a process of application and review. Only in the event of a favorable action is the inventor granted the patent.

A patent is not granted automatically. A patent must be claimed, and the claim may or may not be allowed by the Patent and Trademark Office (PTO). The application and review process requires public documentation of the process, method, or design of the invention. The public disclosure allows others to innovate by developing their own inventions. The knowledge behind the invention is shared by the public.

Many patent claims are rejected because they make only minor modification to existing technology. The invention must be not only an original and useful, but also a significant innovation.

Given the high threshold and limitations, most software innovations do not qualify for patent protection. The incremental nature of software development generally precludes the developer from claiming that the software is significantly unique. The Patent and Trademark Office must determine if an application for patent satisfies minimum criteria of novelty and nonobviousness.

Patent protection for computer software can be difficult. Prior to the 1981 Supreme Court case of *Diamond v. Diehr and Lutton,* it was difficult to obtain a patent on software because much of the software consisted of performing procedures that could be done manually and involved mathematical equations or formulas, which are not patentable. However, the Supreme Court pronounced that it was possible for a patent to be granted for a process that incorporates a computer program, as long as the process itself could be patented.

Since patents are granted to the inventor of a product, this frequently creates problems for the employer, because this means that the patent will be granted to the individual employee. As a result, employers must be careful to have all employees who are responsible for product creation, sign agreements whereby:

- The employee agrees to pursue a patent at the request of an employer, and that
- the rights to all patents for products created while in the company's employ are assigned to the employer.

Of course, this generally requires the employer to pay the costs of obtaining the patent.

Copyrights

Historically, protection of technology resided exclusively under the patent law. During the 1980s, the copyright law also became a major force in protecting computer technology. Copyright law originally was concerned with the protection of the creative expressions of artists and authors. Its transition into computer technology has been the source of much litigation. As we enter the next century, the field of software copyright law has settled considerably. The application of copyright laws to cyberspace is likely to create new and exciting issues for years to come.

Initially, there was a question whether computer software was even copyrightable. Now, most countries in the world simply accept that software can be copyrighted and this issue is not generally litigated. Computer software and other types of electronic information are particularly susceptible to piracy. It is extremely easy to make an exact duplicate of the original. Preventing piracy was a major driving force in granting copyright protection to computer software. Most software litigation is still concerned with one party claiming software piracy, where the second party is alleged to have extensively copied the first party's software program.

A copyright gives the creator of a work the right to copy or reproduce the form in which an idea is expressed and to distribute it. The expression must be reduced to a concrete form, i.e., written or recorded where it can be read or visually perceived. Copying or reproducing that expression, without the consent of the owner of the copyright, constitutes copyright infringement, which will result in monetary damages and even in fines and imprisonment.

Copyrights protect literary works; musical works; and the words; dramatic works; and their music; pantomimes; choreographic, pictorial, sculptural, and graphic works; motion pictures; audiovisual works; and sound recordings.

The Computer Software Copyright Act was passed in 1980, and amended the Copyright Act of 1976 to specifically include computer software programs in its list of creative works to be protected under copyright. Prior to the amendment, there was often controversy on whether programs met the definition of the types of literary and artistic works covered under copyright law.

The 1980 Act defines a *computer program* as "a set of statements or instructions to be used directly or indirectly in a computer in order to bring about a certain result." Computer programs are classified as literary works, and includes both the binary code and source codes of a software program. Because copyrighted software that is bought can be copied or adapted by an owner for individual use, and the copies transferred by the owner, it has become common practice for the owners of copyrights to license the use of the software, rather than sell the software outright. Under a licensing arrangement, the owner of the copyrighted software (the licenser) gives permission to another (licensee) to use the software, rather than ownership rights.

Copyright protection is automatically afforded when a work is created. However, registering a copyright gives the creator greater protection. Unlike patents, which are granted only to the individual inventor, the employer—not the employee—owns the copyright if the work is created while in the employer's employ. This is referred to as *work for hire.*

Work for hire includes work prepared by an employee within the scope of his regular employment duties, and work specifically contracted for or commissioned with an independent contractor if stated in a written agreement that creations are work for hire. If the ownership of the material eligible for copyright is not clearly stated in such a written agreement with a nonemployee, the copyright belongs to the creator and therefore it is important for companies to pay careful attention to this issue.

An individual spends a considerable amount of money in developing computer programs. The cost of duplicating programs is essentially negligible. If the software cannot be copyrighted, the creator must recover all costs and profits on the sale of the first unit of the software package. This model of pricing is acceptable only if the software product is uniquely suited to the needs of only a single entity, such as customized software, and the entity can afford the expense. Otherwise, the software is likely to cost an exorbitant amount of money. The per-unit price decreases significantly if multiple entities can benefit from the software package. By being able to copyright software, the creator can spread the development costs over multiple copies of the software package.

Patent law generally imposes too high a requirement of inventiveness for most computer programs. The trade secret laws require true confidentiality and most software packages can't satisfy this requirement either. Copyright laws impose only few conditions and protect the creator's rights against unauthorized copying.

A copyright can be granted only by the federal government. For an item to be copyrightable, it must satisfy the following criteria:

- The work must be "original" and should be a "work of authorship." The work must not be copied from another. The work does not necessarily have to be unique, but it must have some original expression. Expression involves the manner in which words or symbols are brought together to convey the information or idea. There must be some personal choice in arranging and selecting the work.

- The work must be fixed in some tangible form of media.

- A copyright does not extend to the idea or processes contained in the work of authorship.

To prove a copyright infringement, the following two criteria must be satisfied:

- The plaintiff must prove that he or she holds a valid copyright.

- The plaintiff's exclusive rights granted by a copyright were violated.

Generally the second point is the source of litigation. The plaintiff's exclusive rights in a copyrightable work include the right to copy, disseminate, display, or prepare derivative work. Litigation frequently focuses on whether the rights of the plaintiff were violated.

Trademarks

Trademarks are marks, names, logos, mottos, or symbols that are distinctive and intended to distinguish a company's goods and services from others. Trademarks can be registered with the federal or state government. These distinctive marks are associated with a manufacturer who has invested in the quality of the goods associated with that mark. Thus a value becomes associated with the goodwill of that product.

To obtain trademark protection, the mark must be distinctive. *Distinctive trademarks* are marks that are fanciful, arbitrary, or suggestive. Generic terms like "soap" are not eligible for trademark. Examples of fanciful trademarks are names like "Pepsi" or "Kodak," which have no particular meaning. Infringement takes place when the trademark is used without the owner's permission or consent. The owner has an interest in maintaining the quality associated with the name, and therefore does not want it used in association with items or products without permission.

Management must understand and convey the rules regarding intellectual property rights to its employees. Failure to do so may result in costly litigation to assert rights of the employer, and any duplication or unauthorized use of patented, copyrighted, or trademarked materials by employees may cause real problems for the company.

Trade Secrets

Trade secret laws have been used extensively by the computer industry. Copyrights and patents are granted by federal law. Trade secret protections are primarily based on state law. Trade secret laws protect the ideas and processes that cannot be copyrighted and that do not meet the criteria of sufficient innovativeness for a patent.

Disclosure is not required or even encouraged by trade secret laws. A company can protect its technology and not share it with its competitors using the trade secret laws. Unlike copyright or patent laws, trade secret laws do not create any type of exclusive rights. A competitor can independently develop and use the same technology. Trade secret laws are only used to enforce confidentiality constraints established by the parties.

The owners of a trade secret must maintain the confidentiality of the information and keep it secret. Protection is available only when a competitor learns about the information through a breach of faith.

Software, like most other technologies, is often developed by employees for employers. Major concerns for employers are keeping trade secrets and maintaining confidentiality. The employer provides the financing and other resources, and the law recognizes that the employer has the right to control the products developed by its employees.

Although some business information or processes developed by a company are not eligible for patent, copyright, or trademark protection, they might nevertheless be protected as trade secrets. Violation of trade secrets is treated as a tort or a civil wrong, for which there is legal recourse. Employers and others who may entrust trade secrets to others normally insist on a nondisclosure agreement, which then gives the owner of the trade secret additional grounds to enforce its rights with respect to the trade secret.

Among the most commonly accepted definitions of trade secrets is articulated in the *Restatement of Torts*. Trade secrets are generally defined as consisting of ". . . any formula, pattern, device or compilation of information which is used in one's business, and which gives him an opportunity to obtain an advantage over competitors who do not know or use it." The types of items included are customer lists, research and development information, marketing materials, pricing information, and production processes and techniques.

Liability is imposed if the trade secret is revealed to a competitor and the party making the disclosure used improper means to obtain the information or breaches a confidence. Problems may arise with respect to trade secrets from two perspectives. First, the owner of the trade secret wants to have procedures in place to safeguard the secrets. Second, the party to whom a trade secret is entrusted wants to make sure that the information is not deliberately or inadvertently revealed by it or its employees.

AVOIDING COMPUTER WASTE AND MISTAKES

Managing computer resources is a key to maintaining profitability and avoiding problems associated with the abuse of computers or mistakes made by computer. Safeguards and procedures must be:

- Established
- Implemented
- Monitored
- Reviewed by management

For example, without proper monitoring, countless hours and resources may be wasted by employees on nonwork-related computer use, such as playing games, sending e-mail, or Internet surfing. Mistakes not only waste resources due to the time consumed in correcting the errors, but may actually cause monetary damage. For example, failure to implement procedures to cross-check information may result in systemic mistakes when the error is carried over into future computations or analysis. If this occurs on a client's project, it may result in a lawsuit and compensatory damages.

Establishment of Procedures

Policies and procedures for the selection and acquisition of equipment that is appropriate for the needs of the company must be established. This prevents costly acquisitions of equipment that is underutilized, goes obsolete, or becomes inadequate in a short time, requiring constant and expensive upgrading. Manuals on use and maintenance of equipment should be made available. In addition, guidelines for the disposal of equipment is needed. Many companies discard equipment or supplies such as diskettes while they still have value or can be reused.

Implementation

Programs must be implemented to maximize the use of the equipment in place, such as adequate training of personnel for the optimal use of equipment capabilities, or is equipment recycled so that value is returned to the company.

Monitoring

Monitoring and measuring the results of the programs implemented for quality and productivity are required to determine whether the programs are working. This involves maintaining records and comparing before-and-after conditions.

Review

Once implemented, procedures and programs must be constantly reviewed and modified if conditions change for optimal use of information technology at all times. Reviews should include the establishment of contingencies in the event of the failure of the procedures implemented.

DIFFERENT TYPES OF COMPUTER CRIME

One of the most vexing problems for information professionals is computer crime. These crimes can be costly to the victim in terms of the damage caused, as well as the costs of replacing equipment, correcting, or minimizing damage.

Computer crime is a serious concern. Computer crime may involve the use of computers in perpetrating traditional crimes such as theft, fraud, and embezzlement. Computer records can be altered, and the intangible nature of the records makes it difficult to detect the crime. Computers also make it possible to commit the crime from a remote location and transfer funds with considerable speed. This type of computer crime can be handled within the traditional criminal legal system. Computer crime may also involve various types of computer abuse, such as:

- Unauthorized access to computer records
- Unauthorized copying or transferring of confidential data

- Modifying or destroying data
- Denying legitimate users from accessing the computer system

Computer crimes fall into two categories. In some instances, the computer is the target or object of the crime, such as when it is vandalized or deliberately infected with a virus. In the second category, computers are the instruments of crime or tools for committing the crime, such as when it is used to steal money from an account. The increase in computer crime has resulted in new state and federal legislation designed specifically to deal with these problems.

Computer crime may be extremely difficult to prevent despite precautions and various security measures. Criminals who commit these acts tend to be sophisticated and are able to cover their "tracks."

Computer as the Target of Crime

Computers may be the target of attacks in the commission of a computer crime. These activities can range from physical attack to manipulation of information. The following is a description of the types of crimes that may be encountered.

Physical Attacks   Physical attacks on computers include vandalism, i.e., actual and deliberate acts of physical destruction by damaging or modifying equipment or by cutting off power. Other physical attacks involve removing equipment and stored data, and causing interference such as electronically jamming equipment.

Unauthorized Access   The unauthorized access to information poses one of the greatest economic and social threats of computer crimes, because of the potential use of the information obtained if it falls into the wrong hands. Gaining access to data without authorization, regardless of whether that information is ultimately used or not may in itself be a crime.

Unauthorized access includes physically observing keystrokes to obtain passwords, browsing and reading information, and eavesdropping by intercepting data. A serious act that has gotten much publicity is the ability to access information by bypassing authorization codes. This is usually done by hacking or cracking codes to access data stored in a computer. Once the code is cracked, the party can then read and copy stored information. This leads to theft of information and, in the case of government secrets, a potentially dangerous event.

Other acts of unauthorized access to information need not involve great sophistication. These include "dumpster diving," i.e., collecting and examining printouts, hardware, or disks that have been discarded.

Invasive Attacks Serious and operationally paralyzing results may arise out of invasive attacks by parties penetrating or inserting damaging software mechanisms into computer operations. *Computer viruses* are essentially replications of useless routines that render programs inoperative and therefore result in the destruction of memory, hard drive, and other storage devices. These are to be distinguished from *worms,* which do not have to be inserted into already existing programs to cause the same problem.

Sometimes these destructive techniques are inserted to cause damage at another time or on a specific date. These have become known as *logic bombs,* where a virus is programmed to "explode" or go into execution at a specific time or event. These are often disguised in the form of a program that is apparently useful, but is used to hide the bomb. Thus it has become known as a *Trojan horse.*

Another technique used by hackers to gain access to computer data is the installation of a hidden program in a computer or network called a *password sniffer,* which is used to record identification numbers and passwords.

In response to these types of invasive attacks on computer systems and networks, Congress passed the Computer Abuse Amendments Act of 1994, which prohibits the transmission of harmful computer programs or codes, such as viruses and worms.

Other types of invasive abuses include inserting false or misleading data or modifying data. Examples of these abuses include accessing and changing employee personnel records.

Abuses can take the form of interfering with access to the computer or its data. This can be accomplished by inundating a system with a saturation attack so that other users cannot obtain access.

Computers as an Instrument of Crime

Crimes using computers as the instrument often involve the crime of theft, i.e., the intentional taking of another person's property without consent. Thefts may be of funds, services, software, and data. Because many transactions are now processed automatically and in large volumes at high speeds, thefts are often hard to detect, and they may be easily masked by sophisticated parties. Sometimes these thefts are not detected for very long periods. As a result, companies always have to be vigilant, implementing audit and other procedures to monitor accuracy and activities.

Theft of Funds   The theft of funds by accessing transfer mechanisms and using computers to hide the theft, such as by alteration or creation of bogus records, are the primary methods of committing fraud. Once access is obtained by hackers, funds can be easily transferred from one account to another. Recent stories tell of thieves who obtain personal identification numbers (PINs) assigned to bank customers by observing the customer or by finding discarded electronic receipts issued by automated teller machines (ATMs), and then withdrawing funds from entire accounts. Such stories have prompted new procedures and research into methods of prevention. Some of the changes made were as simple as printing no more than the last four digits of the account number on the receipt, instead of the full number.

Theft of Services   This applies to the unauthorized use of computers, i.e., accessing the computer without authority, or using the computer for other than authorized (work-related) purposes. Sometimes, the activity is viewed as computer waste, and the subject of employee discipline, instead of as a crime. This would probably be the way that innocuous activities like playing games on the computer or surfing the Internet would be treated. However, because a cost is associated with this in terms of lost productivity and the actual costs of operating the computer, this is in fact theft of services.

The more serious forms of theft of services take place when company computers are used by employees not just for personal purposes, like sending personal e-mail, but when personal business/commercial operations are conducted using company computer facilities. The monitoring of these activities brings into focus issues on privacy, which are discussed later in this chapter.

Theft of Software   The unauthorized copying of software is often referred to as software piracy. The problem may arise either when the company's own proprietary software is copied, or when software obtained by a company for its own use is copied without permission of the owner of a patent or copyright. This may result in patent or copyright infringement. While the company may not have authorized the employee to make a copy, the employer may be open to suit by the owner of the patent or copyright.

When packaged software is purchased, the purchaser is given a license to use the software. However, additional copies of the software cannot be transferred to others for use in another computer within the same company unless a site license is obtained. (See the section on copyrights for a discussion on licensing of copyrights.) The site license allows copies of the software to be copied a limited number of times and used by different employees at a specific location. There is sometimes a nominal fee charged for each additional copy made.

Theft of Data   Access is sometimes obtained for the purpose of misappropriating or exploiting the data. The data may have significant value to outside parties, such as trade secrets, or obtaining confidential financial data on individuals for the purpose of selling that information to brokers.

USING SALES AND CONTRACTS AS PROTECTION

Sale of goods is covered by the Uniform Commercial Code (UCC), and the sale of services is covered by common law and other statutes. Goods are defined by the UCC as objects that are movable at the time of identification to the contract. Computer hardware clearly falls into the definition for the sale or lease of goods.

Sale of preexisting computer software packages has generally been treated by the courts as a transaction involving goods. Mass-marketed and prepackaged software are considered goods.

For custom-designed software, the issue is not always clear-cut. Similarly, when the agreement is for both delivery of goods and services, there may be uncertainty as to its legal treatment. Courts generally look at either the *primary purpose* of the transaction or use the *gravamen-of-the-action* standard in distinguishing between a goods or services contract.

Warranties

Express and implied warranties are involved in all types of computer-related transactions.

An *express warranty* is a promise that becomes part of the basis of the bargain between the transacting parties. It is created by an affirmative action and is enforceable. Certain criteria have to be satisfied before a statement or a representation is considered an express warranty. All representations made by the seller during negotiation should not be considered express warranties. The law makes a distinction between statements that are pure "sales talk" and representations intended to induce reliance. The seller is given some latitude in exaggerating the product, and the law does not protect a totally naïve buyer. The buyer is expected to be able to discriminate between exaggerations and express warranties.

Under the Uniform Commercial Code, there is an implied warranty of merchantability. There is also an implied warranty that goods are fit for a particular purpose. The implied *warranty of merchantability* states that goods are fit for the ordinary purpose for which such goods are normally used. The *implied warranty* that goods are fit for a particular purpose exists only when the seller knows what the buyer intends to do with the product, and the buyer is relying on the seller's judgment and expertise that the product is fit for that particular purpose. Implied warranties play a significant role in consumer transactions and contracts. However, implied warranties are typically disclaimed in commercial contracts.

In the computer industry, technical specifications are generally considered express warranties and are enforced in contracts. Examples of technical specifications that have previously been enforced by courts include the storage capacity or the processing speed of a computer system. A vendor cannot simply exclude express warranties based on technical specifications by general-purpose language in the contract.

Express warranties of suitability are enforceable when the vendor promises that the product meets the needs of the buyer. Contracts often contain exclusionary language that eliminates express warranty for suitability for a particular purpose. When the buyer desires such warranty, the best course is to insist that the seller explicitly provide such assurances.

Express limited warranties are generally provided in contracts. These warranties state that the product is free of specified defects, such as programming errors, and excludes other warranties. The buyer's remedy is frequently limited to replacing or fixing the product; the financial liability is often limited to the price of the product.

The *parol evidence rule* precludes the use of oral evidence to contradict the written terms of an agreement. Additional representations that do not alter the terms of the contract, however, are often permitted.

Computer viruses are programs extraneous to the main programs, intentionally introduced to the computer system, whose purpose is to destroy, disrupt, or alter a computer system. Computer viruses raise a number of legal issues. Besides penalties in criminal law, developers and manufacturers may be affected by a virus introduced into their systems.

Vendors can transfer the risk related to computer viruses by disclaiming any warranty regarding them. Vendors may also limit warranty to the lack of knowledge of viruses. Few vendors expressly warrant that their software is free of viruses, especially in cases involving electronic communications and transfers.

The introduction of a virus into a computer system is argued to be similar to trespass and property damage. Most states have criminal penalties only if the introduction of the virus is intentional. States also allow civil penalties on the theory of tort. Tort law requires either intention or negligence on the part of the vendor. Once aware of the presence of a virus, the vendor has a duty to notify the individuals who may be at risk.

The vendor of a system is under no obligation to update or revise its product. Sometimes, however, a vendor commits itself to providing upgrades. The vendor usually requires the buyer to pay an additional fee for the upgrade.

Fraud

Fraud may be claimed when one party fails to disclose material facts or makes false representation on which another party relies. To prove fraud, the following must be established: One party knowingly misrepresents material facts with the intent to deceive, and another party relies on the representation to its detriment.

Frequently, fraud is deemed to exist even if the misrepresentation is not intentional, but represented a reckless disregard of the facts. Allegations of fraud frequently occur in computer contract disputes. Allegation of fraud creates significant advantages during litigation. For example, one might be able to overcome some contract disclaimers.

When the fraud is intentional, such as when the manufacturer or developer intentionally misrepresents the performance characteristics of a computer system, there can no longer exist the presumption that the parties assented to the obligations in the contract. Each party is presumed to have relied to some extent on the honesty of the other.

The issue of fraud in contracts becomes more complex when the intentional misrepresentation of facts is not so clear. Generally, such claims of fraud are not sufficient to circumvent contract disclaimers.

UNDERSTANDING THE SCOPE
OF PRODUCT LIABILITY

Sometimes the developer, distributor, or manufacturer of a product may be held liable for damages to third parties for negligence, strict liability, or contract warranty. The seller may be liable for negligence for foreseeable harm if the product is capable of inflicting substantial harm if defective.

Strict liability goes a step further. Even if the manufacturer has taken all possible care, the manufacturer can still be held liable if the defect causes substantial harm. One aim of strict liability theory is to provide manufacturers with the incentive to design and manufacture defect-free products. A second reason sometimes given for strict liability is the "deep pockets" theory; these manufacturers essentially act as insurance companies in the event of harm.

Product liability, in most states, is limited to physical harm or damage to property; economic loss is generally not included. For this reason, the computer industry has not, so far, experienced substantial litigation in this area. Typically, litigation has involved physical damages caused by computer-assisted machinery and robots. Physical harm caused by computer keyboards has been another source of product liability litigation.

THE RIGHT TO PRIVACY

An issue inescapably intertwined with our ability to collect and use data as well as the need to monitor these activities is the individual's right to privacy. Under traditional tort law, an individual may recover for invasion of privacy, i.e., when a party intrudes into a person's place of business. The problem with computer crimes of this nature is that the intrusion is not physical in the way that is necessary in the tort area. To deal with this issue, a plethora of federal legislation has appeared on the subject.

The privacy issue spills over to the monitoring of employee activities that is necessary to manage and prevent computer waste, and to detect crimes. Monitoring is cited by employees as a major reason for job-related stress. Some employers have taken the position that they will monitor all e-mail and computer usage; others have explicitly decided that e-mail and other computer communications are private, and will not be monitored by the company. Yet others have taken the position that monitoring will not occur unless the company has substantial reason to believe that an abuse is occurring.

Federal laws permit e-mail to be monitored. When e-mail has been deleted, procedures exist for the retrieval of the messages from hard drives, and may be subject to subpoena as part of business records in a lawsuit. These types of problems have surfaced when employees have exercised poor discretion or outright wrongful behavior and have used company e-mail facilities to send out inappropriate messages, thereby potentially subjecting the company to liability if the company fails to stop the behavior. These types of matters have a direct impact on employer–employee relationships, and therefore managers must strike a balance between the employee's right and desire for privacy and the needs of the workplace.

Federal Legislation on Privacy

The violation of many federal statutes not only results in civil penalties, but may also subject the violator to criminal prosecution. Some of the legislation involves information or data in the hands of the government, and others involve information in the hands of nongovernment entities. The objective of this legislation is to prevent unauthorized access to confidential information, and to give notice to individuals when information has been given out. Many states also have legislation governing these issues. The actual and pending legislation should be reviewed.

Government Information The following legislation regulates the handling of information and data collected by the federal government or its agencies:

- The *Freedom of Information Act of 1966* entitles individuals to access government information about themselves.

- The *Criminal Control Act of 1973* protects individuals from the dissemination of information collected by certain state criminal systems.

- The *Privacy Act of 1974* provides individuals with certain safeguards where the federal government is collecting information about them. It applies to all federal agencies, except the CIA and law enforcement. Specifically, government agencies originating, using, or otherwise disseminating information about individuals must ensure the accuracy of the information, and take steps to prevent misuse of the information. The individual's permission must be obtained before it can be used for a purpose other than the original purpose for which it was collected. Information must be provided on what data are being compiled and how they will be used. There must be a procedure or method for correcting inaccuracies.

- The *Tax Reform Act of 1976* protects the privacy of the financial information filed with the Internal Revenue Service.

Other Information   Various other pieces of legislation are available that regulate the access and dissemination of information in the hands of federal nongovernment entities. They are as follows:

- The *Fair Credit Reporting Act of 1970* entitles consumers to be informed about any credit investigations that are being done, the kind of data being collected, and the names of the entities or individuals receiving reports.
- The *Right to Financial Privacy Act of 1978* prevents disclosure of customer financial information to the federal government without customer authorization.
- The *Electronic Fund Transfer Act of 1978* regulates the rights and obligations of parties using electronic methods of transferring funds, and requires that financial institutions notify a customer if a third party gains access to the customer's account.
- The *Counterfeit Access Device and Computer Fraud and Abuse Act of 1984* covers instances of unauthorized retrieval of data from the computer files of a financial institution or a credit-reporting agency by third parties.
- The *Electronic Communications Privacy Act of 1986* contains prohibitions against the interception of information transmitted by electronic means.

Corporate Privacy Policies

As stated earlier, many companies have different policies on privacy that take into consideration business needs and the needs of employees and customers. Failure to implement a fair and appropriate policy can lead to employee discontent and discourage customers who fear the misuse or unauthorized release of information obtained from them, all of which affect the profitability of the business. The policies implemented must be sensitive to the needs of all affected, and should cover the issues of what data are collected, what notice should be given, and how the data are to be used. In addition, any policy to be effective must take into account who has access to the data, and under what conditions that information is to be accessed or released.

Other Abuses

Other potentially damaging abuses do not rise to the level of a crime, nor are they invasions of privacy. But they may involve the willful failure to input data, or the omitting or entering of erroneous data. Equally damaging is the unauthorized release of data.

OTHER ETHICAL AND LEGAL ISSUES

Other concerns related to information technology include health issues. Employment and use of technology and equipment have lead to discussion and complaints of physical ailments related to this use. Among the complaints most often heard are those related to having activities monitored by management, physical ailments related to repetitive hand movements such as with the use of keyboards, problems related to the eyes and headaches, and backaches from long periods of time at the computer.

Implementation of security measures to prevent unauthorized access is needed from constantly changing passwords to upgrading and installing the latest security measures.

Employers and users of technology have to be concerned with these issues because it affects the welfare and well-being of employees. With the welfare of the workers comes the economic issues of lost time from work, lowered productivity, and insurance and other claims stemming from work-related health issues.

The solutions to these health issues have been to design the work environment or even the job and its tasks to minimize the adverse effects. The area of study known as *ergonomics* may include choosing furniture that supports the individual, minimizing glare from computer monitors, and designing the steps needed to accomplish a task to change the repetitive movements that may lead to some of the injuries or ailments.

CONCLUSION

The objective of any program that seeks to meet ethical standards of business conduct and legal compliance must take into account protection of individual privacy rights and the protection of the information system and data from crime. Prevention of the kinds of abuses that result in damage, legal consequences, loss of customer confidence, and other problems can be accomplished only by employing a number of strategies. Monitoring has to play a role in the overall strategy, but employee and staff education and involvement of the workforce in the issue will more likely yield the results desired.

In addition, it is probably advisable for companies to set up narrow areas of access for its employees. For example, people in the sales department should be limited to accessing only the information on sales accounts or even only on the customers they service within a region.

Leadership and role models must be provided from the top on these issues. Among the things that can be done are the issuance of an ethics policy developed with staff and employee participation, discussions and education on issues of security practices, and legal developments and improvement of processes with input from those who deal with these issues daily.

16
CONSULTING STRATEGIES

CHANGES IN CONSULTING

With the increased use of personal computers and distributed computing, the role of information systems professionals has changed significantly in the last decade. In the past, data processing and the role of information systems were centralized. Now the trend is toward decentralized computing. End-users no longer want IS professionals to do the data processing work for them; rather they want IS to provide training, support, and guidance, along with problem-solving skills and *consults*.

We define *consultants* as problem solvers who work with different clients. The term "consultant" refers to both internal and external consultants. *Internal consultants* work with "clients" from different areas and levels within a single organization. *External consultants,* on the other hand, work with clients from multiple organizations. Internal consultants are generally employees of an organization, whereas external consultants generally work on a contract basis. Consultants, internal or external, must be experts in their field. They must excel at what they do.

DEFINING THE CONSULTANT–CLIENT RELATIONSHIP

A consultant acts as a problem solver for the client. Clients have many expectations from an IS consultant. As an information system consultant, you are a source of technical expertise and should work as a partner with the client. This is a significant departure from the traditional way IS professionals performed their duties. In a partnership, you and the client share equal responsibility for problem solving.

Elements of a Consultant–Client Relationship

The information systems consultant:

- Is a problem-solver.
- Acts as a partner of the client. Both share equal responsibility in the outcome.
- Understands the client's perspective.
- Creates an environment of mutual trust.
- Avoids technical jargon and communicates in the client's language and at his/her level.
- Helps the client define and understand the problem.
- Encourages the client to generate and present solutions.
- Garners the client's commitment and support by building enthusiasm for solving the problem.
- Expects conflicts, learning how to creatively manage conflicts without engaging in personal attacks, finger-pointing, or political battles.

Consultants cannot serve clients if they do not understand the clients' problems. This requires consultants to see things from the clients' perspective and understand the clients' point of view. The technical solution to the problem will not be successful if the consultant does not pay careful attention to the human side of the relationship and create an environment of trust and respect. It also requires the information systems consultant to communicate with the client at the client's level and in the client's language. In other words, you should avoid using technical phrases and jargon.

As an information systems consultant, you have to define and classify the problem. While clients may be aware that a problem exists, they may not completely understand its severity and magnitude. You can help your clients better understand the problem by dividing the problem into manageable components. It will be easier to garner client support and commitment by making them see the problem and building enthusiasm to solve the problem. The client should be encouraged to propose solutions. More sophisticated users might even want to assume the primary responsibility for developing and implementing the solution. The consultant should ensure that the problem is kept in focus and on track.

Conflict naturally occurs in such situations. Managing conflict and keeping it from poisoning the entire project is essential. A good consultant expects conflict and deals with it creatively. He/she acts as a facilitator when tensions occur. Do not get involved in finger-pointing and political or personal battles. If you want to be successful, do not take anything personally.

CHARACTERISTICS OF INFORMATION SYSTEMS CONSULTANT

A successful IS consultant must have technical expertise in several specialties and working knowledge of a broad range of technologies. The current business environment encourages distributed and local computing. As computing gets decentralized, the information systems professional is likely to encounter a variety of technologies. Expertise in a single specialty does not help you when you encounter different clients using vastly different technologies.

Cross-training should be an integral part of information systems training. If an information systems department consists only of highly specialized individuals, the specialists can act as trainers in educating the other staff members. As an added benefit, the relationship among staff members improves and a more cooperative and cohesive group results. Cross-training also enables the information systems department to service clients even if a specialist leaves the firm or is away on vacation. The information systems department has greater flexibility in project assignments. The most important benefit of cross-training the information systems professionals is their familiarity with a broad range of technologies. This decreases the likelihood that they will improperly apply technology because it is the only one they know.

Important Consulting Skills

- Ability to work with a wide range of technology.

- Regular cross-training to update skills.

- Good communication skills, especially listening to others and understanding the client's perspective.

- Skill in making formal and informal presentations.

- Ability to write letters, reports, etc., in simple business English.

- A network of relationships to achieve objectives without using formal authority.

- Working knowledge of the client's business.

- Regular reading not only of computer publications but also of the clients' trade and industry publications.

- Attendance at seminars and conferences in the clients' industry to gain knowledge as well as to build and maintain a network.

Successful consultants possess good communication skills, the most important part of which is listening. Listening helps the consultant understand not only the problem, but also the client's perspective. Both are, of course, essential in formulating a solution.

To get your point across, you should be skillful in making formal and informal presentations. You must be comfortable in front of an audience and be able to maintain their interest. Written communication skills are a must. You frequently need to write letters, memos, reports, etc., in simple business English, avoiding technical jargon.

An effective consultant maintains a network relationship through regular, deliberate contact with individuals across functional and hierarchical lines. These relationships help you accomplish objectives without using formal authority. As an added benefit, building coalitions with the right individuals helps in minimizing resistance and conflict, and maintains momentum to complete the project work.

While information systems professionals typically possess technical expertise, they often lack business skills. Many IS professionals see their role as that of a technical consultant and are not interested in the business side of their organization. This is a serious mistake. Actual business experience, working outside information systems, is a strong asset. Regular contact with past, current, and potential clients helps you understand their special needs and concerns.

While most information systems professionals keep current by reading computer publications, most consultants do not read trade and industry publications of their clients. Extra effort to read such publications will greatly enhance the consultant's effectiveness. Consultants may also want to consider attending seminars and conferences in their clients' industry. Understanding current issues and trends that affect your clients is invaluable. Furthermore, it allows you to communicate with clients in their language.

ESTABLISHING A CONSULTING PRACTICE

Accounting and Tax Requirements

The accounting, tax, and legal requirements of setting up and maintaining a business can be overwhelming. As an independent consultant and business person, you are expected to manage your tax affairs. Fulfilling tax requirements is likely to be your greatest administrative worry. Enlisting the help of a Certified Public Accountant (CPA) and an attorney is essential. Depending on the jurisdiction, you typically need to be concerned about:

- Federal withholding for income taxes, FICA, Medicare, unemployment taxes, etc.
- State withholdings for income taxes, unemployment taxes, etc.
- Local withholdings for income taxes, etc.

As an employee, your employer deducts the appropriate federal, state, and local taxes from your paycheck. However, as an independent consultant, you make these payments. You are generally required to make quarterly payments of estimated taxes to the appropriate federal, state, and local authorities. As a self-employed consultant, you are required to pay for the employers' as well as the employees' portion of FICA and Medicare.

If you plan to hire employees, you need to be familiar with payroll tax requirements. You will need to withhold federal, state, and local income taxes from your employees' paychecks. These taxes must be remitted promptly or you incur significant penalties. The frequency with which these taxes must be remitted depends on the magnitude of taxes.

The IRS and most state tax agencies provide publications, forms, and instructions for tax filings on the World Wide Web. These documents are generally available for download in the *portable document format (PDF)*. The National Association of Computerized Tax Processors (NACTP) web site contains links to the IRS and state tax sites. NACTP's web site is located at:

http://www.nactp.org/taxforms.htm

The IRS web site can be accessed directly at:

http://www.irs.ustreas.gov

The following are some of the IRS publications of interest to small business owners:

- Pub. 334: *Tax Guide for Small Business*
- Pub. 583: *Starting a Business and Keeping Records*
- Pub. 509: *Tax Calendar*
- Form 1040ES: *Estimated Tax for Individuals*
- Form SS-4: *Application for Employer Identification Number*
- Pub. 15: *Circular E, Employer's Tax Guide*
- Pub. 463: *Travel, Entertainment, Gift, and Car Expenses*
- Pub. 505: *Tax Withholding and Estimated Tax*
- Pub. 533: *Self-Employment Tax*
- Pub. 1976: *Independent Contractor or Employee*

The Small Business Administration (SBA) is an excellent source of help. It provides information about starting and expanding your business and provides links to other useful sites. SBA's web site is located at:

http://www.sbaonline.sba.gov

Sales and Marketing

Since it is impossible to stay in business without clients, successful consultants know the importance of marketing services. While marketing services can sometimes be frustrating and difficult, it is essential to market oneself consistently. Most new consultants take a passive role in marketing themselves and soon find that they have wasted time and money without gaining new clients. To succeed, the consultants should actively market their services.

Passive marketing techniques include mass mailings and Yellow Page ads. Such techniques frequently do not work for professionals. Most clients ignore "junk" mail and frequently do not use Yellow Pages to find computer consultants.

Mass mailing can be a useful technique if you mail to individuals with whom you have had some prior contact. For example, you might consider doing a mass mailing to former inactive clients or mail to an audience before whom you have made a speech. Some points to consider include:

- You are likely to achieve your mass mailing goals only if you target your mailing list to people with whom you have had some sort of contact.

- Try to target a narrow, specific audience. Do not describe yourself as a generalist. Let your audience know your specialty and how you can help your specific target group. Many consultants do not want to lock themselves out of potential business and are hence afraid to commit themselves to a narrow field. It is generally not advisable to claim that you can do everything for every one; this approach just does not work.

- If a mass mailing is done, try to personalize your mail and avoid the mass-mailed look. For example, use stamps rather than metered mail. Handwritten rather than typed information is likely to grab a potential client's attention.

- Include some type of a free offer, such as a free consultation.

- Mention in your letter that you will be making a follow-up call in a few days. A follow-up call can tremendously improve the response rate from mass mailings.

Note: The typical response rate from such mailings is very small and generally does not exceed 1 to 2 percent.

Print advertising, such as advertising in magazines, journals, and newspapers, can sometimes be effective. The key to print advertising is consistency. The same ad should appear in the same location week after week and month after month. Sporadic ads are not effective. This means that you should have a large budget. Print advertising is expensive and you have to spend considerable sums of money for an extended period. For many consultants, print advertising just may not be cost-effective.

The best way to obtain new clients is through active marketing and networking. Referrals from satisfied clients are the only way to stay in business over time. Of course, if you are new to consulting, you have no satisfied clients to provide referrals. Nonetheless, if you expect to stay in business, you must get referrals. One way to get referrals is to involve yourself in activities in which your prospective clients are involved. It is a good idea to join professional associations and actively participate in their activities.

From the time you begin to diligently market your services, it takes anywhere from six months to a year before the results start to pay off. It frequently takes three to five meetings with a prospective client before you are able to close the sale. If you don't realize that an extended time period is needed to establish a consulting practice, you are likely to be very frustrated.

Once your efforts begin to pay off and you have a few clients, it is tempting to stop marketing. Successful consulting means continuous and consistent marketing. Set aside some time, perhaps one day a week or two days per month, exclusively for marketing. You need to continuously maintain contact with prospective clients. Even if a prospective client does not become an actual client, he/she may in turn provide you with a lead and refer you to another prospective client. Always ask for referrals. Only an active and aggressive marketing approach helps you win clients.

Many consultants try to avoid doing the sales work themselves by hiring a sales representative. This is generally a satisfactory approach for larger organizations. However, most consultants, especially those running a one-person operation, are unlikely to get satisfactory results through this approach. Most good salespersons are able to make considerably more money working for the larger organizations. It is unlikely to be cost-effective for a small or single-person consulting firm to hire and retain qualified sales professionals.

Using Brokers

Corporate clients often prefer using brokers rather than hiring individual consultants. Brokers help by matching the needs of the client with the skills of the consultant. A corporate manager does not have to interview candidates and check their references. A manager also does not have to call up consultants who might be busy on other engagements. Convenience is the key reason for using brokers.

A contract consulting broker can be good place to get started. It means you get immediate work without all the hassles of marketing your services.

It also means that you get paid; collecting money from clients on your own can be a major nuisance. The broker assumes the responsibility for collecting the funds. This, of course, assumes that the broker is reputable. Some brokers lack ethics and may not pay the consultant. Check the broker's reputation before signing a contract.

A major benefit of working as a consultant for a broker is your ability to pick and choose assignments. You are in control of your career and can take on assignments that interest you and benefit your career in the long run.

Contract brokers typically advertise in the Sunday employment classifieds. These companies typically have salaried employees as well as independent consultants working for them. They pay the consultant some percentage, typically 70 to 80 percent, of the hourly rate they bill their clients. Such consulting arrangements can best be classified as temporary employment lasting anywhere from weeks and months to even years. The tax regulations typically require brokers to treat the consultants as employees and withhold taxes. Of course, consultants are typically paid a higher rate and often don't receive fringe benefits, such as health insurance.

Checking the broker's reputation is essential. Ask other consultants for referrals. Generally, it is inadvisable to maintain a long-distance relationship with a broker. Most brokers want the consultants to have at least three to five years' experience as salaried employees, preferably with a *Fortune* 500 firm.

At your initial meeting, the broker tries to assess your technical competence, and you have the opportunity to see if you are comfortable working for the broker. You should have a good idea of what the market rate is for the type of services you perform for the broker. The offer that the broker makes is almost always too low. You should let the broker know what you expect and remain firm. Don't negotiate the rate. The broker has much more negotiating experience and can convince you into accepting a lower rate. Don't accept a lower rate unless you are sure that no other broker can get you that rate. Of course, this assumes that you have properly researched the market rate and you know your worth.

Establishing a Rate and Billing

Determining the rate at which your services should be billed is often difficult for a consultant. You don't want to charge too much and price yourself out of the market. At the same time, you don't want to charge too little and sacrifice your profitability. Once you have determined the billing rate, you wonder how many of the actual hours worked should be billed. What is considered billable time? Answers to these questions are critical and can mean the difference between success and failure—the difference between profitability and loss.

You can take several approaches to setting rates and billing clients. A common approach is for the consultant to bill the client for time and materials. The rate to charge for time can be based on the rate typically charged by other consultants or a markup based on expenses.

GLOSSARY

Application Program   Computer software written specifically to process data in an information system. It performs tasks and solves problems applicable to a manager's work.

Artificial Intelligence (AI)   Thinking and reasoning software based on information inputted by a human expert. The reasoning process involves self-correction. Significant data is evaluated and relevant relationships uncovered. The computer learns which kind of answers are reasonable and which are not. Artificial intelligence performs complicated strategies that determine the best or worst way to accomplish a task or avoid an undesirable result. Examples of applications of AI are tax planning and capital budgeting analysis.

Audit Software   Computer programs designed to examine and test a company's accounting records. Some packages aid in gathering evidence, performing analytical tests, sampling data, appraising internal control, audit scheduling, and printing exception reports. The software is used by internal auditors.

Automatic Programming   The process of using one program to prepare another.

Automatic Recovery Program   A program enabling a system to continue functioning even though equipment has failed.

Background Processing   Execution of lower-priority programs while the system is not being used by higher-priority programs.

Batch Process   Combining several commands to be run at a later time by a software program without user intervention.

Baud   Serial information transfer speed with which a modem receives and sends data.

Benchmarking   Searching for new and better procedures by comparing your own procedures to that of the very best.

Block Diagram   A diagram using symbols to explain the interconnections and information flow between hardware and software.

Budgeting Models   Computer-based mathematical models generating all kinds of corporate budgets (e.g., cash flow, profitability). The models help managers look at a variety of what-if questions. The resultant calculations provide a basis for choice among alternatives under conditions of uncertainty.

Buffer   The area of a computer's memory set aside to hold information temporarily.

Business Process Reengineering (BPR)   An approach aimed at making revolutionary changes as opposed to evolutionary changes by eliminating nonvalue-added steps in a business process and computerizing the remaining steps to achieve desired outcomes.

Catalog   A directory of locations of files.

Cellular Manufacturing   Groups of machinery that are closely associated with each family of parts.

Chain Links   A series of linked data items.

Computer-Aided Design (CAD)   The use of a computer to interact with a designer in developing and testing product ideas without actually building prototypes.

Computer-Aided Design and Manufacturing (CAD/CAM)   A computerized system to both integrate part design, as with CAD, and to generate processing or manufacturing instructions.

Computer-Aided Manufacturing (CAM)   A manufacturing system utilizing computer software that controls the actual machine on the shop floor.

Computer-Integrated Manufacturing (CIM)   Computer information systems utilizing a shared manufacturing database for engineering design, factory production, and information management.

Computer Numerically Controlled (CNC) Machines   Stand-alone machines controlled by a computer.

Continuous Improvement (CI)   Also called *kaisen* in Japanese, the never-ending effort for improvement in every part of the firm relative to all its deliverables to its customers.

Control Chart   A graphical means of depicting sample characteristics—such as means, ranges, and attributes—over time; used for process control.

Corporate Planning Model   A computer-based integrated business planning model in which production and marketing models are linked to the financial model. It is a description, explanation, and interrelation of functional areas of a business (accounting, finance and investments, marketing, production, management, economics) expressed in terms of mathematical and logical equations so as to generate a variety of reports including financial forecasts. Corporate planning models may also be used for risk analysis and what-if experimentation. The goals of the model include improving the quality of planning and decision making, reducing the decision risk, and favorably influencing the future corporate environment.

Cyber Investing   Investing on the Internet, such as online trading.

Cyberspace   Originally used in *Neuromancer*, William Gibson's novel of direct brain–computer networking, a term that refers to the collective realms of computer-aided communication.

Data Interchange Format (DIF) File   A system to transfer computer files from one program to another.

Data Item   A piece of information entered into the database.

Database   The logical arrangement of information in the computer.

Database Management Software   Computer programs used to manage data in a database. They provide for defining, controlling, and accessing the database. The software allows managers to enter, manipulate, retrieve, display, select, sort, edit, and index data.

Debug   The process of tracing and correcting flaws in a software program or hardware device. Computerized routines may be used to find bugs.

Decision Support System (DSS)   A branch of a management information system that provides answers to management problems and that integrates the decision maker into the system as a component. DSS software provides support to the manager in the decision-making process. It analyzes a specific situation and can be modified as the manager desires. Examples of applications include planning and forecasting.

Economic Order Quantity (EOQ)   The amount that should be ordered to minimize the total ordering and carrying costs.

Expert Systems   Computer software involving stored reasoning schemes and containing the decision-making processes of business experts in their specialized areas. The software mimics the way human experts make decisions. The expert system appraises and solves business problems requiring human intelligence and imagination that involve known and unknown information. The components of the expert system include a knowledge base, inference engine, user interface, and knowledge acquisition facility.

File   An organized collection of records.

Financial Analysis Software   Software capable of taking financial data (e.g., online information on the World Wide Web) and performing trend and ratio calculations. Investment and credit decisions are based on the analysis results.

Financial Model   A functional branch of a general corporate planning model. It is essentially used to generate pro forma financial statements and financial ratios. A financial model is a mathematical model describing the interrelationships among financial variables of the firm. It is the basic tool for budgeting and budget planning. Also, it is used for risk analysis and what-if experiments. Many financial models are built using special modeling languages such as IFPS or spreadsheet programs such as Excel.

Flexible Manufacturing System (FMS)   Computer-controlled process technology suitable for producing a moderate variety of products in flexible volumes.

Flow Chart   A systems analysis tool that graphically presents a procedure in which production symbols are used to represent operations and data flow.

Graphic Software   A program showing business information in graphic form, including charts and diagrams. This enhances the understanding of the information including trends and relationships.

Hard Copy   A printed computer report, message, or listing.

Hypertext   A database approach linking related data, programs, and pictures.

Information System (IS)   A computer-based or manual system that transforms data into information useful in the support of decision making.

Integrated Software   A software package that combines many applications into one program. Integrated packages can move data among several programs utilizing common commands and file structures. An integrated package is recommended when identical source information is used for varying managerial purposes and activities.

Interface   A means of interaction between two computer devices or systems that handle data (e.g., formats, codes) differently. A device that converts signals from one device into signals that the other device needs.

Internet   An international network connecting smaller networks linking the computers of different entities.

Intranet   Internal company web sites, developed by the company itself.

Just-in-Time (JIT) Manufacturing   A manufacturing approach that produces only what is necessary to satisfy the demand of the preceding process (a demand-pull system).

Local Area Network (LAN) The linking of computers and other devices for inter-site and intercompany applications in a small geographic area.

Manufacturing Resource Planning (MRP II) An integrated information system that steps beyond first-generation MRP to synchronize all aspects (not just manufacturing) of the business.

Master Production Schedule (MPS) A time-phased statement of how many finished items are to be manufactured. It is obtained by disaggregating the production plan and is the primary input to *material requirement planning (MRP).*

Material Requirement Planning (MRP) A computer-based information system designed to handle ordering and scheduling of dependent-demand inventories (such as raw materials, component parts, and subassemblies, which are used in the production of a finished product).

Menu A list of commands that may be run.

Mnemonic A symbol representing and resembling a word concept, so arranged as to facilitate memory of its meaning.

Modeling Languages Programming languages, usually English-like, that are used to solve a specific task and generate various reports based on the solution and analysis. For example, financial planning modeling languages, such as IFPS (Integrated Financial Planning System), are computer software packages that help financial planners develop a financial model in English terms (not requiring any computer programming knowledge on his/her part), perform various analyses such as what-if analysis, and further generate pro forma financial reports.

Module The conceptual organization of a computer system by function. A module may constitute an entire system or a portion of a system (i.e., payroll processing).

Multitasking The simultaneous execution of two or more computer functions.

Network (1) Interconnected nodes (points where working units interreact [link] with others). (2) Connection of computers and devices.

Neural Networks A technology in which computers actually try to learn from the database and operator what the right answer is to a question. The system gets positive or negative response to output from the operator and stores that data so that it makes a better decision the next time. While still in its infancy, this technology shows promise for use in fraud detection, accounting, economic forecasting, and risk appraisals.

Online Searching Use of a computer retrieval system to obtain information from a database such as on the Internet.

Operations Management (OM)   Also called *production/operations management,* the design, operation, and improvement of the productions/operations system that creates the firm's primary products or services.

Optimal Character Recognition   A computer tool that recognizes typed or printed characters on paper so that they can be recorded on disk.

Prompts   On-screen questions that require a response.

Real-Time   Computer processing of data in connection with another process outside the computer.

Record   One entry of a file that contains possibly many *fields* or *data items.*

Relational Database   A database consisting of relationships between data items.

Reorder Point   An inventory level that triggers a new order.

Report Structure   A structure that defines report formatting information for a group of accounts.

Simulation   An attempt to represent a real-life system via a model to determine how a change in one or more variables affects the rest of the system; also called what-if analysis.

Speech Recognition Software   A program in which verbal commands activate the computer to perform functions.

Spreadsheet   A table of numbers arranged in rows and columns to make accounting, finance, marketing, and other business calculations. Spreadsheets facilitate end-result summary numbers, what-if experimentations, and projections.

Statistical Software   A computer program making quantitative calculations such as standard deviation, coefficient of variation, regression analysis, correlation, and variance analysis.

Tax Software   Tax modules for preparing federal and state income tax returns. Tax planning modules exist to examine tax options and alternatives to minimize the company's tax liability in current and future years. What-if tax situation scenarios may be evaluated.

Template   A computer-based worksheet that includes the relevant formulas for an application but not the data. It is a blank worksheet on which data is saved and filled in as needed for a future business application and to solve problems. Templates are predefined files, including cell formulas and row and column labels for specific spreadsheet applications. Templates allow for the referencing of cells and formulations of interrelated formulas and functions. They are reused to analyze similar transactions.

Terminal   An input–output device allowing a user to communicate directly with a computer.

Thinking Software   Computer programs used by managers preparing written reports, including specialized analyses of corporate operations. The software contains aids to improve writing skills and idea formulation so that managers can create an outline and written report. The information is labeled, organized, and structured.

Time Software   A computer program that tracks hours worked by employees by function, operation, or activity. It prepares an analysis of the variance between budgeted and actual hours, as well as trends in actual hours over a stated time period (e.g., quarterly comparisons).

Total Quality Management (TQM)   Using quality methods and techniques to strategic advantage within firms.

Utility Program   A program supporting the processing of a computer such as a diagnostic and tracing program.

Wide Area Network (WAN)   A network comprising a large geographic area.

World Wide Web (WWW)   The Internet system for worldwide hypertext linking of multimedia documents, making the relationship of information that is common between documents easily accessible and completely independent of physical location.

A
SELECTED INVESTIGATIVE SERVICES AND BACKGROUND VERIFICATION COMPANIES

Accurate Data Services
http://www.acudata.com/

The Alexander Information Group
http://www.alexinfogp.com/

Application Profiles, Inc.
http://www.ap-profiles.com/

Barrientos & Associates
http://www.emcsat.com/

Confidential Research Associates
http://www.mjrcomp.com/cra/

EMPFacts Factual Data
http://www.employmentscreen.com/

Indepth Profiles—A Division of Canode Personnel Services
http://www.idprofiles.com/

Informus Corp.
http://www.informus.com/

Integri-Net
http://www.integri-net.com/

On-Line Screening Services, Inc.
http://www.onlinescreening.com/

Pre-Employment Screening, Inc.
http://www.ddpes.com/

SafeHands
http://www.safehands.com/

StafTrack
http://www.staftrack.com/

USDatalink
http://www.usdatalink.com/

B

SELECTED TESTING SERVICES
FOR INFORMATION
TECHNOLOGY PROFESSIONALS

BOOKMAN CONSULTING INC.
Teckchek
www.teckchek.com/index.html
Tel: (212) 819-1955

Bookman Consulting provides testing for several programming languages including C, C++, COBOL, Oracle, Visual Basic, etc., in North America, Europe, and Africa.

PROVE IT!
TechTests
www.proveit.com/
Tel: (800) 935-6694

Prove It! provides an interactive online skills assessment test to determine the proficiency of programming professionals. The test is available through the Internet, and the results of a candidate's performance are available immediately. Tests are available for Access, C, C++, CICS/COBOL App., COBOL Programming, DB2, HTML, Informix, Novell NetWare, Oracle, Oracle DBA, PC Skills Survey, SCO UNIX System Administrators, SCO UNIX Users, UNIX Users, Visual Basic, Windows, and others.

SELECTED OUTSOURCING VENDORS IN INFORMATION TECHNOLOGY

AFFILIATED COMPUTER SERVICES
2828 North Haskell
Dallas, TX 75204
(214) 841-6381

AMERIQUEST TECHNOLOGIES INC.
Three Imperial Promenade
Santa Ana, CA 92707
(714) 437-0099

ANDERSEN CONSULTING
69 West Washington Street
Chicago, IL 60602
(312) 580-0069

AT&T GLOBAL INFORMATION SOLUTIONS
1700 South Patterson Boulevard
Dayton, OH 45479
(513) 445-5000

CAP GEMINI AMERICA INC.
1114 Avenue of the Americas
New York, NY 10036
(212) 944-6464

COMPASS COMPUTER SERVICES
2085 Midway Road
Carrollton, TX 75248
(214) 788-7100

COMPUTER HORIZONS CORP.
49 Old Bloomfield Avenue
Mountain Lakes, NJ 07046-1495
(973) 402-7400

COMVESTRIX CORP.
1100 Valley Brook Avenue
Lyndhurst, NJ 07071
(201) 935-8300

CONTEMPORARY COMPUTER SERVICES
200 Old Knickerbocker Avenue
Bohemia, NY 11716
(516) 563-8880

THE CONTINUUM COMPANY
9500 Arboretum Boulevard
Austin, TX 78759-6399
(512) 338-7600

CSC
118 MacKenan Drive
Cary, NC 27511
(919) 469-3325

CYNTERGY
656 Quince Orchard Road
Gaithersburg, MD 20878-1409
(301) 926-3400

DATA GENERAL CORP.
4400 Computer Drive
Westborough, MA 01580
(508) 898-5000

Digital Equipment Corp.
111 Power Mill Road
Maynard, MA 01754
(508) 493-5111

Electronic Data Systems Corp.
5400 Legacy Drive
Plano, TX 75024
(214) 604-6000

Entex Information Services
6 International Drive
Rye Brook, NY 10573-1058
(914) 935-3600

GTE Information Services Inc.
201 North Franklin Street
Tampa, FL 33602
(813) 273-4700

Hewlett-Packard Co.
3000 Hanover Street
Palo Alto, CA 94304
(415) 857-1501

IBM/ISSC
150 Kettletown Road
Southbury, CT 06488
(203) 262-2619

I-Net Inc.
1255 West 15th Street
Plano, TX 75075
(214) 578-6100

Inacom Corp.
10810 Farnam Drive
Omaha, NE 68154
(402) 392-4456

INTEGRATED SYSTEMS SOLUTIONS CORP.
44 South Broadway
White Plains, NY 10601
(914) 288-3400

ISOGON CORP.
330 7th Avenue
New York, NY 10001
(212) 376-3293

KEANE INC.
Ten City Square
Boston, MA 02129-3798
(617) 241-9200

LITTON COMPUTER SERVICES
5490 Canoga Avenue
Woodland Hills, CA 91365-4040
(818) 715-5227/(800) 252-6527

MCC CORP.
535 Mountain Avenue
Murray Hill, NJ 07974-2011
(908) 582-9500

MCI COMMUNICATIONS CORP.
1801 Pennsylvania Avenue, NW
Washington, DC 20036
(202) 872-1600

MICROAGE INFORMATION SYSTEMS
2400 South MicroAge Way
Tempe, AZ 85282
(602) 804-2000

OCTEL NETWORK SERVICES INC.
17080 Dallas Parkway
Dallas, TX 75248
(214) 733-2700

POLICY MANAGEMENT SYSTEMS CORP.
One PMS Center
Blythewood, SC 29016
(803) 735-4000

SHL SYSTEMHOUSE/MCI CORP.
50 O'Conner Street, Suite 501
Ottawa, Ontario, Canada K1P 6L2
(613) 236-9734

TECHNOLOGY & BUSINESS INTEGRATORS
50 Tice Boulevard
Woodcliff Lake, NJ 07675
(201) 573-9191

UNISYS CORP.
Township Lane
Blue Bell, PA 19422
(215) 986-4011

XEROX BUSINESS SERVICES
70 Linden Oaks Parkway
Rochester, NY 14625
(800) 432-0412

D

SAMPLE OUTSOURCING AND PERSONNEL CONTRACTS*

FORM A: EMPLOYMENT AGREEMENT FOR TECHNICAL EMPLOYEES

Please read this Contract carefully. This Contract sets forth the fundamental legal and ethical obligations you must observe as a Technician exposed to extremely confidential technologies and strategic data in carrying out your development and research. Firm maintains that this Contract is fair and equitable in light of the interests of the parties thereto. This Contract is lengthy as an attempt has been made to protect the interests of both you and Firm by being as explicit as possible.

This Contract, effective as of the date below, between Firm and Technician:

SECTION 1
SCOPE OF DUTIES

1.1 <u>Employment by Firm as Sole Occupation.</u> Other than the exceptions set forth in this Contract, you agree to dedicate your full working time, attention, aptitudes, and effort solely for carrying out the job duties that Firm may engage you for. You are precluded from taking on any other work activities or provide any services of a business or professional nature, regardless

---

*This appendix was solely prepared and edited by David Erlach, Ph.D., J.D., Assistant Professor of Accounting at Queens College, CUNY.

of whether you are paid or not, for any entity other than Firm, unless Firm has given you advance permission in writing. It is Firm's policy to prohibit its work force from working for any competing business during the employment period, including off hours, weekends, during vacation, regardless of how minimal that employment may be.

1.2 <u>Noninterference with Third-Party Rights.</u> Firm is hiring you with the recognition that (1) you are at your free will to enter into employment with Firm and (2) only Firm is entitled to reap benefit from your work product. Firm has no interest in infringing upon or using any other entity's patents, trade secrets, copyrights, or trademarks in a manner that would be unlawful. You must be vigilant and not misuse proprietary rights that Firm cannot legally use.

1.3 <u>Continuance of Employment.</u> The conscientious observance of this Contract by you shall always be a condition of your employment. Either you or Firm can terminate your employment at any time. As a professional courtesy, please give at least two weeks' notice in the event you no longer wish to be employed by Firm. Firm reserves the exclusive right to modify any work duties, personnel, or employee benefits at any time.

SECTION 2
OWNERSHIP OF EMPLOYEE DEVELOPMENTS

2.1 <u>Existing Proprietary Rights.</u> The following patent, patent applications, copyrights, trade secrets, and trademarks are the sole intangible interests that you own, or have any right to, at the time this Contract is executed: (list proprietary rights).

2.2 <u>Ownership of Work Product.</u>

    a. Firm shall retain title to all Work Product [as per Section 2.2 (e)]. All Work Product is deemed work made for hire by you, and owned by Firm.

    b. If any of the Work Product is not, under applicable law, work made for hire by you for Firm, or if ownership of legal right and title of the intellectual property, the applicable intellectual property rights shall not rest with Firm, you agree to assign without further remuneration, the ownership of all Trade Secrets (as per Section 3.2), domestic or international copyrights, and patentable inventions to Firm, its successors, and assigns.

c. Firm, its successors, and assigns, shall be able to obtain and hold under their name, any Work Product and other protection available in the foregoing.

d. You agree to engage in, upon Firm's request, during or after your employment, any supplementary acts as may be needed or desired to defend Firm's ownership in the Work Product. Upon request, you shall:

(1) Create, acknowledge, and deliver any requisite affidavits and documentation of assignment and conveyance;

(2) Acquire and assist in the effectuation of copyrights, and if pertinent, patents with respect to the Work Product in any jurisdiction, whether domestic or abroad.

(3) Furnish testimony in connection with any legal proceeding relating to the right, title, or interest of Firm in any Work Product; and

(4) Carry out any other necessary acts to effectuate the purposes of this Contract.

Firm shall compensate for all reasonable out-of-pocket costs incurred by you at Firm's request with respect to this Contract, inclusive of a reasonable hourly or daily payment for services rendered after your employment has been terminated, unless you are being compensated at the time in any other form.

e. For purposes of this Contract, "Work Product" refers to all intellectual property rights, including Trade Secrets, copyrights, patents, findings and betterments, and other intellectual property rights, in any programming, documents, technology, or other Work Product that pertains to the commercial interests of Firm and that you generate, cultivate, or deliver to Firm during any time you are employed by Firm. Work Product also includes any intellectual property rights, in programming, documents, technology, or other Work Product that is now part and parcel of any of the systems or products, including development and support systems, of Firm insofar as you generated, cultivated, or delivered such Work Product to Firm before the date on this Contract while you were employed as an independent contractor or personnel of Firm. You hereby, without recourse, surrender for the benefit of Firm and its assignees any moral rights in the Work Product as construed by relevant law.

Clearance Procedure for Proprietary Rights Not Claimed by Employer. If you ever desire to produce or generate, on personal time with personal resources, anything that may be construed as Work Product, but to which you maintain you have the right to the personal benefit of, you must follow the authorization method set forth in this section to ascertain that Firm has no claim to proprietary rights that may arise.

Prior to commencing any development work with your personal resources, Firm must be given advance written notice of your intent and you must furnish a description of your development project. Unless there is a different written agreement signed by Firm prior to receipt, Firm shall have no obligation of confidence with respect to this description. Firm will decide, in good faith, within thirty days after receiving documentation of your intent, whether the development is claimed by Firm. If Firm decides that it does not claim such development, you will receive written notice to that effect, and you will have ownership of the development insofar as what has been disclosed to Firm. You should furnish for further authorization any substantial change or amelioration so a determination can be made as to whether the change or amelioration relates to the commercial interests of Firm.

Authorization under this process does not eliminate your need to get Firm's written permission before engaging in activities of a business or professional nature for the advantage of any entity other than Firm, as per Section 1.1 of this Contract. In this way, Firm retains the right to control development work you may intend to engage in for remuneration after hours, as contrasted with work that is avocational or of insignificant nature that you pursue in your off time.

SECTION 3
CONFIDENTIALITY

3.1 Consequences of Entrustment with Sensitive Information. You must realize that your position with Firm necessitates significant obligations and trust. Firm is depending on your ethical integrity and strict loyalty, and Firm anticipates trusting you with extremely confidential, restricted, and proprietary data that involves Trade Secrets (as per Section 3.2). You must be aware that it may be difficult to separate these Trade Secrets from commercial activities that you may contemplate pursuing after you are no longer employed by Firm, and in certain circumstances, you may not be able to engage in commercial activities if they are construed to be in competition with those of Firm, because of the possibility that Firm's Trade Secrets will be divulged. You are under legal and ethical obligations to safeguard and maintain Firm's proprietary rights for use solely for Firm's benefit, and these obligations may result in strict limitations on your freedom to engage in certain types of commercial activities of a personal nature, either during or after being employed by Firm.

3.2 <u>Trade Secrets Defined.</u> For purposes of this Contract, a "Trade Secret" is informational material including, among others, technological data, formulas, programs, tools, processes, techniques, hand-drafted plans, monetary data, product plans, or customer and/or supplier lists that: (1) acquire commercial worth, even if potential, by virtue of being kept private, and not easily accessible by typical means by other entities or individuals who can derive commercial value from their dissemination or utilization; and (2) are the target of practical efforts to retain their secrecy.

3.3 <u>Restrictions on Use and Disclosure of Trade Secrets.</u> You agree not to utilize or disseminate any of Firm's Trade Secrets during the term of your employ, and for a reasonable time thereafter as long as the relevant information remains a Trade Secret, irrespective of whether the Trade Secrets are in written or other physical form, unless needed to accomplish any work tasks for Firm.

3.4 <u>Screening of Public Releases of Information.</u> Furthermore, and without any aim to curtail your other obligations under this Contract in any way, you are prohibited, while employed by Firm, from disseminating any private information as to the technology relevant to Firm's proprietary products and manufacturing techniques (especially technology that is currently being established, modified, or ameliorated), unless you have received prior written approval from Firm. You must present to Firm for examination any research in the area of science and technology that you intend to submit for publication in a magazine or journal readily accessible to the public, and a copy of any public speeches that relate to your work tasks for Firm, before such text is released or such speech delivered. Firm retains the authority to censor, prohibit, or amend any portion of such articles or speeches that may reveal Firm's Trade Secrets or other private information or be in conflict with Firm's commercial interests.

SECTION 4
RETURN OF MATERIALS

Upon Firm's request, and always at the end of your employment period, you must relinquish to Firm so it may do as it wishes all notes, handbooks, computer programs, commercial documents, software, and any other documents or information that relate to Firm's business, or your work tasks for Firm. You may not keep any copies of these items. You must relinquish to Firm so it may do as it wishes all materials that pertain to Firm's Trade Secrets. The terms of Section 4 are meant to apply to all materials established, modified, or ameliorated by you, as well as to all material provided to you by any entity or individual with respect to your employment.

SECTION 5
PARTIAL RESTRAINT ON POST-TERMINATION
COMPETITION

5.1 <u>Factual Background.</u> Firm anticipates infusion of substantial time, effort, and money to strengthen the worth and attractiveness of its technical staff's talents. Both this infusion and your personal remuneration indicate Firm's anticipation of realizing a substantial return as the sole user of your services, skills, and assistance in the future, without any risks that Firm's competitors may undertake to coax you to leave Firm and unethically reap the benefit of Firm's investment. The partial limitations set forth in Section 5.2 does not furnish total protection for Firm's investments, development efforts, product strategy, and proprietary data, but Firm believes that in conjunction with the other stipulations of this Contract, it is the fairest and most reasonable criterion allowable under applicable law to safeguard Firm's interests, giving proper regard to both your interests and the interest of the firm.

5.2 <u>Covenant Not to Compete.</u> Firm requires its technical staff to accept and observe and heed the following partial limitation on post-termination competition, which you agree to honor:

> FOR A PERIOD OF _____ MONTHS AFTER THE DISCONTINUATION OF YOUR EMPLOYMENT, YOU ARE BARRED FROM COMPETING WITH THE FIRM BY ENGAGING IN (SPECIFY ACTIVITIES OR BUSINESS) IN THE FOLLOWING AREAS:

The running of the _____ month periods enumerated in this Contract shall be tolled and suspended by the period of time you are engaged in occupational tasks that a court of competent jurisdiction later finds to violate the terms of this partial limitation. This partial limitation shall only apply if, within the eight months prior to the discontinuation of your employment, you in effect work in the specialty set forth in the agreement on behalf of Firm in function having some nexus to the activity set forth in this covenant.

5.3 <u>Contingent Benefits.</u> After your employment with Firm terminates, you must immediately provide written notice to the Firm if you receive any employment offer you would like to accept, if the employment might begin during the restrictive period set forth in Section 5.2. The writing must include: (1) a comprehensive description of the terms of the job offer, including the title of your position, and your remuneration, and (2) affirmation of your desire to accept the offer if Firm so permits. After you have properly advised Firm, Firm shall have thirty days to choose either

1. To relieve you from the conditions in Section 5.2, but solely as related to your particular employment offer, as set forth in your notice to Firm; or

2. To demand for complete conformity with Section 5.2, and to furnish you with these Special Benefits:

   a. remuneration in an amount equal to the base salary in terms of the relevant job offer, plus

   b. any bonus forthcoming to you as part of the relevant job offer, if such bonus is not dependent on any other event, condition, or situation of the company extending you the job offer.

(Alternative Provision)

2. To demand for complete conformity with Section 5.2; and to furnish you with these Special Benefits: _____% of your salary from Firm during the _____ months prior to the end of your employment, prorated weekly. While you are receiving these Special Benefits from Firm, you are obligated to industriously seek other employment possibilities that are compatible with your education, background, and work experience. You shall receive these Special Benefits from Firm only during the restriction period set forth in Section 5.2, and solely for the time period that you remain unemployed as per Section 5.2.

Any choice by Firm to relieve you from Section 5.2 as to one job offer will not relieve you from Section 5.2 as to any subsequent job offers, including transfers, reassignments, or relocation, by the same or different employers.

SECTION 6
PROHIBITION AGAINST UNFAIR BUSINESS PRACTICES

6.1 <u>Unfair Business Practices.</u> Professional research and development can be prone to unfair business practices. As an example, Trade Secrets can be misused or disseminated, and copies of reports can be used in an unethical fashion. Corporate spying is a significant issue for enterprises that rely on sensitive technology for success in business. Employees undertaking research and development can be the mark of, or associated with, unfair business practices, in light of the particular allure of the technology, programming, product development tactics, and other lucrative opportunities and information they come across in the course of their employment. It is unjust for Firm's former personnel to hire Firm's current personnel utilizing information or knowledge obtained while in Firm's employ. Firm places considerable importance in choosing, preparing, and promoting qualified individuals for jobs of great responsibility. The time, labor, and capital infused by Firm into its work force should not be sabotaged by an individual operating in a stealthy fashion. It would also be unjust for Firm's current personnel to engage in a competing business while still on Firm's payroll.

6.2 <u>Refraining from Harmful Actions.</u> During your period of employment with Firm, you must abstain from any activity that may hurt Firm or its commercial interests, unless Firm gives permission in advance. Your obligation to uphold and boost Firm's business requires you to prevent any unnecessary commercial difficulties for Firm. This responsibility is quite generalized, in light of the difficulty in foreseeing all likely scenarios. All uncertainties should be handled by getting Firm's advice as to how to navigate the situation at hand. For instance, during your period of employment with Firm, you are prohibited from recruiting any other personnel to engage in a different enterprise. Firm cannot block you from pursuing other career interests, but should you start up or join a different enterprise, you must promptly advise Firm to that effect, so that Firm's current endeavors are not unnecessarily interrupted, and to prevent the chance that Firm's Trade Secrets and confidential matters are not placed in jeopardy of being disseminated.

6.3 <u>Reporting Instances of Unfair Business Practices.</u> During your employment with Firm, if you become aware of, or conjecture that unfair business practices may be taking place, you must promptly notify Firm. This responsibility is quite generalized, as with Section 6.2, in light of the difficulty in foreseeing all likely scenarios. All uncertainties should be handled by getting Firm's advice as to how to navigate the situation at hand. For instance, Firm should be immediately apprised if an individual who is an employee of Firm, or has been an employee of Firm within the last two years, establishes contact with you or any other personnel of Firm with an offer to engage in a different enterprise. This contact encompasses any interchange not established by you or by the personnel getting the job offer, where you are aware that the occasion to partake in an enterprise may be at hand. This obligation also pertains to incidents where a third party, such as a business colleague, initiates contact with you or any other personnel of Firm at the request of an employee of Firm.

SECTION 7
IMPLEMENTATION

7.1 <u>Severability.</u> The components of this Contract shall be interpreted as agreements exclusive of one another and as responsibilities distinct from and unlike one another and as responsibilities distinct from any other Contract between you and Firm. Any assertion that you may have against Firm is not a defense to enforcement of the Contract by Firm.

7.2 <u>Survival of Obligations.</u> The accords in Sections 2 through 7 of this Contract shall outlive the discontinuance of your employment, irrespective of which party causes the discontinuance and the surrounding circumstances.

7.3 <u>Specific Performance and Consent to Injunctive Relief.</u> Irreparable damages are presumed if you violate any accord in this Contract. The thorough conformity with all areas of this Contract is a requisite condition for your employment, and Firm is counting on total conformity. Losses would likely to be unverifiable if you violated any agreement in this Contract. This Contract is aimed at the protection of the proprietary rights of Firm in many crucial ways. The simple threat of misappropriation of Firm's technology would be greatly damaging, since that technology is essential to Firm's commercial interests.

Consequently, you concur that any court of competent jurisdiction should speedily condemn any violation of this Contract, at the Firm's request, and you specifically relieve Firm from the obligation of posting bond with respect to temporary or interlocutory injunctive relief, insofar as allowed by law.

7.4 <u>Notices.</u> All obligatory communications under this Contract shall be written, and considered delivered when (1) it is personally delivered, (2) deposited in the U.S. mail with proper postage and address, or (3) sent through Firm's interoffice mail, if you are still personnel of Firm at the time.

7.5 <u>Related Parties.</u> This contract shall inure to the benefit of, and be binding upon, Firm, and its subsidiaries and affiliates, along with their successors and assigns, and you, with your executor, administrator, heirs, and legatees.

7.6 <u>Merger.</u> This Contract supplants and takes precedence over all previous and concurrent accords, agreements, or understandings, whether verbal or in writing, express or implied, insofar as they differ, clash, or are at variance or disharmony, with the terms of this Contract. This Contract does not propose to amend or hinder the standards, rules, and procedures that Firm may intermittently impose, such as Firm's Statement of Policy Relating to Conflicts of Interest and Business Ethics, of which a signed copy should already be in your possession.

7.7 <u>Choice of Law.</u> This Contract shall be executed and enforced under the laws of the State (Commonwealth) of _____.

    In witness whereof, you, as Firm's employee, have executed this Contract, Firm has accepted your undertaking.

EMPLOYEE/TECHNICIAN

Signature

Social Security No.

Address:

Date:

Accepted:
EMPLOYER/FIRM:

Firm Representative

FORM B: PART-TIME PROGRAMMER CONTRACT

This Part-Time Programmer Contract ("Contract"), executed this _____ day of _____, 20__ , between _____ ("Firm"), a (enter organization type), and _____, ("Programmer"), a resident of the State (or Commonwealth) of _____.

WITNESSETH

Whereas, Firm would like for Programmer to render particular computer programming services on an as-needed basis, including services with respect to the planning and development of particular computer software in the area of _____.

Whereas, Firm and Programmer affirm that the Program Materials are expected to become proprietary products owned by Firm, and to be licensed by Firm to third parties, with discretionary additional fees; and

Whereas, both Firm and Programmer wish to put in writing the terms and circumstances of their accord, including each party's rights to Program Materials;

Now therefore, in consideration of the premises hereof and the mutual agreements and terms hereinafter set forth and other good and valuable consideration, the receipt and adequacy of which are hereby acknowledged, the parties to this Contract, with intent to be legally bound, agree as follows:

SECTION 1
PROGRAMMING SERVICES

1.1 On the terms and conditions set forth in this Contract, Firm engages Programmer to carry out the duties enumerated in Exhibit A (omitted), during the term of this Contract, on an as-needed basis, and Programmer hereby accepts such engagement. Without mutual agreement to the contrary, all duties will be performed at Firm's premises. Programmer agrees to use his/her optimum effort, at a level congruous with others having comparable education, work experience, and mastery in the software industry, in carrying out the duties and responsibilities required under this Contract.

1.2 Programmer is not restricted from undertaking other engagements during the term of this Contract, but agrees to reject work that creates a conflict of interest with the area of business that Programmer is assigned to by Firm.

1.3 Programmer will be supervised by _____, and follow the instructions of this supervisor, or his/her managers.

1.4 Programmer will carry out work duties for Firm at Programmer's assigned work area on Firm's premises.

SECTION 2
TERM OF CONTRACT

2.1 The term of this Contract will be for one year from the date at the beginning of this agreement. Firm expects that it will require Programmer's services for no more than _____ days of _____ hours each per month. Regardless, the actual services will be comprised of specified work tasks or results to be achieved, and will be performed at times satisfactory to both parties on an as-needed basis.

2.2 Regardless of any termination of this Contract, the terms of Sections 6, 7, and 8 of this Contract shall remain in full effect.

SECTION 3
COMPLIANCE

3.1 The parties anticipate that Programmer, although a part-time contractor, may be categorized as an employee for particular legal and tax purposes. Therefore, if applicable, Firm shall pay and report federal and state income taxes withheld, FICA taxes, and unemployment insurance required with respect to Programmer.

3.2 As a part-time contractor, Programmer is ineligible for health insurance, disability insurance, or any other benefits as per the terms of Firm's plans and programs.

SECTION 4
COMPENSATION

4.1 Firm agrees to pay Programmer at $_____ (per hour)/_____ (per day) for each hour/day of services rendered by Programmer during the duration of this Contract. Programmer shall present Firm with a monthly invoice for services rendered during the preceding month; however, unless otherwise agreed in writing by Firm's Controller, Firm's liability under this Contract for all services performed thereunder shall be limited to $_____.

4.2 Programmer shall keep time records and work reports as per Firm's specifications.

SECTION 5
OBLIGATION FOR EXPENSES

5.1 Firm shall provide a work space and resources including equipment, materials, and services it deems necessary for Programmer to properly render services.

5.2 Programmer is not entitled to any remuneration for expenses.

SECTION 6
OWNERSHIP OF PROGRAM MATERIALS

6.1 Programmer affirms that all Program Materials, and other data conceived by Programmer under this Contract or provided by Firm to Programmer shall be owned by the Firm. Programmer explicitly affirms that all copyrightable material created under this Contract shall be deemed works made for hire by Programmer for Firm and that such material shall be the exclusive property of the Firm.

6.2 As far as any such material, under relevant law, may not be considered work made for hire by Programmer for Firm, Programmer consents to assign and, upon its creation, automatically assigns to Firm the legal title of such material, inclusive of any copyright or other intellectual property rights in such materials, without requiring any further remuneration. Firm has the right to acquire and hold in its own name any copyrights with respect to such materials.

6.3 Programmer shall perform any acts that may be deemed required by Firm to evidence more completely transfer of ownership of all materials referred to in Section 6 to Firm to the fullest degree possible, inclusive of, with no limitation, by executing subsequent assignments in writing in a format solicited by Firm.

6.4 Insofar as any preexisting rights of Programmer are encompassed in the Program Materials, Programmer gives to Firm the irrevocable, perpetual, nonexclusive, international royalty-free right and license to (1) utilize, execute, display, disseminate copies of, and prepare derivative works based upon such preexisting rights and any derivative works thereof and (2) grant permission to others to engage in any of the foregoing.

6.5 Programmer represents and warrants that it has the proper privilege and power to carry out its duties and to grant the rights and licenses herein, and that it has not assigned nor has purported to assign any right, title, or interest to any technology or intellectual property right that would create a conflict of interest with this Contract. Programmer promises and agrees that it will not execute any such Contracts.

SECTION 7
PROTECTION OF PROPRIETARY MATERIALS

7.1 Beginning with the execution date of this Contract, and continuing for as long as the information remains a Trade Secret (as per Section 7.2), Programmer shall not utilize, disseminate, or allow any individual or entity to acquire any Trade Secrets of Firm, including any materials developed or produced under this Contract (regardless of whether the Trade Secrets are in tangible [written] form or not), unless explicitly allowed by Firm.

7.2 As per this Contract, "Trade Secrets" encompasses all of, part of, or any phase of any scientific technical data, plan, method, formula, or amelioration relating to the evolvement, strategy, construction, or operation of _____ that is valuable, and of which the competitors of the Firm have no general knowledge.

7.3 Irreparable harm shall be assumed if Programmer breaches any component of this Contract for any reason. This Contract is designed to safeguard Firm's proprietary rights with respect to the Program Materials, and any abuse of such rights would result in significant harm to Firm's interests. Therefore, Programmer affirms that a court of competent jurisdiction should promptly enjoin any violation of this Contract, upon Firm's request.

SECTION 8
RETURN OF MATERIALS

8.1 At Firm's request, and at termination of this Contract, Programmer shall relinquish to Firm all notes, reports, files, drafts, handbooks, computer software, and other materials and copies thereof, with respect to the Program Materials or provided by Firm to Programmer, including any materials that include any Trade Secrets. This section is set up to cover all materials made or put together by Programmer, as well as to any materials provided to Programmer by Firm or any other individual or entity, that concern Program Materials.

SECTION 9
SCOPE OF AGREEMENT

9.1 This Contract is meant by the parties to be a final rendition of their agreement, and it constitutes an entire understanding between the parties as to the subject of this Contract, regardless of any statements or agreements previously made. Amendments to this Contract may be made only in a written document signed by the parties.

9.2 For purposes of enforcing this Contract, all sections thereof, except Section 4.1, shall be deemed as covenants independent of one another and as obligations separate from any other contract or agreement between the parties.

SECTION 10
TERMINATION

This Contract may be terminated by either party with ___ days' written notice to the other party. If this Contract is terminated by either party before its originally intended expiration, Firm has the duty to remunerate Programmer at the rate established in Section 4.1, for services rendered before the date of such termination.

SECTION 11
GOVERNING LAW

This Contract is made, interpreted, and governed under the laws of the State (Commonwealth) of _____.

In witness whereof, the parties to this Contract have caused it to be duly executed on the day and year written below.

(Programmer)

By:

Title:

Date: _____, 20__

Correspondence at:

(address)

(Firm)

By:

Title:

Date: _____, 20__

Correspondence at:

(address)

(Exhibit A)

FORM C: EMPLOYEE EXIT PROCEDURES

To: (Employee)
    (Address)

1. As a result of your employment with _____, you have been made privy to certain sensitive and private data of Firm of significant value, including computer source code, algorithms, user handbooks, formulas, modification reports, and training methods for Firm's computer programs (collectively known as "Proprietary Data"). This information is protected by trade secret and copyright legislation.

2. You have been involved in the formation of the Proprietary Data as a result of your employment with Firm. As per the terms of the employment contract enacted on _____, 20__, you specifically affirmed that all right, title, and interest in any of your work product developed during your employment with Firm were owned by Firm as works made for hire as per federal copyright law. Additionally, you executed an accord to assign and convey all copyright and other proprietary interests to Firm.

(Alternative Provision)

2. You have contributed to the formation of Proprietary Data as a result of your employment with Firm. As set forth in Firm's Statement Regarding Proprietary Data, all right, title, and interest in any of your work product developed during your employment with Firm, reside with Firm.

3. You have a legal duty to abstain from any further use or dissemination of Proprietary Data of Firm as long as such data continues to encompass trade secrets of Firm. Furthermore, Firm claims the copyright in all such work under federal copyright legislation and deems such information as unpublished works. Firm reserves all of its rights in the Proprietary Data, and you are prohibited from utilizing such data in a manner conflicting with (1) confidentiality obligations under the trade secret policies of the Firm and any confidentiality agreement executed by employee, or (2) Firm's copyright interest in such work product.

4. You are forbidden to take with you any Proprietary Data or other material belonging to Firm upon conclusion of your engagement with Firm, and by your signature below, you affirm that you have delivered back to Firm all such Proprietary Data and other materials that were within your possession or dominion at any time during your work with Firm.

5. You affirm that the unpermitted dissemination or utilization of any Proprietary Data of Firm could result in permanent damage and substantial injury to Firm, which may be troublesome to assess with certainty or to recompense through damages. Accordingly, in any petition to a court of competent jurisdiction brought by Firm seeking injunctive or other fair relief to prevent such unpermitted utilization or dissemination, you affirm that you shall not offer evidence or otherwise claim that such relief is not applicable.

6. You affirm that you have read, signed, and been furnished with a copy of (1) Policies of Firm Regarding Proprietary Data, Conflicts of Interest, and Ethics and (2) any confidentiality agreement you may have signed. Furthermore, you affirm that you understand your responsibilities and duties under (1) and (2) above, and with respect to all Proprietary Data of Firm and that you will not take any actions inconsistent thereupon.

7. You further understand and concur that your signature constitutes your verification and agreement with the matters contained in this Agreement.

(Firm)

By:

Human Resource Director

Acknowledged and agreed to:

Employee

Date: _____, 20__

FORM D: CONFIDENTIALITY CONTRACT

This Confidentiality Contract ("Contract") is entered into this _____ day of _____, 20__, between _____ (Firm), located at _____, and the individual signing as "Receiver."

1. <u>Definitions.</u> For purposes of this Contract, "Findings" shall mean the findings referred to in Attachment A (omitted), as well as any other findings categorized "confidential" by Firm or provided to Receiver by Firm with reference to this Contract. Such findings exclude any data that (1) has been acquired by Receiver from a source independent from Firm, (2) has become available to the public at large through a means other than nonpermissible disclosure by Receiver or its employees, or (3) is unilaterally developed by Receiver without any reliance on any information or materials provided by Firm. "Materials" shall include all memos, notes, records, handbooks, disks, or other documentation containing any data provided to

Receiver by Firm with respect to this Contract. "Permissible use" refers to the purposes described in Attachment B (omitted).

2. <u>Limited Use.</u> Receiver affirms that it is to be given access to the information and material solely for purpose of permissible use. Receiver agrees that (1) it will not utilize the information, (2) will keep the material confidential, and (3) will not duplicate or amend the data, or any copy, except as explicitly allowed by Firm. Receiver shall confine its dissemination of the Information and Materials to personnel of its own enterprise whom Firm could reasonably expect to have a bona fide need to get such Information and Materials so as to effect the permitted use.

3. <u>Proprietary Protection.</u> Firm shall have exclusive proprietorship of all right, title, and interest in and to the Information and Materials, including ownership of all copyrights and trade secrets that apply, subject only to rights and privileges explicitly bestowed by Firm. Firm claims and reserves all rights and benefits given under United States and international copyright law in all software programs and documentation embodied in the Materials as copyrighted works. The reversal of the binary or object code version of such software is verboten without Firm's consent in writing. The Information, including the source code version of all software that may be embodied in the Materials, is deemed to consist of substantial trade secrets of the company. Receiver affirms that, in the case of any violation of this Contract, Firm will not have a sufficient remedy in money or damages. Firm shall therefore have the right to obtain an injunction against such violation or breach from any court of competent jurisdiction promptly upon petition. Firm's right to such relief shall not impinge on its right to obtain other remedies.

4. <u>Disclaimer.</u> Except as may otherwise be set forth in a signed, written, accord between the parties, Firm makes no representation or guarantee as to correctness, copiousness, status, suitability, or performance of the Information or Materials, and Firm shall in no way be liable to Receiver as a result of its utilization of the Information and Materials.

5. <u>Term and Termination.</u> Upon the earlier of the Firm's solicitation or the completion of the permitted use, Receiver shall immediately return or destroy all materials and terminate all subsequent use of the Information. At Firm's request, Receiver shall immediately affirm that such activity has been undertaken. The limitations contained in this Contract shall remain effective until three years after the delivery or the purging of all Materials.

6. <u>General.</u> The explanation and implementation of this Contract shall be governed by the laws of the State (or Commonwealth) of _____, as it applies to a Contract executed, delivered, and performed solely in such State (or Commonwealth). Receiver may not sell, transfer, assign, or sub-contract any right or obligation without the consent of Firm in writing.

In witness whereof, the parties have caused this Contract to be executed as follows:

FIRM   RECEIVER

_____   _____
By   By

_____   _____
Title   Title

_____   _____
Date   Date

(Attachment A)

(Attachment B)

FORM E: ADVISEMENT CONTRACT

This Advisement Contract (this "Contract") mutually agreed upon the _____ day of _____, 20__, between the User, a (identify entity), having its primary place of commerce at _____ (here-inafter "User"), and Advisor, a (identify entity), having its primary place of commerce at (hereinafter "Advisor").

SECTION 1
TERM AND TERMINATION

1.1 <u>Term.</u> This Contract commences as of the date shown above, and will remain active through the conclusion of each Job Arrangement (as defined in Section 3.1). The first Job Arrangements are appended as the First Addendum (omitted).

1.2 <u>Termination of Job Arrangements.</u> The User may, at its unilateral discretion, abort the progress of any Job Arrangement, or any part of such Job Arrangement, upon thirty days' advance written communication. Upon receipt of such communication, Advisor shall inform User of scope of performance to date, and assemble and furnish to User any material completed as of that date in the form requested by User. Advisor shall receive proper remuneration for all work engaged in until this date.

1.3 <u>Continuation.</u> Regardless of any termination of this Contract, Sections 5, 6, and 7 shall continue.

SECTION 2
INDEPENDENT CONTRACTOR STATUS

2.1 <u>Intent.</u> It is the parties' aim that Advisor be an independent contractor. There is nothing in this Contract that shall be interpreted as to create an employer–employee relationship between User and Advisor, or any of Advisor's workers or representatives.

2.2 <u>Non-restrictive.</u> Advisor maintains the ability to engage in other employment while this Contract is in effect. User maintains the ability to engage its own work force in similar work tasks, or different work tasks while this Contract is in effect.

SECTION 3
SERVICES TO BE PERFORMED BY ADVISOR

3.1 <u>Advisement Requests.</u> All duties performed by Advisor shall be set forth in an Advisement Request signed by duly authorized agents of each party. Each Advisement Request shall enumerate, among other items, the specific task(s) to be undertaken, how many of Advisor's labor force will be working on the relevant Advisement Contract, the length of time each person will be working on the engagement, and proper remuneration. Advisor retains the discretion to accept, modify, or reject any Advisement Request.

3.2 <u>Performance of Obligations.</u> Advisor, with the concurrence of its work force, will choose the methods, wherewithal of performing the work for User, and any other particulars necessary for fulfilling the Contract obligations. User will have no authority whatsoever to dictate how the services of Advisor shall be performed. User may require Advisor's work force to constantly adhere to all of User's safety procedures. User shall have the right to utilize comprehensive supervision of duties performed by Advisor, in order to generate an acceptable work product. Supervision encompasses the authority to monitor work, and give feedback as to specific aspects of work done, and ask for review and change in the ambit of the Advisement Contract.

3.3 <u>Assignment of Work Force.</u> User may meet with and ask questions of the work force Advisor has chosen to undertake User's work. If User concludes that any member of the work force is not properly qualified based on particular skills, past experience, or accomplishments, Advisor must make a realistic attempt to substitute a different, properly qualified individual.

3.4 <u>Scheduling.</u> Advisor shall try to schedule work activity for User to a feasible extent. If any of Advisor's work force is unable to perform their duties for any reason beyond Advisor's control, Advisor shall try to substitute another properly qualified individual within a reasonable time, but Advisor shall not have any liability if it cannot find a substitute individual, in light of other engagements and previous commitments.

3.5 <u>Reporting.</u> User will inform Advisor of the parties to whom Advisor's supervisor will keep abreast of daily progress. User and Advisor shall plan out proper procedures for carrying out the work tasks at User's location. User shall systematically furnish to Advisor a review of work Advisor has done.

3.6 <u>Work Location.</u> Advisor's work force will perform all duties for User at User's premises, except when mutually agreed that certain work tasks should be engaged in off-premises. User shall provide work space, proper facilities, and other services or goods Advisor or its work force reasonably deem necessary to properly carry out their responsibilities. User is aware of possible necessity to train Advisor's work force in the particular procedures utilized at User's site. When User deems additional training is required, User shall properly remunerate Advisor for training time for its work force, unless previously agreed in writing.

SECTION 4
REMUNERATION

4.1 <u>Rates.</u> A list of all fees for Advisor's work shall be included in each Job Arrangement. Absent communication to the contrary, Advisor retains the right to amend the fees for any Job Arrangement with no less than sixty days' notice, without prior notice for a new Job Arrangement, and without prior notice for a change in any Job Arrangement that has already taken effect.

4.2 <u>Estimates.</u> Estimates of fees for a particular project may be set forth in a Job Arrangement, but such estimates are not binding on the part of Advisor. Advisor shall promptly notify User if the fees to be charged will be higher than the estimate, and User has the option to cancel the Job Arrangement at that time, and effectuate payment only for services received from Advisor up until that point.

4.3 <u>Billing.</u> Advisor shall submit billing statements to User every seven days, for services rendered and expenses incurred for that time period. Each billing statement shall itemize fees charged by name of Advisor's employee(s) who rendered services under the Contract at hand, and shall categorize all expenses.

4.4 <u>Date for Remittance of Remuneration.</u> User must pay the total amount of each billing statement within fifteen days of receipt.

4.5 <u>Expenses and Costs.</u> Unless otherwise stipulated in this Contract or the relevant Job Arrangement, Advisor bears the responsibility for all costs necessary to properly perform services that User has contracted for.

SECTION 5
ADVISOR'S PERSONNEL

5.1 <u>Payment to Advisor's Personnel.</u> Advisor is solely responsible for remunerating its employees. Advisor shall pay and fully account for, with respect to all employees assigned to a particular Job Arrangement, all federal and state withholding taxes, FICA taxes, and unemployment insurance applicable to these employees. Advisor is solely responsible for any work-related benefits (medical insurance, pension plan contributions, etc.) to which employees are entitled. Advisor agrees to indemnify and hold harmless User, User's corporate officers, management, personnel and agents, and User's benefit plan administrators, against any and all claims and costs relating to such remuneration, withholding and FICA taxes, and any work-related benefits; on the condition that User (a) promptly notify Advisor of any such claims as soon as User becomes aware of them; (b) cooperate with

Advisor in resolving such claims; and (c) not unilaterally settle such claims, unless Advisor has previously consented in writing.

5.2 <u>Workers' Compensation.</u> Regardless of any other workers' compensation or other insurance held by User, Advisor shall obtain workers' compensation coverage in an amount that meets the legal requirements of any jurisdiction in which Advisor's employees are engaging in work for User.

5.3 <u>Advisor's Agreements with Employees.</u> Advisor shall acquire and have available written covenants with each of its employees who undertake any of User's work resulting from any Job Agreement. Such covenants shall explicitly state how Advisor will meet all provisions of this Contract, and shall state that Advisor's employees have no standing as employees of User, and cannot receive any benefits from any User benefit plan.

5.4 <u>State and Federal Taxes.</u> Neither Advisor nor Advisor's work force are User's employees. Consequently, User shall not:

    a. withhold FICA taxes from Advisor's payments.

    b. contribute towards state or federal unemployment programs for Advisor or its work force.

    c. withhold any payroll taxes from payments to Advisor.

    d. contribute towards disability insurance with respect to Advisor.

    e. procure workers' compensation insurance coverage for Advisor or its employees.

SECTION 6
INTELLECTUAL PROPERTY RIGHTS

6.1 <u>Confidentiality.</u> Advisor shall keep in strict confidence, and will utilize and divulge only as permitted by User, all delicate information that it collects in the process of performing contractual obligations for User under a Job Arrangement. Advisor must require its work force to maintain the same level of confidentiality. User shall take practical measures to highlight for the benefit of Advisor and its work force any delicate or sensitive information. These parameters shall not be deemed to apply to (1) data known and accepted by the general public; (2) information normally released by User without any restriction; or (3) information approved for dissemination by Advisor or its work force without restriction. Regardless, Advisor and its employees may utilize and divulge information (1) in the event of a subpoena by a court of law or other governmental branch or (2) as may be required to protect Advisor's interest in this Contract, but in each instance only after Advisor has duly notified User, and User has had a reasonable opportunity to prevent such information from being disseminated.

6.2 <u>Ownership of Work Product.</u> All copyrights, trade secrets, patents, or other intellectual property rights associated with ideas, methods, scholarly or professional creations developed by Advisor or its employees in the course of performing the Contract, belong to the User, and are deemed to be a work product developed for the User, as per Title 17 of the United States Code. Advisor automatically assigns, as does its employees, any and all legal rights and interests that may have been acquired from that work product, without any remuneration for said rights. At request of User, Advisor and its employees shall take all actions necessary to properly and legally effectuate such assignment.

6.3 <u>Residual Rights of Employees.</u> Regardless of any of the aforementioned, Advisor and its employees may legally use and disclose work skills, methods, ideas, or techniques acquired during the performance of a Job Assignment for User, unless such use may lead to the disclosure of sensitive or classified information of User.

SECTION 7
HIRING OF ADVISOR'S EMPLOYEES

7.1 <u>Additional Value from Hiring.</u> User affirms that Advisor provides a unique service in the selection and assignment of employees for User's work. User also affirms that User would gain additional and significant advantage, and Advisor would lose the benefits of its employees, if User makes an offer of employment to Advisor's employees after being introduced to User by Advisor.

7.2 <u>No Hiring Without Prior Authorization.</u> Unless Advisor has previously given written authorization, User shall not make an offer of employment to any Advisor's employees who have worked for User under a Job Arrangement, until a period of one year has elapsed since the completion of the last Job Arrangement between the two parties.

7.3 <u>Hiring Fees.</u> If User hires any employee of Advisor, who has performed services for User, User shall pay Advisor, within one year of such employment, a hiring fee of 25% of the total first year salary and other compensation User pays such employee, as a fee for added benefit derived by User.

SECTION 8
LIMITATIONS

8.1 <u>Disclaimer.</u> Advisor does not make any express or implied warranties, as to the work product of its work force or the results derived from their work, including, without limitation, any implied warranty of merchantability or fitness for particular purpose or use. Advisor shall not be liable for consequential, incidental, special, or indirect damages, or negligence that is not intentional or reckless, irrespective of whether it has been alerted to the possibility of such losses.

8.2 <u>Total Liability.</u> User concurs that Advisor's obligation for damages shall not be greater than the total payment for services under the relevant estimate or, absent an estimate, in the authorization for the contracted services.

8.3 <u>Events Beyond Advisor's Control.</u> Advisor shall not be liable to User for any failure or slowdown caused by unusual, unexpected, or uncontrollable events, including User's inability to communicate proper information, travel delays, labor strikes or slowdowns, or shortages of gasoline, materials, or machinery.

SECTION 9
GENERAL PROVISIONS

9.1 <u>Communications.</u> Any communication under this Contract from one party to the other can be effectuated by personal delivery of written notice, or by certified or registered mail, with return receipt requested. Communications sent by mail shall be sent to the addresses designated by the parties at the outset of this Contract, but Advisor or User can change such address by written communication as per this section. Notices delivered in person are deemed communicated when received. Communications sent by mail are deemed communicated 48 hours after mailing.

9.2 <u>Anti-Discrimination Clause.</u> Advisor affirms that in the course of performing this Contract, it will not discriminate or allow discrimination based on gender, race, religious belief, or ethnic origin in any way prohibited by United States law.

9.3 <u>Insurance.</u> Insofar as Advisor's employees may perform labor at User's premises, User shall maintain comprehensive general liability insurance, including broad form property damage coverage, with limits of no less than one million dollars combined single limit for bodily injury and property damage for each incident.

9.4 <u>Entire Agreement of the Parties.</u> This Contract supersedes any and all Contracts, oral or written, between the parties with respect to rendering of services by Advisor for User and contains all the covenants of rendering of services in any manner whatsoever. Advisor and User affirm that no representations, inducements, agreements, or promises, orally or otherwise, have been made by any party or any agent of any party, that are not contained herein, and that no agreement, statement, or promise not contained in this Contract shall be valid or binding. Any modification to this Contract is effective only if written, and signed by the party to be charged.

9.5 <u>Partial Invalidity.</u> If any component of this Contract is found to be invalid, void, or unenforceable by a court of competent jurisdiction, the remaining contractual provisions will remain in effect without any impairment or invalidation.

9.6 <u>Parties in Interest.</u> This Contract is enforceable only by Advisor and User. The terms of this Contract are not assurance with respect to compensation, further engagement, or benefits of any kind to Advisor's employees assigned to User's work, or any beneficiary of such employee, and no such employee or any beneficiary thereof, shall be a third-party beneficiary as per the terms of this Contract.

9.7 <u>Governing Law.</u> This Contract will be governed and regulated under the laws of the State (or Commonwealth) of _____.

9.8 <u>Successors.</u> This Contract shall inure to the benefit of, and be binding upon, Advisor and User, their successors, and assigns.

ADVISOR: USER:

_____   _____
(Business Name)   (Business Name)

_____   _____
by: by:
    (signature)   (signature)

_____   _____
Typed Name   Title   Typed Name   Title

Social Security/_____   Social Security/_____

Taxpayer ID No._____   Taxpayer ID No._____

FORM F: EMPLOYEE'S ACKNOWLEDGMENT OF FIRM'S RIGHTS IN WORK PRODUCT

This Contract is offered by me (undersigned) for the advantage of _____, its subsidiaries, associates, successors, and assigns (collectively, "Firm") and has the effect of a legally binding Contract for the acknowledgment and transfer of all "Work Product" that Firm may come across.

    For purposes of this Contract, "Work Product" refers to all intellectual property rights, trade secrets, copyrights (both domestic and international), patents, and other intellectual property rights in software, computer programs, documents, technology, or any other work product that is conceived with respect to my Work. Additionally, any legal rights in preexisting software, computer programs, documents, technology, or other Work Product furnished to Firm during my period of employ or engagement shall immediately become part of the Work Product under this Contract, regardless of whether it is directly attributable to my "Work." For purposes of this

Contract, "Work" refers to (1) any of Firm's work tasks I have been engaged in, and (2) any other usable work output that is relevant to Firm's commercial interests, and is created in the course of my employment with Firm. For purposes of this part of the Contract, Work may take place after regular business hours, in a location other than one belonging to Firm, without supervision, whether by myself or with colleagues. Unless stated to the contrary in a later document signed by Firm, this Contract applies to all Work Product resulting from endeavors before or after the date of this Contract.

Firm owns all legal rights in the Work Product. In this respect, all Work Product is considered Work made by me for remuneration by Firm. If any of the Work Product should not, as a result of law or an accord between the parties, be categorized as Work made by me for remuneration by Firm, or if all rights of ownership do not vest solely in Firm, I will assign, without further remuneration, the ownership thereof to Firm. I surrender without recourse for Firm's advantage any moral rights in the Work Product that are legally recognized. Firm has the option to acquire and keep, in whatever capacity it chooses, copyrights, registrations, and any other legal protection that pertains to the Work Product.

At Firm's request I will engage in, during work hours or after-hours, any work tasks that may be required to transfer, perfect, and defend Firm's ownership of the Work Product, including by (1) executing, acknowledging, and providing any solicited affidavits and documentation of conveyance, (2) getting and/or assisting in enforcing copyrights, trade secrets, and (if relevant) patents applicable to the Work Product in any jurisdiction, both domestic and international, and (3) giving testimony in any legal proceeding that affects Firm's rights in any Work Product.

During my employment as well as afterwards, I will not utilize or disseminate any of Firm's trade secrets unless required to carry out my work responsibilities for Firm. Legally, a "trade secret" is a form of intangible property, the misappropriation of which is a tort and crime in most jurisdictions. The trade secret need not be in writing in order to be afforded legal protection. A trade secret is significant, privileged information or ideas that Firm gathers or utilizes so as to keep itself competitive in the market, including classified information that Firm obtains from clientele, vendors, or representatives. Trade secrets include technological data as manufacturing or operating procedures, machinery design, product standards, computer software in source code format, and other proprietary bodies of knowledge, and commercial data such as selling, pricing, and other business strategies, customer lists, and financial statements generated for internal use. These limitations are not applicable to information that is of general public knowledge or any information duly retrieved from a totally independent origin.

I affirm that my employment with Firm will not be at variance with any remaining duties I may have with any previous employer. I also affirm to generate all Work Products in a fashion that avoids even the look of infringement on a third party's claims to intellectual property.

At Firm's desire and, always at the end of my engagement, I will relinquish to Firm all notes, records, plans, handbooks, software, or other documentation, apparatus, and media that relates to Firm's commercial interests or my Work or encompassing any Work Product, including any copies. I consent to attest in writing, at the solicitation of Firm, that these acts have been executed.

This Contract does not eradicate or amend any other contract or duty relating to any other consistent facet of the conditions of my Work. This Contract may not be amended or waived unless such actions are in a written document, signed by Firm. This Contract shall be governed by the laws of the State (Commonwealth) of _____.

EMPLOYEE:

_____

Signature

_____

Name (typed or printed)

_____

Social Security Number

_____

Current Address

_____

SAS No. 48: The Effects of Computer Processing on the Examination of Financial Statements

Statement of Auditing Standards (SAS) No. 48, *The Effects of Computer Processing on the Examination of Financial Statements* (sections 9 and 10) states:

> The auditor should consider the methods the entity uses to process accounting information in planning the audit because such methods influence the design of the accounting system and the nature of the internal accounting control procedures. The extent to which computer processing is used in significant account applications, as well as the complexity of that processing, may also influence the nature, timing and extent of audit procedures. In evaluating the effect of an entity's computer processing on an examination of financial statements, the auditor should consider matters such as:
>
> a. The extent to which the computer is used in each significant account application.
>
> b. The complexity of the entity's computer operations, including the use of an outside service center.
>
> c. The organizational structure of the computer processing activities.
>
> d. The availability of data. Documents that are used to enter information into the computer for processing, certain computer files, and other evidential matter that may be required by the auditor may exist only for a short period or only in computer readable form. In some computer systems, input documents may not exist at all because information is directly entered into the system. An entity's data retention policies may require the auditor to request retention of some information for his review or to perform audit procedures at a time

481

when the information is available. In addition, certain information generated
by the computer for management's internal purposes may be useful in performing substantive tests (particularly analytical review procedures).

e. The use of computer-assisted audit techniques to increase the efficiency of
performing audit procedures. Using computer-assisted audit techniques may
also provide the auditor with an opportunity to apply certain procedures to an
entire population of accounts or transactions. In addition, in some accounting
systems, it may be difficult or impossible for the auditor to analyze certain data
or test specific control procedures without computer assistance.

The auditor should consider whether specialized skills are needed to
ascertain the effect of computer processing on the audit, to understand the
flow of transactions, to understand the nature of internal accounting control procedures, or to design and perform audit procedures. If specialized
skills are needed, the auditor should seek the assistance of a professional
possessing such skills, who may be either someone on the auditor's staff or
an outside professional. If the use of such a professional is planned, the
auditor should have sufficient computer-related knowledge to communicate the objectives of the other professional's work; to evaluate whether the
specified procedures will meet the auditor's objectives; and to evaluate the
results of the procedures applied as they relate to the nature, timing, and
extent of other planned audit procedures. The auditor's responsibilities
with respect to using such a professional are equivalent to those for other
assistants.

THREE AUDIT SOFTWARE PACKAGES

This appendix provides three illustrative audit software packages of interest to the reader.

- *Price Waterhouse's (PW) Controls* facilitates the documentation, evaluation, and testing of internal controls. The software expedites the collection and summarization of controls in place, appraises their effectiveness, and identifies areas of risk exposure. Auditors can use PW Controls to document particular business processes. Control weaknesses are identified, with resultant recommendations for improvement. The auditor can view control effectiveness at different levels within the company (e.g., by activity or by business unit). A comparison and analysis may be made of the relative control performance of different operating units.

- *American Institute of Certified Public Accountants's (AICPA) Interactive Data Extraction and Analysis (IDEA)* software displays, evaluates, manipulates, and extracts data from computer systems for both audit and financial decision making. It allows for inquiries to data files, arithmetic computations, sampling (random, systematic, interval, or monetary), fraud detection, highlights unusual items, and compares records or transactions to predetermined criteria for reasonableness. The software enables the creation and analysis of reports. IDEA improves audit effectiveness and efficiency.

- *Business Foundations's Internal Operations Risk Analysis* software evaluates a client's areas of risk and internal control structure. It is an expert system developed around a 180-question interview. Based on the answers to the questions, the software prepares a management report highlighting the strengths and weaknesses in the operations of the business. A risk rating (high, medium, low) is assigned to categories of risk. Relevant management and analytical reports are generated. Operational areas evaluated by the software include working environment, objectives, planning, and personnel. It has database capabilities. It recommends corrective steps for problem areas. There is also an upgrade for industry-specific components.

INDEX